T0184174

Lecture Notes in Computer Science   12480

Founding Editors

Gerhard Goos
Karlsruhe Institute of Technology, Karlsruhe, Germany
Juris Hartmanis
Cornell University, Ithaca, NY, USA

Editorial Board Members

Elisa Bertino
Purdue University, West Lafayette, IN, USA
Wen Gao
Peking University, Beijing, China
Bernhard Steffen
TU Dortmund University, Dortmund, Germany
Gerhard Woeginger
RWTH Aachen, Aachen, Germany
Moti Yung
Columbia University, New York, NY, USA

More information about this subseries at http://www.springer.com/series/7407

Bartosz Balis · Dora B. Heras et al. (Eds.)

Euro-Par 2020: Parallel Processing Workshops

Euro-Par 2020 International Workshops
Warsaw, Poland, August 24–25, 2020
Revised Selected Papers

 Springer

Editors
Bartosz Balis
AGH University of Science and Technology
Krakow, Poland

Dora B. Heras
CiTIUS
Santiago de Compostela, Spain

Additional Workshop Editors *see next page*

ISSN 0302-9743 ISSN 1611-3349 (electronic)
Lecture Notes in Computer Science
ISBN 978-3-030-71592-2 ISBN 978-3-030-71593-9 (eBook)
https://doi.org/10.1007/978-3-030-71593-9

LNCS Sublibrary: SL1 – Theoretical Computer Science and General Issues

© Springer Nature Switzerland AG 2021
This work is subject to copyright. All rights are reserved by the Publisher, whether the whole or part of the material is concerned, specifically the rights of translation, reprinting, reuse of illustrations, recitation, broadcasting, reproduction on microfilms or in any other physical way, and transmission or information storage and retrieval, electronic adaptation, computer software, or by similar or dissimilar methodology now known or hereafter developed.
The use of general descriptive names, registered names, trademarks, service marks, etc. in this publication does not imply, even in the absence of a specific statement, that such names are exempt from the relevant protective laws and regulations and therefore free for general use.
The publisher, the authors and the editors are safe to assume that the advice and information in this book are believed to be true and accurate at the date of publication. Neither the publisher nor the authors or the editors give a warranty, expressed or implied, with respect to the material contained herein or for any errors or omissions that may have been made. The publisher remains neutral with regard to jurisdictional claims in published maps and institutional affiliations.

This Springer imprint is published by the registered company Springer Nature Switzerland AG
The registered company address is: Gewerbestrasse 11, 6330 Cham, Switzerland

Workshop Editors

Laura Antonelli
ICAR-CNR Italy
Italy
laura.antonelli@icar.cnr.it

Andrea Bracciali
University of Stirling
UK
abb@cs.stir.ac.uk

Thomas Gruber
Friedrich-Alexander-Universität
Germany
thomas.gruber@fau.de

Jin Hyun-Wook
Konkuk University
South Korea
jinh@konkuk.ac.kr

Michael Kuhn
Otto von Guericke University Magdeburg
Germany
michael.kuhn@ovgu.de

Stephen L. Scott
Tennessee Tech University
USA
sscott@tntech.edu

Didem Unat
Koc University
Turkey
dunat@ku.edu.tr

Roman Wyrzykowski
Czestochowa University of Technology
Poland
roman@icis.pcz.pl

Workshop Editors

Preface

Euro-Par is an annual, international conference in Europe, covering all aspects of parallel and distributed processing. These range from theory to practice, from small to the largest parallel and distributed systems and infrastructures, from fundamental computational problems to full-fledged applications. It also covers architecture, compiler, language, and interface design and implementation, as well as tools, support infrastructures, and application performance aspects. The Euro-Par conference itself is complemented by a workshop program, where workshops dedicated to more specialized themes, to cross-cutting issues, and to upcoming trends and paradigms can be easily and conveniently organized with little administrative overhead.

This year, 11 workshop proposals were submitted, and after a careful revision process, which was led by the workshop co-chairs, all of them were accepted. Three workshops were withdrawn due to a low number of submissions, or due to the decision to conduct the Euro-Par 2020 conference in the online format as a consequence of the COVID-19 pandemic. Two more of them were cancelled after the review process.

The workshops took place on the two days before the Euro-Par conference and the program included papers belonging to the following 6 online workshops:

1. Challenges and Opportunities of HPC Storage Systems (CHAOSS)
2. Workshop on Future Perspectives of Decentralised Applications (FPDAPP)
3. Workshop on Algorithms, Models and Tools for Parallel Computing on Heterogeneous Platforms (HETEROPAR)
4. Workshop on Parallel and Distributed Computing for Life Sciences: Algorithms, Methodologies and Tools (PDCLIFES)
5. Workshop on Parallel Programming (PARAMO)
6. Workshop on Resiliency in High Performance Computing with Clouds, Grids, and Clusters (RESILIENCE)

The total number of submissions was 51 from 15 different countries. Each workshop had an independent program committee, which was in charge of selecting the papers. The workshop papers received more than three reviews per paper on average (170 reviews in total). Out of the 51 submissions, 27 papers were selected to be presented at the workshops. So, the acceptance rate was 53%.

The success of the Euro-Par workshops depends on the work of many individuals and organizations. We therefore thank all the workshop organizers and reviewers for the time and effort that they invested. The effort was specially intense this year due to the pandemic situation. We would also like to express our gratitude to the members of the Organizing Committee and the local staff, especially the volunteer students, who helped us and successfully adapted to the new situation. Sincere thanks are due to Springer for their help in publishing the proceedings. This volume includes the papers of the 6 workshops organized into 4 track sections (FPDAPP, HETEROPAR, PARAMO,

RESILIENCE), and also a section called Complementary Papers that includes the 3 papers from CHAOSS and PDCLIFES.

Lastly, we thank all participants, panelists, and keynote speakers of the Euro-Par workshops for their contribution to a productive meeting. It was a pleasure to organize and host the Euro-Par workshops 2020 in Warsaw.

November 2020   Bartosz Balis
                                                      Dora B. Heras

Organization

Euro-Par Steering Committee

Chair

Luc Bougé   ENS Rennes, France

Vice-chair

Fernando Silva   University of Porto, Portugal

Full Members

Marco Aldinucci	University of Turin, Italy
Dora Blanco Heras	CiTIUS, University of Santiago de Compostela, Spain
Emmanuel Jeannot	Inria Bordeaux, France
Christos Kaklamanis	Computer Technology Institute, Greece
Paul Kelly	Imperial College London, UK
Thomas Ludwig	University of Hamburg, Germany
Tomàs Margalef	Universidad Autònoma de Barcelona, Spain
Wolfgang Nagel	Dresden University of Technology, Germany
Francisco Fernández Rivera	CiTIUS, University of Santiago de Compostela, Spain
Krzysztof Rządca	University of Warsaw, Poland
Rizos Sakellariou	University of Manchester, UK
Henk Sips	Delft University of Technology, The Netherlands
Leonel Sousa	University of Lisbon, Portugal
Domenico Talia	University of Calabria, Italy
Massimo Torquati	University of Pisa, Italy
Phil Trinder	University of Glasgow, UK
Denis Trystram	Grenoble Institute of Technology, France
Felix Wolf	Technical University of Darmstadt, Germany
Ramin Yahyapour	GWDG, Göttingen, Germany

Honorary Members

Christian Lengauer	University of Passau, Germany
Ron Perrott	Oxford e-Research Centre, UK
Karl Dieter Reinartz	University of Erlangen-Nuremberg, Germany

Euro-Par 2020 Organization

Co-chairs

Krzysztof Rzadca   University of Warsaw, Poland
Maciej Malawski   AGH University of Science and Technology, Poland

Workshops

Bartosz Baliś   AGH University of Science and Technology, Poland
Dora Blanco Heras   CiTIUS, University of Santiago de Compostela, Spain

Logistics

GlobalCongress

Additional Reviewers

Abdelhafez, Hazem
Antonelli, Laura
Barbara, Fadi
Campagna, Rosanna
Chasapis, Konstantinos
Cuomo, Salvatore
Dolz, Manuel F.
Faloci, Francesco
Guzzi, Pietro Hiram
Ito, Yasuaki
Lepore, Cristian
Mathà, Roland
Mehran, Narges
Mercanti, Ivan
Murgia, Maurizio
Nikolskiy, Vsevolod
Rodríguez-Sánchez, Rafael
Spadafora, Chiara
Takafuji, Daisuke
Thamsen, Lauritz
Vitaletti, Andrea

Euro-Par 2020 Organization

Additional Reviewers

Contents

ParaMo - Workshop on Parallel Programming Models in High-Performance Cloud

**Resilience - 13th Workshop on Resiliency in High Performance
Computing with Clouds, Grids, and Clusters**

Complementary Papers

FPDAPP - Second International Workshop on Future Perspective of Decentralised APPlications

International Workshop on Future Perspectives of Decentralised Applications (FPDAPP)

Workshop Description

Blockchain technologies (BCTs) make agreement amongst untrusted parties possible, without the need for certification authorities. Proposed frameworks have been put forward in sectors as diverse as finance, health-care, notarization, intellectual property management, identity, provenance, international cooperation, social good, and security to cite but a few. Smart contracts, i.e. self-enforcing agreements in terms of executable software running on blockchains, have been developed in several contexts. Such an under-definition computational model introduces innovative aspects such as the economics and trust of the decentralized computation relying on the shared contribution of peers and their decentralized consensus.

This third edition of FPDAPP offered a venue for presenting and discussing the latest applications of BCTs, their technical aspects, the novel decentralized computation model, and the possible impact on society, business, and the public sector.

FPDAPP is traditionally hosted at Euro-Par, with the aim to foster cross-fertilization between the blockchain and the distributed/parallel computing communities, which share several interests and can strongly contribute to each other's development.

FPDAPP 2020 received 10 papers for review. After a thorough peer-reviewing process, with at least three reviews per paper, 6 papers were accepted for publication, presented at the workshop, and published in this volume.

Due to the exceptional international situation due to the Covid-19 pandemic, FPDAPP 2020 was held remotely, through video conferencing provided by the main conference. We want to particularly thank the authors, reviewers, participants, the program committee, and the Euro-Par organization for their efforts this year, which, despite difficulties, contributed to maintaining the submission rate, the quality of the papers, and the interest of the on-line presentations and discussion.

Organization

Program Chairs

Andrea Bracciali	University of Stirling, UK
Claudio Schifanella	University of Turin, Italy

Program Committee

Fadi Barbara	University of Turin, Italy
Stefano Bistarelli	University of Perugia, Italy
Guido Boella	University of Turin, Italy
Monika Di Angelo	Technische Universität Wien, Austria
Nadia Fabrizio	CEFRIEL, Italy
Alberto Guffanti	University of Turin, Italy
Luca Mazzola	Hochschule Luzern - Informatik, Switzerland
Carlos Molina-Jiménez	University of Cambridge, UK
Federico Pintore	University of Oxford, UK
Massimiliano Sala	University of Trento, Italy
Yilei Wang	Ludong University, China
Aleš Zamuda	University of Maribor, Slovenia

Additional Reviewers

Francesco Faloci
Cristian Lepore
Ivan Mercanti
Maurizio Murgia
Chiara Spadafora
Andrea Vitaletti

Blockchain Utility in Use Cases: Observations, Red Flags, and Requirements

Tommy Koens$^{(\boxtimes)}$ and Erik Poll

Radboud University, Nijmegen, The Netherlands
{tkoens,E.Poll}@cs.ru.nl

Abstract. On a global scale blockchain is persistently proposed in thousands of use cases by corporates, governments, and academics. However, there is a lack of systematic evaluation of these use cases and the utility of blockchain. In this work we systematically evaluate fifteen use cases that use blockchain. Based on our evaluation we observe six recurring problems in these use cases. These problems either relate to the utility of blockchain in the use case, or to how well-documented a use case description is. We point out four red flags that, whenever they occur in a use case description, signal that blockchain may be a sub-optimal solution for that use case. Notably, one of these red flags indicates that there are no clear requirements in the use case descriptions that warrant the use of blockchain. We address this by proposing a set of requirement templates for any use case that includes a transaction system.

Keywords: Blockchain · Use case · Evaluation · Red flags · Requirements

1 Introduction

It is estimated that global spending on blockchain reaches 9.2 billion US dollars in 2021 [7]. Indeed, there is much attention from corporate institutions, governments, and academics to blockchain. Many use cases have been proposed that use blockchain in, for example, healthcare [43], and cloud computing [33]. Such use cases advocate blockchain as a solution to a particular use case problem. There is, however, a lack of a systematic evaluation of use cases and the utility of blockchain. To address this we make the following three contributions:

1. We systematically evaluate fifteen use cases that apply blockchain based on a decision scheme which we improve. From our evaluation we observe six recurring problems, including that there is a bias towards decentralisation, fallacies on blockchain properties occur, and there are no requirements that warrant the use of blockchain.

© Springer Nature Switzerland AG 2021
B. Balis et al. (Eds.): Euro-Par 2020 Workshops, LNCS 12480, pp. 5–17, 2021.
https://doi.org/10.1007/978-3-030-71593-9_1

2. From these six observations we introduce four red flags. Raising such a flag signals that blockchain may be a sub-optimal solution for a use case; blockchain is a sub-optimal solution when alternative technologies can be used. These red flags also allow for a quick evaluation of a use case description. We apply these red flags to the fifteen use cases and evaluate our findings.

3. Red flag 1 'no clear requirements' is raised for all fifteen use case descriptions. We argue that defining use case requirements must precede any technological choice. We address this by proposing a set of requirement templates for any use case that includes a transaction system.

2   Background

Bitcoin [30] and Ethereum [41] are two examples of a decentralised transaction system. Both systems use blockchain to create a public and permissionless ledger. This type of ledger allows for an unbounded number of pseudonymous participants to reach consensus on the state of a ledger. By contrast, private and permissioned ledgers, such as Corda [17], allow a select number of known participants to view the content of the ledger. Also, a select number of participants can participate in creating and verifying transactions. In this research we evaluate use cases that aim to use either Bitcoin or Ethereum. We use Bitcoin as an example to describe a public and permissionless ledger because such a description is sufficient for our research. In a public and permissionless ledger participants may own one ore more tokens (e.g. bitcoins). Participants can propose a change of ownership by means of transactions (txs). To prevent a participant from spending a token twice, transactions are bundled in a one megabyte (MB) block by participants called miners. A miner that creates a new block attempts to solve a difficult cryptographic puzzle which is easy to verify. The probability of solving this puzzle increases with the amount of computational power a miner has. As such, miners may form a mining pool in which they combine their computational power.

Occasionally two miners find a block at the same time which may contain, possible, conflicting transactions. Here the chain of blocks branches into a fork. To address a fork, a rule in Bitcoin exists stating that only the chain with the most cumulative work (i.e. a solved puzzle) is valid. If one of the branches is extended by another block, then that branch becomes the new and valid chain, and the shorter branch is discarded by all network participants.

Currently there are four main challenges with public and permissionless ledgers. First, the transaction throughput in blockchain is limited. Bitcoin can process 7 transactions per second. Although improvements have been proposed for blockchain to increase transaction throughput, such as an increase in block size or off-chain payments, these solutions could lead to centralisation [24]. Second, some devices can not store the blockchain as it is too large, for example IoT devices. Although this can be addressed by light-clients, it would also lead to centralisation as a large group of nodes is now dependent on a small group of nodes to update the ledger [15]. Third, transaction finality is probabilistic.

There is a probability that a transaction will be removed from the ledger due to the appearance of a fork. Only when time progresses there is an increased probability that the transaction will remain on ledger. Fourth, transaction cost may exceed the value of tokens being transferred in a transaction. This makes that blockchain may not be suitable for specific use cases, for example, a use case that deals with micro-transactions.

2.1 Blockchain Decision Schemes

Blockchain has been proposed in use cases where its usefulness is questionable. To address this, decision schemes have been proposed to determine if blockchain should be applied. We use the scheme by Koens and Poll [22] as they propose a new scheme based on an evaluation of 30 of such schemes. They show that there are contradictions between some of these schemes, whereas other schemes are biased towards blockchain. Their scheme allows for determining if blockchain is an optimal solution, and which alternative technologies can be used.

Their scheme involves nine conditions, where each condition either leads to another condition or leads to a *technology* that is considered the optimal solution for a use case. We briefly introduce these conditions in their respective order.

1. Need to store state? When state should not be stored then there is *no need for a database*.
2. Is there a single writer? If only a single writer exists then a *central database* can be used.
3. Need to control functionality? Controlling functionality is being able to determine which and how many functions a system can perform. For example, determining how the data is stored in a database. If control of functionality is required then a *shared central database* can be used.
4. Can you use a third party (TP)? If a third party can be used then a *shared central database* can be used.
5. Is there transaction (tx) interaction? This refers to the interdependency between transactions. For example, an account holding zero tokens can only send tokens by means of tx_2 once it receives tokens first from another transaction tx_1. Transaction tx_1 therefore must be stored on the ledger first before transaction tx_2 can occur. If there is no need for transaction interaction then a *distributed database* should be used.
6. Are the participants known? This refers to if the identity of the participants should be known in a use case. If the identity of the participants should be known then the following question appears:
7. Can anyone join the network? If participants are known and anyone can join the network, a *permissioned ledger* should be used, such as Ripple [4]. If the participants are known and only a limited set of participants can join the network, then a *permissioned ledger* such as Corda [17] should be used.
8. Transaction throughput matters? Blockchains currently can not process a large amount of transactions per second [28], which may be a limitation for a use case.

9. Store large amount of data? Another limitation may be the need for storing large amount of data. Blockchains currently can not store large amount of data [28].

Our Improvements to the Decision Scheme. We make three improvements to the scheme of Koens and Poll [22]:

1. We omit condition 3 from the scheme. A third party can be used if functionality needs to be controlled, which is related to the condition 4. If a third party can not be used then functionality can not be controlled. Therefore, the condition regarding the control of functionality is already included in the condition of being able to use a third party.
2. We find that all use cases can use a third party. According to the decision scheme a *shared central database* should be used. However, use cases 4 and 8 argue that the problem of the use case lies within centralisation itself. Even though it would be technically feasible to use a third party in these use cases, a third party seems not to be suitable because of trust issues. Therefore we add another condition: a. Is a centralised solution based on a single third party (TP) suitable?
3. Conditions 8 and 9 concern potential limitations of blockchain. Blockchain is proposed as a solution when none of these limitations matter. Otherwise, there currently is no solution available. However, these are not the only current limitations, as discussed in Sect. 2, which is why we add two more conditions: a. Transaction finality matters? and b. Transaction cost matters?

3   Related Work

In our research we make six observations, see Sect. 4.1. Observations 1–6 have been made separately in the literature but are unrelated, for example in [10] and [22] in which fallacies about blockchain and blockchain limitations are discussed separately. In our work the six observations are a set of recurring problems in the fifteen use cases. In addition, our observations support each separate observation made in the literature. A description of the fallacies that occur, see Sect. 4, are furthermore described in the literature, for example in [38]. In our research we go beyond this description as we observe that these fallacies are used as a rationale to apply blockchain, and we argue in Sect. 4 that these fallacies can not be used as an argument for applying blockchain.

In Sect. 4.2 we propose and discuss four red flags. We did not find any existing work that proposes similar red flags. Also, the observed relationship between red flags 3 and 4 is new in the literature.

Use case requirements have been proposed for particular domains, such as healthcare [43], and internet service architecture [33]. Other use cases requirements have been proposed that are set by an external party [31]. These requirements are limited to a specific use case that is using blockchain. In Sect. 4.3 we propose a set of requirement templates. Our set of requirements can be used for any use case that includes a transaction system. This is useful because our requirements can be used to 1. prevent raising any of the red flags, and 2. determine the feasibility of using blockchain.

4   Use Case Evaluation

We conduct our research based on the Design Science Research (DSR) methodology. DSR is a research paradigm in which a researcher aims to answers questions via the creation of artefacts, thereby contributing new knowledge to the literature [18]. Such artefacts may include models, methods, constructs, and design theories [19]. In our research these artefacts are the red flags in Sect. 4.2 and the requirement templates in Sect. 4.3. We use a case study as our research method [14]. We use the improved version of the decision scheme, as discussed in Sect. 2, to systematically evaluate fifteen use cases that use blockchain. All use cases propose to use either the Bitcoin blockchain or the Ethereum blockchain. We choose five use cases that apply blockchain in identity management, five use cases in IoT, and five use cases in business process management, see Table 1. We choose these topics as they are one of many application domains of blockchain [1] and because we find these interesting, and because the use case address a topic other than cryptocurrencies. Besides this, we aim to choose the use cases randomly to prevent a bias in evaluating the use cases.

Table 1. Overview of use cases (UCs) evaluated

UC	Author(s)	Area of application
1	Zyskind et al. [44]	Identity management
2	Augot [5]	Identity management
3	Raju et al. [37]	Identity management
4	Al-Bassam [2]	Identity management
5	Liu et al. [25]	Identity management
6	Huh et al. [21]	Internet of Things
7	Özyilmaz and Yurdakul [32]	Internet of Things
8	Manzoor et al. [27]	Internet of Things
9	Huang et al. [20]	Internet of Things
10	Alblooshi et al. [3]	Internet of Things
11	Weber et al. [40]	Business process management
12	Prybila et al. [36]	Business process management
13	López-Pintado [26]	Business process management
14	Haarmann [16]	Business process management
15	Viriyasitavat [39]	Business process management

We aim to answer all scheme questions for each use case. The results of our evaluation are shown in Table 2, where Y stands for 'yes', N stands for 'no', and

U stands for 'unknown'. Here, 'unknown' means that the use case description does not provide an answer to the scheme question. In what follows we discuss our evaluation in more detail.

Table 2. Decision scheme results per use case

Scheme question	Use cases														
	1	2	3	4	5	6	7	8	9	10	11	12	13	14	15
1. Need to store state?	Y	Y	Y	Y	Y	Y	Y	Y	Y	Y	Y	Y	Y	Y	Y
2. Is there a single writer?	N	N	N	N	N	N	N	N	N	N	N	N	N	N	N
3. Can you use a third party?[a]	Y	Y	Y	Y	Y	Y	Y	Y	Y	Y	Y	Y	Y	Y	Y
4. Is a TP solution suitable?[a]	N	N	N	N	N	N	Y	Y	N	N	N	N	N	N	Y
5. Tx interaction?	Y	Y	Y	Y	Y	Y	Y	Y	Y	Y	Y	Y	Y	Y	Y
6. Writers known?	Y	Y	Y	Y	Y	Y	Y	Y	Y	Y	Y	Y	Y	Y	Y
7. Can anyone join the network?	U	U	Y	Y	U	U	U	U	U	N	N	Y	U	N	Y
8. Tx throughput matters?	U	U	U	U	U	Y	Y	Y	U	U	U	Y	Y	U	U
9. Store large amount of data?	Y	Y	U	Y	Y	Y	Y	Y	Y	N	Y	N	N	U	U
10. Tx finality matters?	U	Y	U	U	U	U	Y	U	U	U	U	Y	U	U	Y
11. Tx cost matters?	U	Y	U	Y	U	U	U	U	U	U	Y	U	Y	Y	Y

[a]The difference between questions 3 and 4 is discussed in Sect. 2.1

4.1   Observations from the Use Case Evaluation

From our evaluation we make the following six observations:

1. The descriptions of the use cases mention a downside of centralisation and none of these descriptions mention a downside of decentralisation.
2. In all use cases fallacies occur on blockchain properties.
3. Some use case descriptions do not address the current blockchain limitations.
4. Blockchain is applied despite that the decision scheme (see Sect. 2.1) suggests other technologies for all use cases.
5. None of the use cases consider other technologies other than blockchain.
6. Clear requirements that warrant the use of blockchain are not specified in the use case descriptions.

Note that observation 1–3 relate to the solution proposed in the use case description. Observations 4–6 relate to the deficiencies of the solution in the use case description. From these six observations we derive red flags, see Sect. 4.2. Also, we address observation 6 by proposing a set of requirement templates derived from observations 1, 2, and 5, in Sect. 4.3. Observations 3 and 4 are likely to be avoided when these requirement templates are applied in use case descriptions. In what follows we will discuss the observations in more detail.

Observation 1. The downsides of *decentralisation* are not discussed in any of the fifteen use cases. The use cases that do not wish to use a third party mention the downsides of *centralisation*, such as lack of trust between participants and a third party, lack of decentralisation, and lack of transparency. However, long before the advent of blockchain it has been argued that there are downsides of decentralisation [12]. In fact, Prud'Homme states that "... there are serious drawbacks that should be considered in designing any decentralisation program" [35]. A downside of fiscal decentralisation, for example, is that it may lead to disparity and adversely affect the distribution of equity, it may jeopardise stability, and it may undermine efficiency [35]. Note that these arguments are blockchain agnostic as they were stated before blockchain was proposed by Nakamoto [30]. As these downsides are not discussed there appears to be a bias towards decentralisation in the use cases. Such drawbacks should be discussed in the use cases, as the downsides of centralisation are also being discussed.

Observation 2. In the use case descriptions fallacies occur on blockchain properties. Such fallacies may lead to misconceptions about the advantages and limitations of blockchain [9]. The following fallacies occur in the use cases:

1. "Blockchain is immutable". Smith [38], for example, argues that a blockchain is not immutable. Indeed, a blockchain must be mutable as forks may occur, as discussed in Sect. 2.
2. "Blockchain is fully decentralised". Bitcoin and Ethereum are not fully decentralised. In fact, the Bitcoin network is largely controlled by 8 mining pools, and the Ethereum network is largely controlled by 5 mining pools [13]. This centralisation contradicts the goal of the Bitcoin network [30], as now participants have to rely on a few third parties processing payments.
3. "Blockchain does not include trusted third parties". Blockchain networks are largely dominated by a limited set of participants, see fallacy 2, and trust is placed in these participants to not to collude.
4. "Blockchain is trustless", and "blockchain increases trust". Lemieux [23], for example, argues that blockchain is a trusted chain of transactions. Also, following the description at fallacy 2, trust is placed in a small group of miners to not to collude.
5. "Blockchain is scalable". In contrast, one of the challenges of blockchain is its transaction scalability [28], as discussed in Sect. 2.
6. "Blockchain is safe and credible". The use cases do not provide a definition of the terms 'safe' and 'credible'. As such, there is no proof for this statement.
7. "Blockchain is anonymous". All use cases propose to use either the Bitcoin blockchain or the Ethereum blockchain. It has been shown that these blockchains do not provide anonymity as identities can be retrieved [29].

Some of these fallacies are used as a rationale to support the use of blockchain in the fifteen use cases. However, as these are fallacies they can not serve as an argument for using blockchain. From observation 2 we derive requirements 5–8, see Sect. 4.3.

Observation 3. The current blockchain limitations, as discussed in Sect. 2, are not sufficiently addressed in some use case descriptions. There appear to be two causes for this. First, blockchain limitations are ignored in the use case descriptions. Second, blockchain limitations are addressed by introducing a centralised solution such as a private blockchain, or a cloud provider. From this observation we derive red flag 4 in Sect. 4.2. Observation 3 leads us to propose the requirement templates 1–4 in Sect. 4.3.

Observation 4. The participants that update the database are known in all use cases where a single third party is not wanted. For these use cases the improved decision scheme, as discussed in Sect. 2, suggests a distributed ledger. However, all fifteen use cases choose to apply a blockchain.

Observation 5. None of the use cases consider alternative technologies other than blockchain. As decentralisation is a recurring theme in all fifteen use cases, see observation 1, at least other technologies should be considered that also achieve decentralisation such as a distributed ledger.

Observation 6. Clear requirements that warrant the use of blockchain are not specified in the use case descriptions. In particular, scheme questions 8, 10 and 11 remain mostly unanswered, see Table 2. To address observation 6 we propose a set of requirement templates for use cases that include a transaction system in Sect. 4.3.

4.2   Red Flags

In this section we propose four red flags for use cases that use blockchain, and we apply these red flags to the fifteen use cases. Blockchain may be a sub-optimal solution for a use case when one of the following flags is raised:

1. There are no clear use case requirements in the use case description.
2. Other technologies than blockchain are not considered.
3. Current blockchain limitations are not addressed.
4. A centralised solution is introduced despite the use case description stating the need for a decentralised solution.

Red flag 1 and 2 measure how well-documented use cases are, whereas red flag 3 and 4 provide technical insight in the utility of blockchain. Red flag 1 is derived from observations 1 and 6, as discussed in Sect. 4.1. Red flag 2 is derived from observations 4 and 5, red flag 3 is derived from observations 2 and 3, and red flag 4 is derived from observation 3, We observe from Table 3 that for all use cases almost all flags are raised.

Red flags 3 and 4 are closely related in the fifteen use cases. Red flag 3 is not raised when current blockchain limitations are addressed, however, this raises red flag 4 for six of the fifteen use cases as a centralised solution is introduced, for example, a cloud provider. Red flag 4 is not raised when no centralised solution is proposed, however, this raises red flag 3 for nine of the fifteen use cases as the current blockchain issues are not addressed. The findings in Sect. 4.1, where we argue that the use cases may also use other technologies, appear to support the validity of raising these flags. This suggests that raising three of the four red flags is a signal that blockchain is a sub-optimal solution for a use case.

Table 3. Red flags raised in each use case

Red flag	Red flag raised in use case[a]														
	1	2	3 .	4	5	6	7	8	9	10	11	12	13	14	15
1. No clear requirements	Y	Y	Y	Y	Y	Y	Y	Y	Y	Y	Y	Y	Y	Y	Y
2. No other tech. considered	Y	Y	Y	Y	Y	Y	Y	Y	Y	Y	Y	Y	Y	Y	Y
3. Blockchain issues not addressed	N	Y	N	Y	Y	Y	N	Y	N	N	N	Y	N	N	N
4. Introduction of a centr. solution	Y	N	Y	N	N	N	Y	N	Y	Y	Y	N	Y	Y	Y

[a]Y: the flag is raised for a use case. N: the flag is not raised.

4.3 Use Case Requirements

Red flag 1 'No clear requirements' is raised for all fifteen use cases. As such, none of the use case descriptions state clear requirements for the use of blockchain. This is a concern as use case requirements have to be defined before choosing any solution. Leaving the requirements implicit imposes a risk to the implementation of the use case, as better solutions may be available. To address this concern we propose a set of requirement templates. We derive requirements 1–4 from observation 3, and requirements 5–8 are derived from observation 2, as discussed in Sect. 4.1. These requirements can be used in any use case that includes a transaction system to verify the feasibility of the use case.

Requirement Templates. Our requirement templates are based on the format proposed in the standard textbook on requirements engineering [11]:
the <system> shall be able to <function> <object>.

1. The <system> shall be able to process <...> transactions per second.
2. The <system> shall be able to store <...> MB of data.
3. The <system> shall be able to finalise transactions in <...> seconds.
4. The <system> shall be able to limit the cost of a transaction to a maximum of <...> US dollar per transaction.
5. The <system> shall be able to provide a data storage that is <...>
   - Mutable. Data stored can be modified and appended.
   - Append-only. Data stored can only be appended.
   - Immutable. Data stored can not be modified or appended.
6. The <system> shall be able to provide user identities that are <...>
   - Known. The legal identity of a participant is known to all participants, for example the true name of a person.
   - Pseudonymous. The identity of a person is disguised by providing a false name, for example a public key.
   - Anonymous. The identity of a person being unknown.
7. The <system> shall be able to include at least <...> parties (for example, 1, 2, etc.) to use the <system>.
8. The <system> shall be able to distribute the capability of modifying the database over <...> (for example, anyone, a limited set of participants)

5   Limitations and Future Work

Our requirement templates are based on an analyses of use cases that are limited to either Bitcoin or Ethereum. Potentially, additional or other requirements can be proposed based on an analyses of use cases that use a blockchain other than Bitcoin or Ethereum. Additional requirements may be derived from an analyses of use cases in other domains, such as energy, health care, and finance. Evaluation of additional use cases based on other decision schemes, for example [42] and [34], could be preceded by using our red flags. Those findings may introduce new red flags, and may support the validity of our red flags.

The need for decentralisation in the fifteen use cases is the opinion of those that performed the research. Looking beyond that opinion, future research should include the opinion of participants (such as consumers of a product) of a use case, and to what extent they believe decentralisation should be applied. Also, the meaning and consequences of decentralisation could be critically discussed in future work. Furthermore, a similar evaluation to our research could be performed of decentralised solutions that are not blockchain based, such as a Directed Acyclic Graph (DAG) [8] and Hashgraph [6].

6   Conclusion

In this research we systematically evaluate fifteen use cases that propose blockchain as a solution. We argue that blockchain is a sub-optimal solution for these fifteen use cases. With billions of US dollars spend on blockchain, this is a concern, as blockchain may be a sub-optimal solution for other use cases, too. We point out four red flags that, whenever they are raised, signal that blockchain is a sub-optimal solution for that use case. Red flag 1, no clear requirements, is raised for all fifteen use cases. We address this by presenting eight requirement templates that can be applied to any use case that includes a transaction system. With these templates, corporates, governments, and academics may become more aware of the need for blockchain, or the lack of any such a need.

References

1. Jaoude, J.A., Saade, R.G.: Blockchain applications-usage in different domains. IEEE Access **7**, 45360–45381 (2019)
2. Al-Bassam, M.: SCPKI: a smart contract-based PKI and identity system. In: Proceedings of the ACM Workshop on Blockchain, Cryptocurrencies and Contracts, pp. 35–40 (2017)
3. Alblooshi, M., Salah, K., Alhammadi, Y.: Blockchain-based ownership management for medical IoT (MIoT) devices. In: 2018 International Conference on Innovations in Information Technology (IIT), pp. 151–156. IEEE (2018)
4. Armknecht, F., Karame, G.O., Mandal, A., Youssef, F., Zenner, E.: Ripple: overview and outlook. In: Conti, M., Schunter, M., Askoxylakis, I. (eds.) Trust 2015. LNCS, vol. 9229, pp. 163–180. Springer, Cham (2015). https://doi.org/10.1007/978-3-319-22846-4_10

5. Augot, D., Chabanne, H., Chenevier, T., George, W., Lambert, L.: A user-centric system for verified identities on the bitcoin blockchain. In: Garcia-Alfaro, J., Navarro-Arribas, G., Hartenstein, H., Herrera-Joancomartí, J. (eds.) ESORICS/DPM/CBT -2017. LNCS, vol. 10436, pp. 390–407. Springer, Cham (2017). https://doi.org/10.1007/978-3-319-67816-0_22
6. Baird, L.: The swirlds hashgraph consensus algorithm: fair, fast, byzantine fault tolerance. Swirlds, Inc., Technical Report SWIRLDS-TR-2016, 1 (2016)
7. Bashir, I.: Mastering Blockchain: Distributed Ledger Technology, Decentralization, and Smart Contracts Explained. Packt Publishing Ltd. (2018)
8. Benčić, F.M., Žarko, I.P.: Distributed ledger technology: blockchain compared to directed acyclic graph. In: 2018 IEEE 38th International Conference on Distributed Computing Systems (ICDCS), pp. 1569–1570. IEEE (2018)
9. Carson, B., Romanelli, G., Walsh, P., Zhumaev, A.: Blockchain Beyond the Hype: What is the Strategic Business Value. McKinsey & Company, pp. 1–13 (2018)
10. de Leon, D.C., Stalick, A.Q., Jillepalli, A.A., Haney, M.A., Sheldon, F.T.: Blockchain: properties and misconceptions. Asia Pac. J. Innov. Entrep. (2017)
11. Dick, J., Hull, E., Jackson, K.: Requirements Engineering. Springer, Cham (2017). https://doi.org/10.1007/978-3-319-61073-3
12. Fisman, R., Gatti, R.: Decentralization and corruption: evidence across countries. J. Public Econ. **83**(3), 325–345 (2002)
13. Gencer, A.E., Basu, S., Eyal, I., van Renesse, R., Sirer, E.G.: Decentralization in Bitcoin and Ethereum networks. In: Meiklejohn, S., Sako, K. (eds.) FC 2018. LNCS, vol. 10957, pp. 439–457. Springer, Heidelberg (2018). https://doi.org/10.1007/978-3-662-58387-6_24
14. Gerring, J.: Case Study Research: Principles and Practices. Cambridge University Press, Cambridge (2006)
15. Gervais, A., Karame, G.O., Capkun, V., Capkun, S.: Is Bitcoin a decentralized currency? IEEE Secur. Priv. **12**(3), 54–60 (2014)
16. Haarmann, S., Batoulis, K., Nikaj, A., Weske, M.: DMN decision execution on the Ethereum blockchain. In: Krogstie, J., Reijers, H.A. (eds.) CAiSE 2018. LNCS, vol. 10816, pp. 327–341. Springer, Cham (2018). https://doi.org/10.1007/978-3-319-91563-0_20
17. Hearn, M.: Corda: a distributed ledger. Corda Technical White Paper, 2016 (2016)
18. Hevner, A., Chatterjee, S.: Design science research in information systems. In: Design Research in Information Systems, pp. 9–22. Springer, Boston (2010). https://doi.org/10.1007/978-1-4419-5653-8_2
19. Hevner, A.R., March, S.T., Park, J., Ram, S.: Design science in information systems research. MIS Q. 75–105 (2004)
20. Huang, Z., Su, X., Zhang, Y., Shi, C., Zhang, H., Xie, L.: A decentralized solution for IoT data trusted exchange based-on blockchain. In: 2017 3rd IEEE International Conference on Computer and Communications (ICCC), pp. 1180–1184. IEEE (2017)
21. Huh, S., Cho, S., Kim, S.: Managing IoT devices using blockchain platform. In: 2017 19th International Conference on Advanced Communication Technology (ICACT), pp. 464–467. IEEE (2017)
22. Koens, T., Poll, E.: What blockchain alternative do you need? In: Garcia-Alfaro, J., Herrera-Joancomartí, J., Livraga, G., Rios, R. (eds.) DPM/CBT -2018. LNCS, vol. 11025, pp. 113–129. Springer, Cham (2018). https://doi.org/10.1007/978-3-030-00305-0_9

23. Lemieux, V.L.: Trusting records: is blockchain technology the answer? Rec. Manage. J. (2016)

24. Lin, J.-H., Primicerio, K., Squartini, T., Decker, C., Tessone, C.J.: Lightning network: a second path towards centralisation of the Bitcoin economy. arXiv preprint arXiv:2002.02819 (2020)

25. Liu, Y., Zhao, Z., Guo, G., Wang, X., Tan, Z., Wang, S.: An identity management system based on blockchain. In: 2017 15th Annual Conference on Privacy, Security and Trust (PST), pp. 44–4409. IEEE (2017)

26. López-Pintado, O., García-Bañuelos, L., Dumas, M., Weber, I., Ponomarev, A.: Caterpillar: a business process execution engine on the Ethereum blockchain. Softw. Pract. Exp. **49**(7), 1162–1193 (2019)

27. Manzoor, A., Liyanage, M., Braeke, A., Kanhere, S.S., Ylianttila, M.: Blockchain based proxy re-encryption scheme for secure IoT data sharing. In: 2019 IEEE International Conference on Blockchain and Cryptocurrency (ICBC), pp. 99–103. IEEE (2019)

28. Meiklejohn, S.: Top ten obstacles along distributed ledgers path to adoption. IEEE Security & Privacy **16**(4), 13–19 (2018)

29. Meiklejohn, S., et al.: A fistful of Bitcoins: characterizing payments among men with no names. In: Proceedings of the 2013 Conference on Internet Measurement Conference, pp. 127–140 (2013)

30. Nakamoto, S.: Bitcoin: a peer-to-peer electronic cash system (2008). https://bitcoin.org/bitcoin.pdf

31. Neisse, R., Steri, G., Nai-Fovino, I.: A blockchain-based approach for data accountability and provenance tracking. In: Proceedings of the 12th International Conference on Availability, Reliability and Security, pp. 1–10 (2017)

32. Ozyilmaz, K.R., Yurdakul, A.A.: Designing a blockchain-based IoT with Ethereum, Swarm, and loRa: the software solution to create high availability with minimal security risks. IEEE Consum. Electron. Mag. **8**(2), 28–34 (2019)

33. Park, J.H., Park, J.H.: Blockchain security in cloud computing: use cases, challenges, and solutions. Symmetry **9**(8), 164 (2017)

34. Peck, M.E.: Blockchain world-do you need a blockchain? This chart will tell you if the technology can solve your problem. IEEE Spectrum **54**(10), 38–60 (2017)

35. Prud'Homme, R.: The dangers of decentralization. In: The World Bank Research Observer, vol. 10, no. 2, pp. 201–220 (1995)

36. Prybila, C., Schulte, S., Hochreiner, C., Weber, I.: Runtime verification for business processes utilizing the Bitcoin blockchain. Future Gener. Comput. Syst. **107**, 816–831 (2020)

37. Raju, S., Boddepalli, S., Gampa, S., Yan, Q., Deogun, J.S.: Identity management using blockchain for cognitive cellular networks. In: 2017 IEEE International Conference on Communications (ICC), pp. 1–6. IEEE (2017)

38. Smith, T.D.: The blockchain litmus test. In: 2017 IEEE International Conference on Big Data (Big Data), pp. 2299–2308. IEEE (2017)

39. Viriyasitavat, W., Da Xu, L., Bi, Z., Sapsomboon, A.: Blockchain-based business process management (BPM) framework for service composition in industry 4.0. J. Intell. Manufa. 1–12 (2018)

40. Weber, I., et al.: On availability for blockchain-based systems. In: 2017 IEEE 36th Symposium on Reliable Distributed Systems (SRDS), pp. 64–73. IEEE (2017)

41. Wood, G., et al.: Ethereum: a secure decentralised generalised transaction ledger. Ethereum project yellow paper, vol. 151, no. 2014, pp. 1–32 (2014)

42. Wüst, K., Gervais, A.: Do you need a blockchain? In: 2018 Crypto Valley Conference on Blockchain Technology (CVCBT), pp. 45–54. IEEE (2018)
43. Zhang, P., Schmidt, D.C., White, J., Lenz, G.: Blockchain technology use cases in healthcare. In: Advances in Computers, vol. 111, pp. 1–41. Elsevier (2018)
44. Zyskind, G., Nathan, O., et al.: Decentralizing privacy: using blockchain to protect personal data. In: 2015 IEEE Security and Privacy Workshops, pp. 180–184. IEEE (2015)

Ants-Review: A Privacy-Oriented Protocol for Incentivized Open Peer Reviews on Ethereum

Bianca Trovò[1,2(✉)] and Nazzareno Massari[3]

[1] Sorbonne Université, Faculté des Sciences et Ingénierie, Paris, France
[2] Atomic Energy and Alternative Energies Commission (CEA), Frédéric Joliot Institute for Life Sciences, NeuroSpin, Cognitive Neuroimaging Unit, Saclay, France
bianca.trovo@protonmail.com
[3] MakerDAO, Community Development, London, UK
nazzareno@nazzarenomassari.com

Abstract. Peer review is a necessary and essential quality control step for scientific publications but lacks proper incentives. Indeed, the process, which is very costly in terms of time and intellectual investment, not only is not remunerated by the journals but it is also not openly recognized by the academic community as a relevant scientific output for a researcher. Therefore, scientific dissemination is affected in timeliness, quality and fairness. Here, to solve this issue, we propose a blockchain-based incentive system that rewards scientists for peer reviewing other scientists' work and that builds up trust and reputation. We designed a privacy-oriented protocol of smart contracts called Ants-Review that allows authors to issue a bounty for open anonymous peer reviews on Ethereum. If requirements are met, peer reviews will be accepted and paid by the approver proportionally to their assessed quality. To promote ethical behaviour and inclusiveness the system implements a gamified mechanism that allows the whole community to evaluate the peer reviews and vote for the best ones.

Keywords: Blockchain · Ethereum · Peer review · Incentivization

1 Introduction

Since the birth of Bitcoin [18] in 2008 as a peer-to-peer electronic cash system, blockchain technologies have spread far beyond the sole cryptocurrency domain, in particular after the implementation of general purpose smart contracts introduced by Ethereum [32]. Besides a growing number of applications ranging from De-Fi, healthcare, music industry, government, identity, to cite but a few, blockchain technology has recently started to catalyse the attention of the scientific community as well [7,24] with the promising potential of being a 'game

---

The two authors contributed equally to this work.

© Springer Nature Switzerland AG 2021
B. Balis et al. (Eds.): Euro-Par 2020 Workshops, LNCS 12480, pp. 18–29, 2021.
https://doi.org/10.1007/978-3-030-71593-9_2

changer' in outdated and broken scientific practices and leading towards open science [2]. Indeed, scholars have pointed out how the intrinsic characteristics of blockchain technology set the basis for a open science infrastructure [15] in which decisional processes are transparent and therefore more democratically accessible to all the stakeholders (researchers, reviewers, funders, taxpayers). Those are: the consensus algorithm [16], a deterministic computational trust that allows for decentralization, for which there are no trusted third parties; the proof of existence (PoE) that via cryptographic hashing and timestamping creates a digital footprint able to keep a traceable chronological record of research objects that cannot be altered or retrieved (due to its property of immutability or append-only) [15]. In particular, a 'blockchainified science' [3] could 'reduce waste' [10], by disclosing each step in the research cycle to 'scientific self-correction' way before the final publication step, and therefore help fixing the current reproducibility crisis in science.

A thorny issue in the academic system that can - and we think it should - be tackled by blockchain concerns the status and accreditation of peer review, the core process of scientific validation currently facing a crisis [11]. In this paper we propose a solution to the problem of reviewers recognition based on the principles of tokenomics [14] and in line with the values of open science.

2   Background

2.1   Peer Review: Present Problems and Mild Solutions

Peer review is still the only quality control mechanism devoted to evaluating scientific outcomes. The purpose of peer review is, to cite [11]: "improving the quality of the published paper, determining the originality of the manuscript, determining the importance of the findings, detecting fraud, and detecting plagiarism.". However, the system is 'flawed' and outdated [25] and presents multifaceted issues [28], here reviewed.

A Slow Multi-Stage Process. The main issues affecting the effectiveness of peer review is the delay between paper submission and journal acceptance for publication. The traditional peer review process is centralized around the journals' editor(s). The author(s) submit the manuscript to the journal where an editorial team assesses if the paper meets the scopes of the journal and novelty criteria. If the editorial decision is to send the manuscript for review, the handling editor personally selects potential reviewers. The authors' identity is usually known to the reviewer but the reviewers' identity is hidden to the authors or among the other reviewers themselves (single-blind review). Reviewers independently conduct their reviews by exposing in their reports strengths and weaknesses of the manuscript and sometimes substantially improving the draft. Depending on if the decision is a major or minor revision, authors are invited to re-submit a corrected or improved version of the manuscript. The same reviewers might be contacted again to continue the same peer review process. This process can take multiple rounds and is a huge time investment both for authors and reviewers. An analysis of all papers published in *PubMed* for a time period of 30 years claims that the median review time is around 100 days [19].

Lack of Recognition and Incentives. Peer reviewing is an invisible activity purely conducted on voluntary basis, neither paid by the journals or officially credited via standard scientific metrics (such as the ones that establish the Impact Factor of an author). Thus, it does not lead to advancements in career or help securing grants. Researchers are motivated to do peer review by a sense of belonging and a desire to 'give back' to the community [30]. A major consequence of not promoting incentives for the quality (and quantity) of peer reviews is to either slow down publication of potentially good research which awaits for validation [12] or let bad science be published through sloppy and uncritical reviews.

Fraud and Misconduct. Due to the 'publish or perish culture' pressures, unethical behaviour from reviewers has been occasionally reported, from abusive behaviour towards authors [1, 25] to identity fraud. Some studies have reported an improvement in the transparency and civility of the review process when open reports are released according to the standards of open peer review [5].

Social and Cognitive Biases. Given the fact that anonymity is usually asymmetrically applied only for reviewers, many power related dynamics can influence the reviewers decision [26], such as gender or cultural discrimination and social prestige of the institution. To solve this problem some journals have implemented double-blind review process (the identity of both authors and reviewers are masked) which seems to reduce the bias towards minorities.

Peer Reviews Need to Be... Reviewed. There is high variability in the reliability and depth of reviews and a recurrent question is: "Who watches the watchers?" [26].

Need for More Reviewers. There is a disproportion between the progressive increase in journal publications and the number of experienced reviewers selected for the task which demands an expansion of the reviewer's pool including early career scientists [1, 30].

Some mild attempts to credit peer review have been handled without much success by journals via attribution of virtual 'badges', certificates of performance, citation in annual editorials [26] where performance, though, is assessed only in terms of quantity of reviews but not quality [30].

Partnering with publishers, the startup *Publons*[1] provides a free metric service for tracking, verification and recognition of publications, peer reviews and journal editing in a single researcher identifier that showcases a record of scientific activity and impact based on authors' productivity.

3   System Concept

In this paper we propose Ants-Review, a new incentivisation mechanism built on Ethereum that issues open peer reviews to validate scientific papers while preserving the anonymity of its contributors. We imagine a final paper originating from the peer review process as a complex system that emerges from the interactions between the authors and the reviewers, a whole that is more than the sum of its parts. Therefore, the name evokes an ant colony as a self-organising organism in which all micro-contributions of the individuals emerge into complex behaviour. The original proposal behind this paper can be found here [27]. Its design and implementation are exposed in the following section.

3.1   Design

Incentivization and Recognition. A popular incentive model for open source software (OSS) is represented by bounties. Bounties are prizes or monetary rewards given for completing a task before a deadline [33]. Examples of such platforms that allow funders (bounty backers) to pay developers (bounty hunters) for open source contributions are *Gitcoin*[2] and *The Bounties Network*[3]. Incentives can be represented by tokens, units of values registered on the blockchain. In the network of the scientific community reviewers provide a service and those who consume it (authors, journals) should be able to contribute with tokens. The amount of tokens reflects material and symbolic recognition of the performed work that can be statistically quantified for author-level metrics measuring the productivity and impact of a researcher. Thus, the system acts also as a reputation builder.

Transparency and Re-Usability of the Records. The peer review history, including reviewers' recommendations and authors' replies, should be openly and permanently accessible to the community (in the form of 'open reports' of open peer reviews) even before articles' publication in order to make editorial decisions more democratic and prevent waste of knowledge. Following the example of models offered by journals peer review consortia, such as the *Neuroscience Peer Review Consortium*[4] and independent companies like *ResearchSquare*[5] and

---

[1] *Publons.* https://publons.com.
[2] *Gitcoin.* https://gitcoin.co.
[3] *The Bounties Network.* https://bounties.network.
[4] *Neuroscience Peer Review Consortium.* http://nprc.incf.org.
[5] *ResearchSquare.* https://www.researchsquare.com.

Peerage of Science[6], that provide a scientific peer review service, peer reviews in Ants-Review will be transferable across journals (like in 'cascading' or 'portable peer reviews').

Accountability via Pseudo-Anonymity. In order to counteract malicious behaviour (see Sect. 2.1) affecting the integrity of the reviews but also to correctly attribute the intellectual contributions making sure there are no conflicts of interest, it is important to be able to track back the identities of the contributors to a peer review report. This is possible if the platform acts like a version control system where commits are permanent and their hashes timestamped. InterPlanetary File System (IPFS) [4] is a peer-to-peer hypermedia protocol for storing data in a distributed file system over the internet which guarantees data immutability and unique file identification via cryptographic hashes. IPFS' hashes are then stored inside the smart contracts' state that is timestamped into the Ethereum blocks where the transactions take place; there, data remains unaltered and indelible. This notarization process is called proof of existence (PoE) and allows manual verification of the existence of the document.

To prevent retaliation for negative peer reviews and to promote the participation of early researchers who might feel intimidated to judge the scientific work of senior authors, the Ants-Review system maintains the privacy of both authors and reviewers in a double-blind approach via Ethereum's externally owned accounts (EOA) addresses and zero-knowledge proof (ZKP), a cryptographic method where a party can prove to another party the possession of certain information, like a secret key, without revealing that information (see Sect. 3.2).

Inclusiveness via Gamification. As a final step we propose that all the community is involved in the process of peer reviewing by abolishing the editorial selection process through 'open participation' (or 'open interaction', 'open platform' [22, 23]). In this way, the pool of reviewers is enriched and allows younger researchers to get the appropriate training through interactive feedback. Moreover, peer reviews could be evaluated, commented, criticised by the other members of the scientific community, enabling a virtuous loop of verification. An interesting addition would be to introduce a rank of peer reviews resulting from the community feedback via a voting process (see Sect. 4.1). It is conceivable that the community members that engage in assessing the quality of peer reviews could be incentivized as well. This solution would create a self-reinforcing ethical behaviour where the fair evaluation of peer reviews would be also in the interest of the agents at play.

3.2   Implementation

The Ants-Review Protocol is divided into different modules responsible for the following functionalities, as shown in the flow-chart (see Fig. 1): *AntsReview,*

---

[6] *Peerage of Science.* https://www.peerageofscience.org.

which manages access management and the core system (see Fig. 1(**a, b, f, h**)); *Privacy*, which maintains the anonymity of the system via AZTEC Protocol (see Fig. 1(**e**)); *Tokenomics*, which manages the incentive mechanism of the system (see Fig. 1(**c, d, e, h**)).

Agents in the platform are: issuers, peer reviewers, approvers and contributors (or Anters, members of the Ants-Review Community).

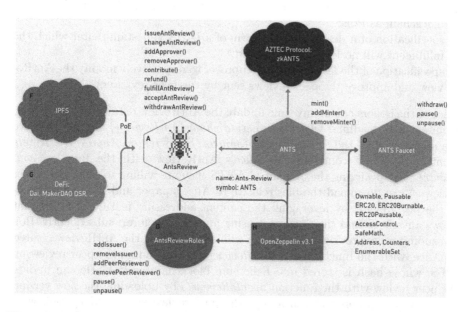

Fig. 1. Exagones represent the protocol's smart contracts. Ellipse represents the smart contract inherited by AntsReview. Clouds represent integrations into the protocol. Rectangles represent the smart contracts' libraries. **a** Core contract of the protocol implementing a bounty system with the functions listed. **b** Module inherited by AntsReview: it manages the access control of the protocol by adding and removing issuers and peer reviewers. **c** Native token used in the protocol. It is linked to (**a**), (**e**) and to (**d**). **d** Faucet to distribute *ANTS* on Kovan Testnet for testing purposes. **e** Integration with Aztec Protocol to wrap (**c**) into *zkANTS* to implement private *ANTS* transactions on Ethereum. **f** Integration with IPFS to upload papers, requirements and peer reviews and store the hash as *PoE* into AntsReview (**a**). **g** Integration with ERC20 tokens like *Dai*, and De-Fi services like MakerDAO DSR to be used in the protocol. **h** Library used by the protocol for secure contract development with the modules listed.

AntsReview. AntsReview (see Fig. 1(**a**)), the core of the smart contracts written in *Solidity*[7], a contract-oriented programming language for writing smart contracts that run on the Ethereum Virtual Machine (EVM), is deployed on

---

[7] *Solidity.* https://solidity.readthedocs.io.

Ethereum Kovan Testnet[8]. AntsReview implements a bounty-like system (based on the *StandardBounties* contract[9]) where Alice (issuer) can issue an AntReview with the function *issueAntReview()*.

In order to create a transparent and openly accessible AntReview, Alice has to complete a series of required tasks:

- upload of the files containing the requirements of the peer review and the paper to be reviewed into IPFS, whose hash is stored into the Ethereum blockchain as PoE;
- specification of a deadline in the form of a UNIX timestamp after which the fulfillment will no longer be accepted;
- specification of the Issuers and an Approver to respectively modify the AntReview and approve the peer reviews sent by the peer reviewers.

Alice or the issuers can at any time update the AntReview details (issuers, paper, requirements, deadline) with the function *changeAntReview()* and add/remove the approver with the functions *addApprover()* and *removeApprover()*. Anters (contributors) can contribute to Alice's AntReview with the function *contribute()*, by specifying the amount of ANTS they are willing to send. Bob (peer reviewer) can download the files relative to Alice's paper and the requirements of the peer review by leveraging the content-addressing feature of IPFS that allows anyone to find the document using an IPFS explorer; subsequently, Bob can submit a peer review before the deadline by fulfilling the AntReview created by Alice, with the function *fulfillAntReview()*, by uploading the peer review on IPFS, whose hash is stored into Ethereum blockchain as PoE. He can update the peer review with the function *updateReview()* by uploading the new version on IPFS. Ted (approver) can accept the peer review submitted by Bob with the function *acceptAntReview()*, by specifying the amount of ANTS that will be transferred as reward from the contract to Bob. If Alice's AntReview does not receive any peer review and the deadline expires, Anters can get a refund with the function *refund()* for their contributions. In order to avoid residual balance, Alice can withdraw ANTS from the AntReview's balance, if the deadline expires, with the function *withdrawAntReview()*, and the contract will transfer the amount specified to Alice and update the balance.

Access management of the Ants-Review protocol is defined and controlled by *AntsReviewRoles* (see Fig. 1(**b**)), implemented by leveraging *AccessControl.sol* by *OpenZeppelin Library*[10] that is used to define the Issuer and Peer Reviewer Roles. AntsReviewRoles also integrates a circuit breaker design pattern via *Pausable.sol* by OpenZeppelin to allow the Pauser Role, granted by default to the owner of the smart contracts, to pause (or unpause) all the functions in case of a security emergency, such as an attack to the smart contracts.

---

[8] *AntsReview.* https://kovan.etherscan.io/address/0x85be8F04482cBB920550d5469E 4dEdD6e1788121.

[9] *StandardBounties.sol.* https://github.com/Bounties-Network/StandardBounties.

[10] *OpenZeppelin Library.* https://openzeppelin.com.

Privacy. The anonymity of an agent in the system is achieved in two ways: via pseudo-anonymity, granted through Ethereum's EOAs that can pseudo-obscure the identity of the agent, and via private transactions allowed by AZTEC [31] Protocol's security layer.

Pseudo-Anonymity. EOAs in Ethereum are controlled via private keys. However, the privacy is limited by the fact that both the blockchain and its transactions are public. Therefore, the details of the transactions are visible to anyone by browsing a block explorer (such as *Etherscan*[11]) and are subject to data mining that could extract value and identify users in the blockchain.

Private Transactions. AZTEC Protocol was conceived to enable privacy on public blockchains. It uses zero-knowledge succinct non-interactive argument of knowledge (zk-SNARKs) [21] and homomorphic encryption [6] to validate encrypted transactions. zk-SNARKs are ZKP that require no interaction between prover and verifier; they are used inside the Ants-Review protocol via the zkANTS token to allow private transactions between the agents. Future developments will allow to leverage on permutations over Lagrange-bases for oecumenical noninteractive arguments of knowledge (PLONK) [9], a universal zk-SNARK construction that reduces gas costs and improves scalability.

Tokenomics. Ants-Review integrates a few *ERC20*[12] tokens, each of whom plays an integral role in the functioning and anonymity of the decentralized protocol. ANTS (see Fig. 1(**c**)) is the primary protocol token and can be staked into an AntReview. It is implemented by inheriting *ERC20.sol* from OpenZeppelin Library with name *Ants-Review* and symbol *ANTS*. A Faucet (see Fig. 1(**d**)) is implemented to distribute ANTS token on Kovan Testnet for testing purposes. zkANTS (see Fig. 1(**e**)) is a wrapper of ANTS that will be used inside the protocol to allow for private transactions among the agents of the protocol, preserving their anonymity as well as the amount of the AntReview reward and the contributions by the Anters. It will be implemented via AZTEC Protocol [31], that uses a cryptographic engine, *ACE.sol*, a contract responsible for validating the set of AZTEC ZKPs and performing any transfer instructions involving AZTEC notes, minted into a zkAsset, that can be converted into ERC20 tokens. In order to implement a zkAsset called zkANTS, *zkAsset.sol*, a contract implementation of a confidential token that follows the EIP-1724 standard[13] will be used as a template to build an AZTEC-compatible asset.

The current state of the art of Ants-Review is represented by version 0.2.0 (MVP) live on Ethereum Kovan Testnet (see Supplementary Material).

4   Discussions

We have described how the Ants-Review protocol can solve the limitations of the current peer review system (see Sect. 2.1). In particular, the lack of recog-

---

[11] *Etherscan.* https://etherscan.io/.

[12] *EIP 20.* https://eips.ethereum.org/EIPS/eip-20.

[13] *EIP 1724.* https://github.com/ethereum/EIPs/issues/1724.

nition, the lack of transparency, fraud and misconduct can be solved via the Ants-Review Protocol (see Section AntsReview in Sect 3.2); the social and cognitive biases can be counteracted via anonymity granted by AZTEC Protocol (see Section Privacy in Sect. 3.2); the slowness of the process, the need for evaluation of the peer reviews themselves and the need for increasing the number of reviewers can be worked out through the creation of the community of Anters.

4.1 Future Developments

An interesting aspect of the protocol is the double function of an AntReview respectively as a bounty and as a pool to stake ERC20 tokens like Dai[14]. Moreover, the duration of peer reviews consents to connect the protocol to De-Fi services with the possibility for the community to accrue interest over time via *MakerDAO Dai Saving Rate* (Pot[15]) or *Compound*[16], to cite a few. Therefore, an ERC20 pool token would be automatically released by the protocol, representing the accrued interest on the Anters' stake over time that can be traded, sold, or held as the Anter desires. A Decentralized Autonomous Organization (DAO) [17,29] could be formed in the future to allow ANTS stakers to participate in the governance of important aspects of the protocol, from smart contracts upgrades to minor changes in settings across the protocol.

Finally, a protocol upgrade inspired by *Discover*[17], a Web3 browser by *Status*[18] and still under investigation would allow Anters to validate peer reviews via an upvote/downvote system that will consent the protocol to automatically pay out the reward to the reviewers based on the votes associated with their peer reviews.

4.2 A New Community-Driven Standard?

As Tennant points out [26], a change is already happening in the publishing industry, especially with new born publishers opening up the review process (*BioMed Central, ELife, Frontiers, PeerJ, F1000 Research*). Recently, pre-print servers, such as *arXiv* and *biorXiv*, started integrating peer review services into their platforms: *PREreview*[19], *PeerCommunityIn*[20], *Review Commons*[21], *PrePrint Review*[22] and the previously mentioned *Peerage of Science*. This dissociation of initial scientific dissemination and scientific validation will force the

---

[14] *Dai.* https://docs.makerdao.com/smart-contract-modules/dai-module/dai-detailed-documentation.

[15] *Pot.* https://docs.makerdao.com/smart-contract-modules/rates-module/pot-detailed-documentation.

[16] *Compound.* https://compound.finance.

[17] *Discover.sol.* https://github.com/dap-ps/discover/blob/master/contracts/Discover.sol.

[18] *Status.* https://status.im/.

[19] *PREreview.* https://www.prereview.org.

[20] *PeerCommunityIn* https://peercommunityin.org.

[21] *Review Commons.* https://www.reviewcommons.org.

[22] *PrePrint Review.* https://elifesci.org/preprint-review.

publishing industry to adapt in order to keep up with the higher quality scientific process offered by those alternative peer review platforms and justify their added value [26]. In our proposal we also decoupled the peer review process from the publishers giving it back to the scientific community and applying incentives from tokenomics. We foresee that the future will evolve towards community-driven peer reviews: peer reviews will be more and more independent from publishers [20], and researchers will be the ones seeking the papers to review to build reputation within the community and not journals.

Enlarging the pool of reviewers to potentially an entire scientific community and accelerating the whole process requires a standard for peer reviews [13]: for example some aspects might be taken over by AI assistants (such as the *Artificial Intelligence Review Assistant (AIRA)* [8] leaving to the reviewers the sole task of evaluating the content of a paper. Building smart contracts for peer reviews might accelerate this novel process of standardization. We hope that soon the value of peer review as a public good will be recognized by research funders and hiring committees.

5   Conclusion

In this paper we addressed a crucial problem within scholarly academic communication: the peer review process. We have shown how blockchain technology could provide an efficient and viable solution to open up possible directions for a paradigm shift in scientific communication. We proposed an incentive mechanism that could solve the problems of lack of acknowledgment and trust during peer reviews. We exposed the architecture of our project for which we adopted cutting-edge tools from the open source blockchain ecosystem.

Supplementary Material. Source code: https://doi.org/10.5281/zenodo. 3971044;
DApp: https://ants-review.on.fleek.co.

Acknowledgements. We would like to thank Andy Tudhope, Mark Beylin, Matteo A. Tambussi, Evan C. Harris and the four external anonymous peer reviewers for useful comments and revisions; the FDAPP 2020 workshop chairs and speakers for questions and feedback; Mitrasish Mukherjee for contributions on the interface.

Declaration of Competing Interest
This work was mainly developed during the ETHTurin Hackathon 2020 and the Gitcoin Kernel Fellowship program 2020. These organizations, as well as the authors' affiliations, had no financial role in the design and implementation of the protocol.

References

1. Albuquerque, U.P.d.: The tragedy of the common reviewers: the peer review process. Revista Brasileira de Farmacognosia **21**(1), 1–3 (2011). https://doi.org/10. 1590/s0102-695x2011005000036

2. b8d5ad9d974a44e7e2882f986467f4d3: Towards Open Science: The Case for a Decentralized Autonomous Academic Endorsement System. Zenodo (2016). https://doi.org/10.5281/zenodo.60054

3. Bartling, S., et contributors to living document: Blockchain for Science and knowledge creation. Zenodo (2016). https://doi.org/10.5281/zenodo.401369. https://www.blockchainforscience.com/2017/02/23/blockchain-for-open-science-the-living-document/

4. Benet, J.: IPFS - Content Addressed, Versioned, P2P File System. arXiv (2014)

5. Bravo, G., Grimaldo, F., López-Iñesta, E., Mehmani, B., Squazzoni, F.: The effect of publishing peer review reports on referee behavior in five scholarly journals. Nat. Commun. **10**(1), 322 (2019). https://doi.org/10.1038/s41467-018-08250-2

6. Buterin, V.: Exploring Fully Homomorphic Encryption (2020). https://vitalik.ca/general/2020/07/20/homomorphic.html

7. Extance, A.: Could Bitcoin technology help science? Nature **552**(7685), 301–302 (2017). https://doi.org/10.1038/d41586-017-08589-4

8. Frontiers: Artificial Intelligence to help meet global demand for high-quality, objective peer-review in publishing (2020). https://blog.frontiersin.org/2020/07/01/artificial-intelligence-to-help-meet-global-demand-for-high-quality-objective-peer-review-in-publishing/

9. Gabizon, A., Williamson, Z.J., Ciobotaru, O.: PLONK: Permutations over Lagrange-bases for Oecumenical Noninteractive arguments of Knowledge. Protocol Labs Research (2019)

10. Glasziou, P., et al.: Reducing waste from incomplete or unusable reports of biomedical research. Lancet **383**(9913), 267–276 (2014). https://doi.org/10.1016/s0140-6736(13)62228-x

11. Gropp, R.E., Glisson, S., Gallo, S., Thompson, L.: Peer review: a system under stress. BioScience **67**(5), 407–410 (2017). https://doi.org/10.1093/biosci/bix034

12. Hauser, M., Fehr, E.: An incentive solution to the peer review problem. PLoS Biol. **5**(4), e107 (2007). https://doi.org/10.1371/journal.pbio.0050107

13. Krummel, M., et al.: Universal principled review: a community-driven method to improve peer review. Cell **179**(7), 1441–1445 (2019). https://doi.org/10.1016/j.cell.2019.11.029

14. Lee, J.Y.: A decentralized token economy: how blockchain and cryptocurrency can revolutionize business. Bus. Horizons **62**(6), 773–784 (2019). https://doi.org/10.1016/j.bushor.2019.08.003

15. Leible, S., Schlager, S., Schubotz, M., Gipp, B.: A review on blockchain technology and blockchain projects fostering open science. Front. Blockchain **2**, 16 (2019). https://doi.org/10.3389/fbloc.2019.00016

16. Mingxiao, D., Xiaofeng, M., Zhe, Z., Xiangwei, W., Qijun, C.: A review on consensus algorithm of blockchain. In: 2017 IEEE International Conference on Systems, Man, and Cybernetics (SMC), pp. 2567–2572 (2017). https://doi.org/10.1109/smc.2017.8123011

17. Morrison, R., Mazey, N.C.H.L., Wingreen, S.C.: The DAO controversy: the case for a new species of corporate governance? Front. Blockchain **3**, 25 (2020). https://doi.org/10.3389/fbloc.2020.00025

18. Nakamoto, S.: Bitcoin: A Peer-to-Peer Electronic Cash System. Whitepaper (2009). www.bitcoin.org

19. Powell, K.: The waiting game. Nature **530**, 148–151 (2016). https://doi.org/10.1038/530148

20. Priem, J., Hemminger, B.M.: Decoupling the scholarly journal. Front. Comput. Neurosci. **6**, 19 (2012). https://doi.org/10.3389/fncom.2012.00019

21. Reitwießner, C.: zkSNARKs in a Nutshell. Ethereum blog (2016). https://chriseth. github.io/notes/articles/zksnarks/zksnarks.pdf
22. Ross-Hellauer, T.: What is open peer review? A systematic review. F1000Research 6, 588 (2017). https://doi.org/10.12688/f1000research.11369.2
23. Ross-Hellauer, T., Görögh, E.: Guidelines for open peer review implementation. Res. Integrity Peer Rev. 4(1), 4 (2019). https://doi.org/10.1186/s41073-019-0063-9
24. Rossum, D.J.v.: Blockchain for research - perspectives on a new paradigm for scholarly communication. Digital Science (2017). https://doi.org/10.6084/m9.figshare. 5607778. www.digital-science.com
25. Smith, R.: Peer review: a flawed process at the heart of science and journals. J. R. Soc. Med. 99(4), 178–182 (2006). https://doi.org/10.1177/014107680609900414
26. Tennant, J.P., et al.: A multi-disciplinary perspective on emergent and future innovations in peer review. F1000Research 6, 1151 (2017). https://doi.org/10.12688/ f1000research.12037.1
27. Trovò, B., Massari, N.: Ants-review: a bounty-like system for open anonymous scientific peer-reviews. Zenodo (2020). https://doi.org/10.5281/zenodo.3828087
28. Walker, R., Silva, P.R.d.: Emerging trends in peer review-a survey. Front. Neurosci. 9, 169 (2015). https://doi.org/10.3389/fnins.2015.00169
29. Wang, S., Ding, W., Li, J., Yuan, Y., Ouyang, L., Wang, F.Y.: Decentralized autonomous organizations: concept, model, and applications. IEEE Trans. Comput. Soc. Syst. 6(5), 870–878 (2019). https://doi.org/10.1109/tcss.2019.2938190
30. Warne, V.: Rewarding reviewers - sense or sensibility? A Wiley study explained. Learn. Publ. 29(1), 41–50 (2016). https://doi.org/10.1002/leap.1002
31. Williamson, Z.J.: The AZTEC Protocol. Whitepaper (2018)
32. Wood, G.: Ethereum: a secure decentralised generalised transaction ledger. Yellowpaper (2017)
33. Zhou, J., Wang, S., Bezemer, C.P., Zou, Y., Hassan, A.E.: Bounties in Open Source Development on GitHub: A Case Study of Bountysource Bounties. arXiv (2019)

Next Generation Blockchain-Based Financial Services

Roberto Moncada[✉], Enrico Ferro[✉], Alfredo Favenza[✉],
and Pierluigi Freni[✉]

Business Model Innovation – LINKS Foundation, 10138 Turin, Italy
{roberto.moncada,enrico.ferro,alfredo.favenza,
pierluigi.freni}@linksfoundation.com

Abstract. This paper explores the transition towards a paradigm in which centralization and decentralization systems coexist in the provision of financial services. The blockchain technology application to the financial industry is giving birth to Decentralized Finance (DeFi). The transition is studied through a cross-chain analysis that allows to compare different blockchain ecosystems characterized by diverse evolution courses. The results show a path dependency linked to the first-mover advantage of the Ethereum blockchain. The analysis also highlights the emergence of new players that propose higher scalability opportunities (e.g., Eos, Tezos) and different design choices in terms of governance. This exploratory study also emphasizes the potential complementarity between the standard financial system and DeFi, discussing the main differences among the financial services provided on-chain and off-chain.

Keywords: Blockchain · Decentralization · Financial service · Decentralized finance · Cryptocurrency

1 Introduction and Underlying Rationale

The modern economic system works through the close interaction among centralized institutions such as governments, Central Banks (CBs), private banks and stock exchanges, not exclusively restricted to national borders. The interdependence of these actors concentrates risks, leading to domino effects whenever a pillar of consolidated economic structures enters a crisis. The blockchain technology was born in response to one of the most severe economic meltdown in recent decades: the 2008 financial crisis. This crisis accentuated some pains of the economic system, such as lack of transparency, traceability and accountability, as well as the need for better wealth distribution and a greater alignment of incentives among the stakeholders of the financial ecosystem. Indeed, the first

This work was conducted as part of the research activity related to an extensive and ongoing effort to understand and map the innovation potential of Distributed Ledger Technologies (DLTs) carried out by OverTheBlock, a permanent observatory on Blockchain technology powered by LINKS Foundation.

© Springer Nature Switzerland AG 2021
B. Balis et al. (Eds.): Euro-Par 2020 Workshops, LNCS 12480, pp. 30–41, 2021.
https://doi.org/10.1007/978-3-030-71593-9_3

blockchain infrastructure was implemented in 2009, after the publication by Satoshi Nakamoto [10] of the whitepaper that also gave birth to the first cryptocurrency, the Bitcoin, proposing an innovative system capable of performing peer-to-peer transactions with no need for trusted third party interventions.

After more than ten years, the blockchain ecosystem has considerably evolved, hosting an increasing number of decentralized financial applications built on numerous blockchain infrastructures. The environment composed of all these applications is defined as Decentralized Finance (DeFi). In particular, blockchain technology grants a transparent and trustless framework, departing from the traditional financial system's paradigm, allowing permissionless access to various financial services, provided that an Internet connection is available.

Therefore, the decentralized nature of DeFi provides a unique solution to solve three critical points of the centralized paradigm. Firstly, decentralization eliminates the necessity of trusted third parties, diminishing the intermediaries' market power derived from the information advantage they develop over transacting parties, leveraging their intermediation services [14]. Secondly, transparency is granted since all users have access to transaction data stored on the blockchains while still maintaining privacy (at least for public blockchains) [5]. Thirdly, DeFi can leverage the blockchain technology to foster financial inclusion, providing the possibility to have access at least to essential financial services (e.g., transaction account, savings deposit) [11].

For the DeFi ecosystem to exist, there must be a circulating medium of exchange that we define as *currency* in the traditional system while in the DeFi context, we call *cryptocurrency*. If, on the one hand, fiat money is generally under the monopolistic control of CBs, on the other, cryptocurrencies represent a form of unregulated and programmable digital money that is consensually accepted by the community members of the blockchain [8]. New transactions, in turn, are performed through the implementation of a consensus algorithm. Hence, it is on the community and algorithm that the DeFi bases its functioning.

However, most financial services' implementation needs the execution of *smart contracts*, conceived by Nick Szabo in 1996 [15] and first implemented on the Ethereum blockchain. Therefore, despite the massive innovative contribution brought by Bitcoin's creation, the birth of DeFi dates back to a later time. In particular, smart contracts automatically trigger self-enforcing actions arising from an agreement among two or more parties. Therefore, whenever the terms set in the agreement are fulfilled, the lines of code contained within the smart contract are executed, and the effects of the contract take place.

Since the first implementation of smart contracts, the DeFi ecosystem has experienced relevant improvements, attracting increasing attention and capital levels by users and developers. Indeed, despite the high volatility of cryptocurrencies, looking at the market capitalization of the principal tokens, the ecosystem has achieved significant aggregated volumes, i.e., about 235 billion US dollar[1].

---

[1] The market capitalization is calculated as the product between the number of tokens in circulation and the value of each token. The value aggregates the capitalization of the top ten native blockchain tokens available in the market. Source: https://coinmarketcap.com/ - accessed 15-05-2020.

In this context, this paper presents an exploratory study of the next generation blockchain-based financial services. In particular, the analysis carried out aims to trace the path outlined by DeFi, showing the present status of this ecosystem, focusing on a cross-chain perspective. Therefore, the study addressed in this work serves as a strategic observation point to comprehend future developments affecting the financial industry and the associated interaction between centralized and decentralized environments. The paper's main contribution lies in delineating the features of DeFi and highlighting its relevance, outlining, for the best of our knowledge, the first transverse representation of an infrastructures' ecosystem to identify the DeFi progress and its future trends.

The paper proceeds as follows. Section 2 deals with blockchain technology within the context of tokenomics. Section 3 presents a discussion about the blockchain infrastructures analyzed in this study. The actual DeFi ecosystem is presented within Sect. 4. Finally, Sect. 5 concludes the paper.

2   Blockchain Technology and Tokenomics

The blockchain represents a subset of the Distributed Ledger Technologies (DLTs). All DLT platforms allow to record and share data across multiple stores, each containing the same contents. Therefore, the community is responsible for maintaining these records, distributed within a network of computer servers called *nodes*. Three main features of the blockchain technology make its innovative potential disruptive. Firstly, the ledger's distributed nature eliminates intermediaries by spreading control over the network among users. Secondly, since the network is born distributed, the community needs to find consensus over new data entries. The *consensus protocol* defines the rules that legitimize the entry of new transactions into the ledger. Thirdly, the validation of new data entries takes advantage of cryptographic methods designed by the platform's developers. Moreover, the consensus mechanism's peculiarities and the cryptographic algorithm determine many essential aspects of the blockchain infrastructure, such as the degree of efficiency and power consumption [16]. Besides, the consensus protocol creates a system of incentives that, in combination with the absence of intermediaries, allow the platform to settle transfers of property rights that can involve cryptocurrencies, as well as a wide variety of assets.

The cryptographic validation of transactions allows the introduction of the concept of *digital scarcity* since property right transfers do not permit to create copies of the exchanged assets. Indeed, if in the case of the Internet, information abundance is due to high fixed costs and low marginal costs of production considering that information is costly to produce but cheap to reproduce [13], assets traded on top of blockchain platforms cannot be replicated at will. Therefore, blockchain technology has the potential to transform society and economy from multiple perspectives through the development of new market design solutions.

Focusing on the financial services sector, blockchain infrastructures provide lower entry barriers for users and developers. Moreover, the blockchain platforms are characterized by alternative monetary policies for individuals who suffer unstable economic conditions due to untrustworthy institutions.

As stated before, the growth experienced by the DeFi ecosystem since the implementation of smart contracts has attracted the attention of new developers. In recent years, many blockchain platforms have been created with the capability not only to execute smart contracts but also to develop decentralized applications (dApps). One of the most fertile fields in terms of dApps development is DeFi, through the conception of applications able to offer standard financial services, often taking a step forward to propose innovative solutions to old-time needs.

In this context, the functioning rules of the blockchain infrastructures and decentralized applications are set by developers during the platforms' design. Even though in most cases, the community has the power to modify relevant aspects of the framework through internal voting, the laws that regulate on-chain operation are designated in such a way as to achieve predefined objectives (e.g., total token supply, users' incentive system). The main result of this dynamic is the shift from economics towards *tokenomics*. Indeed, while in economics changes are applied in a dynamic fashion by maneuvering key variables to approach the desired objectives through the observation of the reaction of the system, in tokenomics, innovation is put forward by designing the rules governing the playground in a way that the stakeholders' behavior aligns with the goal pursued [7]. As a result, DeFi falls, by definition, within the field of tokenomics, allowing users to have access to financial services through the exploitation of dApps and to interact with the other members of the community to manage the ecosystem.

3   Blockchain Infrastructure Analysis

The fields of application of DLT and, in particular, blockchain technology are certainly not limited to cryptocurrencies and DeFi. Nevertheless, remaining within this paper's scope, this section presents the analysis of a series of blockchains upon which the exploratory study on DeFi is based. This analysis aims to present the technical scenarios within which the DeFi ecosystem has proliferated in the last years, paving the way for subsequent research that wants to investigate the conditions that favor and hinder the decentralized financial realm's growth.

Figure 1 shows eight blockchains: Bitcoin, Ethereum, Tron, Stellar, Eos, Tezos, Neo and Cardano. The selection criteria of the blockchains are essentially three. The first one concerns the market capitalization of the blockchain's native tokens, while the second one has to do with the platforms' nature. In particular, the sampling concentrates on permissionless and public permissioned platforms where DeFi has developed the most. Finally, the third one regards the objectives of the blockchains. Indeed, the analysis focuses on platforms that aim at reshaping the financial industry from multiple perspectives. Specifically, the figure provides data about nine variables that aim to delineate the platforms' governance features, outlining the principal factors that make each of them unique. First of all, the figure indicates the accessibility of blockchain platforms since we can primarily distinguish between permissionless and permissioned blockchains. In the first case, users do not need any approval to join or leave the network and have access to an identical copy of the ledger. In the second case, the nodes have to be pre-selected by a network administrator to join and operate inside the community [8]. Moreover, permissioned blockchains can also be divided into two other categories: public and closed (or private). While in the public case, anyone can access and view the contents of the blockchain even though only the pre-selected nodes can enable transactions, in the closed case, the access is restricted to the components of the community and, in addition, the transactions can be validated only by the blockchain administrator.

BLOCKCHAIN	BITCOIN	ETHEREUM	TRON	STELLAR	EOS	TEZOS	NEO	CARDANO
Accessibility	Permissionless	Permissionless	Permissionless	Permissionless	Permissioned (Public)	Permissionless	Permissioned (Public)	Permissionless + Permissioned
Consensus Mechanism	PoW	PoW → PoS	DPoS	SCP	BFT-DPoS	LPoS	DBFT	Ouroboros PoS
Cryptocurrency Issuance Method	Mining	Pre-Mined (72 million) + Mining	Pre-Mined (65 billion)	Pre-Mined (100 billion)	Pre-Mined (700 million)	Pre-Mined (≈763 million)	Pre-Mined (50 million)	Pre-Mined (30 million)
Cryptocurrency Symbol	BTC	ETH	TRX	XLM	EOS	XTZ	NEO	ADA
Cryptocurrency Total Supply	Limited (21 million)	Unlimited	Limited (100 billion)	Unlimited	Unlimited	Unlimited	Limited (100 million)	Limited (45 billion)
Blockchain Uses	Transaction Platform	Fuel Issuer + Smart Contracts and dApps Deployment	Web Decentralisation + Smart Contracts and dApps Deployment + Entertainment Industry	Transaction Platform + Smart Contracts Deployment	Transaction Platform + Smart Contracts and dApps Deployment	Self-Amending + Smart Contracts and dApps Deployment	Assets Digitalisation + Smart Contracts and dApps Deployment	Fuel Issuer + Smart Contracts and dApps Deployment
Target Audience	Individuals + Businesses	Individuals + Businesses	Individuals + Businesses	Individuals + Businesses	Individuals + Businesses	Individuals + Businesses	Individuals + Businesses	Individuals + Businesses
Market Capitalisation	≈ € 178.6 B	≈ € 23.6 B	≈ € 1 B	≈ € 1.4 B	≈ € 2.5 B	≈ € 2 B	≈ € 700 M	≈ € 1.5 B
Creation Year	2008	2014	2017	2014	2018	2018	2014	2017

Fig. 1. Blockchain infrastructures analysed with respect to nine qualitative and quantitative variables.

Figure 1 also shows that all the blockchains selected are permissionless or public. Only Cardano represents an exception since it incorporates both a centralized and decentralized governance layer. This criterion of selection follows the logic according to which permissionless and public blockchain infrastructures represent the real innovative contribution to the financial industry by decentralizing the services provided. Indeed, DeFi benefits, with respect to Centralized Finance (CeFi), include transparency, autonomy (i.e., non-custodial management of assets), financial inclusion and tradability (i.e., no requirements to commit to entire high-value investment at once[2]) [1]. Conversely, financial services supplied on permissioned and private blockchains do not significantly differ from the CeFi paradigm except, in most cases, in terms of efficiency deriving from more significant scalability opportunities [12].

The second variable deals with the consensus protocol, indicating the specific validation mechanism of new data entries in every blockchain analyzed.

---

[2] In most cases, transactions conducted on blockchain platforms can involve purchases and sales of portions of assets. For instance, the smallest unit of Bitcoin tradable on the market is called a *satoshi* and corresponds to the one-hundred-millionth part (100.000.000) of a Bitcoin, i.e., 0.00000001 BTC.

Zhang and Lee (2019) [16], studying the main consensus protocols, distinguish between *probabilistic-finality* and *absolute-finality* mechanisms. Proof-of-Work (PoW), Proof-of-Stake (PoS) and Delegated Proof-of-Stake (DPoS) protocols fall within the first category, while Practical Byzantine Fault Tolerance (PBFT) and Ripple protocols belong to the second one. Moreover, they conclude that PoW, PoS and DPoS are more suitable for public and permissionless blockchains than PBFT and Ripple that, instead, apply better in a permissioned (private) framework. In the context of DeFi, where platforms aim to attract the largest possible number of users, one can expect that the relative blockchain infrastructures are presumably based on probabilistic-finality consensus mechanisms.

Furthermore, as mentioned in Sect. 2, the consensus protocol of a blockchain is also responsible for the platform's efficiency, determining the number of transactions performed per second (TPS). Generally, the more transactions a blockchain can perform in a specific time frame, the less decentralized the blockchain is since the consensus mechanism will be based on few consensus nodes that support the platform's wellness (e.g., Eos blockchain). Bach et al. (2018) [3] carry out a comparative analysis of typical blockchain consensus protocols. They focus the analysis on different algorithmic steps of the consensus mechanisms (e.g., scalability, the system of incentive and security), confirming the indirect proportionality between efficiency and decentralization degree of blockchain platforms by reporting TPS numbers of the *high-profile* blockchain infrastructures (i.e., those with the highest market capitalization of native cryptocurrencies).

The variables between the third and the fifth deal with characteristics directly related to the native cryptocurrencies of the blockchains: the issuance method (which differentiates between *pre-mined* tokens and *mining* activities regardless the consensus protocol applied), the token symbol and the total supply of tokens. In the issuance method, pre-mining activities are typically associated with Initial Coin Offering (ICO) funding mechanisms. In particular, ICOs have emerged in the last years as a novel instrument through which ventures sell tokens to fund initial development, although no commitment is made to their future price [4]. Moreover, ICOs have allowed new blockchain platforms to trigger network effects in relatively short times through the prospect of future positive revenues (e.g., Eos, Tezos and Cardano), instead of waiting for them to develop independently (e.g., Bitcoin, Ethereum). The implementation of ICOs, in turn, also affects design decisions regarding the total supply of tokens.

The variable *blockchain uses* highlights the main on-chain activities that, in most cases, also involve developers' attention (e.g., dApps deployment and smart contracts). In the context of DeFi, as described previously, the development of dApps and the implementation of smart contracts are of primary importance to provide access to financial services, leveraging the blockchain technology's decentralized nature. The variable *target audience*, instead, identifies the main actors who take advantage of the services provided on the blockchains. However, note that, even though only individuals and businesses have been identified, this does not preclude other actors (e.g., institutional players) from fruitfully exploiting the benefits deriving from the use of these frameworks.

The last two variables show the market capitalization of each blockchain's native cryptocurrency and the platforms' creation year. In particular, concerning the market cap, the values are expressed in US Dollars and are calculated as the product between the number of tokens issued by the platform and the current price per coin[3]. Moreover, the cryptocurrency market cap can also be used to measure the volume of investors' attention drawn by each blockchain. As a result, the data presented within Fig. 1 shows how the Bitcoin blockchain has attracted the largest amount of capital in the DeFi ecosystem (and, by extension, in the blockchain environment), despite the inefficiency of its infrastructure compared to other platforms (e.g., Eos, Stellar). Therefore, network effects still play a more influential role within the blockchain ecosystem than infrastructure features (e.g., efficiency, power consumption) in attracting investors.

4   DeFi Ecosystem

In terms of financial services, the transition from the traditional financial industry to DeFi is not straightforward. Moving from a centralized ecosystem to a globally inclusive financial system, not all the features remain constant. Numerous changes happen, creating a network characterized by more or less disruptive elements concerning the standard environment. In this framework, this section aims to present the actual DeFi ecosystem from a cross-chain perspective, highlighting the main differences between the financial services provided within DeFi and those offered in the traditional financial system. The principal financial services taken into consideration in this study are *borrowing and lending, exchange, deposit/asset management, derivatives* and *stablecoin issuance*.

After having selected the platforms to analyze following the criteria described in Sect. 3, the categories of financial services have been designated in such a way as to encompass most of the financial operations carried out both in DeFi and CeFi. The methodology applied results in a comprehensive framework of the actual DeFi ecosystem that can also provide a strategic observation point to observe future developments. For the best of our knowledge, this analysis represents the first cross-chain study of the DeFi ecosystem within a context where other studies generally refer to single-chain frameworks [2].

In the context of the eight blockchains presented in Sect. 3, Fig. 2 shows the DeFi ecosystem in terms of services provided within each blockchain platform. As stated earlier, most of the financial services offered by DeFi require the implementation of smart contracts and specific protocols generally performed by dApps. In this framework, the Bitcoin blockchain is the only one, among the eight platforms analyzed, that does not allow to execute smart contracts and, in turn, to develop dApps. However, as also discussed in the previous section,

---

[3] Note that the source of this information is the same as indicated in footnote 1.

given the Bitcoin's impact in terms of network effects, which caused its considerable appreciation since 2012, it represents one of the DeFi ecosystem's cornerstone. Moreover, the situation outlined by the figure below shows the monopolist role played by the Ethereum blockchain inside the DeFi environment. Indeed, Ethereum has generated strong network effects as in the Bitcoin case, being the first blockchain to implement smart contracts and develop dApps.

Consequently, despite the relative inefficiencies compared to other platforms, the positive feedback loops generated by the increasing dimension of the blockchain environment in terms of dApps have always attracted more attention by users and developers[4]. Nevertheless, more recent infrastructures (e.g., Eos, Tezos) have started to expand their network in terms of the number of on-chain dApps and financial services offered. Consequently, the effects deriving from the emergence of other blockchains within the DeFi environment are twofold. First of all, emerging platforms can attract on-chain users of other infrastructures, offering higher performances to face increasing scalability requirements. Secondly, a more prosperous DeFi environment composed of many blockchains can bring to an expansion of the decentralized network at the expense of the CeFi ecosystem.

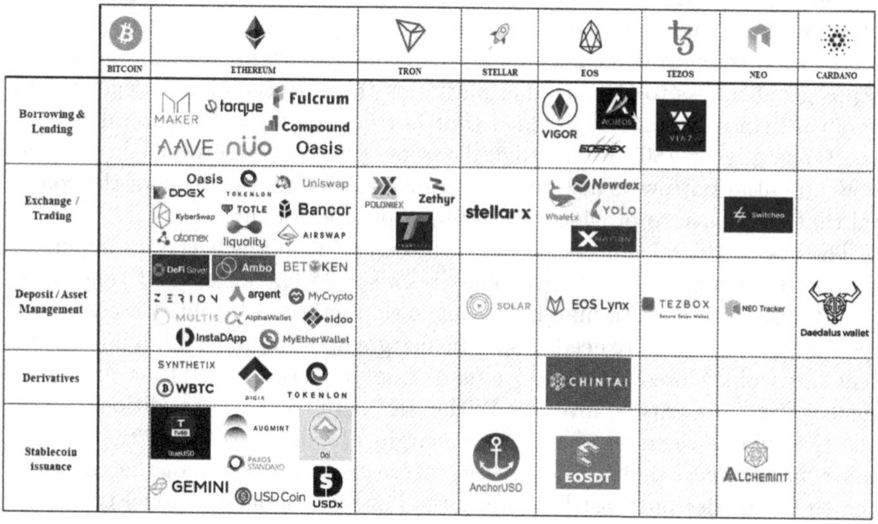

Fig. 2. DeFi ecosystem survey across eight blockchain infrastructures.

Within the set of categories of financial services selected, payment gateways were not mentioned since they can be considered as a standard integration of deposit service granted by traditional financial institutions like private banks. However, in the case of DeFi that principally makes use of cryptocurrencies,

---

[4] However, it has to be considered that the Ethereum blockchain is planning to make a change in the consensus mechanism from PoW to PoS to increase the efficiency of the platform, as shown in Fig. 1 above.

conditions may change. Indeed, since their price tends to fluctuate, it is not easy to think of these tools as widespread means of payment. Instead, they should be conceived as assets and, therefore, as *digital assets* utilized by users to take advantage of the financial services made available by dApps. In this context, the introduction of stablecoins has marked the DeFi ecosystem, since they grant access to digital assets with minimal fluctuation rates and peg either to fiat currencies (e.g., US Dollars) or to digital assets (e.g., USDC, TUSD). Consequently, the launch of this type of tool has created an essential incentive in moving simple payment transactions on the DeFi ecosystem.

In this framework, DAI represents the first stablecoin issued through the borrowing and lending platform of MakerDAO, developed on top of the Ethereum blockchain. Examples of fiat-backed stablecoins are SDUSD, provided by the Neo blockchain through the dApp Alchemint, and ANCT, issued by AnchorUSD and built upon the Stellar blockchain. On the other hand, instances of crypto-backed stablecoins are EOSDT issued by the Eos blockchain and USDx provided by dForce developed on top of the Ethereum blockchain.

Concerning borrowing and lending services, in DeFi, differently from CeFi, the money deposited in platforms is used to finance borrowers without substantial restrictions. Therefore, deposit activity collapses into borrowing and lending category, since lenders can earn interests just depositing fiat money or digital assets in the framework's wallet (i.e., generating passive income). In particular, dApps grant access to P2P lending platforms that use the money deposited by users to finance borrowers provided that borrowers can over-collateralize their loan (generally at 150%) with digital assets. Besides, these on-chain projects allow potential borrowers also to become margin traders by virtue of the collateral that they have to provide in order to apply for a loan.

The ease with which users have access to margin trading activities highlights another important point of divergence between decentralized and centralized ecosystems. Within CeFi, margin trading is characterized by elitist access, since a potential trader usually needs a specific margin account and a minimum investment threshold. Moreover, to receive funds from brokerage firms, the trader must be recognized as a trusted investor. Within the CeFi context, in addition, margin calls take place whenever the trader's margin account falls below the *maintenance margin level* due to a consistent decrease in the value of the collateral (i.e., the securities purchased spending the borrowed money). In DeFi, instead, the collateral is represented by a certain amount of digital assets pre-deposited by the borrowers. The margin call automatically occurs when these assets' value falls below a predefined threshold, via smart contracts, without the necessity of trusted third party interventions. For this reason, within DeFi, we can talk about *permissionless initiation of margin calls* and *permissionless provision of margin call liquidity* [9]. Regarding the DeFi ecosystem, Fulcrum and Nuo represent two examples of borrowing and lending dApps developed on top of the Ethereum blockchain, which also offer margin trading services.

When it comes to exchanging activities, they can be considered the *alter ego* of trading in the CeFi framework. Indeed, thinking of cryptocurrencies as digital assets, the exchange among native tokens of different blockchains represents an investment choice to take advantage of rising and decreasing trends in the various digital asset markets. Moreover, as also seen before, many dApps provide more than one financial services. For instance, the dApp Nuo mentioned above grants also access to exchange activities. Another interesting example is Tokenlon, an exchange platform built on top of the Ethereum blockchain, which also issues the token *imBTC* that is a derivative pegged to the value of BTC.

The dApps that deal with deposit and asset management are applications that allow managing funds and digital assets. Indeed, in the DeFi ecosystem, dApps are generally non-custodial, which means no specialized institution is entitled to make financial and commercial decisions regarding assets belonging to customers. Moreover, since asset management activities also include the possibility of transferring tokens from an account to another, payment activities can be considered part of this category. In this context, Instadapp is an interesting dApp, developed upon the Ethereum blockchain, that grants access to asset management activities and connects many DeFi protocols allowing users to interface with a series of financial services. MakerDAO, Compound and Uniswap are three examples of interconnections made available by Instadapp.

DeFi derivatives represent another exciting field of this growing financial ecosystem. In the CeFi framework, derivatives are contracts among two or more parts whose value depends on the underlying financial assets upon which the parts have an agreement. As such, derivatives can be viewed as secondary securities, since they have no intrinsic value. Instead, in the DeFi environment, derivatives represent synthetic tokens able to reproduce the underlying assets' fluctuations. In particular, DeFi derivatives are obtained through a set of practices that fall within the *asset tokenization* field. One of the main applications of asset tokenization is the *wrapping process*. This procedure allows to obtain wrapped tokens, starting from an original token (e.g., ETH, BTC) through a transformation process carried out by smart contracts. The wrapping procedure also provides additional functionalities to the transformed tokens. A prominent example of this type of activity is present on the Ethereum blockchain, and in particular, it is applied in the ecosystem of tokens based on the ERC20 (Ethereum Request for Comment-20) standard. Indeed, the ERC20 standardized format makes possible the interaction between users who own ERC20 tokens.

Moreover, it is also worth noting that user interaction also occurs across different DeFi platforms (even though always developed upon the Ethereum blockchain) that recognized the same standardized format. An example of asset tokenization dApp is Chintai, built on top of the Eos blockchain, allowing businesses to issue, manage and trade tokenized assets. Another example of this category is Digix, a dApp based on the Ethereum blockchain that issues tokens pegged to the value of gold (i.e., 1 DGX = 1 g of real gold). Besides, also the Tezos blockchain is entering the world of digital derivatives through the issuance of wrapped BTC tokens, named *tzBTC* [6].

Finally, Fig. 3 summarizes the information collected within the study, showing how, just a few years after the first execution of smart contracts in 2014, the DeFi ecosystem is expanding across the blockchain environment. Therefore, whenever a box that connects a financial service with a blockchain is colored, at least one dApp provides that specific service upon the related infrastructure.

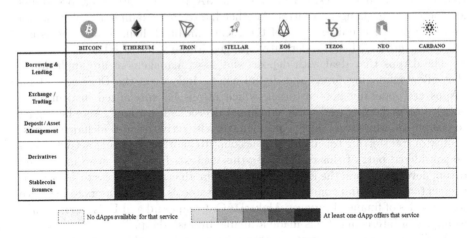

Fig. 3. DeFi ecosystem map across eight blockchain platforms.

5   Conclusion and Next Steps

The exploratory study about next generation blockchain-based financial services presented in this work allows understanding how and towards which way the financial industry is evolving. The blockchain technology application in this sector has brought to the creation of an ecosystem composed of dApps able to reproduce standard financial services and go a step further, proposing innovative solutions for this industry's evolution. The results presented describe a rapidly changing ecosystem, actually driven by the Ethereum blockchain and followed by prominent projects with broad potential in terms of efficiency and ecosystem prosperity. Therefore, the study addressed in this work provides a strategic observation point to better comprehend the future developments affecting the financial industry. This exploratory study also represents an initial step within the research field that treats the transition from centralized to decentralized systems. Further analysis will focus on a multiple perspectives' study with the aim to define which degree of complementarity among centralization and decentralization can maximize their respective strengths and minimize the weaknesses. Therefore, subsequent work will broaden the research horizon to in-between realities that present combinations of decentralized and centralized governance layers while preserving the blockchain's principles. This type of analysis will enhance comprehension about the future perspectives of DeFi, delineating the profile of potential future successful actors in the next-generation financial industry.

References

1. Centralized vs. decentralized finance—how does DeFi stack up? (2020). https://www.elev8con.com/centralized-vs-decentralized-finance-how-does-defi-stack-up/. Accessed 22 May 2020
2. Alethio: The DeFI series—an overview of the ecosystem and major protocols (2019). https://medium.com/alethio/the-defi-series-an-overview-of-the-ecosystem-and-major-protocols-da27d7b11191. Accessed 26 July 2020
3. Bach, L., Mihaljevic, B., Zagar, M.: Comparative analysis of blockchain consensus algorithms. In: 2018 41st International Convention on Information and Communication Technology, Electronics and Microelectronics (MIPRO), pp. 1545–1550. IEEE (2018). https://doi.org/10.23919/MIPRO.2018.8400278
4. Catalini, C., Gans, J.S.: Initial coin offerings and the value of crypto tokens. Technical reports, National Bureau of Economic Research (2018). https://doi.org/10.3386/w24418
5. De Filippi, P.: The interplay between decentralization and privacy: the case of blockchain technologies. J. Peer Prod. (7) (2016)
6. Foxley, W.: Wrapped Bitcoin aims to kick-start DeFi on Tezos blockchain (2020). https://www.coindesk.com/wrapped-bitcoin-aims-to-kickstart-defi-on-tezos-blockchain. Accessed 25 May 2020
7. Freni, P., Ferro, E., Moncada, R.: Tokenization and blockchain tokens classification: a morphological framework. In: 2020 IEEE Symposium on Computers and Communications (ISCC), pp. 1–6. IEEE (2020)
8. Houben, R., Snyers, A.: Cryptocurrencies and blockchain. Bruxelles: European Parliament (2018). https://doi.org/10.2861/263175
9. Kistner, K.J.: How decentralized is DeFi? A framework for classifying lending protocols (2019). https://medium.com/hackernoon/how-decentralized-is-defi-a-framework-for-classifying-lending-protocols-90981f2c007f. Accessed 25 May 2020
10. Nakamoto, S.: Bitcoin: a peer-to-peer electronic cash system. Whitepaper (2008). http://www.bitcoin.org/bitcoin.pdf
11. Ohnesorge, J.: A primer on blockchain technology and its potential for financial inclusion. No. 2/2018, Discussion Paper (2018). https://doi.org/10.23661/dp2.2018
12. Rupp, M., Kumar, P., Scholten, U., Turner, D.: Comparing public (permissionless) and private (permissioned) blockchains - what is best for banking and payment services (2019). https://www.real-sec.com/2019/12/comparing-public-permissionless-and-private-permissioned-blockchains-what-is-best-for-banking-and-payment-services/. Accessed 22 May 2020
13. Shapiro, C., Varian, H.R.: Information Rules: A Strategic Guide to the Network Economy. Harvard Business Press (1998)
14. Stiglitz, J.E.: Information and the change in the paradigm in economics. Am. Econ. Rev. **92**(3), 460–501 (2002). https://doi.org/10.1257/00028280260136363
15. Szabo, N.: Smart contracts: building blocks for digital markets. EXTROPY. J. Transhumanist Thought **16**(18), 2 (1996)
16. Zhang, S., Lee, J.H.: Analysis of the main consensus protocols of blockchain. ICT Express (2019). https://doi.org/10.1016/j.icte.2019.08.001

A Digital Voting System
for the 21st Century

Davide Casaleggio[1], Vincenzo Di Nicola[2]🆔, Michele Marchesi[3]🆔,
Sebastiano Missineo[4], and Roberto Tonelli[3(✉)]🆔

[1] Rousseau Association, Milan, Italy
davide@casaleggio.it
[2] Montreal, Canada
[3] DMI, University of Cagliari, Cagliari, Italy
marchesi@unica.it, roberto.tonelli@dsf.unica.it
[4] Strateghia Ltd., Rome, Italy
missineo@strateghia.it

Abstract. We present Terminus, a voting system based on blockchain
technology. Terminus relies on technology solutions pioneered by Monero,
a privacy-focused Blockchain, and on specifically designed operational
procedures: this guarantees full anonymity of the vote and addresses
several concerns of digital voting systems. Terminus was tested at an
event of an Italian political movement, and will be used to carry out
polls to drive some of the political decisions of this movement. We also
introduce an evaluation framework for DLT voting systems, and use it
to compare existing systems.

Keywords: e-voting · DLT · Monero

1 Introduction

Voting is an action we perform in several different situations: some examples
are song contests (e.g., Eurovision), reality shows (e.g., Big Brother), associa-
tions/councils (e.g., residents meeting), company's decisions (e.g. shareholders
meeting) or politics (e.g., country elections). Wherever allowed, digital voting
systems have been introduced as tools to make it easier for voters to express
their choice and to reduce the huge costs of voting in person. However, most
digital voting solutions in use nowadays are centralized and affected by a number of problems (e.g., certification of results). Some solutions are available and
have been adopted in some cases on traditional online voting, but these are out
of scope of this paper.

Recently, the introduction of digital ledger technologies (DLT), and in particular of blockchain, led to a renewed interest in e-voting, because they provide
high levels of immutability, accessibility and reliability, and are typically open
source.

V. Di Nicola—Independent researcher.

© Springer Nature Switzerland AG 2021
B. Balis et al. (Eds.): Euro-Par 2020 Workshops, LNCS 12480, pp. 42–53, 2021.
https://doi.org/10.1007/978-3-030-71593-9_4

In this paper, we analyze the key properties a remote digital voting system must exhibit, and provide an evaluation framework to compare voting systems based on DLT. Using this framework, we compared some of the most recent and popular e-voting systems based on DLT, with our proposal of Terminus, a voting system based on Monero technology, a privacy-preserving blockchain able to guarantee a very high degree of anonymity [13]. We then describe Terminus solution in deeper detail, and a live test which was performed after its deployment.

2 Requirements of an E-Voting System

Voting systems can be used for a variety of purposes, from shareholders meetings, to contests, to political voting – both non-binding and political election. A common requirement is that only qualified voters can cast their vote, and that this vote is counted just once. In most situations, voting must be anonymous, and the voting system must guarantee this.

Though there is no accepted standard on how to evaluate an e-voting system, several recent proposals reported evaluation criteria quite similar to each other [7,10,14].

Starting from these criteria, we summarized them, resulting in the following criteria a remote digital voting system must satisfy:

1. **Immutability:** No one can neither delete nor modify votes. Known also as "Integrity" [7].
2. **Egality:** Each vote must be equal to each other (in some kinds of voting, however, votes might be weighted). No voter can have his/her vote counted more than once. Each voter must receive one and only one ballot.
3. **Eligibility:** Only the voter can add his/her vote; no one else can add votes.
4. **Anonymity:** No one must know what a voter has voted for, unless specified otherwise. Known also as "Privacy" [10], [14].
5. **Blindness:** During the voting session, no one must know where the votes are going to. In other words, results must not be visible in real time. Known also as "Fairness" [10], [14] or "Data Confidentiality and Neutrality" [7].
6. **No forgery:** Ballots cannot be forged, and their number must be exactly equal to the number of voters. This property can be further detailed (for instance, prescribing that a voter cannot vote more than once), but here we will consider it as a single criterion.
7. **Verifiability:** Auditors – or even voters themselves – must be able to verify that the number of ballots is exactly equal to the number of voters, that each voter has received one and only one ballot, and that votes are correctly counted. Known also as "Auditability" [7].
8. **Cost:** Deployment, management and maintenance cost are reasonably low. Known also as "Affordability" [14].
9. **Scalability:** The system is able to manage very many voters, even political elections.

We added three more criteria to the above quoted ones, targeted to practical implementation and usage of the e-voting system. They are the **10. Stability** of the approach, that is the probability that the system is long-lived, the **11. Openness** of the system – it must be open source, or with inspectionable code, a feature very important to get the needed trust that the system always works properly – and the presence of **12. Actual use cases**, or at least test demonstrators, of the system.

Using these criteria, we defined a framework to evaluate e-voting systems based on DLT, especially targeting political elections.

Each criterion is evaluated using an integer scale from 1 to 5, meaning that the criterion is:

1. unsatisfied or poorly satisfied.
2. only partially satisfied.
3. fairly satisfied, but it might be better.
4. satisfied for the most part.
5. totally satisfied.

It would be possible to further weight by importance these criteria, but to the purposes of this work we assume that all criteria have the same weight. The actual comparative evaluation of existing voting system and of our proposal is reported in Sect. 5.

3   Existing E-Voting Systems Based on DLT

Despite the interest and the promises of DLT for implementing better voting systems, the number of actual systems in advanced development, or already deployed, is not high. Among these, the most popular and mature DLT voting systems we found are: Agora, Vocdoni, Voatz, Follow My Vote, Polys and Colony.

Agora [1] is a project started in 2015 by a Swiss-based voting technology company which developed an end-to-end verifiable voting solution for governments and institutions. Bryan Ford, who served as the Director of the Lausanne's Swiss Federal Institute of Technology (EPFL) Decentralized and Distributed System Lab (DEDIS) gave a key contribute. Agora is maintained by a team of cryptographers of Losanna Institute of Technology already accustomed with blockchain technology. It runs on a custom blockchain with various architectural levels and with three main components: Skipchain, Cotena and Valeda. Skipchain manages consensus, with high throughput and efficient transaction validation. Cotena is the component which stores cryptographic Skipchain proofs. Valeda validates Skipchain and Cotena data by means of cryptographic proofs. The Cotena layer is also used to anchor the system to the Bitcoin blockchain, since Cotena periodically stores a hash of the most recent Skipblock in a Bitcoin transaction `OP_RETURN` opcode, which enables anyone to verify that all data remained unaltered. Agora's architecture has different interconnected layers, is quite complex and is anchored to the Bitcoin blockchain. Agora piloted the first test of

Blockchain voting in a national government vote during Sierra Leone Presidential Elections in 2018, where results were counted on blockchain separately from official counting after the vote took place on paper ballots.

Vocdoni [6], which in Esperanto translates to "to give voice", is perhaps the most advanced among DLT voting systems, being very recent, and based on systematic usage of Zero Knowledge proofs. Vocdoni aims to build a general-purpose voting system, seen *"as a collective signaling mechanism that gives cryptographic guarantees about its integrity and its outcome"*. Its architecture is quite complex. The voting is handled by a Tendermint blockchain called "vochain". Data integrity is provided by Ethereum blockchain, data availability is provided by IPFS/Swarm. To date, we are not aware of real use cases of Vocdoni.

Voatz [5] is one of the first voting systems, and is that with most real use cases, being used by several counties and states in the USA. It is based on an app able to perform biometric identification of the voter. The e-voting process is quite traditional, but is registered on the Voatz blockchain, built using the HyperLedger blockchain framework. The Voatz blockchain is permissioned, run by selected nodes managed by the stakeholders of the election, such as the major political parties, NGOs, non-profits and independent auditors, etc. Voatz approach is proprietary, and has been security audited by independent third parties.

Follow My Vote (FMV) [3] is an open-source project based in USA whose code is available on GitHub. Most of the code is written in Python language, and the system is based on BitShares blockchain. The system provides the voters the possibility to monitor election results in real time and also to consequently act in order to change their mind according to partial results and to change the previous vote. Depending on the election rules this feature can be turned off. Voters register with an ID card issued by a public authority and receive a ballot for voting on the specific election they qualify to vote in. It uses a Registrar to pair the ID Key with a Blinded Token for anonymous voting.

Polys [4] is a Russian voting system based on Ethereum technology. It is in advanced development, but with already several use cases because the use of its beta version is presently free. The system is patented and proprietary, though they plan to release also an open source version. The voting is performed on a permissioned Ethereum blockchain, with added nodes managed by "trusted representatives" (TR) of the voting organization, or of interested parties. The vote anonymity is guaranteed by a Shamir's Secret Sharing schema involving private keys generated by the TRs, which is used to encrypt votes. The voting choices are in turn obscured with homomorphic encryption using the exponential ElGamal cryptosystem. Voters are provided of an app to generate their private key, and cast their unique vote after exchanging information with TRs nodes. Once cast, it is impossible to change one's vote. If the number of voters is high, homomorphic decryption can have performance issues, though they can be solved by partitioning the voters across different voting systems which run concurrently.

Colony [2] is peculiar among the considered platforms, because it is more a platform for community collaboration, rather than a true voting system. It is completely based on Ethereum, and is aimed to manage the polls of decentralized communities working on this blockchain. For this reason, it does not support anonymous voting, but only blind voting, until the poll is closed and the votes are revealed.

The literature includes many other proposals of voting systems based on DLT. However, despite the fact that some of these look quite sound and innovative, they are still under study or development. A recent paper on an e-voting system reports and describes some of these works [14]. Finally, it is worth quoting that Estonia performs e-voting using a traditional system, but with the register of voters stored on a blockchain (ksi blockchain) to ensure their integrity and to protect them against insider threats.

4   Our Proposal, the Terminus Platform

Work on Terminus started in 2017, as a way to use blockchain technology to increase transparency and trust of the Rousseau voting platform, used by the Italian 5-star Movement to ask its members to define political decisions.

The use of a public blockchain was quickly ruled out, because of its cost and voting recording time. In fact, the cost is linked to the price of the underlying cryptocurrency and on the number of transactions to be processed, and is way too volatile. The recording time too can be subject to unpredictable delays. For instance, November and December 2017 saw a major congestion of the Bitcoin network. Transactions remained unconfirmed for several days, if not eventually disappearing from the mempool [8].

So, we opted for a hybrid permissioned blockchain solution. In such solution:

- Sealers are nodes run by pre-authorized separate entities, which can create ("seal") transaction blocks. In addition, by choosing anonymous blockchain technologies, such as Monero or Zcash, sealers cannot distinguish data in the underlying transactions, thus preventing a malicious sealer to effectively tamper the voting session.
- Supporters are secondary nodes which can be run by everyone. They have access to the blockchain: they cannot create blocks, but can watch them and be aware if something suspicious happens.
- Rules could be put in place so that a subset of supporter nodes are eventually promoted to sealer nodes.

This approach resembles the dynamics existing at the United Nations Security Council. A set of predetermined sealer nodes (akin to the UN Security Council 5 permanent members) and a set of supporter nodes that are temporarily promoted to sealer nodes (akin to the UN Security Council 10 non-permanent members).

As the underlying blockchain to run the platform, we chose the technology behind Monero as the most suitable one for a digital and remote voting system. As a cryptocurrency, Monero proved its strength in highly adversarial environments. It has an extreme degree of privacy protection, and its community strives to increase it even further. We are by far not the first ones to think that the technological prowess behind Monero can be applied to voting. In fact, we took inspiration from the CryptoNote protocol [13] (on which Monero is based) that uses an optimized version of the Ring Signature scheme described by Fujisaki and Suzuki [11]. The key application mentioned in the paper is actually anonymous voting.

We believe in anonymity first: this must be the main key pillar of any digital voting solution. It is important to stress that anonymity is native to the Monero protocol, and it is very well battle-tested. Other technologies, such as Bitcoin, try to achieve anonymity by adding second layers (e.g., Lightning Network); however, as of today, such incremental approaches do not provide the same guarantees as of native solutions. Table 1 reports a summary of the key features a digital voting solution must satisfy, along with their technical solutions. Roles (such as Administrator and Custodian) are described in the following section.

Table 1. The key features a digital voting solution must satisfy.

Key feature	Solution
No external entity can add/remove/modify votes	Native to blockchain technologies
No one must know what a voter has voted (anonymity)	Ring Signatures of voters
No one must know where the votes are going to (results must not be visible in real time)	Stealth address of Vote Receivers + Vote Receivers private keys safe management by external Custodians
Ballots cannot be forged, and its number must be the same of voters	Blockchain tokens generated before voting session begins
Each voter must receive one and only one ballot	Blockchain tokens sent by the Administrator to voters before voting session begins
Auditor must be able to verify the 2 points above (number of ballots == number of voters; each voter has received one and only one ballot) without relinquishing anything in voter anonymity and vote visibility	Auditor has access to voters view keys, thus verifying that Administrator has indeed sent one token to each voter
No voter can have his/her vote counted more than once	Native to blockchain technologies
Each vote must be equal to each other	Token fungibility

We forked what at the time was the stable version of Monero (v0.13.0.4). In our permissioned solution, we removed all transaction fees (i.e., they were set to zero) and all their relative checks. Also, for the sake of scalability, regarding the consensus protocol we opted for a Proof-of-Authority (PoA) approach with pre-approved sealer nodes.

Before the voting session, all sealer nodes start mining at startup with same fixed-difficulty (100), and block rewards are sent to a special wallet called "Admin wallet". Only a total of N vote tokens (where N is the number of Voters) are created. In our solution, 1 forked XMR equals to 1 vote token.

The Admin Wallet initially hoards the N tokens of the permissioned Blockchain, to be used as vote tokens; then, before the voting session starts, the Admin Wallet distributes each vote token to the N Voters, creating N transactions of 1 forked XMR as amount. Our system uses one blockchain for each voting session: this prevents people from using unspent vote tokens of a previous election in a new one. In addition, in order to further guarantee that no additional vote tokens are created, during a voting session block rewards are zeroed out. Also, if, by any chance, a "disturber" Voter sends a fractional token value to the Vote Receiver, such vote will not be counted.

We then introduced a few tweaks on the wallet side in order to allow vote transactions to be mined. To this purpose, we forked what at the time was the stable version of Monerujo (v1.10.10), a high-quality Monero light wallet [12].

We also created a dashboard where the Administrator can distribute the vote tokens (before the voting session starts), and can calculate results, without having to perform all the operations from the command line (after the voting session is over). For sake of demonstration, for the Proof of Concept the dashboard also allowed the Administrator to create Vote Receivers keys, and start/end the voting session: these are aspects that can be solved through improvements as discussed in later Sect. 6.

4.1 Roles in the System

Terminus voting process makes use of several roles, which are key to ensure voting fairness and trust. These roles are:

- **Voters**: the people who vote. In a real-world paper voting analogy, Voters are akin to electors.
- **Vote Receivers** (for ease of readability, also simply called "Receivers"): entities who receive the votes. In a real-world paper voting analogy, Vote Receivers are akin to candidates.
- **Administrator**: entity which, before voting session begins, grants one ballot to each Voter. In a real-world paper voting analogy, Administrator is akin to poll clerks that give a ballot to each eligible voter.
- **Auditor**: entity which ensures no foul play is done by the Administrator. In a real-world paper voting analogy, Auditor is akin to scrutineers that ensure there is no malpractice. Any Voter might also be an Auditor.
- **Custodians**: entities which, before voting session begins, create Receivers private keys, publish Receivers public keys, but cannot show Receiver private keys. In a real-world paper voting analogy, Custodians are akin to militaries that protect the ballot box to be closed till the end.
- **Sealer Nodes**: Entities which run the underlying blockchain software solution and can create ("seal") blocks. In a real-world paper voting analogy,

it is a combination of poll clerks and scrutineers that ensure no vote is added/deleted/modified during the voting session.

– **Supporters**: entities which run the underlying blockchain software solution but can only watch.

4.2 Voting Process

Before starting the voting session, the network must be configured. To this purpose, it is needed to setup a minimum number of Sealer Nodes, able to run the permissioned blockchain. For evaluation purposes, 5 nodes are enough, possibly located on the cloud, running a modified version of "monerod", the Monero daemon software. Real polls would require a bigger number of Sealer Nodes, each managed by an independent organization, in order to ensure the stability and trust of the system.

Before each session, the Vote Receivers are set up. The Administrator had access to a server where, through a simple dashboard, s/he will:

1. Create Vote Receivers wallets
2. Start a voting session
3. Enable Voters
4. Stop a voting session
5. Calculate results

Presently, the Administrator keeps locally all the Vote Receivers keys. Of course, this is not acceptable in a real-life voting system: the proper way to address Vote Receiver key management is discussed in later Sect. 6 with the introduction of a custodial system.

The voting session needs that voters install on their smartphones and use an application. Each voter must create a Voter wallet, send the Voter wallet address to the Administrator, receive a vote token by the Administrator, and eventually send the vote token to one of the admissible Vote Receivers (voting options).

After the voting session, the results are processed by simply counting the number of tokens received by each Vote Receiver.

4.3 Proof of Concept

On March 10, 2019, at Villaggio Rousseau in Milan we showcased a simple Proof of Concept: voters were asked to pick one of four choices of food they would have liked to eat at the end of the event. Each of the food choices (pizza, apple, oranges, sweets) had a Vote Receiver wallet associated to them. There was only one voting session, and at the end results were published. Had additional voting sessions been scheduled, the whole process would have been recreated from scratch (i.e., "one voting session, one blockchain").

Before starting the voting session, we had to configure the network. For demonstration purposes, we setup 5 instances of a modified version of monerod on AWS. We bound the daemon on localhost and linked directly every Sealer to every other one through SSH tunnels. At the end, we had a total of 20 tunnels (5 nodes, with 4 connections each).

For this demonstration, the Vote Receivers were:

1. Pizza Margherita
2. Apples (Mele)
3. Oranges (Arance)
4. Sweets (Caramelle)

The voting session lasted 1 h (from 10:00 am to 11:00 am). During such time, 67 attendees of Villaggio Rousseau volunteered to install and use on their Android phones the voting wallet. Each attendee ("Voter") created a Voter wallet, sent the wallet address to the Administrator, received a vote token by the Administrator, and sent the vote token to one of the four Vote Receivers.

Fig. 1. The results of the demonstration voting session (in Italian).

At 11:00 am on March 10, the Administrator stopped mining on each node, thus terminating the voting session. Results were immediately announced by publishing the balance of each Vote Receiver wallet. A total of 67 Voters took part to the 1-h voting session demonstration. 53 of them actually cast a vote. The output of the vote is shown in Fig. 1. By the way the system has been designed, there is no way of knowing who the 14 people who did not cast their vote were.

5   Comparative Evaluation

Using the framework reported in Sect. 2, we evaluated the voting systems reported in Sect. 3, together with Terminus. We were unfortunately unable to actually install, use and test these systems, except for Terminus. So, the evaluation is based on the information gathered collecting the information on the Web site of these systems, and on other Web sources.

The evaluation was made by polling seven blockchain app programmers, working at our department or at other firms, and taking the median value of the answers. The result is reported in Fig. 2. There is no room for a thorough discussion of these results. Basically, the scores of the voting systems do not differ much. The most advanced systems – Agora, Vocdoni, Voatz and Polys – are somewhat penalized for being very complex and, with the exception of Vocdoni, quite closed. FMV and Colony are quite simple, and are not intended for large-scale, anonymous, blind voting. Terminus was conceived to be simple, easy to manage and scalable, hence the good score.

#	Criterion	Terminus	Agora	Vocdoni	Voatz	FMV	Polys	Colony
1	Immutability	4	4	3	3	3	4	4
2	Egality	4	4	4	3	4	4	4
3	Eligibility	4	4	4	5	5	4	4
4	Anonymity	4	4	5	3	3	4	1
5	Blindness	5	4	5	4	4	5	4
6	No forgery	5	5	5	4	5	5	5
7	Verifiability	4	4	4	3	4	4	4
8	Cost	4	2	2	2	3	2	4
9	Stability	4	4	3	3	3	4	4
10	Openness	5	3	4	1	5	1	5
11	Scalability	4	4	3	5	3	3	1
12	Actual use cases	2	4	1	5	3	4	2
	TOTAL SCORE	49	46	43	41	45	44	42

Fig. 2. Comparative evaluation of the considered voting systems, using the proposed framework.

Clearly, there are strong threats to the validity of the comparative analysis. The main threat is that the evaluation of most systems is not based on testing the actual system, but on information gathered on the Web. Another threat is the obvious bias of the authors, though we tried to be as impartial as possible. Nevertheless, we believe that this evaluation might be a good starting point for demonstrating the usefulness of the proposed evaluation framework for DLT-based voting systems.

6   Discussion and Further Improvements

So far, we have discussed the core of the technology behind Terminus. Though, in order for the system to achieve important properties of voting systems, some operational procedures must be introduced.

For example, in order to prevent visibility of voting trends, it is not enough to rely on Vote Receivers stealth addresses. In fact, if a Vote Receiver has access to his/her private keys, s/he can see in real-time the voting session results: s/he might decide to leak results, or take advantage of this knowledge. All of this can be effectively solved by introducing the role of Custodians: that is, independent people in charge of protecting secrets. Let's consider N Custodians, and a safe environment where Vote Receiver private keys are created. These keys are then split into N shares using algorithms such as Shamir's Secret Sharing, and a threshold of M ($M \leq N$) is set. That is, it would require at least M Custodians to be able recreate the Vote Receivers private keys. The corresponding Vote Receivers public keys are generated along with the private keys, and they can obviously be shared with the world so that Voters know where to send their transaction to. Such custody schemes are today well used in the cryptocurrency world to protect wealth [9]: they involve safe procedures and hardware (e.g. HSM), which can be also directly applied in this case.

Additional operating procedures, not necessary but useful, would require the Voter to share his/her view keys with the Administrator, and the Administrator to share them to the whole public. This way, any Voter can - on his/her own - verify that the number of ballots created by the Administrator is indeed correct (no ballot forgery) and that each Voter has received one and only one ballot.

Further improvements regard voting session termination. Voting session duration must be known, and cannot be extended. For example, if it is set to last 12 h, and the system creates blocks every 10 s, then the last block of the voting session must be block number 4,319. The sealers won't mine any block greater or equal to number 4,320.

A big issue which is not addressed in this work, and by any of the other considered voting system, is its ability to prevents or mitigate the risk of buying and selling votes. This bribing problem also exists in traditional remote voting (as in the case of voting via physical mail), and in other electronic voting systems. In fact, it is very easy to sell a vote in systems that use ballot paper and mail, or to sell a username and a password. The proposed solution opens up ways to mitigate the issue, and will be the main focus of future research and developments of the solution.

Finally, it is also worth mentioning that Terminus relies on the concept of digital identities, which must be created beforehand. Digital Identities Management goes beyond the scope of this voting system; however, appropriate solutions may be integrated on Terminus and improve the overall platform, both in Voter experience and in its reliability.

7   Conclusion

In this paper we described the issues of e-voting platforms using blockchain (DLT) technology, and the quality criteria such platforms should exhibit. From these criteria, an evaluation framework for these platforms is introduced and applied. We also presented Terminus, a new e-voting platform based on the privacy-preserving blockchain technology of Monero.

The elements of innovation, compared to the state of the art, are that this, to our knowledge, is the first paper explicitly targeted to analyze and compare DLT-based voting systems. Moreover, compared with existing and proposed approaches, Terminus aims to be much simpler, open and yet very scalable. This is obtained with a solution which is solid, auditable and tamper-proof, and maintains total voters' anonymity.

Future work will be performed in two directions. The first is to extend and tune our evaluation framework, including weighting of the criteria. We will also evaluate more voting systems, using a panel of experts and a Delphi technique approach. The second direction is to make the needed improvements to Terminus, especially on the consensus protocol and protection against denial-of-service attacks or spam voting. We will also examine the introduction of the possibility to vote more than once, keeping as valid only the last vote. This would improve the resistance against voting bribery or blackmailing.

Acknowledgements. The Terminus platform was developed with a grant by Associazione Rousseau. The evaluation framework was funded by Sardegna Ricerche, project "CriptoVoting" (RICERCA 2-26), POR FESR 2014-2020, Asse 1, Azione 1.1.3, 2nd call.

References

1. Agora homepage (2020). https://www.agora.vote/. Accessed 4 June 2020
2. Colony homepage (2020). https://colony.io/. Accessed 4 June 2020
3. Follow my vote homepage (2020). https://followmyvote.com/. Accessed 4 June 2020
4. Polys homepage (2020). https://polys.me/. Accessed 4 June 2020
5. Voatz homepage (2020). https://voatz.com/. Accessed 4 June 2020
6. Vocdoni homepage (2020). https://vocdoni.io/. Accessed 4 June 2020
7. Bistarelli, S., Mercanti, I., Santancini, P., Santini, F.: End-to-end voting with non-permissioned and permissioned ledgers. J. Grid Comput. **17**, 97–118 (2019)
8. CCN: 700 million stuck in 115,000 unconfirmed bitcoin transactionse (2017). https://www.ccn.com/700-million-stuck-115000-unconfirmed-bitcoin-transactions/. Accessed 4 June 2020
9. Di Nicola, V.: Custody at Conio – part 2 (2020). https://medium.com/conio/custody-at-conio-part-2-21e976f86384. Accessed 4 June 2020
10. Dimitriou, T.: Efficient, coercion-free and universally verifiable blockchain-based voting. Comput. Netw. **174** (2020)
11. Fujisaki, E., Suzuki, K.: Traceable ring signature. In: Okamoto, T., Wang, X. (eds.) PKC 2007. LNCS, vol. 4450, pp. 181–200. Springer, Heidelberg (2007). https://doi.org/10.1007/978-3-540-71677-8_13
12. m2049r: Monerujo: an android monero wallet (2019). https://www.monerujo.io/. Accessed 4 June 2020
13. van Saberhagen, N.: Cryptonote v 2.0 (2013). https://cryptonote.org/whitepaper.pdf. Accessed 4 June 2020
14. Zhang, S., Wang, L., Xiong, H.: Chaintegrity: blockchain-enabled large-scale e-voting system with robustness and universal verifiability. Int. J. Inf. Secur. **19**(3), 323–341 (2019). https://doi.org/10.1007/s10207-019-00465-8

Trustless, Censorship-Resilient and Scalable Votings in the Permission-Based Blockchain Model

Sebastian Gajek and Marco Lewandowsky$^{(\boxtimes)}$

Flensburg University of Applied Sciences, Flensburg, Germany
{sebastian.gajek,marco.lewandowsky}@hs-flensburg.de

Abstract. Voting systems are the tool of choice when it comes to settle an agreement of different opinions. We propose a solution for a trustless, censorship-resilient and scalable electronic voting platform. By leveraging the blockchain together with the functional encryption paradigm, we fully decentralize the system and reduce the risks that a voting provider, like a corrupt government, does censor or manipulate the outcome.

Keywords: Voting · Functional encryption · Blockchain · Hyperledger

1 Introduction

In many countries, the de facto mechanism to realize democratic choices are votings. It is well-known that voting systems are subjected to attacks, which threaten democratic decision-making [10]. This includes vote-buying, ballot-stuffing, destruction or invalidation of ballots, mis-recording of votes, aggravating the voting access or tampering with the electronic voting machines [9,11]. The commonality of all these threats is to affect the outcome of the voting. For important decisions (e.g. presidential or shareholder elections) one tries to reduce the threats by recruiting trusted helpers and the engagement of neutral observers. These entities are appointed by a central authority, like the government or a corporation, and are crucial to the election process. Centralized trust is fragile. Even if their implementation is cost-efficient, the history has shown that central authorities can misuse their responsibility and power to influence the outcome of an election to their favor.

1.1 Previous Work

Electronic voting systems and their security properties have been actively studied in the research community, since their introduction in the celebrated work of Chaum [3,5,15]. Due to their scalability and fault-tolerance properties [4], it

Supported by the European Commission through H2020 project FENTEC (grant no. 780108).

© Springer Nature Switzerland AG 2021
B. Balis et al. (Eds.): Euro-Par 2020 Workshops, LNCS 12480, pp. 54–65, 2021.
https://doi.org/10.1007/978-3-030-71593-9_5

Table 1. Comparison of different e-voting protocols in the blockchain.

Properties	[21]	[13]	[22]	[29]	[20]	This work
Fairness	✗	✓	✗	✓	✓	✓
Eligibility	✓	✓	✓	✓	✓	✓
Privacy	✓	✓	✓	✓	✓	✓
Individual verifiability	✓	✓	✓	✓	✓	✓
Universal verifiability	✓	✓	✓	✓	✓	✓
Trustlessness	✗	✗	✓	✗	✓	✓
Scalability	✗	✗	✗	✗	✗	✓
Receipt-Freeness	✗	✗	✗	✓	✗	✗
Coercion-Resistance	✗	✗	✗	✗	✗	✗
Vote Type	Any	Any	Yes-no	Any	Any	Any

turns out that the blockchain is a promising tool for electronic voting systems [7]. Even if blockchain-based e-voting systems come with some compromises [14,24], their main advantage is the provision of a tamper-proof way to achieve a publicly verifiable consensus that makes it interesting even for governmental institutions, which aim to extend the involvement of citizens in local community decisions [28]. It has been verified in practice that particular solutions are able to handle hundreds of thousands of voters [18].

A lightweight solution for an Etherium-based e-voting protocol, which focuses on reducing trust against the voting provider, is given by Lai et al. [20]. Their protocol works in a way that key managers have to agree on a common key using secret sharing techniques, which is then used by eligible voters to create obfuscated addresses for available candidates. In order to prevent double voting, a one-time ring signature has to be created by every voter. Because ballots are stored as normal transactions to obfuscated addresses within the network, verification and tallying has to be processed off-chain by every interested party after the key managers publish their secret keys. The fact that expensive computations have to take place outside the blockchain in order to reduce gas costs may exclude low power devices from verifying the results. Liu et al. propose a voting protocol within the permissioned and permissionless blockchain model [21]. A voter casts a ballot by encrypting the vote with the organizer's public key before the inspector signs it. The system thus assumes to trust both parties not to violate ballot and voter privacy. An implementation based on the blockchain framework Ethereum is given in [2]. With regard to today's gas prices and Ethereum's throughput, the system is unsuitable for frequent or large-scale elections. Hardwick et al. propose a voting scheme in the permission-based blockchain model, satisfying the basic notions of fairness, eligibility, privacy and verifiability [13]. Their protocol uses the blockchain as a transparent ballot box. The system relies on a central certification authority to authenticate voters and give permission to access the network. Hence, an authority when byzantine, breaks the link between voter identity and vote and therefore violates the ballot privacy. Their implementation within a private Ethereum chain requires a non-negligible amount of gas per vote, which makes the approach less appealing for frequent votings like in DAOs. McCorry et al. propose a variant of the Open Vote Network (OVN) in the permissionless blockchain model [22]. The OVN is a self-tallying protocol, which avoids a central counting authority. A self-tallying protocol converts tallying into an open procedure, which allows any voter or a third-party observer to perform the tally computation once all ballots are cast. This removes the role of a tallying authority from an election as anyone can compute the tally without assistance. Unfortunately, self-tallying protocols have a fairness drawback as the last voter can compute the tally before anyone else, which results in both, adaptive and abortive issues. Moreover, the protocol is limited to boardroom votes, where board members take a yes-no decision. Their implementation in Ethereum shows suitable gas costs for 40 voters, but does not scale with larger numbers. Yu et al. propose a platform-independent approach [29]. To achieve the comprehensive goal, the authors employ Paillier encryption to enable ballots to be counted without leaking candidature information in the ballots. To leverage the homomorphic property for summation of votes, an administrator decrypts the plain text sum. If byzantine, the administrator can use the same decryption key to decrypt each encrypted ballot and break the ballot privacy. A proof-of-knowledge is employed to convince the voting system that the ballot is valid without revealing its content. Linkable ring signatures are used to ensure that the ballot is from one of the valid voters, while no one can trace the owner of the ballot. To this end, a voter needs to download the public keys of all other voters, which entails a space allocation linear in the number of voters. Their reference implementation in Hyperledger Fabric allows handling millions of voters, provided that they are grouped in sufficient batches.

A comparison of the above mentioned e-voting schemes by their properties can be found in Table 1.

1.2 Our Contribution

We propose a solution for a trustless voting system based on Hyperledger Fabric [1]. By trustless, we mean a system in which byzantine parties, including the voting organizer, are unable to manipulate the outcome of an election. A bit more precisely, malicious organizers are prevented from opening ballots before the official tallying. We leverage techniques from functional encryption [26] and implement decentralized *off-chain opening oracles* in order to allow voters to encrypt their votes and store them secretly within the blockchain. This technique already leads to censorship-resilience of the cast votes, as the blockchain guarantees the immutability of the storage. Off-chain oracles, like for example time-triggered servers, open the encrypted ballots by writing their decryption keys into the blockchain. Only if a sufficient subset of keys, matching a predefined quorum policy, has been stored, the blockchain or any other auditing entity is capable of opening and publicly tallying the ballots. This way we fully decentralize the opening phase and lift the byzantine fault-tolerance properties of blockchains to the off-chain perimeter. Furthermore, we introduce *off-chain anonymizer oracles*, which cooperatively unlink the encrypted vote from the user's identity and enforce the eligibility to cast a single vote. To instantiate the oracles, we leverage techniques from threshold blind signatures [17], which allows us to scale the byzantine fault-tolerance of the voting system by making adjustments to the threshold parameter. Only if the eligible voter receives sufficient signatures from the anonymizer oracles, she can unblind and reconstruct an anonymous voting credential, which is necessary to submit her encrypted vote.

2 Preliminaries

2.1 Trust Model

Our goal is to provide a platform in which voters are not required to put their trust in the honest behavior of individual system components, a property to which we refer as *trustlessness*. Our approach to provide such a trustless voting system is built upon the decentralization of critical security components and entities. For example, we decentralize the need to trust a single eligibility-controlling entity, and by leveraging threshold blind signatures, we distribute the voter admission process over several authorities. At the same time, we also ensure that each voter is only able to cast a single ballot. Further, we make use of distributed multi-authority functional encryption to prevent that a single authority is able to open ballots without prior agreement of other authorities. Another aspect of our trustless voting system leverages the blockchain as a distributed ballot box and tamper-resistant tallying entity. The blockchain operating principle ensures that no malicious node is able to add or remove ballots, or write a wrong decryption result to the blockchain, on its own. While public blockchains are considered as trustless networks, we decide to use a hybrid between public and (trusted) private blockchain, because of performance reasons. However, we claim that with the permission-based blockchain Hyperledger Fabric, this trustlessness also holds to some degree [27]. With a proper selection of voting providers which host the peer nodes, e.g. well-known companies, the trust can be minimized as it can be assumed that they do not help each other tampering with the data and risk their reputation in the process.

2.2 Cryptographic Building Blocks

In order to protect the voter's privacy, we use a decentralized multi-authority functional encryption system with inner-product functionality, for short, decentralized inner-product predicate encryption DIPPE = (DIPPE.GlobalSetup, DIPPE.AuthSetup, DIPPE.KeyGen, DIPPE.Encrypt, DIPPE.Decrypt). The reason of using this scheme is to ensure that no single authority is able to decrypt, and therefore break the secrecy of the ballot, on her own. For our prototype we use the scheme of Michalevsky et al. [23] as it best fits our need for an adaptive secure scheme with excellent decryption performance that doesn't scale with the number of authorities.

To implement the voter's eligibility check, we utilize a t-out-of-n threshold blind signature scheme TBS = (TBS.ParGen, TBS.KeyGen, TBS.Sign, TBS.Verify). We require the blindness property to prevent that authorities make conclusions about the voter's identity as soon as the ballots are published to the blockchain. In addition, we use the threshold property to prevent that voters request more than one signature from distinct authorities and therefore contradict our one–person–one–vote approach. For our implementation we use the scheme of Kuchta et al. [19]. While the base version of this scheme requires a trusted dealer, the TBS.KeyGen can be *completely decentralized* through a distributed key generation protocol [12]. For formal definitions we refer the reader to the appropriate articles.

3   System Model

Key Authority (Opening Oracle): There exists a set of n_{KA} off-chain key authorities $\boldsymbol{KA} := \{KA_1, \ldots, KA_i, \ldots, KA_{n_{KA}}\}$, with each KA_i owning an identity $\mathcal{I}_{KA_i} := \{sk_{KA_i}, pk_{KA_i}, cert_{KA_i}\}$, consisting of a private key, public key and certificate. Key authorities fulfill two tasks within the voting system. First, for every voting vid, where KA_i has been registered as a responsible key authority, the authority creates a new key pair $(pk_{KA_i,vid}, sk_{KA_i,vid})$ consisting of public and private key. While the private key is kept secret, the public key is published to the blockchain. The second task relates to the opening process. In order to open the encrypted ballots, every responsible key authority KA_i has to generate a decryption key $sk_{KA_i,vid,v}$ using the private key $sk_{KA_i,vid}$ and a policy vector $\boldsymbol{v}$, and sends it to the blockchain.

Signer Authority (Anonymizer Oracle): There exists a set of n_{SA} off-chain signer authorities $\boldsymbol{SA} := \{SA_1, \ldots, SA_i, \ldots, SA_{n_{SA}}\}$, with each SA_i possessing an identity $\mathcal{I}_{SA_i} := \{sk_{SA_i}, pk_{SA_i}, cert_{SA_i}\}$, consisting of a private key, public key and certificate. Main task of the signer authority SA_i is to create a signature σ_{vid,V_i} over a ballot for an eligible voter V_i. To prevent a double voting attack, each SA_i keeps track of already issued signatures.

Registrar: There exists a set of n_R off-chain registrars $\boldsymbol{R} := \{R_1, \ldots, R_i, \ldots, R_{n_R}\}$, with each R_i owning an identity $\mathcal{I}_{R_i} := \{sk_{R_i} pk_{R_i}, cert_{R_i}\}$ that consists of a private key, a public key and a certificate issued by an organization of the network. A registrar's main responsibility is the registration of new votings at the system.

Voter: There exists a set of n_V off-chain voters $\boldsymbol{V} := \{V_1, \ldots, V_i, \ldots, V_{n_V}\}$, with each V_i possessing two types of identities. First, an individual voter identity $\mathcal{I}_{V_i} := \{sk_{V_i}, pk_{V_i}, cert_{V_i}\}$ and second, an anonymous identity $\mathcal{I}_{anon} := \{sk_{anon}, pk_{anon}, cert_{anon}\}$, which is shared between all voters. Both identities consist of a certificate and a pair of public and private key. While $\mathcal{I}_{V_i}$ is uniquely bound to a voter and can be used to authenticate herself, the intention of $\mathcal{I}_{anon}$ is to protect the privacy of the voter. Since we operate in a permission-based blockchain model, every request has to be signed by an authorized identity of the network. We use this approach of a shared identity, which can only be used to submit ballots to the blockchain, to bypass the membership check and to disguise the real origin of the request. To participate at a given voting *vid*, the voter fetches the corresponding voting description from the blockchain, casts an encrypted ballot, gets enough signatures from the signer authorities and submits all together to the blockchain.

Peer: There exists a set of n_P peers $\boldsymbol{P} := \{P_1, \ldots, P_i \ldots, P_{n_P}\}$, with each peer P_i owning an identity $\mathcal{I}_{P_i} := \{sk_{P_i}, pk_{P_i}, cert_{P_i}\}$ consisting of a certificate and a pair of public and private key. Peers are part of Hyperledger Fabric and are mainly responsible for maintaining the distributed ledger. Further, they provide the communication endpoint for all off-chain entities in the system. The application functionality is included within their smart contracts and can be invoked by appropriate entities.

Ordering Service (Orderer): There exists a set of n_O ordering nodes $\boldsymbol{O} = \{O_1, \ldots, O_{n_O}\}$. The ordering service is a modular component of Hyperledger Fabric and its main responsibility is the block creation process. It collects all transactions and sorts them into blocks. At the time of writing this article the recommended decentralized ordering service is based on RAFT [25], which is only crash-fault-tolerant. An orderer that tolerates byzantine errors is already planned for a future release.

Organization: There exists a set of n_{Org} organizations $\boldsymbol{Org} = \{Org_1, \ldots, Org_i, \ldots, Org_{n_{Org}}\}$, with each Org_i owning a key pair consisting of public and private key. Organizations are superior entities within the context of Hyperleder Fabric. Every network participant whether it is a client or a peer, has to obtain a signed certificate from an organization in order to operate within the network.

4 Protocol

The voting system consists of four protocols: *Setup*, *Pre-Voting*, *Voting* and *Tallying*.

4.1 Setup

Preparation of the Hyperledger Fabric Network. This step encompasses the creation of the cryptographic material for organizations, smart-contracts and common configuration (genesis block) required to bootstrap the network peers. As this is standard process we refer the reader to the Hyperledger Fabric documentation [16].

Preparation of Off-Chain Entities. In order to operate within the permission-based blockchain, each network participant has to obtain a digital certificate from an organization. The certificate encompasses information such as the public key, a type (registrar, voter, ...) to limit the operation set and possibly other metadata of the entity. During this step, each organization may also verify the physical identity of the requester. Details of the issuance policy as well as the decentralized implementation of the certification protocol (e.g. through an MPC protocol [6]) are out of scope.

Registration of Signer Authorities. In order to fulfill their special purpose of ensuring the voter's eligibility, signer authorities need to perform an additional set up of the threshold blind signature scheme. Due to our focus on a decentralized voting platform, signer authorities, across organizational boundaries, start by engaging the common execution of the TBS.KeyGen($\cdot$) algorithm, with output the set of secret keys sk_{TBS,SA_i} for each signer authority SA_i and public key components, which form the common public key pk_{TBS}. Note that in order to be completely decentralized, the preceding execution of a distributed key generation protocol may be necessary. Public key components are then stored within the blockchain (Fig. 1).

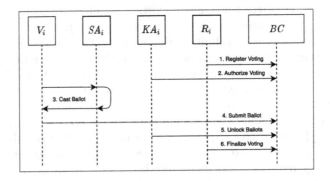

Fig. 1. Protocol flow of our voting system. Due to clarity of presentation, the setup protocol is left out. Components of Hyperledger Fabric are summarized as blockchain (BC) and its state is assumed to be known by every party.

4.2   Pre-voting

Register Voting. In our system, a registrar R_i is capable of scheduling new votings. To do so, the registrar sends a signed request containing metadata like vid, title, expiration date, a set of eligible voters, a set of possible choices **opt** and a policy π, which specifies a set of responsible key authorities, to the blockchain.

Authorize Voting. Trustlessness within our system relies on the decentralization of critical entities. In case of key authorities this approach ensures that there is no single authority, which is capable of opening the encrypted ballots on her own. Now, in this sub-protocol the virtual ballot box is prepared. Therefore, every key authority KA_i, mentioned within the policy π of a registered voting, generates a new functional encryption key pair $\{sk_{vid,KA_i}, pk_{vid,KA_i}\} \leftarrow$ DIPPE.AuthSetup(pp, i) using the public parameters pp of the scheme. While the private key sk_{vid,KA_i} is stored locally, the public key pk_{vid,KA_i} is distributed to a blockchain peer in a signed request. If the blockchain is able to verify that the requesting key authority is part of the voting policy, it accepts and links the public key to the voting description, which is stored within the blockchain.

4.3   Voting

Cast Ballot. To cast a new ballot, the voter V_i first fetches the appropriate voting description from the blockchain and calls $ballot_{vid,V_i} \leftarrow$ DIPPE.Encrypt($pp, \boldsymbol{x}$, opt_{vid,V_i}) using her choice $opt_{vid,V_i} \in \boldsymbol{opt}$, the public keys $\{pk_{KA_m,vid}\}_{m \in \pi}$, a policy vector $\boldsymbol{x}$ derived from the policy π, and the scheme's public parameter pp. In order to prevent double voting, the ballot $ballot_{vid,V_i}$ has to be signed by a set of at least t signer authorities. Note that the signing of the voter's ballot has to be done blindly in order to disguise associations from the ballot to the voter. The signer authorities check whether the voter is eligible to participate at the voting vid and if that is the case, V_i with input her encrypted ballot $ballot_{vid,V_i}$ and the set of signer authorities engages in the protocol TBS.Sign($\cdot$), while in the end V_i obtains a signature σ_{vid,V_i} and all participating signer authorities learn nothing about the ballot. Further, signer authorities locally keep track of already issued blind signatures and in consequence, a valid signature can only be obtained once per voter V_i and voting id vid.

Submit Ballot. The voter now votes by submitting the ballot $ballot_{vid,V_i}$ together with the signature σ_{vid,V_i} to the blockchain. Note that it is mandatory for a voter at this point, to utilize her anonymous identity I_{anon} in order to sign the request to the blockchain. Otherwise, it breaks the voter's privacy as soon as the ballot is opened. The blockchain accepts the ballot if TBS.Verify(pk_{TBS}, $ballot_{vid,V_i}, \sigma_{vid,V_i}$) outputs 1.

4.4   Tallying

Unlock Ballots. In order to unlock an expired voting, key authorities have to send decryption keys to the blockchain. To do so, each responsible key authority KA_i first fetches the voting description from the blockchain, and generates a decryption key $sk_{KA_i,vid,v} \leftarrow$ DIPPE.KeyGen($pp, i, sk_{KA_i,vid}, \{pk_{KA_m,vid}\}_{m \in \pi}$, $vid, \boldsymbol{v}$) using its own private key sk_{vid,KA_i}, the public keys $\{pk_{KA_m,vid}\}_{m \in \pi}$ of all responsible key authorities, and an attribute vector $\boldsymbol{v}$ derived from the policy π. The decryption key $sk_{KA_i,vid,v}$ is then distributed to the blockchain. The blockchain verifies that the key authority KA_i is indeed responsible for this voting and if that is the case, the blockchain links the decryption key to the stored voting description.

Finalize Voting. Up to now, the blockchain contains all encrypted ballots and the corresponding decryption keys from the key authorities. So the final step is the actual decryption. This is a transparent, either automated or triggered process, which takes place within the peer's smart contract. During this step, the choice opt_{vid,V_m} of voter V_m is revealed by calculating $opt_{vid,V_m} :=$ DIPPE.Decrypt($ballot_{vid,V_m}, \{sk_{KA_i,vid,v}\}$) and the result is stored within the blockchain. With all ballots now open, the tallying can be performed by anyone.

5   Security Analysis

In this section, we analyze and informally argue security of our voting system.

Ballot Privacy: Ballot privacy means that an adversary is not able to reveal the way, a specific voter has voted. Our system ensures ballot privacy due to the fact that voters submit their ballots using a distinct anonymous identity, which is shared between all voters and therefore disguises the real user behind it. Even if ballots, which are stored within the blockchain, become publicly visible, an inference to a specific voter can not be established anymore. In order to prevent double voting, a ballot has to be submitted together with a signature over the ballot, created by a set of signer authorities. The blindness property of the threshold blind signature scheme ensures that even a (minority) set of malicious signer authorities is not able to learn the structure of the ballot and as a consequence, break the privacy as soon as the ballot is published to the blockchain.

Fairness: Fairness means that an adversary is not able to obtain intermediate results of a voting before its expiration date. This property is ensured within our system as long as no majority of malicious key authorities collude. The reason is that all ballots, which enter the system, are encrypted client-side using an IND-CPA secure functional encryption scheme and in order to open ballots, which are stored within the blockchain, decryption keys from multiple key authorities are required.

Eligibility: The eligibility property limits the voting attendance to voters that are entitled to it. Each voter within our system possesses a digital identity, which she obtains in exchange to a proof of her real identity. When registering a new voting at the system, a registrar is able to define the set of voters that are able to participate. The enforcement of the eligibility property is then performed by the signer authorities as they only create signatures in exchange for a proof of identity, for voters whose name is on the list.

Verifiability: Verifiability means that interested parties are able to validate that results are correctly tallied. Here, we differentiate between two types of verifiability.

Individual Verifiability: Individual verifiability means that every distinct voter is able to assure herself that the own ballot was correctly counted. Our system benefits from the fact that the decryption (ballot opening) is a transparent process, which is done by the smart contract. During this step, all necessary decryption keys are made public. Furthermore, voting data never leaves the blockchain and Hyperledger Fabric prevents that smart contracts are changed on single peers in order to manipulate the outcome.

Universal Verifiability: Universal verifiability allows every interested party to verify the election result. The same argumentation, which was given for the individual case, is also applicable for the universal one. Every party that mistrust the result, is able to recalculate the outcome by decrypting and tallying the stored ballots herself.

Receipt-Freeness and Coercion-Resistance: The two properties of receipt-freeness and coercion-resistance are closely related to each other, as they enable protection against coercion or profit intentions of the voter, e.g. vote buying. Receipt-freeness, basically, is the absence of information of the voter that can be used to prove to an attacker the way she voted. Coercion-resistance assumes a stronger attacker, which not only cooperates with the voter in form of sharing secret information, but is also able to adaptively interact with the voter by preparing messages for her [8]. Our system is vulnerable to such type of attacks, due to the fact that all encrypted ballots are stored publicly within the blockchain. If the voter cooperates with an attacker by providing the random coins, which are used to encrypt the ballot, the attacker is able to make associations between the voter and her choice as soon as the ballots are opened.

Double-Voting-Resistance: Double-voting is the threat in one–person–one–vote systems that a voter is able to submit more than just one ballot. In our system, double-voting is prevented as long as a majority of signer authorities act honestly. The reason is that a ballot can only be submitted in combination with a valid signature, issued by a set of signer authorities. Signer authorities, however, will only issue signatures once for every eligible voter. We require that the used threshold blind signature scheme fulfills the unforgeability property, which prevents that valid signatures can be illegitimately cast by unauthorized entities.

Censorship-Resistance: Our system is censorship-resistant in the sense that there is no solely responsible voting provider that is able to manipulate the outcome of the voting by adding undetected forgeries, declining to accept ballots from voters or even hiding ballots from the counting process. This follows from the fact that the blockchain itself is immutable and allows modifications only if a quorum of voting providers agree.

Reliability: Attacks on the voting system in order to force malfunction or even the destruction of submitted ballots, and in consequence a change in the outcome of the election, are an actual threat. The fact that our voting system is built on top of a decentralized blockchain ensures protection against data loss, as a copy of the database is stored redundantly on each peer.

6   Conclusions and Future Work

In this paper, we proposed a trustless, censorship-resilient and scalable electronic voting system based on Hyperledger Fabric. Our system allows the parametrization of the number of peers in order to decrease the required tallying time of the ballots. A preliminary performance evaluation showed that Hyperledger Fabric is basically a good choice for such a system, because the smart contract hardly limits the performance of the underlying voting program. When considering large-scale votings like for example, the federal election 2017 in Germany with around 61,69 million eligible voters, our voting system needs approximately 8,77 h to perform the whole counting process with 512 peers (single-threaded on

3,60 GHz CPU) per organization, which is within the time frame of traditional, manual tallying processes. As future work remains a completion of the system, as it is only partially implemented up to this point and further, a performance analysis using the BFT based orderer. It would be interesting to investigate optimizations that can be applied, e.g. faster schemes and finally, a formal security analysis is still pending.

References

1. Androulaki, E., et al.: Hyperledger fabric: a distributed operating system for permissioned blockchains. In: Proceedings of the Thirteenth EuroSys Conference, EuroSys 2018, Porto, Portugal, 23–26 April 2018, pp. 30:1–30:15 (2018)
2. András, S.I.: Implementing an e-voting protocol with blind signatures on ethereum (2018). http://medium.com/coinmonks/implementing-an-e-voting-protocol-with-blind-signatures-on-ethereum-411e88af044a
3. Binu, V.P., Nair, D.G., Sreekumar, A.: Secret sharing homomorphism and secure e-voting. CoRR abs/1602.05372 (2016). http://arxiv.org/abs/1602.05372
4. Cachin, C., Vukolic, M.: Blockchain consensus protocols in the wild (keynote talk). In: Richa, A.W. (ed.) 31st International Symposium on Distributed Computing, DISC 2017, Vienna, Austria, LIPIcs, 16–20 October 2017, vol. 91, pp. 1:1–1:16. Schloss Dagstuhl - Leibniz-Zentrum für Informatik (2017)
5. Chaum, D.: Untraceable electronic mail, return addresses, and digital pseudonyms. Commun. ACM **24**(2), 84–88 (1981)
6. Chida, K., et al.: Fast large-scale honest-majority MPC for malicious adversaries. In: Shacham, H., Boldyreva, A. (eds.) CRYPTO 2018. LNCS, vol. 10993, pp. 34–64. Springer, Cham (2018). https://doi.org/10.1007/978-3-319-96878-0_2
7. CoinBundle Team: Using blockchain for: Voting (2019). https://medium.com/coinbundle/using-blockchain-for-voting-3287817291dc
8. Delaune, S., Kremer, S., Ryan, M.: Coercion-resistance and receipt-freeness in electronic voting. In: 19th IEEE Computer Security Foundations Workshop, (CSFW-19 2006), Venice, Italy, 5–7 July 2006, pp. 28–42 (2006)
9. Democratic National Committee: Democracy at risk: The 2004 election in Ohio (2005)
10. Freedom House: Freedom in the world 2019 (2019). https://freedomhouse.org/sites/default/files/Feb2019_FH_FITW_2019_Report_ForWeb-compressed.pdf
11. Freeman, S.F.: The unexplained exit poll discrepancy. University of Pennsylvania Graduate School of Arts and Sciences, Center for Organizational Dynamics Research Report, pp. 04–09 (2004)
12. Gennaro, R., Jarecki, S., Krawczyk, H., Rabin, T.: Secure distributed key generation for discrete-log based cryptosystems. J. Cryptology **20**(1), 51–83 (2007)
13. Hardwick, F.S., Gioulis, A., Akram, R.N., Markantonakis, K.: E-voting with blockchain: an e-voting protocol with decentralisation and voter privacy. In: IEEE International Conference on Internet of Things (iThings) and IEEE Green Computing and Communications (GreenCom) and IEEE Cyber, Physical and Social Computing (CPSCom) and IEEE Smart Data (SmartData), iThings/GreenCom/CPSCom/SmartData 2018, Halifax, NS, Canada, 30 July - 3 August 2018, pp. 1561–1567. IEEE (2018)
14. Heiberg, S., Kubjas, I., Siim, J., Willemson, J.: On trade-offs of applying block chains for electronic voting bulletin boards. IACR Cryptology ePrint Archive 2018, 685 (2018). https://eprint.iacr.org/2018/685

15. Hirt, M., Sako, K.: Efficient receipt-free voting based on homomorphic encryption. In: Preneel, B. (ed.) EUROCRYPT 2000. LNCS, vol. 1807, pp. 539–556. Springer, Heidelberg (2000). https://doi.org/10.1007/3-540-45539-6_38

16. Hyperledger: A blockchain platform for the enterprise - hyperledger fabric (2019). https://hyperledger-fabric.readthedocs.io/

17. Juang, W., Lei, C.: Blind threshold signatures based on discrete logarithm. In: Concurrency and Parallelism, Programming, Networking, and Security: Second Asian Computing Science Conference, ASIAN 1996, Proceedings, Singapore, 2–5 December 1996, pp. 172–181 (1996)

18. Kshetri, N., et al.: Blockchain-enabled e-voting. IEEE Softw. **35**(4), 95–99 (2018)

19. Kuchta, V., Manulis, M.: Rerandomizable threshold blind signatures. In: Yung, M., Zhu, L., Yang, Y. (eds.) INTRUST 2014. LNCS, vol. 9473, pp. 70–89. Springer, Cham (2015). https://doi.org/10.1007/978-3-319-27998-5_5

20. Lai, W., Wu, J.: An efficient and effective decentralized anonymous voting system. CoRR abs/1804.06674 (2018). http://arxiv.org/abs/1804.06674

21. Liu, Y., Wang, Q.: An e-voting protocol based on blockchain. IACR Cryptology ePrint Archive 2017, 1043 (2017). http://eprint.iacr.org/2017/1043

22. McCorry, P., Shahandashti, S.F., Hao, F.: A smart contract for boardroom voting with maximum voter privacy. In: Kiayias, A. (ed.) FC 2017. LNCS, vol. 10322, pp. 357–375. Springer, Cham (2017). https://doi.org/10.1007/978-3-319-70972-7_20

23. Michalevsky, Y., Joye, M.: Decentralized policy-hiding ABE with receiver privacy. In: Lopez, J., Zhou, J., Soriano, M. (eds.) ESORICS 2018. LNCS, vol. 11099, pp. 548–567. Springer, Cham (2018). https://doi.org/10.1007/978-3-319-98989-1_27

24. Nasser, Y., Okoye, C.I., Clark, J., Ryan, P.Y.A.: Blockchains and voting: Somewhere between hype and a panacea (a position paper) (2018)

25. Ongaro, D., Ousterhout, J.K.: In search of an understandable consensus algorithm. In: 2014 USENIX Annual Technical Conference, USENIX ATC 2014, Philadelphia, PA, USA, 19–20 June 2014, pp. 305–319 (2014)

26. Sahai, A., Waters, B.: Fuzzy identity-based encryption. In: Cramer, R. (ed.) EUROCRYPT 2005. LNCS, vol. 3494, pp. 457–473. Springer, Heidelberg (2005). https://doi.org/10.1007/11426639_27

27. Pereira, S.: How can corporations trust each other in a consortium blockchain. https://hackernoon.com/how-can-corporations-trust-each-other-in-a-consortium-blockchain-5919a3691801

28. Swiss Post: Swiss post's e-voting solution: Electronic voting and elections for Switzerland. https://www.post.ch/en/business/a-z-of-subjects/industry-solutions/swiss-post-e-voting

29. Yu, B., et al.: Platform-independent secure blockchain-based voting system. In: Chen, L., Manulis, M., Schneider, S. (eds.) ISC 2018. LNCS, vol. 11060, pp. 369–386. Springer, Cham (2018). https://doi.org/10.1007/978-3-319-99136-8_20

P2T: Pay to Transport

Fadi Barbàra[(⊠)] and Claudio Schifanella

University of Turin, Turin, Italy
{fadi.barbara,claudio.schifanella}@unito.it

Abstract. We present Pay To Transport (P2T), a protocol that lets customers buy an item remotely in an atomic, privacy preserving and trustless manner. P2T needs only basic features of a blockchain scripting language and does not need any tracking systems, arbitrator or deposit to preserve its security properties. For this reason the protocol can be implemented on any permissionless blockchain, regardless of its scripting language, without additional trust. Merchants' and transporters' addresses are public, but in P2T the parties never pay those addresses directly. Therefore P2T maintains the privacy of customers, merchant and transporters.

Keywords: Blockchain · Transportation · P2SH · Bitcoin · Privacy

1 Introduction

As humans, we exchange value for goods since the specialization of labor. Value has been represented in many forms, for example using gold, money and even rocks. We started doing it physically in markets, and recently we moved to remote exchanges using online web-stores. Remote exchanges are undoubtedly useful, less physically hazardous and more convenient and efficient with respect to the previous in-person method, but the shift to remote exchanges had undesired consequences.

One of those consequences is the *de facto* loss of privacy and security. Today, services that centrally collect and store users' data have a far wider reach for sharing that data than they had before the internet. Third-party services can use data both for legitimate and non-legitimate purposes, and an aggressive sharing of data increases the probability of non-legitimate uses. Examples of non-legitimate uses are unfair prices or insurance premiums, stigmatization of people and, in the worst case, the unfair punishment of people in non-honest states [4]. Furthermore, any service that stores data centrally is potentially the target of malicious attacks. In this regard, then, private data is a liability for both the user giving it and the service collecting it. We claim that it would be better for all the parties involved not to have the data in the first place.

© Springer Nature Switzerland AG 2021
B. Balis et al. (Eds.): Euro-Par 2020 Workshops, LNCS 12480, pp. 66–77, 2021.
https://doi.org/10.1007/978-3-030-71593-9_6

Nowadays, people can use blockchains to exchange value in a more (but not completely) private manner to defend themselves from some of these attacks, but there is not a private or anonymous method or protocol for the shipping of some good from the merchant to the customer: generally the shipping still forces customers to share their personal data (e.g. their address or their identity) with the service they are buying from. The result is that people still have to trust services not sharing their data with other data collectors even if they use a blockchain based payment system.

Proposed methods to exchange goods using a blockchain for both the exchange of value and the shipment agreement still require private data sharing or additional trust. For example, some methods rely on tracking and the result of tracking is posted on a blockchain [3]. Generally, this involves external objects (typically a GPS) to signal the position of the package. In those settings, the GPS operates like some form of trusted oracle. This is both a trust and a privacy problem. In fact, both the company supplying the product and the client receiving it have to trust that nobody tampered with the GPS. Furthermore, a throwaway GPS sensor can be more expensive than the purchased item the transporter is carrying: this makes transportation costs higher than the item's cost. Therefore GPS-based tracking are not feasible for inexpensive items.

Our contribution. To solve the current lack of privacy, security and trust in delivery systems, we present a protocol that doesn't require sharing private data but is still secure against non-honest participants. More specifically, our contributions are:

- We present Pay to Transport, denoted as P2T, a protocol that lets a merchant M and a customer C to remotely exchange value (*coins*) for goods using any permissionless blockchain;
- We analyze P2T and informally prove how the protocol respects the properties presented in Sect. 3, including privacy, atomicity and trustlessness, even without any arbitrator or deposit;
- We present a proof-of-concept implementation[1] which uses the Bitcoin blockchain.

The paper proceeds as follows. In Sect. 2 we present the literature on the topic of delivery transportation using a blockchain. In Sect. 3 we introduce the concepts needed to understand the protocol. In Sect. 4 we introduce the protocol using only one transporter. In Sect. 5 we analyze P2T and then we conclude.

2   Related Works

While there are multiple papers about the use of a blockchain system on a supply chain (see e.g. [7] for a survey), we decided to analyze only those papers that explicitly study the use of a transporter.

---

[1] See code at https://gitlab.com/disnocen/pay-to-transport.

2.1   Proof of Delivery

In [6], Hasan et al. analyze what they call a Proof of Delivery system to trade and track sold items between two parties. The system relies on five agents. The first three agents are directly involved with the shipment of the item and they are the Seller, the Buyer and the Transporter. The others are external parties not directly involved in the exchange, they overview the process. Those are the Arbitrator and the Smart Contract Attestation Authority. The Arbitrator is a trusted third party involved in case of a dispute and solve the issues off the chain. The smart contract authority is responsible to attest that the smart contract complies with the terms and conditions signed by the involved parties in the agreement form. Each involved party puts an equal deposited collateral which he risks to lose if he behaves maliciously.

In the solution proposed by the authors the third parties (the arbitrator and the SC authority) are not prevented from colluding with one of the parties. In particular, the arbitrator handles the data off chain, so there is no transparent way to inspect his judgment. Furthermore, both the systems require that all parties, arbitrator and the smart contract authority included, know both the physical address and blockchain address of the buyer, so privacy is not guaranteed.

2.2   Lelantos

The solution proposed by Al Tawi et al. [2] also uses a smart contract deployed by the Lelantos system itself to manage the shipment. A single smart contract is used by all customers, merchants and couriers. A customer C is able to redirect shipment between different couriers by using a specific smart contract function. C sends new delivery addresses in encrypted form using the long term public key of the currently designated delivery courier. The public keys are vouchered by Lelantos itself.

The customer C does not declare in advance which couriers he will use. Furthermore, C won't contact any Currier before the shipment. While this process achieve anonymity for the customer C, the Lelantos protocol is interactive and requires both C and all the delivery couriers to pay attention to the delivery smart contract.

3   Preliminaries

Labeled Wallets and Derived Blockchain Addresses. It is possible to create multiple public/secret key pair (and therefore addresses) starting from a single secret, called *base*. An example of this behavior is given, e.g. in the Bitcoin blockchain, from BIP32 address generation format [10]. The wallet generates new addresses starting from the base and a label. Therefore it is possible to index those addresses via the label.

In this paper we use the label format of [5]. Given a secret (private) key $\mathbf{sk}$ and a generation point g in the elliptic curve, the public key $\mathbf{pk}$ is computed as

$\mathbf{pk} = g^{\mathbf{sk}}$. The couple $(\mathbf{sk}, \mathbf{pk})$ is the base in our wallet. The derived key pair with label x from base $(\mathbf{sk}, \mathbf{pk})$ is written as $(\mathbf{sk}[x], \mathbf{pk}[x])$ an it is given by

$$\mathbf{sk}[x] := \mathbf{sk} + H_1(x) \quad \mathbf{pk}[x] := \mathbf{pk} + g^{H_1(x)}$$

where H_1 is (the numerical representation of) the hash function implemented in the blockchain. For example H_1 in Bitcoin is the SHA256, while H_1 in Tezos is Blake2b[2]. We call $\mathbf{sk}[x]$ the *derived secret key* and $\mathbf{pk}[x]$ the *derived public key*. Blockchain addresses are derived in a deterministic way using particular encoding $Enc(\cdot)$ of the hash of the public key. So if P is the address generated by the public key $\mathbf{pk}$, then the *derived address* is

$$d_{addr}(P, x) = Enc(H_2(\mathbf{pk}[x]))$$

where H_2 is generally different from H_1.

Conditional Transactions. It is possible to make transactions that include conditional statements based on time (or block numbers): one branch of the transaction is used if it is redeemed before a certain time (or a certain block); the other branch is used if it is redeemed later. Throughout the paper we denote these as *conditional transactions*. It is possible to build conditional transactions for the majority of the blockchains, including Bitcoin and derivatives, Ethereum or Tezos. In the repository of this paper, we put a way to build conditional transactions in the case of Bitcoin transactions.

In P2T we use two kinds of conditional transaction constructions between non-trusting parties A and B: conditional transactions with secrets and without secrets. One way to build transactions that use secrets is through hash-lock contracts [1]. In short, given pre-computed secret s and hash $h = H(s)$, where $H(\cdot)$ is a hash function, the party who builds the transaction (say A) adds the presentation of the preimage of h among the conditions to redeem that transaction. The other participant (say B) must then reveal the secret s (such that $h = H(s)$), in addition to putting his signature, to redeem the transaction. A hash-lock contract can be put in either (or both) of the branches of a conditional transaction.

More formally, let v be the value (sometimes called *amount*) of a transaction and let the string x be a particular encoding of the order placed by the customer C. Then, given $i = 1, 2$, s and h as above we denote with the ordered 5-tuple $(A, B, v, t, (h, i))$ the conditional transaction toward the address $d_{addr}(P_A, x)$ with secret s which is redeemable by:

---

[2] Although there are multiple hash functions implemented in Tezos, including SHA256, the Blake2b function is used for the most important cryptographic operations (such as signature checks). See the code at the URL https://gitlab.com/tezos/tezos/-/blob/master/src/lib_crypto/secp256k1.ml.

1. a *multisig*[3] between parties (A, B), i.e. by using a joint signature with the keys related to addresses $d_{addr}(P_A, x)$ and $d_{addr}(P_B, x)$, before time t, or
2. the signature of party A alone using the private key relative to address $d_{addr}(P_A, x)$ after time t .

If $i = 1$, then the hash-lock contract is put in the first branch of the transaction. Otherwise, if $i = 2$, the hash-lock contract is in the second branch. Finally, note that not all conditional transactions use secrets in P2T. In those cases we will write $(A, B, v, t, \texttt{null})$ or more simply (A, B, v, t).

Transportation Protocol Properties. Using the terminology explained in Table 1.1 of [9] we want P2T to satisfy the following cryptographic properties:

- **Privacy**: keeping information secret from all but those parties that are authorized to see it
- **(Customer) Anonymity**: the customer is able to conceal his identity
- **Entity Authentication**: corroboration of the identity of an entity
- **Receipt**: acknowledgment that information has been received;
- **Confirmation**: acknowledgment that services have been provided
- **Plausible Deniability**: an external party can not prove that a customer C bought an item I from a merchant M and it has been delivered by a transporter T without the active collaboration of at least one of those parties.

Similarly to [6] we also focused on these logistic properties:

- **Punctuality**: every action and deliver has a maximum allowed time
- **Honesty**: following the protocol is the most rewarding behavior
- **Atomicity**: no party involved can lose money even if other parties misbehave

Finally we want P2T to satisfy this property:

- **Trustlessness**: it is not necessary for one participant to trust the others

In Sect. 5 we show how the P2T protocol satisfies all these requirements.

Notation. Parties are addressed with their initial letter, e.g. the merchant is denoted by M. In the previous sections we already introduced the notation for keys, addresses and conditional transactions. We explain here the notation used for the time constraints.

Given an ordered couple of parties (P, Q) and a transporter T, we denote with δ_T^{PQ} (an estimate of) the time that T needs to go from the pick up point of P to the pick up point of Q. Note that in principle going from P's pick up point

---

[3] Even if in some blockchains such as Ethereum, there is no concept of multisignature, it is still possible to build smart contracts that have functions behaving like a multisignature. See for example https://github.com/unchained-capital/ethereum-multisig. Furthermore, in other blockchains it is possible to create *aggregate signatures* that act as a multisignature but leaving only one signature as blockchain footprint, further increasing privacy. See for example [8].

to Q's one can be different from going from Q's pick up point to P's. For this reason the couple (P, Q) is ordered and $\delta_T^{PQ} \neq \delta_T^{QP}$. Because the transporter has to wait at his pick up point for the customer or others to take the package, we put ϵ_T the maximum time that T can wait before he returns the package. We also put $\tilde{\delta}_T^{PQ} = \delta_T^{PQ} + \delta_T^{QP} + \epsilon_T$ as the whole time that T needs to go from P's pick up point to Q's and back plus the waiting time. Of course $\tilde{\delta}_T^{PQ} = \tilde{\delta}_T^{QP}$, but we will use both notations. We use $\tilde{\delta}_T^{PQ}$ when T goes from P to Q and then he goes back to P and vice versa. This lets us be more explicit in the description of all the time constrained payments needed to support the fact that C can refuse the delivered package in the end.

4 Transportation Protocol

The P2T protocol involves three parties: a merchant M, a customer C and a transporter T. Public keys $\mathbf{pk}_M$ and $\mathbf{pk}_T$ and blockchain addresses P_M and P_T of M and T respectively are public and known in advance to all the parties (e.g. those information are in the contact internet pages of the parties). Note that a protocol for the shipment of a product from M to C is different from a protocol for returning that product *after* the acceptance of the delivered package: in this paper we focus only on the shipment protocol. Therefore the shipped package can be accepted or refused by C on the spot only. Of course, it is possible to adapt this protocol in case of a product return, treating it as a shipment from C to M, but this is not discussed here (Fig. 1 and 2).

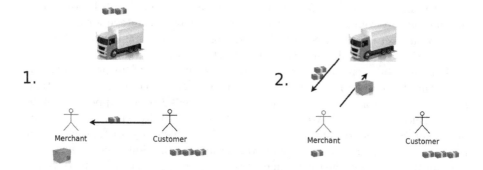

Fig. 1. Phases one and two of the Basic Protocol with One Transporter. **1.** C pays M the transportation costs, **2.** T physically goes to M, pays M and receive the package

Broadly speaking, the P2T protocol works as follows. The transporter T goes to merchant M, pays M the cost of the item (ad interim payment) and takes charge of the package. The transporter then brings it to his own pick up point (e.g. T's company headquarters). Finally, customer C goes to T's pick up point, pays T the cost of the item plus transportation costs and takes his package. C does not have to reveal his own physical address nor his identity to perform these actions.

Algorithm 1. Basic protocol

1: C decides on I and M
2: C and M engage T, C accepts c_T
3: T generates r, T computes $R := H(r)$
4: T sends R to C
5: C pays c_T to M
6: CT1: C sends conditional transaction $(C, T, c_I, t_1 + \tilde{\delta}_T^{TM}, (R, 1))$
7: CT2: T sends conditional transaction $(T, M, c_I - c_T, t_1 + \delta_T^{TM}, \texttt{null})$
8: M gives package to T and *at the same time* CT3: T and M send conditional transaction $(M, T, c_I - c_T, t_1 + \tilde{\delta}_T^{TM} + \delta_T^{TM}, (R, 2))$
9: **if** C accepts the package **then**
10:    C and T spend CT1 (so T releases r)
11:    M spends CT3 using r
12: **else**
13:    T brings package back to M
14:    T and M send money from CT3 to T's address
15: **end if**

Since a system of "simple" transactions (e.g. P2PKH in Bitcoin or transactions between Externally Owned Accounts in Ethereum) would not give sufficient guarantees to any of the parties involved, we based every passage of coins and product on time constraints and spendability conditions (see Sect. 3), coded in the transactions. Building transactions this way, we accomplish two things. On the one hand we accomplish a traceable coordination of multiple parties without using external tracking devices. On the other hand, C doesn't need to be on line after the first payment to M and from that payment on the P2T protocol is non interactive from his point of view. This is a huge advantage for C since in this way he can use a device once (for example a public computer in a library) without the need to subsequently check the status of his order.

Fundamental steps of the P2T protocol are summarized in pseudo-code in Algorithm 1 and it works as follows. Customer C decides to buy an item I at time t_0 from the webstore of the merchant M, and he needs I to be shipped to a place which is more close to him. We assume that the cost for the item is c_I, and throughout the protocol the cost of the transportation is assumed to be c_T for each chosen transporter T. An order from C can have multiple information, such as the item's identification number, the item's quantity or the maximum date of delivery which we denote as t_2 (see below for a constraint on t_2). C is required also to provide a blockchain address P_C both as the (only) identification for that shipment and to prove he has enough coins to pay for the item I. On the other hand, C is *not* required to provide a delivery address nor any other identifying information. We emphasize that a blockchain address created specifically for this trade cannot be considered as an identifying element for the customer C. In fact, assuming that C is keen on maintaining its privacy, this address can be funded using the particular technologies of blockchain projects. Examples are the z-shielded transactions in Zcash, the use of a large number of *mixins* in Monero, CoinJoins or similar technologies in Bitcoin or, in general, the use of mixers. Furthermore, this address is used directly only once, so there is no risk of address reuse.

Based on the information provided by C, M and C agree on a transporter T[4]. During the agreement, C specifies what we call the *minimal required zone* (MRZ). A MRZ is the minimal information needed by T to estimate delivery costs and date of delivery. For example, if T charges the same delivery costs and estimates the same delivery time for a whole country, then C communicates only the country where he intends to pick up the item I. Therefore by the agreement T must take the item I from M and take it to his pick up place before date t_2. Here $t_1 + \tilde{\delta}_T^{TM} - \epsilon_T \leq t_2 \leq t_1 + \tilde{\delta}_T^{TM}$ where t_1 is the occurrence of the first payment from C to M (see below for details). Of course, if C and M agree on T, they also agree on the additional costs c_T. All parties M, C and T provide to each other some contact information for possible notifications, e.g. for the arrival of the package at T's pick up place[5]. As soon as T has been decided and engaged in transport, T generates a random number r and creates $R = H(r)$ where H is a hash function. T sends R to C using the contact information provided before. R is the puzzle for the secret, as described in Sect. 3.

After this step, M checks that there are at least $c_I + c_T$ funds in P_C[6] and if so M creates a bill contract x that he sends to C. In x there are some static information about M, i.e. information that persists for more than one order, and some dynamic information regarding the specific order. In particular, the address P_T of T is included in x. C verifies that the information on x are sound and if he agrees on them he sends the equivalent of c_T to address $d_{addr}(P_M, x)$. We call this transaction the *non-redeemable commitment transaction of C* and it is done at time t_1. This payment represents three things about C: it is a proof that C controls the funds in address P_C, it is a proof that C accepts all terms written in x and, being non redeemable by C, it is an incentive not to spam M with fake requests which would result in a DoS attack.

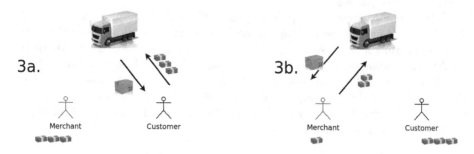

Fig. 2. Possible endings of the Basic Protocol with One Transporter. **3a.** C physically goes to T and if the package is intact, then C accepts it and pays T, **3b.** otherwise, if C refuses the package, T gives M the package back while M returns T his money.

---

[4] T can be chosen from a billboard or by some convention between the merchant M and T himself.

[5] The contact information should not reveal identity of C. For example C can use a throwaway e-mail address or a burner phone.

[6] The merchant M can do that because the blockchain is public.

When the merchant M receives the payment from customer C, he is sure that C has serious intentions in buying the object, but he does not know anything about T. For this reason M sends $H(x)$ to T waiting for his commitment transaction.

Before doing that, T needs a commitment from C, so C sends another commitment transaction, this time to T. This commitment transaction is different from the previous one because it is redeemable by C. This is a $(C, T, c_I, t_1 + \tilde{\delta}_T^{TM}, (R, 1))$ conditional transaction with secret R in the first branch of the transaction (see Sect. 3) and we call it CT1. C has to do this payment before time $t_1 + \delta_T^{TM}$, otherwise T cannot go to M in time and T risks to delay the whole shipment process. In case C is too slow to pay, T decides to abort the protocol and notifies other parties. In case T can commit to M, he sends $c_I - c_T$ coins to address $d_{addr}(P_T, x)$ doing a redeemable conditional commitment transaction without secret $(T, M, c_I - c_T, t_1 + \delta_T^{TM})$ which we call CT2. M considers valid T's coin transfer only if the transaction is built in the way described above, otherwise M aborts the protocol and notifies C of that.

After the merchant M saw the payment, he produces and physically prints a visual representation V (e.g. a QRcode) of $H(x)$ and use it to seal the package. At time $t_1 + \delta_T^{TM}$, T can take this package with item I inside it from M. If M is not malicious, the package of item I is in perfect conditions and T verifies that V is the visual representation of $H(x)$ (recall that T has received $H(x)$ before to create address $d_{addr}(P_T, x)$), both M and T sign the transaction from $d_{addr}(P_T, x)$ to $d_{addr}(P_M, x)$. This is a $(M, T, c_I - c_T, t_1 + \tilde{\delta}_T^{TM} + \delta_T^{TM}, (R, 2))$ conditional transaction CT3 with secret R in the second branch. At this stage, M has received (but cannot use yet) $c_T + (c_I - c_T) = c_I$ coins, so the merchant has received the full price of the item I and the item is shipped. The second conditional transaction with a secret is done to account for the case in which C could refuse the package.

T takes the package to his pick up point. When T and C physically meet at T's pick up point, C checks that the package is intact, that the seal V is not broken and that it represents $H(x)$. If that is case, then C and T spends their conditional transaction CT1 sending funds to an address belonging to T. This way T has to reveal r such that $R = H(r)$ and M can use it to spend CT3. On the other hand, if there is some problem with the package, C refuses the package and T has to bring it back to M. T is sure he can have his coins back because of the conditional transaction CT3.

5   Analysis

Privacy and Anonymity. From C's point of view, P2T is highly private. In fact, the customer C provides to the merchant M and the transporter T only a public key with funds and a geographical zone (the MRZ) where he intends to pick the package. Depending on the blockchain method used, the source of funds can be obfuscated in a way to detach it from the real identity of C (see Sect. 3). Therefore P2T satisfy also customer anonymity. Note that privacy and anonymity comes at a cost for C. M could steal funds of C and never give him any product, gaining c_T. While this is the case, we assume C won't use merchants or transporters that have any or a bad reputation for big payments. On the other hand, even if C loses funds, he only loses transportation costs. Still, this is better than today's policy for which C must pay the whole cost in advance, and therefore he risks losing both the cost of the item c_I and the delivery cost c_T.

Authentication and Deniability. In the P2T protocol there is an intrinsic authentication method. In fact, the public addresses and keys of the merchant M and the transporters T are public and the payments are made to addresses deriving from those public keys using the homomorphic properties of the construction of the addresses. The fact that the entities are able to spend these funds in the derived addresses is proof of their identity. Furthermore, since all entities use derived addresses and not their publicly accessible addresses, an external observer cannot prove that the parties involved have completed a particular exchange thanks to the hardness of the discrete logarithm problem assumption[7]. Therefore all parties can plausibly deny their involvement in an order.

Confirmation and Receipt. The use of the blockchain and the particular way parties following the protocol build the addresses and transactions gives both the receipt and confirmation of orders and payments. Furthermore, by following the state of the blockchain the entities involved can track the state of the order by seeing which payments have been already done.

Punctuality. This also provide the punctuality property of P2T: time constraints in the transactions force parties to respect all prearranged times or they risk losing funds.

Atomicity and Honesty. Transactions are constructed taking into account the possible dishonesty of each participant. Since every transaction is atomic, if a participant does not respect the protocol (that is, he is not honest), he does not receive the coins that would be due to him. Each participant is therefore encouraged to be honest. In other words, following the protocol is the most rewarding behavior.

Trustlessness. In P2T, participants do not have to trust the others. This is due to the particular constructions of the transactions. We analyze the protocol from the point of view of each of the participants.

From the point of view of the merchant M, there is no way to lose both the money and the product. In fact, once the product has been given to the transporter T, the transaction CT3 assures the merchant that (if customer C accepts the package) he will be able to spend his coins. This is because M

---

[7] This is the underlining assumption for the construction of public keys on all blockchain projects.

supervises the creation of this transaction (M and T are in the same place at the same time) and can verify that the hash placed by T is the same as the one in transaction CT1. Furthermore M will know about the preimage of the hash the moment T redeems CT1. If, on the other hand, C does not accept the product, theoretically T may decide not to return the package to M. But this would not be a rational choice for T. The transporter, in fact, does not know what is contained in the package (therefore a priori may not be interested in the article) and he is therefore encouraged to return it in order to redeem the money stuck in the multisig with M.

As far as the transporter T is concerned, he is interested in not losing the money invested to earn the transport commissions. T cannot lose money in CT2 (its first transaction) since it is atomic and T only executes it after CT1 has been confirmed. T risks losing money in CT3 if C doesn't accept the package and M doesn't show up for the return. In this case the time-lock would expire and M could redeem the transaction. This is not possible because M must also solve the hash-lock contract, and to solve it M needs the preimage revealed by T. T reveals this secret only if C accepts the package. In this regard, note that if the secret had been created by C, T would not have had the same assurances. In fact, given the anonymity of C, he and M could be the same entity, or colluding. If that were the case, then C could refuse the package and M could still redeem the coins in CT3 because he is aware of the preimage.

Finally, C doesn't need to trust anyone too. Once the shipping costs have been paid (which C agrees to lose if the package is refused) C creates and sends the atomic transaction CT1. On the scheduled date, C goes to the pick up point of T and decides whether to accept the package and sign the transaction with T or to refuse the package. In this latter case, C only has to wait for the time-lock to expire in order to use its coins again: in the meantime T cannot spend them because they are in a multisig.

6   Conclusion and Future Works

We present P2T, a payment protocol for the exchange of coins and physical goods. P2T is trustless, privacy preserving and preserves the anonymity of customers without using external tracking systems, arbitrators or deposits. The protocol uses mechanisms common to all blockchain protocols, so that it is possible to implement it in all these projects. We implemented a proof of concept that uses the Bitcoin blockchain and that can be found online. In addition to privacy and anonymity, the protocol satisfies other properties such as plausible deniability and encourages participants' honesty by using atomic transactions. In the future we intend to extend the treatment of the P2T protocol by giving a more formal analysis of these properties. We also plan to extend the protocol to use more than one transporter and to include the inverse case of the return of a product. In fact, a protocol for the return of the product would mirror the proposed one by exchanging the roles of the merchant and the customer, keeping that of the transporter the same. In the future version of P2T, payments can make use of the payment channel such as Lightning Network (on Bitcoin) or Raiden Network (on Ethereum). The implementation on payment channels would make payments faster and increase privacy since most transactions would never appear on blockchain.

References

1. Hashlock - Bitcoin Wiki. https://en.bitcoin.it/wiki/hashlock
2. AlTawy, R., ElSheikh, M., Youssef, A.M., Gong, G.: Lelantos: a blockchain-based anonymous physical delivery system. In: 15th Annual Conference on Privacy, Security and Trust (PST). IEEE, August 2017. https://doi.org/10.1109/pst.2017.00013
3. Ellis, S., Juels, A., Nazarov, S.: ChainLink, A Decentralized Oracle Network, September 2017
4. Garg, S., Goldwasser, S., Vasudevan, P.N.: Formalizing data deletion in the context of the right to be forgotten. In: Canteaut, A., Ishai, Y. (eds.) EUROCRYPT 2020. LNCS, vol. 12106, pp. 373–402. Springer, Cham (2020). https://doi.org/10.1007/978-3-030-45724-2_13
5. Gerhardt, I., Hanke, T.: Homomorphic payment addresses and the pay-to-contract protocol. ArXiv abs/1212.3257 (2012)
6. Hasan, H.R., Salah, K.: Blockchain-based solution for proof of delivery of physical assets. In: Chen, S., Wang, H., Zhang, L.-J. (eds.) ICBC 2018. LNCS, vol. 10974, pp. 139–152. Springer, Cham (2018). https://doi.org/10.1007/978-3-319-94478-4_10
7. Juma, H., Shaalan, K., Kamel, I.: A survey on using blockchain in trade supply chain solutions. IEEE Access 7, 184115–184132 (2019)
8. Maxwell, G., Poelstra, A., Seurin, Y., Wuille, P.: Simple Schnorr multi-signatures with applications to Bitcoin. Des. Codes Crypt. 87(9), 2139–2164 (2019). https://doi.org/10.1007/s10623-019-00608-x
9. Menezes, A.J., Katz, J., Van Oorschot, P.C., Vanstone, S.A.: Handbook of Applied Cryptography. CRC Press, Routledge (1996)
10. Wuille, P.: Hierarchical deterministic wallets (2012). https://github.com/bitcoin/bips/blob/master/bip-0032.mediawiki

HeteroPar - 18th International Workshop on Algorithms, Models and Tools for Parallel Computing on Heterogeneous Platforms

Workshop on Algorithms, Models and Tools for Parallel Computing on Heterogeneous Platforms (HeteroPar)

Workshop Description

Heterogeneity is emerging as one of the most profound and challenging characteristics of today's parallel environments. From the macro level, where networks of distributed computers, composed of diverse node architectures, are interconnected with potentially heterogeneous networks, to the micro level, where deeper memory hierarchies and various accelerators are increasingly common, the impact of heterogeneity on all computing tasks is increasing rapidly. Traditional algorithms, programming environments and tools, designed for legacy homogeneous systems, will at best achieve a small fraction of the efficiency and the potential performance that we should expect from parallel computing in tomorrow's highly diversified environments. Therefore, efficiently using these new and multifarious parallel architectures requires new ideas, innovative algorithms, and other specialized or unified programming environments and tools.

The 18th edition of the workshop (HeteroPar'2020) took place on August 25, 2020, in Warsaw, Poland, organized for the 12th time in conjunction with the Euro-Par annual international conference. Because of the COVID-19 pandemic, HeteroPar'2020 was held as a virtual event. The format of the workshop included two keynotes and 9 technical presentations. The workshop was well attended, featuring a healthy average of 40 attendees throughout the day.

This year the workshop received 16 submissions from 6 countries. After a thorough peer-reviewing process that included discussion and agreement among reviewers whenever necessary, the Program Chair selected 9 papers for presentation at the workshop. The review process focused on the quality of the papers, their innovative ideas and their applicability to heterogeneous computing. The topics addressed in the accepted papers include domain-specific languages for numerical algorithms, virtualization for CUDA applications, unified memory in CUDA, porting CUDA codes to AMD GPUs, management of heterogeneous cloud resources, GPU implementation of graph neural networks, GPU and CPU signal processing for a wildlife tracking system, parallelization of the k-means algorithm on CPU-GPU platforms, and a portable solver for systems of linear equations.

The Program Chair thanks all the authors, the Program Committee and the Steering Committee for their diligent efforts in ensuring the high quality and continued success of this workshop. Special thanks are due to the Euro-Par organizers for hosting the HeteroPar community, and especially to the workshop chairs Dora Blanco Heras and Bartosz Baliś, for their help and support.

Organization

Steering Committee

Alexey Kalinov	Cadence Design Systems, Russia
Alexey Lastovetsky	University College Dublin, Ireland
Yves Robert	École Normale Supérieure de Lyon, France
Leonel Sousa	Universidade de Lisboa, Portugal
Denis Trystram	Université Grenoble Alpes, France

Program Chair

Roman Wyrzykowski	Częstochowa University of Technology, Poland

Program Committee

Marc Baboulin	University of Paris-Saclay, France
Michael Bader	TU München, Germany
Jorge G. Barbosa	University of Porto, Portugal
Olivier Beaumont	INRIA Futurs Bordeaux, LABRI, France
George Bosilca	University of Tennessee, USA
Jesús Carretero	Universidad Carlos III de Madrid, Spain
Louis-Claude Canon	Université de Franche-Comté, France
Maciej Drozdowski	Poznań University of Technology, Poland
Toshio Endo	Tokyo Institute of Technology, Japan
Edgar Gabriel	University of Houston, USA
Aleksandar Ilic	Technical University of Lisbon, Portugal
Emmanuel Jeannot	Inria, France
Helen Karatza	Aristotle University of Thessaloniki, Greece
Jacek Kitowski	AGH University of Science and Technology, Poland
Joanna Kołodziej	National Research Institute NASK, Poland
Tomáš Kozubek	Technical University of Ostrava, Czechia
Marco Lapegna	University of Naples, Italy
Hatem Ltaief	KAUST, Saudi Arabia
Ravi Reddy Manumachu	University College Dublin, Ireland
Ami Marowka	Bar-Ilan University, Israel
Rafael Mayo	Universidad Jaume I, Spain

Iosif Meyerov   Lobachevsky State University of Nizhni
                                  Novgorod, Russia
Koji Nakano   Hiroshima University, Japan
Raymond Namyst   University of Bordeaux and Inria, France
Dana Petcu   West University of Timişoara, Romania
Loïc Pottier   University of Southern California, USA
Radu Prodan   University of Klagenfurt, Austria
Enrique S. Quintana Ortí   Technical University of Valencia, Spain
Thomas Rauber   Universität Bayreuth, Germany
Matei Ripeanu   The University of British Columbia, Canada
Rizos Sakellariou   University of Manchester, UK
Thomas Scogland   Lawrence Livermore National Laboratory, USA
Vladimir Stegailov   Russian Academy of Science and MIPT/HSE
                                  University, Russia
Przemysław Stpiczynski   Maria Curie Sklodowska University, Poland
Łukasz Szustak   Częstochowa University of Technology, Poland
Bora Uçar   ENS Lyon, France
Ramin Yahyapour   University of Göttingen and GWDG, Germany

Balanced and Compressed Coordinate Layout for the Sparse Matrix-Vector Product on GPUs

José Ignacio Aliaga[1], Hartwig Anzt[2,3], Enrique S. Quintana-Ortí[4(✉)], Andrés E. Tomás[1,5], and Yuhsiang M. Tsai[2]

[1] Dpto. de Ingeniería y Ciencia de Computadores, Universitat Jaume I, Castellón de la Plana, Spain
[2] Steinbuch Centre for Computing, Karlsruhe Institute of Technology, Karlsruhe, Germany
[3] Innovative Computing Lab, University of Tennessee, Knoxville, USA
[4] DISCA, Universitat Politècnica de València, Valencia, Spain
quintana@disca.upv.es
[5] Dpto. de Informática, Universitat de València, Valencia, Spain

Abstract. We contribute to the optimization of the sparse matrix-vector product on graphics processing units by introducing a variant of the coordinate sparse matrix layout that compresses the integer representation of the matrix indices. In addition, we employ a look-ahead table to avoid the storage of repeated numerical values in the sparse matrix, yielding a more compact data representation that is easier to maintain in the cache. Our evaluation on the two most recent generations of NVIDIA GPUs, the V100 and the A100 architectures, shows considerable performance improvements over the kernels for the sparse matrix-vector product in cuSPARSE (CUDA 11.0.167).

Keywords: Sparse matrix-vector product · Sparse matrix data layouts · Sparse linear algebra · High performance computing · GPUs

1 Introduction

The sparse matrix-vector product (SpMV) is a fundamental operation for the iterative solution of sparse linear systems since it is usually the computationally most expensive building block in stationary schemes as well as Krylov subspace methods [10].

The SpMV is, in general, a memory-bound operation which means that its performance is strongly determined by the memory access volume and the access pattern dictated by the algorithmic realization of the kernel and the memory bandwidth of the target computer architecture. In this context, the irregularity of the memory accesses turns the parallel optimization of SpMV into a challenging task.

© Springer Nature Switzerland AG 2021
B. Balis et al. (Eds.): Euro-Par 2020 Workshops, LNCS 12480, pp. 83–95, 2021.
https://doi.org/10.1007/978-3-030-71593-9_7

A particular factor which directly influences the implementation and (parallel) performance of SpMV is the data layout of the sparse matrix. The coordinate format (COO) [10] is likely the most intuitive layout: for each non-zero matrix entry, this scheme maintains a 3-tuple with the entry's row and column indices and its numerical value. The compressed sparse row format (CSR) [10] is a flexible alternative that reduces the indexing overhead with respect to COO by storing only starting/ending indices (pointers) for each matrix row, while keeping the same information for the column indices and values as COO. A plethora of application-specific sparse matrix layouts have been proposed over the past decades; see [2–5,8,9] among many others. In general, these solutions deliver high performance for some problem domains and/or computer architectures but perform poorly and/or require expensive transformations of the matrix format for others.

In [7] we introduced a balancing parallelization scheme for GPUs optimized for matrices with an irregular row distribution of the non-zero entries. In brief, this scheme: 1) is based on the standard CSR format; 2) requires an inexpensive pre-processing step; and 3) consumes only a minor amount of additional memory compared with significantly more expensive GPU-specific sparse matrix layouts. The new balancing approach departs from the conventional parallelization across matrix rows by instead distributing the workload evenly among the thread teams while avoiding race conditions via atomic transactions with efficient support by hardware in recent GPU architectures. In [6], we extended the idea to the COO format, showing that the resulting kernel is superior to some of the most popular SpMV implementations based on both COO and CSR.

In this paper, we continue our effort towards the optimization of SpMV on GPUs by making the following contributions:

- We propose orthogonal (independent) enhancements of the balancing COO-based scheme in [7] that result in a compressed storage format for the matrix data (indices and values), thus reducing the memory traffic and improving performance.
- We develop a high performance realization of this scheme for the most recent generations of NVIDIA GPUs (Volta and Ampere).
- We provide a complete evaluation of the new kernel in comparison with highly optimized implementations of SpMV, based on COO and CSR, from in NVIDIA cuSPARSE (those in CUDA 11.0.167). Following standard practice, this analysis is performed both from the perspective of memory consumption and GFLOPS (billions of floating-point arithmetic operations, or flops, per second).

The idea of compressing the indexing information to reduce the pressure on memory bandwidth is not original. In this sense, our approach is slightly related to the compressed sparse blocks (CSB) format [3], which partitions the sparse matrix into a regular grid of sparse blocks, each of which is stored in CSR format with the block indices compressed as offsets to a reference. In comparison, we also maintain the indices as offsets, encoded using a shorter number of bits. However, our scheme is based on COO instead of CSR; we divide the nonzero matrix entries (instead of the matrix itself) into regular chunks; we couple this partitioning with a balanced workload distribution for GPUs; and we also explore the compression of the numerical data using a look-ahead table.

The rest of the paper is organized as follows. In Sect. 2, we review the COO format and introduce our new balancing and compressed variant for GPUs based on it. In Sect. 3, we evaluate a standalone implementation of the new scheme for SPMV in comparison with the GPU kernels in NVIDIA cuSPARSE. In addition, in that section, we also assess the impact of the scheme when the SPMV kernel is integrated into the biconjugate gradient stabilized method (BICGSTAB) [10]. Finally, in Sect. 4, we offer some concluding remarks and a brief discussion of open research lines.

2   Balanced and Compressed SpMV

2.1   COO Format

Consider the SPMV $y := A \cdot x$, where A is an $n \times n$ sparse matrix with n_z non-zero entries and x, y are both vectors with n components. The COO format employs three vectors: say a, i and j, each of dimension n_z, to maintain the values of the non-zero elements of the matrix and their row and column index coordinates, respectively. In a direct parallelization of the COO-based SPMV on a GPU, each thread operates with a single nonzero element of the matrix, performing the multiplication with the corresponding entry of x, and using *atomic operations* to accumulate the partial result on the appropriate component of y. The performance of this initial approach can be improved if each thread computes several elements of the result vector, as typically 2 or 4 elements suffice for the compiler to aggregate enough memory access operations to overlap transfer and arithmetic operations. The excerpt of CUDA-like code in Listing 1.1 illustrates this approach for a COO-based SPMV with A stored using vectors a, i, and j. There each thread computes K accumulations of the form $y_i := y_i + a_{ij} \cdot x_j$, involving K nonzero matrix elements. Note that, for simplicity, we assume that n_z is an exact multiple of B·K, where B denotes the number of threads per block. Otherwise, the matrix can be padded with explicit zero elements.

In practice, the number of iterations in the loop of the SpMV_kernel in Listing 1.1 is small, and the whole loop should be unrolled to attain high performance. For that purpose, it is convenient to pad each matrix row with zeros so that its dimension becomes an exact multiple of K.

A second "loop" is implicit in the GPU code as the B threads of a block perform the operations for a *chunk* of B · K matrix elements. In current NVIDIA GPUs, the number of threads in a block is limited to 1,024 and must be over 192 for good performance. The compromise value B = 256 is rather optimal and provides some advantages from the perspective of the compression technique introduced in the next subsection.

Finally, a third (outermost) "loop" is also implicitly present, for the $\lceil n_z/(\text{B} \cdot \text{K}) \rceil$ thread blocks. With this approach, the GPU hardware scheduler will dynamically assign blocks to each chunk of the matrix. This is important because the

```
1  #define W 32      // Warp size
2  #define B 256     // Number of threads per block
3  #define K 4       // Number of elements per thread
4
5  void SpMV(int n, int nz, int *i, int *j, double *a, double *x, double *y)
   {
6      cudaMemset(y, 0, sizeof(double) * n);
7      int nc = nz / (B * K);
8      dim3 tb(W, B / W);
9      SpMV_kernel<<<nc, tb>>>(i, j, a, x, y);
10 }
11
12 __global__ void SpMV_kernel(int *i, int *j, double *a, double *x, double
      *y){
13     int     p = blockIdx.x, q = threadIdx.y * W + threadIdx.x;
14     double v = 0.0;
15     for (int l = 0; l < K; l++) {
16         int t = (p * B + q) * K + l;
17             v += a[t] * x[j[t]];
18     }
19     int row = i[p * B + q];
20     atomicAdd(y + row, v);
21 }
```

Listing 1.1. CUDA code for the SPMV with a simple balancing parallelization scheme and A stored in coordinate format.

execution time of the threads can be quite different given the variations in the access cost to the vectors x and y. The reason is that, although each thread process the same number of elements, the matrix pattern can result in very different cache hits and misses during the accesses to the input vector x. Also, the ordering of the matrix elements can introduce an important number of cache misses in the update of the result vector y. In addition, atomic operations must be used to avoid race conditions in this update. Although atomic primitives have efficient support in modern GPU hardware, they introduce contention among the threads introducing further variations to the execution time.

In principle, the COO format does not enforce any specific ordering of the matrix elements. However, a random ordering will result in poor locality during the accesses to the result y. In contrast, a row-major ordering (such as that used in CSR) renders excellent locality during the same accesses, but with higher contention among threads. To avoid this, a segmented scan is implemented using the intra-block communication primitives available on NVIDIA's GPU. The fragment of CUDA code in Listing 1.2 shows this reduction. There, the variable v stores the values that have to be accumulated and the variable row their corresponding row indices.

This solution mimics the highly parallel variant of the classic prefix sum: each thread communicates the accumulated value as well as the row index for that value to the thread in the next level of the hierarchy. The accumulation continues if the received row index matches the index of the row assigned to the receiving thread. Assuming a row-major ordering (i.e., consecutive row indices), the thread with the lowest identifier participating in the accumulation of elements for each row accumulates the partial products for all the products in that row. Only this thread issues a global memory access operation to write the final value to the main memory.

```
1 #define W 32      // Warp size
2 for (int l = 1; l < W; l *= 2) {
3     int     s = __shfl_down_sync(0xffffffff, row, 1);
4     double t = __shfl_down_sync(0xffffffff, v, 1);
5     if (row == s && threadIdx.x + l < W) v += t;
6 }
7 int prev = __shfl_up_sync(0xffffffff, row, 1);
8 if (threadIdx.x == 0 || row != prev) atomicAdd(Y + row, v);
```

Listing 1.2. CUDA code that performs the accumulation on y.

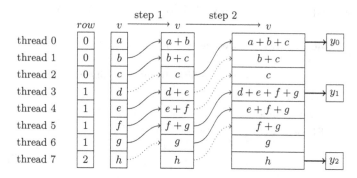

Fig. 1. Diagram of a segmented scan of 8 elements using 8 threads

Figure 1 shows a reduced example using only 8 threads. The first column represents the contents of the *row* variable in each thread and the last column corresponds to the result vector y. The columns in between show the value of v at each step of the loop. Each arrow represents the messages sent among threads, using a dotted line when the received value is not added because it comes across a row boundary. The solid arrows are atomic additions to y in main memory.

This reduction scheme requires 11 communication operations for adding the values for all rows compared with 5 communications in a regular reduction which only computes one sum. Therefore, it is only sub-optimal when the matrix elements processed by a warp pertain to the same row. However, this case is avoided by the compression technique introduced in the next subsection.

2.2   Compression

Following the balanced thread distribution, each block of threads processes exactly a chunk of B · K nonzero elements of the sparse matrix. If the matrix elements are ordered row-wise and, by columns inside each row, (as is the case in the CSR format,) each chunk will likely present a significant number of repeated row indices in vector i as well as clustered column indices in vector j. In addition, for some applications, many of the matrix values are repeated. For these reasons, it may be beneficial to use different encodings for each chunk, reducing (compressing) the amount of memory required to store the sparse matrix. This approach avoids thread divergence as the same format is used for all the elements in a chunk. At the same time, the compression level may not be optimal as it needs to account for the values accessed by several threads.

To implement this compression, a handful of auxiliary vectors are required, all of the length $\lceil n_z/(\mathtt{B} \cdot \mathtt{K}) \rceil$ (that is, vectors with one element per chunk). The first vector contains a 1-byte entry per block to specify which particular format is used for that block. Table 1 shows a summary of the possible encodings for a matrix with double precision (DP) floating point data. The row index and element value combinations can be represented by a single bit each, while the column index requires two bits in each 1-byte entry of the vector.

Table 1. Possible encodings of the chunk data for DP data.

	None	8 bits	16 bits	32 bits	64 bits
Row index	×	×			
Column index		×	×	×	
Element value		×			×

Two additional integer vectors then contain the baseline (reference) row and column indices of the elements in the chunk, which correspond to those for the top-leftmost nonzero entry of the sparse matrix in the chunk. Finally, as the space occupied by distinct chunks will be often different, a vector of integers is used to point to the start of each chunk.

Instead of the three original COO vectors (i, j and a), the data of the matrix elements in a chunk are maintained in a *blob* (Binary Large OBject), with the B row indexes first; followed by the $\mathtt{B} \cdot \mathtt{K}$ column indexes; and finally the $\mathtt{B} \cdot \mathtt{K}$ values. Those blobs are stored contiguously in memory with no alignment issues provided B and $\mathtt{B} \cdot \mathtt{K}$ are both integer multiples of 8 for DP data (or 4 for single precision values). The values of i and j are stored as offsets relative to the baseline element of the chunk.

For $\mathtt{B} \leq 256$, the row index is encoded using one byte only as most matrices contain at least one element per row. If this is not the case, each empty row is padded with an explicit zero element. If the whole chunk corresponds to a unique row, it is not necessary to store any value for the individual elements, and a regular sum reduction is used instead of the segmented scan. Depending on the nonzero pattern of the matrix, the column index is encoded using 8, 16, or 32 bits. For sparse matrices arising in non-graph applications, the non-zero entries in a row usually appear in clusters, allowing to use fewer bits to encode the column indices. While converting the matrix, a lookup table (LUT) is built containing the 256 most frequent values. If all value entries in the chunk are covered by the LUT, only one byte per element is used to index the right element in the LUT instead of storing the actual floating point values.

Figure 2 shows an example corresponding to a small chunk ($\mathtt{B} = 8$ and $\mathtt{K} = 1$) in compressed COO format. The original COO data is represented left of the arrow and the different elements in the compressed COO format on the right.

In this figure, each column from the blob corresponds to the respective original vector. The first column contains the (row) i indices as an offset to the row baseline. Similarly, the second column contains the (column) j indices as an offset to the column baseline. Finally, the third column contains an index to the LUT where the double precision values are stored. The values of the row and columns offsets are different for each chunk/element but the LUT is common to the whole matrix.

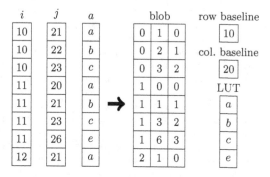

Fig. 2. Example of one chunk in Compressed COO format. In the last column, row/col. baseline specify the offset to be added to the first/second index of each block to obtain the corresponding i/j index; and LUT contains the different values encountered in vector a, which are indirectly referenced via the third entry of the blob.

3   Experimental Results

3.1   Setup and Memory Savings

For the experimental evaluation of the new compressed realization of SpMV, we selected 60 test matrices from the Suite Sparse Matrix Collection [1]. The chosen benchmarks have row/column dimensions larger than 900,000 and arise in a variety of scientific problems excluding graph applications. (Although the adjacency matrices associated with graphs have excellent compression properties, we do not consider them to be interesting use cases for the SpMV kernel as there are more efficient algorithms for graph manipulation.) The test matrices along with some key properties are listed in Table 2.

Figure 3 visualizes the memory overhead of COO and Compressed COO with respect to CSR, assuming a DP floating point representation for the numerical values with all three formats, and a 32-bit integer representation for the indices in CSR and COO. There are some matrices with clustered indices/repeated numerical entries where the compression schemes are especially efficient and, as a result, Compressed COO uses less memory than CSR. For the rest of the matrices, except in two cases, the overhead of Compressed COO over CSR is always smaller than that of regular COO.

Table 2. Test matrices

Matrix	n	n_z	n_z/n	Matrix	n	n_z	n_z/n
1. af_shell10	1,508,065	52,259,885	34.7	31. Geo_1438	1,437,960	60,236,322	41.9
2. atmosmodd	1,270,432	8,814,880	6.9	32. Hamrle3	1,447,360	5,514,242	3.8
3. atmosmodj	1,270,432	8,814,880	6.9	33. Hardesty1	938,905	12,143,314	12.9
4. atmosmodl	1,489,752	10,319,760	6.9	34. Hook_1498	1,498,023	59,374,451	39.6
5. atmosmodm	1,489,752	10,319,760	6.9	35. HV15R	2,017,169	283,073,458	140.3
6. audikw_1	943,695	77,651,847	82.3	36. kkt_power	2,063,494	12,771,361	6.2
7. bone010_M	986,703	23,888,775	24.2	37. ldoor	952,203	42,493,817	44.6
8. bone010	986,703	47,851,783	48.5	38. Long_Coup_dt0	1,470,152	84,422,970	57.4
9. boneS10_M	914,898	18,489,474	20.2	39. Long_Coup_dt6	1,470,152	84,422,970	57.4
10. boneS10	914,898	40,878,708	44.7	40. memchip	2,707,524	13,343,948	4.9
11. Bump_2911	2,911,419	127,729,899	43.9	41. ML_Geer	1,504,002	110,686,677	73.6
12. cage14	1,505,785	27,130,349	18.0	42. nlpkkt120	3,542,400	95,117,792	26.9
13. cage15	5,154,859	99,199,551	19.2	43. nlpkkt160	8,345,600	225,422,112	27.0
14. circuit5M_dc	3,523,317	14,865,409	4.2	44. nlpkkt200	16,240,000	440,225,632	27.1
15. circuit5M	5,558,326	59,524,291	10.7	45. nlpkkt240	27,993,600	760,648,352	27.2
16. Cube_Coup_dt0	2,164,760	124,406,070	57.5	46. nlpkkt80	1,062,400	28,192,672	26.5
17. Cube_Coup_dt6	2,164,760	124,406,070	57.5	47. nv2	1,453,908	37,475,646	25.8
18. CurlCurl_3	1,219,574	13,544,618	11.1	48. Queen_4147	4,147,110	316,548,962	76.3
19. dgreen	1,200,611	26,606,169	22.2	49. rajat31	4,690,002	20,316,253	4.3
20. dielFilterV2real	1,157,456	48,538,952	41.9	50. Serena	1,391,349	64,131,971	46.1
21. dielFilterV3real	1,102,824	89,306,020	81.0	51. ss	1,652,680	34,753,577	21.0
22. ecology1	1,000,000	4,996,000	5.0	52. StocF-1465	1,465,137	21,005,389	14.3
23. ecology2	999,999	4,995,991	5.0	53. stokes	11,449,533	349,321,980	30.5
24. Emilia_923	923,136	40,373,538	43.7	54. t2em	921,632	4,590,832	5.0
25. Flan_1565	1,564,794	114,165,372	73.0	55. thermal2	1,228,045	8,580,313	7.0
26. Freescale1	3,428,755	17,052,626	5.0	56. tmt_unsym	917,825	4,584,801	5.0
27. Freescale2	2,999,349	14,313,235	4.8	57. Transport	1,602,111	23,487,281	14.7
28. FullChip	2,987,012	26,621,983	8.9	58. vas_stokes_1M	1,090,664	34,767,207	31.9
29. CurlCurl_4	2,380,515	26,515,867	11.1	59. vas_stokes_2M	2,146,677	65,129,037	30.3
30. G3_circuit	1,585,478	7,660,826	4.8	60. vas_stokes_4M	4,382,246	131,577,616	30.0

We ran all the following experiments in this section using DP arithmetic on two distinct generations of NVIDIA accelerators:

- A V100 GPU with compute capability 7.0, furnished with 16 GB of main memory, 128 KB L1 cache per streaming processor, and 6 MB of L2 cache. The bandwidth to memory bandwidth is 900 GB/s and the theoretical peak performance is 7.8 DP TFLOPS.
- An A100 GPU with compute capability 8.0, equipped with 40 GB of memory, 1.5 GB/s main memory bandwidth, and a theoretical peak performance of 19.5/9.7 DP TFLOPS with/without DP tensor cores, respectively.

All the codes were compiled using CUDA version 11.0.167.

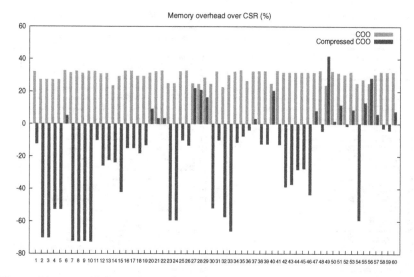

Fig. 3. Memory overhead with respect of the CSR format using DP arithmetic.

3.2 Performance of SpMV

We first compare the computational efficiency of our realization of SpMV against the codes in NVIDIA cuSPARSE. This native library from NVIDIA offers three routines for this computational kernel, two based on CSR and one based on COO. In the following comparisons, we include only the default CSR SpMV algorithm from cuSPARSE as the second CSR-based variant delivers very similar performance for the chosen test matrices. We do not include results for other formats, such as ELL or Hybrid-ELL, which were available in earlier versions of cuSPARSE but are no longer included in the last version of the library.

Figure 4 shows the performance evaluation of NVIDIA's codes against our Compressed COO implementation which applies the memory-reduction techniques described in Sect. 2 to diminish the indexing overhead for the row/column indices as well as data values. The results in the figure, in terms of GFLOPS, show a large performance improvement using Compressed COO for matrices with clustered indices/repeated values. Concretely, we are able to achieve up to 170/250 GFLOPS on the V100/A100 GPUs, respectively. While the compressed COO almost always outperforms the cuSPARSE COO and the cuSPARSE CSR kernels (except for a few outliers where the performance is on par or negligibly lower), the median speed-up over its competitors is 1.4× and 1.25–1.3× on the V100 and the A100 GPUs, respectively. Even though the median speed-up over cuSPARSE CSR and cuSPARSE COO is almost identical, we note that the performance ratios for the distinct problems are more consistent when comparing the COO formats.

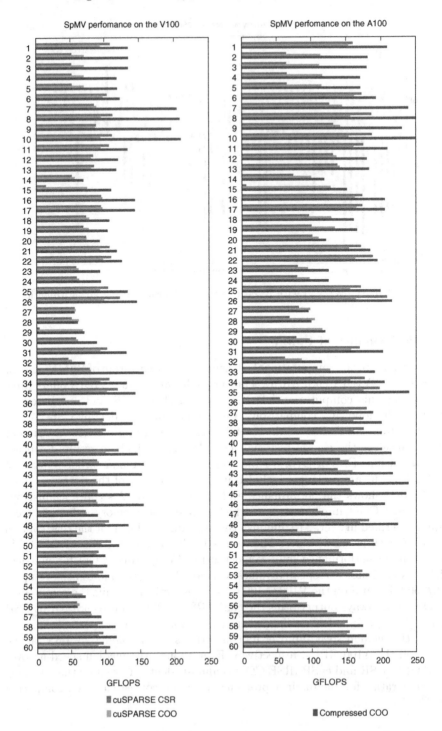

Fig. 4. Performance of the new compressed realization of SpMV against those in cuS-PARSE on NVIDIA V100 and A100 GPUs (left and right, resp.)

3.3   Effect on BICGSTAB

We next evaluate the impact of the new compressed kernels for SPMV when integrated into an iterative solver for sparse linear systems based on a Krylov subspace method. For this purpose, we select a BICGSTAB implementation based on CUDA. In the comparison, the BiCGSTAB solver employs the three different SPMV realizations analyzed in the previous subsection: compressed COO, cuSPARSE CSR, and cuSPARSE COO. For a performance comparison, we execute a fixed number of iterations and measure the GFLOPS for the linear systems constructed from the same test cases selected for the standalone evaluation of SPMV.

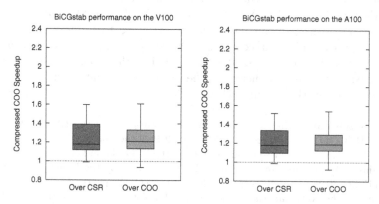

Fig. 5. Performance of the BICGSTAB solver with the new compressed realization of SPMV against those in cuSPARSE on NVIDIA V100 and A100 GPUs (left and right, resp.)

Our experiments with the BiCGSTAB solver using the three SPMV kernels show that the performance benefits of the faster SPMV kernel execution carry over to the BiCGSTAB solver. The acceleration of the BiCGSTAB solver depends on the specific problem and how much the SPMV kernel contributes to the overall runtime cost. In that sense, the speed-ups of BiCGSTAB correlate to a scaled version of the SPMV speed-up values reported in Fig. 4, damped with the problem-specific ratio between SPMV kernel cost vs. BiCGSTAB solver cost. In the end, equipping the BiCGSTAB solver with the compressed COO SPMV kernel improves the overall iterative solver performance for virtually all problems with a median speed-up of about 1.2× on both architectures, see Fig. 5.

4   Concluding Remarks and Future Work

We have adopted our previous balancing approach for SPMV to (virtually) divide the matrix contents into chunks (blocks) of nonzero entries of the same size; map these to the thread blocks; and prevent race conditions via efficient atomic operations. On top of this technique, in this work, we have proposed a new compression scheme that reduces the amount of indexing information that is associated with a COO-based realization of SpMV while maintaining the balanced distribution. For this purpose, the indices of each entry inside the same chunk are maintained as offsets with respect to a baseline row/column index pair, allowing the use of 8-bit encodings for the row indices, and 8/16/32-bit encodings for the column indices depending on the chunk. In addition, the observation that the numerical values in the sparse matrices arising in scientific applications present a considerable number of repetitions, motivates the design of a compression scheme that employs a look-up table.

The experimental results show the benefits of the new format, demonstrating a consistent advantage over the native implementation of the SpMV kernel in NVIDIA's cuSPARSE (CUDA 11.0.167) on the V100 and A100 GPUs.

The matrix format in this paper can be extended to support more efficient encodings. For example, matrix values could be stored in different precisions. Or even not stored at all for graph adjacency matrices that contain a large number of entries equal to one. Furthermore, the presented format is suitable for very large-scale matrices that require 64-bit indices.

Acknowledgements. This work was partially sponsored by the EU H2020 project 732631 OPRECOMP and project TIN2017-82972-R of the Spanish MINECO. Hartwig Anzt and Yuhsiang M. Tsai were supported by the "Impuls und Vernetzungsfond" of the Helmholtz Association under grant VH-NG-1241 and by the Exascale Computing Project (17-SC-20-SC), a collaborative effort of the U.S. Department of Energy Office of Science and the National Nuclear Security Administration. The authors would like to thank the Steinbuch Centre for Computing (SCC) of the Karlsruhe Institute of Technology for providing access to an NVIDIA A100 GPU.

References

1. Suitesparse matrix collection (2018). https://sparse.tamu.edu. Accessed Sept 2020
2. Bell, N., Garland, M.: Efficient sparse matrix-vector multiplication on CUDA. NVIDIA Technical report NVR-2008-004, NVIDIA Corporation, December 2008
3. Buluç, A., Williams, S., Oliker, L., Demmel, J.: Reduced-bandwidth multithreaded algorithms for sparse matrix-vector multiplication. In: Proceedings of the IEEE International Parallel & Distributed Processing Symposium, pp. 721–733 (2011)
4. Choi, J.W., Singh, A., Vuduc, R.W.: Model-driven autotuning of sparse matrix-vector multiply on GPUs. In: Proceedings of the 15th ACM SIGPLAN Symposium on Principles and Practice of Parallel Programming, PPoPP 2010, pp. 115–126 (2010)
5. Filippone, S., Cardellini, V., Barbieri, D., Fanfarillo, A.: Sparse matrix-vector multiplication on GPGPUs. ACM Trans. Math. Softw. **43**(4), 1–49 (2017)
6. Flegar, G., Anzt, H.: Overcoming load imbalance for irregular sparse matrices. In: Proceedings of the Seventh Workshop on Irregular Applications: Architectures and Algorithms, IA3 2017 (2017)
7. Flegar, G., Quintana-Ortí, E.S.: Balanced CSR sparse matrix-vector product on graphics processors. In: Rivera, F.F., Pena, T.F., Cabaleiro, J.C. (eds.) Euro-Par 2017. LNCS, vol. 10417, pp. 697–709. Springer, Cham (2017). https://doi.org/10.1007/978-3-319-64203-1_50

8. Grossman, M., Thiele, C., Araya-Polo, M., Frank, F., Alpak, F.O., Sarkar, V.: A survey of sparse matrix-vector multiplication performance on large matrices. CoRR abs/1608.00636 (2016). http://arxiv.org/abs/1608.00636
9. Liu, W., Vinter, B.: CSR5: an efficient storage format for cross-platform sparse matrix-vector multiplication. In: Proceedings of the 29th ACM on International Conference on Supercomputing, ICS 2015, pp. 339–350. ACM, New York (2015)
10. Saad, Y.: Iterative Methods for Sparse Linear Systems, 2nd edn. SIAM, Philadelphia (2003)

High-performance GPU and CPU Signal Processing for a Reverse-GPS Wildlife Tracking System

Yaniv Rubinpur and Sivan Toledo[✉]

Blavatnik School of Computer Science, Tel-Aviv University, Tel Aviv, Israel
stoledo@tau.ac.il

Abstract. We present robust high-performance implementations of signal-processing tasks performed by a high-throughput wildlife tracking system called ATLAS. The system tracks radio transmitters attached to wild animals by estimating the time of arrival of radio packets to multiple receivers (base stations). Time-of-arrival estimation of wide-band radio signals is computationally expensive, especially in acquisition mode (when the time of transmission of not known, not even approximately). These computation are a bottleneck that limits the throughput of the system. The paper reports on two implementations of ATLAS's main signal-processing algorithms, one for CPUs and the other for GPUs, and carefully evaluates their performance. The evaluations indicates that the GPU implementation dramatically improves performance and power-performance relative to our baseline, a high-end desktop CPU typical of the computers in current base stations. Performance improves by more than 50X on a high-end GPU and more than 4X with a GPU platform that consumes almost 5 times *less* power than the CPU platform. Performance-per-Watt ratios also improve (by more than 16X), and so do the price-performance ratios.

Keywords: GPU · CUDA · Digital signal processing · Arrival-time estimation

1   Introduction

ATLAS is a reverse-GPS wildlife tracking system, targeting mostly regional movement patterns (within an area spanning kilometers to tens of kilometers) and small animals, including small birds and bats [18,21]. ATLAS is a mature collaborative research effort: 6 systems have been set up and are operating in 5 countries on 3 continents. The first system has been operating for about 6 years almost continuously and has produced ground-breaking research in Ecology [4,20].

ATLAS tracks wild animals using miniature radio-frequency (RF) transmitting tags attached to the animals [17,19]. The transmissions are received by ATLAS base stations that include a sampling radio receiver and a computer

© Springer Nature Switzerland AG 2021
B. Balis et al. (Eds.): Euro-Par 2020 Workshops, LNCS 12480, pp. 96–108, 2021.
https://doi.org/10.1007/978-3-030-71593-9_8

running Linux or Windows. The computer processes RF samples to detect transmissions from tags and to estimate the time of arrival (ToA) of the transmissions. It reports the reception times to a server via an internet connection, usually cellular. The server estimates the location of a tag from ToA reports of the same transmission by different base stations [21].

The signal processing that ATLAS base stations performs is computationally demanding and is one of the main limiting factors of the throughput of the system (the number of tags that it can track and the number of localizations per second that it can produce). The signal-processing algorithms were initially optimized for single-threaded on CPUs, but no significant effort has been made to exploit multiple cores effectively.

This paper presents a new implementation of the ATLAS signal-processing code[1] designed to effectively exploit graphical processing units (GPUs). Our aim in developing this implementation was to significantly improve the throughput of the system and to reduce the power consumption of base stations. Reduced power consumption reduces the cost and complexity of base stations that rely on solar and wind energy harvesting, such as those deployed in the shallow Wadden sea; it is not particularly important in base stations connected to the power grid. High throughput is useful in most base stations. As part of this project, we also exposed a little more parallelism in the original CPU implementation, but it was not our intention to make it as parallel as possible, because that would have little value to users (who should use the GPU implementation) and would necessitate replacing our simple single-threaded task scheduler with a complex concurrent one.

We also evaluate the performance of both the (slightly improved) CPU code and the new GPU code on real recorded data. The evaluations, performed on two CPU platforms and on three GPU platforms, show dramatic improvements relative to our baseline, a high-end desktop CPU that is typical of the computers in current base stations. The improvements are both in terms of absolute performance (more than 50X with a high-end GPU and more than 4X with a GPU platform that consumes almost 5 times *less* power than the CPU platform), in terms of performance-per-Watt ratios (more than 16X), and in terms of price-performance ratios. However, because we did not attempt to achieve top multicore performance on CPUs, these results should not be taken as fair comparisons of the hardware platforms; they are meant mainly to demonstrate the level of performance that is achievable on such tasks on GPUs using a single-threaded scheduler coupled with GPU data parallel tasks.

2   Background

ATLAS tags transmit a fixed unique pseudorandom packet every second, 2 s, 4 s, or 8 s. The packets are 8192-bit long and the bitrate is around 1 Mb/s. The data

---

[1] The current CPU and GPU versions of the code are available, along with the data files requires to run the code, at http://www.tau.ac.il/~stoledo/Tools/atlas-dsp-heteropar2020.zip.

is frequency modulated (FSK); ATLAS can also use phase modulation, but this is beyond the scope of this paper (see [12] for details). The sampling receiver in each base station sends a continuous stream of complex RF samples, usually at 8 or 8.33 Ms/s, to a computer. The samples are placed in a circular buffer. A high-level scheduler repeatedly extract a block of samples from the buffer and processes it. The size of the circular buffer allows for processing delays of more than 10 s; this simplifies the scheduler and the signal-processing code considerably relative to in-order stream processing with hard deadlines.

The signal processing aims to detect whether packets from specific tags appear in the block, to estimate the precise (sub-sample) time of arrival (ToA) of each packet, to estimate the (relative) power of the packet, and to estimate a signal-to-noise ratio that is correlated with the variance of the ToA estimate. This data is sent to a server that estimates the locations of the tags [21].

The scheduler creates two kinds of tasks for the signal-processing code. *Searching-mode* (acquisition-mode) tasks process blocks of 100 ms and try to detect packets from all the tags that have not been detected in the past few minutes. The set of tags to search for can consist of over 100 tags. Since all tags transmit on one or two frequencies, the FSK demodulation step is performed only once or twice per block of samples, but the number of pseudorandom codes that must be correlated with the demodulated signals can be over 100. *Tracking-mode* tasks aim to detect an 8 ms packet from one particular tag in a block of about 12 ms of samples. These tasks perform demodulation and correlate the demodulated signal with one pseudorandom code.

Normally, the scheduler allocates 50% of the processor's time to searching and 50% to tracking, in an amortized sense, simply to avoid starvation of one of the tasks. If one of the queues is empty, all the processing resources are devoted to the other queue.

The scheduler is sequential; it generates one task at a time and performs it to completion, devoting to it all the cores except for one that handles incoming samples. This simplifies its algorithms but places all the responsibility to efficiently utilize multiple cores to the signal-processing code.

Graphics cards (GPUs) that can run general-purpose code, sometimes called GPGPUs, have emerged as effective accelerators of computationally-intensive tasks [9]. This paper focuses on GPUs produced by the market leader, NVIDIA. NVIDIA GPUs contains a large number of simple cores (execution units) under the control of a smaller number of instruction schedulers. In the Jetson TX2 GPU, for example, 256 cores are organized into *warps* of 32 cores that are controlled by a single instruction scheduler. The warps are organized into *streaming multiprocessors* (SMs; two in the TX2). All the cores in a warp perform the same operation at the same time, so the code must exhibit a high degree of data parallelism. Larger NVIDIA GPUs use the same basic structure, but with different numbers of cores and SMs. Many NVIDIA GPUs can only operate directly on data stored in the GPUs memory, not in the computer's main memory. NVIDIA GPUs have a memory hierarchy that includes a small block of so-called *shared* memory that is private to an SM; on the TX2, its size is 64 KB. Data-movement engines called *copy engines* in the GPU move data between main memory and GPU memories and within GPU memories.

NVIDIA GPUs run programs written in CUDA, an extension of the C language. CUDA programs express GPU computations using an abstraction called a *kernel*. A kernel operates on a small piece of data (say one element of an input array and one element of an output array). CUDA programs invoke kernels on entire arrays concurrently.

3   Signal Processing in ATLAS

The signal-processing building blocks that are performed on each task are as follows:

1. Conversion of the complex RF samples, represented by pairs of 16-bit integers, to a single-precision (`float`) complex vector x. The complex samples are usually element-wise by a complex input vector l representing a local-oscillator signal, to shift the center frequency so that transmissions are centered at zero. That is, we replace $x \leftarrow x \odot l$ (for all i, $x_i \leftarrow x_i \cdot l_i$).
2. Next, a bandpass FIR (finite impulse response) filter, represented here by a circulant matrix that H_{BP}, is applied, to produce $y \leftarrow H_{\text{BP}}x$. We use filters with 200 coefficients.
3. Two short (8 samples) matched filters are applied to y, one that represent a single-bit (chip) period at the frequency representing a 1 symbol and one that represent a single-bit period at the frequency that represents a 0 symbol. We denote their outputs by $f_1 = H_1 y$ and $f_0 = H_0 y$.
4. The vectors f_1 and f_0 are used to demodulate the transmission in two different ways, with and without normalization,

$$d = (|f_1| - |f_0|) \oslash (|f_0| + |f_0|) , \quad u = (|f_1| - |f_0|)$$

(elementwise absolute value, elementwise subtraction and addition, and elementwise division). These signals are real.
5. The algorithm applies exactly the same steps to a *replica* of the transmission we are trying to detect, a synthetic noise-free zero-padded signal $r^{(c)}$ that represents an FSK packet with the same modulation parameters and a pseudo-random bit sequence c. The resulting demodulated vector is denoted $d^{(c)}$; it is computed once and stored. The lengths of d, u and $d^{(c)}$ are identical.
6. We cross-correlate d with $d^{(c)}$. The cross correlation vector is also real.
7. We compute the value and location j of the maximum of the absolute value of the cross correlation vector, $j = \arg\max_i |\text{xcorr}(d, d^{(c)})|$. The elements of $\text{xcorr}(d, d^{(c)})$ around j are subsequently interpolated to estimate the arrival time of the incoming signal. We also compute quantities that are used to estimate the signal-to-noise ratio (SNR) and the power of the signal. Assuming that the nonzero part of $d^{(c)}$ spans its first n elements, we compute

$$w_c = \sum_{i=0}^{n} d_i^{(c)} d_{i+j} , \quad q = \sum_{i=0}^{n} d_{i+j}^2 , \text{ and } p_c = \sum_{i=0}^{n} d_i^{(c)} u_{i+j} .$$

For details on how power and SNR are estimated and how they are used, see [12,15].

4 High-Performance Design and Implementations

We use algorithms that minimize the operation counts that the signal-processing building-blocks perform. In particular, we use the fast-Fourier transform (FFT) to compute cross-correlation and to apply FIR filters with many coefficients, so $xcorr(d, d^{(c)}) = ifft(fft(d) \odot fft(d^{(c)}))$. We compose FIR filters that are applied in a sequence ($H_{BP}H_1$ and $H_{BP}H_0$) and we use FFTs to apply long FIR filters (filters with many coefficients). We use the overlap-add method to apply medium-length filters and cross correlations. This reduces the operation count from $\Theta(m \log m)$ to $\Theta(m \log n)$ when applying a filter of length n to a block of m RF samples. We pad inputs to lengths that are a product of small integers, usually 2, 3, and 5; this ensures that applying FFT is as inexpensive as possible.

We also use high-performance implementation principles in both the CPU implementation in C and in the GPU implementation in CUDA. In most cases the principles are applicable to both implementations; we highlight the differences when this is not the case.

We use comprehensive high-performance FFT libraries to compute FFTs. On CPUs, we use FFTW [7]; on GPUs, we use NVIDIA's cuFFT. The implementations allocate arrays when they are needed and reuse them aggressively. In general, they are never released. For example, demodulation of a block of RF samples of a certain size is always done using the same temporary arrays; for other sizes, we use other arrays. This reduces memory-allocation overheads and allows us to preplan all the FFT calls (both FFTW and cuFFT requires calls to be *planned* in order to achieve high performance). Allocated arrays are aligned on cache-line boundaries in the CPU implementation and are allocated in GPU memory in the GPU implementation. Auxiliary vector, like $fft(d^{(c)})$, are computed when needed but stored indefinitely, to avoid recomputation. Loops are aggressively fused in the CPU implementation and kernels are aggressively fused in the GPU implementation. This reduces data movement (e.g., cache misses) and allows elimination of some temporary arrays. On the GPU, a library called CUB [13] enables fusion of kernels with reductions (e.g., sums), which are otherwise challenging to implement efficiently in CUDA. In the CPU implementation, we batch cross correlation operations: a single call to FFTW computes many cross-correlation vectors. This exposes "embarrassing" parallelism (completely independent operations) that FFTW should be able to easily exploit, at least in principle.

CUB uses shared memory to achieve high performance; it requires the caller to allocate this memory, which our code does. In kernels that do not use CUB we do not use shared memory because they implement low data-reuse data-parallel operations over large vectors. cuFFT might also use shared memory, but if it does, it allocates it internally.

5 Experimental Evaluation

This section presents our experimental evaluation of the effectiveness of GPUs for our task, in terms of both performance and energy efficiency.

5.1 Methodology (Test Data)

To test the codes, we modified the CPU-based DSP C code so that it stores all its inputs and outputs in files. We then ran the ATLAS base station code in an ad-hoc mode (that is, not as part of a localization system) on a computer connected to a USRP B210 sampling radio and configured the base station to detect a tag that was present in the room. This produced files that contained the RF samples that were processed in both searching and tracking mode, inputs that represent filter coefficients and the signal to correlate with, and the outputs of the signal-processing algorithms.

Next, we wrote a C program that reads these files, calls the signal processing routines on the recorded data, measures their running time and optionally the power consumption of the computer and its components, and stores the results in files. The program can use the recordings in both single-code single-RF-window mode and in batch mode that processes many codes in one call. The former is typical of tracking mode and the latter of searching mode. The program checks that the returned results are identical, up to numerical rounding errors, to those returned by the full base station run that detected the tag correctly. This ensures that all the results that we report represent correct executions of the algorithms. The code then stores the running times and the power measurements, if made, to log files.

We also tested that the new CUDA-based code works correctly when called from Java through the JNI interface and detects transmissions from tags and their arrival times. This test was performed on the Jetson TX2 computer described below and the same URSP B210 radio.

5.2 Platforms

We evaluated the code on several platforms using both the CPU code and the GPU code.

Our baseline is a small form-factor desktop computer, representative of those currently used in ATLAS base stations, with an Intel i7-8700T CPU. This CPU has 6 physical cores running at clock frequencies between 2.4 and 4 GHz and thermal design power (TDP) of 35 W. This CPU was launched in Q2 2018 and is fabricated in a 14 nm process. The computer ran Linux kernel version 5.3. We compiled the code using GCC version 7.5. Both our code and FFTW version 3.3.8 were compiled using the optimization options that are built into FFTW. The code that was produced ran slightly faster than code compiled with only -O3 -mtune=native.

Our main target is a low-power Jetson TX2 computer [2,6], which has a 256-core NVIDIA Pascal GPU, four ARM Cortex-A57 cores and two ARM Denver2 cores, launched in Q2 2017 using a 16 nm process. The Cortex-A57 cores were designed by ARM and the Denver2 cores were designed by NVIDIA for higher single-threaded performance; both use the same 64-bit ARMv8 instruction set. It also has 8 GB of memory that both the CPU and GPU can access, with 59.7 GB/s memory bandwidth. The TX2 ran Linux kernel 4.9.140-tegra. We used nvcc version 10.0.326, CUDA library 10.0.130, gcc 7.4.0, and FFTW 3.5.7. CUB version 1.8.0 was used on all platforms.

We measured power consumption on the TX2 using two ina3221 current sensors built into the TX2 module and a third built into the motherboard [5]. Each sensor senses current on three different rails, and all the measurements are available by reading special files exposed by the driver under /sys/bus/i2c/drivers/ina3221x. The values that we report are the maximum value observed during the computation.

The power-vs-performance profile of the TX2 can be adjusted by turning cores on or off and by changing their clock frequency. NVIDIA defined several standard modes, which we use below in our tests. Table 1 describes these modes. The nominal TDP of the TX2 ranges from 7.5 W for the highest power efficiency mode, to 15 W for the highest performance modes. Both the TX2 module and the motherboards include power sensors that we use to measure the power consumption directly in our tests.

Table 1. Standard power modes on the Jetson TX2.

Mode name	Denver2 cores	A57 cores	GPU frequency
Max-Q	—	4 × 1.2 GHz	0.85 GHz
Max-P All	2 × 1.4 GHz	4 × 1.4 GHz	1.12 GHz
Max-P ARM	—	4 × 2.0 GHz	1.12 GHz
Max-P Denver	2 × 2.0 GHz	—	1.12 GHz
Max-N	2 × 2.0 GHz	4 × 2.0 GHz	1.30 GHz

We also ran the GPU code on two additional platforms. One is an NVIDIA GeForce 1050 GTX GPU. This GPU uses the Pascal architecture, 640 cores running at 1.455 GHz, and 2 GB of RAM. The TDP is 75 W. It was plugged into a desktop running Windows 10 with a quad-core Intel i5-6500 CPU; we used CUDA 10.1, nvcc version 10.1.168, Microsoft's C++ compiler (cl) version 19.00.24210 for x64. The last GPU platform that we used is an NVIDIA Titan Xp GPU. This GPU also uses the Pascal architecture and has 3840 cores running at 1.582 GHz. It has 12 GB of memory and a high-bandwidth memory interface. The thermal design power is 250 W. It was plugged into a server with a 10-core Intel Xeon Silver 4114 CPU running Linux. We used CUDA and nvcc 10.0.130 and gcc 4.9.2.

5.3   Results

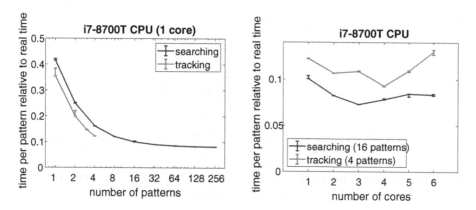

Fig. 1. The performance of the DSP code on one CPU core (left) and its speedup on multiple cores. The vertical bars show the minimum and maximum values over 10 experiments, and the actual data points are median results of the 10 experiments. The number of RF windows is 10 in the searching experiments and 100 in the searching experiments.

Figure 1 shows the performance of our C implementation on the baseline platform, which has an Intel i7-8700T CPU. We present the performance in terms of the ratio of processing time per pattern relative to the length of the RF window. That is, if the code takes 1 s to process one 100 ms window of RF samples and to correlate the demodulated signal with 16 different code patterns, then we report the performance as $(1/16)/0.1 = 0.625$. A ratio of 1 implies that the base station can search for one tag continuously, that searching for 2 tags would drop 50% of the RF samples, and so on. A ratio of 0.1 implies that the station can search continuously for 10 tags without dropping any RF sample, and so on. Lower is better.

The results on one core (Fig. 1 left) show that the performance per pattern improves significantly when we process multiple patterns in one window of RF samples (which is how the experiment was structured, since this is typical given how ATLAS systems are usually configured). This is mostly due to the amortization of the cost of demodulation over many patterns. The graph on the right in Fig. 1 that using 2 or 3 cores improves performance relative to using only one core, but the improvement is far from dramatic or linear. Using 4 or more cores actually slows the code down relative to 2 or 3 cores. The parallelization in the CPU code is only within FFTW and it does not appear to be particularly effective in this code, perhaps due to the length of the FFTs.

Performance on the TX2 is excellent on the GPU but poor on the CPU, as shown in Fig. 2. Our CUDA code running on the TX is about 4.3 times faster than the single-core i7 code and about 3 times faster than the i7 multicore runs. However, even at the highest performance mode, the TX's CPU cores perform about 4 times worse than the i7.

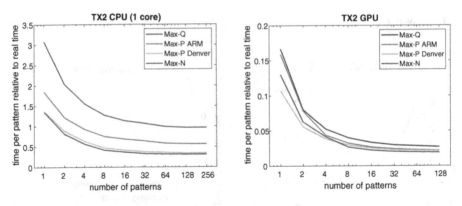

Fig. 2. Searching performance on the Jetson TX2 on both the ARM cores (left) and the GPU (right) under four standard power configurations.

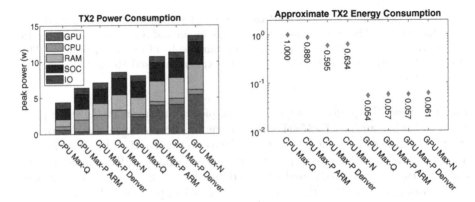

Fig. 3. Power consumption during searching tasks (left), broken down by system component, and approximate total energy consumption during searching with 16 patterns, normalized to the largest energy expenditure (right). Both graphs show the data for searching on either the CPU or the GPU of the Jetson TX2 and under four standard power configurations. The rated accuracy of the power sensors is 2% for values above 200 mW and 15% for smaller values.

We also measured the power consumption of the TX2 while it was running our code. The results, shown in Fig. 3, indicate that when running the GPU code, the GPU is the largest power consumer, but the memory and other parts of the system-on-chip (most probably the memory interface) consume a lot of power, about 50% of the total. The CPU and IO interfaces also consume power, but not much. In the C-code runs, the GPU is essentially off; the CPU, memory, and system-on-chip are the largest power consumers. The graph on the right in Fig. 3 shows that the CUDA code is about 10 times more energy efficient than the C code running on the CPU, for the same task.

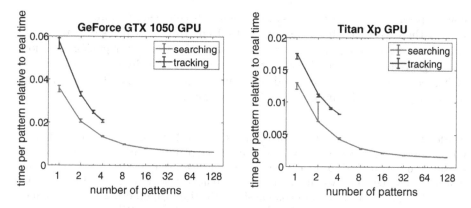

Fig. 4. The performance of two desktop GPUs, a low-end (and somewhat old) GeForce GTX 1050 and a high-end Titan Xp.

Figure 4 shows that our CUDA code is also very effective on desktop and server GPUs. A low-end GPU 12.8 times faster than a single x86_64 desktop core that is 2 years newer. A server GPU is 51.4 times faster than the desktop CPU.

6   Related Work

Alawieh et al. [1] and Hendricks et al. [10] compare the performance of several types of compute nodes, including GPUs, CPUs, and FPGAs, in the context of RF ToA estimation, with application to a location estimation system called RedFIR. Their requirements are more demanding, in the sense that RedFIR requires real-time processing of a stream of samples, whereas we buffer samples for a few seconds and use a priority scheduler to simplify the signal-processing code. It is well known that real-time scheduling on GPUs is challenging [22]; our scheduler allows ATLAS to avoid the difficulty. Also, RedFIR does not rely on periodic transmit schedules, whereas ATLAS reduces the computational load by tracking tags rather than just searching for them. Finally, signal processing in RedFIR is a bit simpler than in ATLAS because they use PSK transmitters, not FSK transmitters. Belloch et al. [3] and Kim et al. [11] present acoustic localization systems that exploit GPUs for ToA estimation.

Our use of cuFFT follows the advice of Střelák and Filipovič [16, Sect. 2.5]. Other CUDA FFT libraries [8,14] appear to be no longer maintained.

7   Discussion and Conclusions

We have shown that by implementing the DSP functionality of an RF time-of-arrival transmitter localization system in CUDA, we can improve the acquisition (searching) throughput of the system by a factor of 4 while reducing power consumption by a factor of 5 or so relative to a baseline single-core C code, even though the C code has been carefully optimized. Table 2, which summarizes the characteristics of our test platforms (as well as of a few newer platforms) show that higher-end GPUs can improve throughput dramatically higher, at the cost of higher power consumption, and sometimes also higher cost. The throughput of tracking modes also improves on GPU platforms.

Table 2. A comparison of GPU platforms. Column 3 shows the number CPU and GPU cores. The 5th column shows the TDP of the platform, either the overall power consumption or, if marked by a +, of only the device itself. The cost in USD is only indicative, and again shows either the total system cost or, when marked by a +, the cost of the device. The rightmost column shows the throughput, defined as the number of codes (tags) that can be searched for without dropping any RF samples, assuming batches of 128 and windows of 100 ms each; this also assumes that only 50% of the time is devoted to searching, the rest to tracking. The performance of the i7 processor assumes that only one of the six cores are used.

Device	Launch	Cores	Fab	W	USD	tput
i7-8700T	Q2 2018	6 × x86	14 nm	35^+	1000	6
Jetson TX2	Q2 2017	6 × ARM +256	16 nm	7.5–15	1000	26
GeForce GTX 1050	Q2 2016	+384	14 nm	75^+	110^+	77
Titan Xp	Q2 2017	+3840	16 nm	250^+	1200^+	315

Our baseline code does not effectively exploit multicore CPU platforms, even though it relies heavily on a (high-quality) parallel multicore FFT library; this alone does not deliver good parallel speedups, perhaps due to the modest size of the tasks. It is likely that a careful parallel multicore implementation, perhaps in OpenMP, can the performance of the C code on multicore CPUs. However, this would entail programming that is at least as complex as our CUDA implementation, and it would still not attain the maximum performance of the GPU code or its power-performance ratio.

Acknowledgements. Thanks to NVIDIA Corporation for the donation of the Jetson TX2. This study was also supported by grants 965/15, 863/15, and 1919/19 from the Israel Science Foundation.

References

1. Alawieh, M., Kasparek, M., Franke, N., Hupfer, J.: A high performance FPGA-GPU-CPU platform for a real-time locating system. In: Proceedings of the 23rd European Signal Processing Conference (EUSIPCO), pp. 1576–1580, August 2015. https://doi.org/10.1109/EUSIPCO.2015.7362649

2. Amert, T., Otterness, N., Yang, M., Anderson, J.H., Smith, F.D.: GPU scheduling on the NVIDIA TX2: hidden details revealed. In: Proceedings of the IEEE Real-Time Systems Symposium (RTSS), pp. 104–115 (2017)
3. Belloch, J.A., Gonzalez, A., Vidal, A.M., Cobos, M.: On the performance of multi-GPU-based expert systems for acoustic localization involving massive microphone arrays. Expert Syst. Appl. **42**, 5607–5620 (2015). https://doi.org/10.1016/j.eswa.2015.02.056
4. Corl, A., et al.: Movement ecology and sex are linked to barn owl microbial community composition. Mol. Ecol. **20**(7), 1358–1371 (2020). https://doi.org/10.1111/mec.15398
5. Corporation, N.: NVIDIA Jetson Linux Developer Guide, 32.4.3 Release, July 2020
6. Franklin, D.: NVIDIA Jetson TX2 delivers twice the intelligence to the edge, nVIDIA Developer Blog, March 2017. https://devblogs.nvidia.com/jetson-tx2-delivers-twice-intelligence-edge
7. Frigo, M., Johnson, S.G.: The design and implementation of FFTW3. Proc. IEEE **93**(2), 216–231 (2005). Special issue on "Program Generation, Optimization, and Platform Adaptation"
8. Govindaraju, N.K., Lloyd, B., Dotsenko, Y., Smith, B., Manferdelli, J.: High performance discrete Fourier transforms on graphics processors. In: Proceedings of the ACM/IEEE Conference on Supercomputing (SC), pp. 1–12, November 2008
9. Greengard, S.: GPUs reshape computing. Commun. ACM **59**(9), 14–16 (2016). https://doi.org/10.1145/2967979
10. Hendricks, A., Heller, T., Schäfer, A., Kasparek, M., Fey, D.: Evaluating performance and energy-efficiency of a parallel signal correlation algorithm on current multi and manycore architectures. Procedia Comput. Sci. **80**, 1566–1576 (2016)
11. Kim, S., Cho, J., Park, D.: Moving-target position estimation using GPU-based particle filter for IoT sensing applications. Appl. Sci. **7**(11), 1152 (2017)
12. Leshchenko, A., Toledo, S.: Modulation and signal-processing tradeoffs for reverse-GPS wildlife localization systems. In: Proceedings of the European Navigation Conference (ENC), pp. 154–165 (2018)
13. Merrill, D.: Cub (cuda unbound) library version 1.8.0, a library of CUDA collective primitives (2018). https://nvlabs.github.io/cub/
14. Mitra, S., Srinivasan, A.: Small discrete Fourier transforms on GPUs. In: Proceedings of the 11th IEEE/ACM International Symposium on Cluster, Cloud and Grid Computing, pp. 33–42, May 2011. https://doi.org/10.1109/CCGrid.2011.14
15. Rubinpur, Y., Toledo, S.: High-performance GPU and CPU signal processing for a reverse-GPS wildlife tracking system (2020). https://arxiv.org/abs/2005.10445
16. Střelák, D., Filipovič, J.: Performance analysis and autotuning setup of the cuFFT library. In: Proceedings of the 2nd Workshop on Autotuning and Adaptivity Approaches for Energy-Efficient HPC Systems (ANDARE), p. 6. ACM (2018). https://doi.org/10.1145/3295816.3295817
17. Toledo, S., et al.: Lightweight low-cost wildlife tracking tags using integrated transceivers. In: Proceedings of the 6th Annual European Embedded Design in Education and Research Conference (EDERC), Milano, Italy, pp. 287–291, September 2014
18. Toledo, S., Kishon, O., Orchan, Y., Shohat, A., Nathan, R.: Lessons and experiences from the design, implementation, and deployment of a wildlife tracking system. In: Proceedings of the IEEE International Conference on Software Science. Technology and Engineering (SWSTE), Beer Sheva, Israel, pp. 51–60, June 2016

19. Toledo, S., Orchan, Y., Shohami, D., Charter, M., Nathan, R.: Physical-layer protocols for lightweight wildlife tags with Internet-of-things transceivers. In: Proceedings of the 19th IEEE International Symposium on a Wolrd of Wireless, Mobile, and Multimedia Networks (WOWMOM), pp. 1–4, June 2018

20. Toledo, S., et al.: Cognitive map-based navigation in wild bats revealed by a new high-throughput tracking system. Science **369**(6500), 188–193 (2020)

21. Weller-Weiser, A., Orchan, Y., Nathan, R., Weiss, M.C.A.J., Toledo, S.: Characterizing the accuracy of a self-synchronized reverse-GPS wildlife localization system. In: Proceedings of the 15th ACM/IEEE International Conference on Information Processing in Sensor Networks (IPSN), Vienna, Austria, pp. 1–12, April 2016

22. Yang, M., Otterness, N., Amert, T., Bakita, J., Anderson, J.H., Smith, F.D.: Avoiding pitfalls when using NVIDIA GPUs for real-time tasks in autonomous systems. In: Proceedings of the 30th Euromicro Conference on Real-Time Systems (ECRTS), pp. 20:1–20:21 (2018). https://doi.org/10.4230/LIPIcs.ECRTS.2018.20

Preparing Ginkgo for AMD GPUs – A Testimonial on Porting CUDA Code to HIP

Yuhsiang M. Tsai[1], Terry Cojean[1], Tobias Ribizel[1],
and Hartwig Anzt[1,2]

[1] Karlsruhe Institute of Technology, Karlsruhe, Germany
[2] Innovative Computing Lab, University of Tennessee, Knoxville, TN, USA
{yu-hsiang.tsai,terry.cojean,tobias.ribizel,hartwig.anzt}@kit.edu

Abstract. With AMD reinforcing their ambition in the scientific high performance computing ecosystem, we extend the hardware scope of the GINKGO linear algebra package to feature a HIP backend for AMD GPUs. In this paper, we report and discuss the porting effort from CUDA, the extension of the HIP framework to add missing features such as cooperative groups, the performance price of compiling HIP code for AMD architectures, and the design of a library providing native backends for NVIDIA and AMD GPUs while minimizing code duplication by using a shared code base.

Keywords: Portability · GPU · CUDA · HIP

1 Introduction

Over the last decade, GPUs have been established as the main powerhouse in leadership supercomputers [1]. GPUs have proven valuable components to accelerate computations not only for machine learning workloads, but also for numerical linear algebra libraries powering computational science [2]. As of today, AMD and NVIDIA are considered the main GPU manufacturers. In the past, software efforts primarily focused on NVIDIA GPUs due to the comprehensive CUDA development environment and the common adoption in HPC centers. With the next leadership supercomputers deployed in the US National Laboratories being equipped with AMD GPUs [2], and the US Exascale Computing Project's mission to provide math functionality on the leadership systems, we extend the scope of the GINKGO library to feature an AMD GPU backend.

In this paper, we report and discuss the effort of porting a CUDA-focused library to the HIP ecosystem. We elaborate on the use of the perl-based script provided by AMD that aims at simplifying the transition process, its pitfalls and flaws. We also assess the performance HIP-based code achieves on NVIDIA architectures when compiled using NVIDIA's `nvcc` compiler.

© Springer Nature Switzerland AG 2021
B. Balis et al. (Eds.): Euro-Par 2020 Workshops, LNCS 12480, pp. 109–121, 2021.
https://doi.org/10.1007/978-3-030-71593-9_9

Transitioning a code base from one architecture to another, and platform portability in general, is an important problem in the software technology ecosystem. In particular, the number of adopters and contributors of community software scales only in the presence of good platform portability. The effort of porting a software stack to new architectures is, for example, described for molecular dynamics algorithm in [7], and for the solution of finite element problems in [12]. Concerning performance portability, the authors of [11] compare the algorithm performance for CUDA, HC++, HIP, and OpenCL backends.

Compared to previous work, we highlight that this work contains the following novel contributions:

- We discuss the porting of linear algebra kernels from CUDA to HIP.
- We add technology to the HIP ecosystem that is lacking but needed, e.g., a subwarp cooperative group concept with shuffle operations.
- We compare the performance of HIP and CUDA kernels coming from the same code base and providing the same functionality.
- Up to our knowledge, GINKGO is the first open-source sparse linear algebra library supporting several matrix types (Coo, Csr, Sellp, Ell, Hybrid), solvers (CG, BiCG, GMRES, etc.), preconditioner (block-jacobi) and factorization (ParILU and ParILUT) on AMD and NVIDIA GPUs.
- We ensure full result reproducibility by archiving all performance results.

Before providing more details about the porting effort in Sect. 3, we recall some background information about CUDA and HIP in Sect. 2. We present the results of the experiments of the same kernels being compiled by CUDA and HIP in Sect. 4. We conclude in Sect. 5 with a summary of this paper.

2   Background

2.1   Compute Unified Device Architecture - CUDA

NVIDIA developed the CUDA programming model and the corresponding nvcc compiler enabling developers to write kernels for GPU architectures using the C or C++ programming language. Also, NVIDIA provides several math libraries, like cuBLAS, cuSPARSE, and cuSOLVER containing ready-to-use numerical algorithms and core functionalities allowing users to easily develop a parallel application without writing device kernel functions.

In Listing 1.1, CUDA uses __global__ as the declaration specifier to tell the compiler this function runs on a GPU and uses execution configuration syntax (<<< >>>) to represent the configuration of grid and block dimensions, execution stream, and dynamically-sized shared memory. Moreover, developers can provide additional information at compile-time to optimize the execution performance like __launch_bounds__ to limit the register usage.

```
1  template <int value>
2  __global__ void dummy_kernel(const int num, int *__restrict__ array) {
3    // kernel_code
4  }
5  int main() {
6    // allocation of memory and calculation of grid/block_size
7    dummy_kernel<4> <<<dim3(grid_size), dim3(block_size)>>>(num, array);
8    return 0;
9  }
```

Listing 1.1. CUDA kernel launch syntax.

2.2 C++ Heterogeneous-Compute Interface for Portability - HIP

As a counterpart to NVIDIA's CUDA ecosystem, AMD more recently developed the GPU compute programming language and library ecosystem "RadeonOpen-Compute" (ROCm). ROCm is the first open-source HPC platform for GPU computing shipping with several math libraries, like rocBLAS, rocSPARSE, roc-SOLVER, etc. This enables users to develop GPU-ready applications in ROCm like in the CUDA ecosystem.

Aside from ROCm, AMD also provides a HIP abstraction that can be seen as a higher layer on top of the ROCm ecosystem, enveloping also the CUDA ecosystem. The idea behind HIP is to increase platform portability of software by providing an interface through which functionality of both, ROCm and CUDA can be accessed. Obviously, this would remove the burden of converting or rewriting code for different hardware architectures, therewith also reducing the maintenance effort for libraries supporting several backends.

In Listing 1.2, HIP uses the same declaration specifier __global__ like CUDA, but a different execution configuration syntax. HIP handles kernels featuring template parameters with the macro HIP_KERNELS_NAME. Although HIP also provides the __launch_bounds__ flag for kernel optimization, the effect differs from the CUDA ecosystem due to the architectural differences between AMD and NVIDIA GPUs.

```
1   template <int value>
2   __global__ void dummy_kernel(const int num, int *__restrict__ array) {
3     // kernel_code
4   }
5   int main() {
6     // allocation of memory and calculation of grid/block_size
7     hipLaunchKernelGGL(HIP_KERNEL_NAME(dummy_kernel<4>), dim3(grid_size),
8                        dim3(block_size), 0, 0, num, array);
9     return 0;
10  }
```

Listing 1.2. HIP kernel launch syntax.

2.3 Difference Between AMD and NVIDIA GPUs

The primary technical difference between AMD and NVIDIA GPUs is the number of threads that are executed simultaneously in a wavefront/warp. In NVIDIA

GPUs, a warp contains 32 threads, in AMD GPUs, a wavefront contains 64 threads. This difference potentially impacts all other parameter configurations and has to be taken into account when designing kernels and setting thread block size, shared memory and register usage, and compute grid size for valid parameter settings and optimal kernel performance.

Less relevant for the kernel design and parameter choice is that GPUs differ in the number of multiprocessors accumulated in a single device and in the memory bandwidth. While these are still relevant for kernel optimization, they rarely impact the correctness of a kernel design. We elaborate on the optimization of kernel parameters in Sect. 3.5.

As of today, AMD's ROCm ecosystem – and the HIP development ecosystem – still lacks some key functionality of the CUDA ecosystem. For example, HIP lacks a cooperative group interface that can be used for flexible thread programming inside a wavefront, see Sect. 3.3.

3   Porting CUDA Functionality to the HIP Ecosystem

Next, we report and discuss how we ported GINKGO's GPU functionality available for CUDA backends to the HIP ecosystem. To understand the technical realization, it is however useful to first elaborate on GINKGO's design.

3.1   Ginkgo Design

A high-level overview of GINKGO's software architecture is visualized in Fig. 1. The library design collects all classes and generic algorithm skeletons in the "core" library which, however, is useless without the driver kernels available in the "omp", "cuda", and "reference" folders. We note that "reference" contains sequential CPU kernels used to validate the correctness of the algorithms and as reference implementation for the unit tests realized using the googletest [6] framework. The "include" folder contains the public interface. Extending GINKGO's scope to AMD architectures, we add the "hip" folder containing the kernels in the HIP language, and the "common" folder for platform-portable kernels with the intention to reduce code duplication, see Sect. 3.2.

To reduce the effort of porting GINKGO to AMD architectures, we use the same base components of GINKGO like config, binding, executor, types and operations, which we only extend and adapt to support HIP.

- config: hardware-specific information like warp size, lane_mask_type, etc.;
- binding: the C++ style overloaded interface to vendors' BLAS and sparse BLAS library and the exception calls of the kernels not implemented;
- executor: the "handle" controlling the kernel execution and the ability to switch the execution space (hardware backend);
- types: the type of kernel variables and the conversion between library variables and kernel variables;

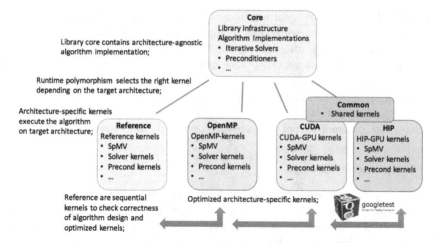

Fig. 1. The GINKGO library design overview. The components added when extending the scope to AMD GPUs are the "HIP" and the "Common" modules.

– operations: a class aggregating all the possible kernel implementations such as reference, omp, cuda and hip, which allows to switch between implementations at runtime.

Moreover, some components are not officially supported by vendors, e.g. complex number atomic_add[1] on CUDA and HIP, and warp-wide cooperative groups on HIP. For the functionality missing in both vendor ecosystems, we implement CUDA device functions providing the functionality and apply the work flow listed in Algorithm 1 to generate corresponding HIP kernels. For components missing only in one vendor ecosystem, we implement kernels providing the same functionality in the other ecosystem. In particular, as the HIP ecosystem currently lacks the warp-wide cooperative groups we make heavy use of, we implement device functions that provides this functionality for AMD architectures, see Sect. 3.3.

3.2   Avoiding Code Duplication

Despite the fact that the HIP ecosystem allows to compile the kernels for both AMD and NVIDIA GPUs, we currently plan to still provide native support in the CUDA ecosystem. This choice is motivated by the wider adoption of CUDA in the high performance computing community on the one side, and the unclear future of this functionality remaining in the HIP ecosystem on the other side. A third reason is that preserving native CUDA support allows to utilize novel CUDA-specific technology, e.g., dynamic parallelism. Extending GINKGO

---

[1] A complex atomic_add involves separate real and imaginary atomic_add and thus is not strictly an atomic operation, as no ordering between the individual components of multiple complex atomic operations is guaranteed.

to AMD GPUs, a primary goal was to avoid a significant level of code duplication. For this purpose, we created the "common" folder containing all kernels and device functions that are identical or the CUDA and the HIP executor except for kernel configuration parameters (such as warp size or launch_bounds). These configuration parameters are not set in the kernel file contained in the "common" folder, but in the files located in "cuda" and "hip" that are interfacing these kernels. This way we can avoid code duplication while still configuring the parameters for optimal kernel performance on the distinct hardware backends.

3.3   Cooperative Groups

CUDA 9 introduced cooperative groups for flexible thread programming. Cooperative groups provide an interface to handle thread block and warp groups and apply the shuffle operations that are used heavily in GINKGO for optimizing sparse linear algebra kernels. HIP [3] only supports block and grid groups with thread_rank(), size() and sync(), but no subwarp-wide group operations like shuffles and vote operations.

For enabling full platform portability, a small codebase, and preserving the performance of the optimized CUDA kernels, we implement cooperative group functionality for the HIP ecosystem. Our implementation supports the calculation of size/rank and shuffle/vote operations inside subwarp groups. We acknowledge that our cooperative group implementation may not support all features of CUDA's cooperative group concept, but all functionality we use in GINKGO.

The cross-platform cooperative group functionality we implement with shuffle and vote operations covers CUDA's native implementation. HIP only interfaces CUDA's warp operation without _sync suffix (which refers to deprecated functions), so we use CUDA's native warp operations to avoid compiler warning and complications on NVIDIA GPUs with compute capability 7.x or higher. We always use subwarps with contiguous threads, so we can use the block index to identify the threads' subwarp id and its index inside the subwarp. We define

$$
\begin{aligned}
\text{Size} &= \text{Given subwarp size} \\
\text{Rank} &= \text{tid \% Size} \\
\text{LaneOffset} &= \lfloor \text{tid \% warpsize / Size} \rfloor \times \text{Size} \\
\text{Mask} &= \sim 0 >> (\text{warpsize} - \text{Size}) << \text{LaneOffset}
\end{aligned}
$$

where tid is local thread id in a thread block such that Rank gives the local id of this subwarp, and ~0 is a bitmask of 32/64 bits, same bits as lane_mask_type, filled with 1 bits according to CUDA/AMD architectures, respectively. Using this definition, we can realize the cooperative group interface, for example for the shfl_xor, ballot, any, and all functionality:

$$
\begin{aligned}
\text{subwarp.shfl\_xor(data, bitmask)} &= \text{\_shfl\_xor(data, bitmask, Size)} \\
\text{subwarp.ballot(predicate)} &= (\text{\_ballot(predicate) \& Mask}) >> \text{LaneOffset} \\
\text{subwarp.any(predicate)} &= (\text{\_ballot(predicate) \& Mask}) \mathrel{!=} 0 \\
\text{subwarp.all(predicate)} &= (\text{\_ballot(predicate) \& Mask}) == \text{Mask}
\end{aligned}
$$

Note that we use the **ballot** operation to implement **any** and **all** operations. The original warp **ballot** returns the answer for the entire warp, so we need to shift and mask the bits to access the subwarp results. The **ballot** operation is often used in conjunction with bit operations like the population count (*popcount*), which are provided by C-style type-annotated intrinsics __popc [11] in CUDA and HIP. To avoid any issues with the 64bit-wide lane masks on AMD GPUs, we provide a single function **popcnt** with overloads for 32 and 64 bit integers as well as an architecture-agnostic **lane_mask_type** that provides the correct (unsigned) integer type to represent a (sub)warp lane mask.

```
 1   template <int Size, typename ValueType>
 2   __global__ void reduce(ValueType *__restrict__ data, int inner_loops) {
 3     auto local_data = data[threadIdx.x];
 4     for (int i = 0; i < inner_loops; i++) {
 5   +   auto group = tiled_partition<Size>(this_thread_block());
 6       #pragma unroll
 7   -   for (int bitmask = 1; bitmask < Size; bitmask <<= 1) {
 8   +   for (int bitmask = 1; bitmask < group.size(); bitmask <<= 1) {
 9   -     const auto remote_data = __shfl_xor(local_data, bitmask, Size);
10   +     const auto remote_data = group.shfl_xor(local_data, bitmask);
11         local_data = local_data + remote_data;
12       }
13     }
14     data[threadIdx.x] = local_data;
15   }
```

Listing 1.3. Reduce kernel. Green part is cooperative group implementation, and red part is legacy implementation

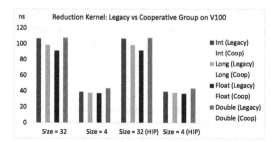
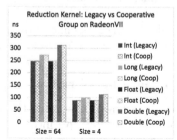

Fig. 2. GINKGO's cooperative groups vs. legacy functions for different data types on V100 (left) and RadeonVII (right). (Color figure online)

To assess the performance of our cross-platform cooperative group implementation, we use the local reduction kernel shown in Listing 1.3 that utilized either the vendor's legacy functionality (red) or GINKGO's cross-platform cooperative group interface (green). In Fig. 2, we report the runtime needed for 100 reduction operations (after a warm-up phase of 10 reductions) on NVIDIA's V100 GPU and AMD's RadeonVII GPU. To exclude the overhead of the kernel launch and memory operations, we run the kernel executing "inner_loops" reductions (line 4 of Listing 1.3) for "inner_loops = 1000" and "inner_loops = 2000" and report the runtime difference. This way, we can isolate the runtime needed for the warp-wide reduction by excluding the overhead of the kernel launch and memory operations. The results identifies GINKGO's cross-platform cooperative group implementation as competitive to the vendor's native implementation. Both implementations use the same strategy for the reduction operation, and both implementations execute the reduction loop (line 7–12 of Listing 1.3) exactly $\log_2(Size)$ times. For the execution time for different values of $Size$, the theoretical performance ratios are $\frac{\log_2(4)}{\log_2(64)} \approx 0.333$ on the RadeonVII and $\frac{\log_2(4)}{\log_2(32)} = 0.4$ on the V100. In the experimental evaluation, we observe average ratios $\frac{\text{runtime}(Size=4)}{\text{runtime}(Size=64)} = 0.360$ and $\frac{\text{runtime}(Size=4)}{\text{runtime}(Size=32)} = 0.394$ for the RadeonVII and the V100 GPUs, respectively.

3.4   Porting via the Cuda2Hip Script

For easy conversion of CUDA code to the HIP language, we use a script based on the hipify-perl script provided by AMD with several modifications to meet our specific needs. First, the script generates the target filename including the path in the "hip" directory. Then AMD's hipify-perl script is invoked to translate the CUDA kernels to the HIP language, including the transformation of NVIDIA's proprietary library functions to AMD's library functions and the kernels launch syntax. Next, the script changes all CUDA-related header, namespace, type and function names to the corresponding HIP-related names. By default, the script hipify-perl fails to handle namespace definitions. For example, the hipify-perl script changes `namespace::kernel<<<...>>> (...)` to `namespace::hipLaunchKernelGGL(kernel, ...)`, while the correct output would be `hipLaunchKernelGGL(namespace::kernel, ...)`. Thus, the script ultimately needs to correct the namespaces generated by the hipify-perl script.

3.5   Porting Workflow

In Algorithm 1, we sketch the workflow we use for porting GINKGO's CUDA backend to HIP. Step 1 introduces a set of variables to represent the architecture-specific parameters such as the warp size (32 on CUDA devices, 64 on AMD devices) and optimization parameters. Step 2 moves the identical kernel codes into the "common" folder we introduced in Sect. 3.2. We include the code in the "common" folder after setting the configuration variables in Step 3 and Step 4. Step 5 runs the script Cuda2Hip script detailed in Sect. 3.4 to generate the corresponding hip files. Ultimately, we modify the hip "config" file in Step 6. After completion of these steps, the validity and correctness of the porting effort is tested. This is realized by invoking GINKGO's unit test framework that employs googletest to check the correctness of the high performance kernels – in particular also the CUDA and HIP backends – against the reference kernels.

We note that GINKGO's cross-platform cooperative group extension presented in Sect. 3.3 dramatically reduces backend-specific implementations and allows to use a shared kernel in "common" for both, the NVIDIA and the HIP backend.

Algorithm 1: GINKGO's porting workflow

1: Use a variable to represent the architecture-specific parameters
2: Move all shared code into a "common" file
3: Set the architecture-specific parameters before including a "common" file
4: Include the "common" file
5: Use the Cuda2Hip script for converting the code
6: Modify the hip file "config" to support different architectures

3.6   Porting Statistics for Ginkgo

With the setup and tools described, extending the scope of GINKGO to cover also AMD GPUs is a smooth process. We acknowledge that some kernels that are heavily tuned for performance needed additional attention, most notably the multiprecision block-Jacobi kernel [4]. Aside from this, the addition of the HIP ecosystem required slight modifications to the library architecture, most importantly the addition of the "common" module containing the kernels that are identical up to parameter settings for the CUDA and the HIP ecosystems. In the left figure of Fig. 3, we visualize how existing code lines are relocated and new code lines are added when extending GINKGO's scope to support also HIP. The exact number of code lines contained in the distinct modules of the extended GINKGO library are listed in the right table of Fig. 3. We note that about one third of the code base is shared between the CUDA and the HIP executor, and that by creating the "common" folder we actually avoided duplicating 4,000 lines of code. The other modules each contain about 5,000 lines of code. While most submodules are comparable in size, the more significant differences for "base" and "component" stem from the differing comprehensiveness of the ecosystems and possibilities of architecture-specific optimization.

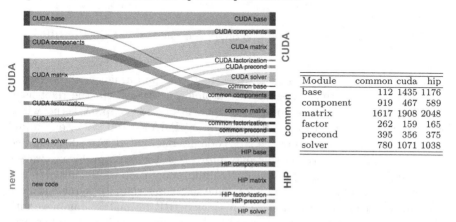

Module	common	cuda	hip
base	112	1435	1176
component	919	467	589
matrix	1617	1908	2048
factor	262	159	165
precond	395	356	375
solver	780	1071	1038

Fig. 3. Left: Reorganization of the GINKGO library to provide a HIP backend for AMD GPUs. Right: (Physical) Lines of code in the "common", "cuda", and "hip" modules of the GINKGO library, ignoring the unit tests.

4   Experiments

To assess how well the HIP ecosystem interfaces to the CUDA technology, we compare HIP code compiled for NVIDIA GPUs with native CUDA code. More precisely, we apply the porting workflow we described in Sect. 3 to high performance sparse linear algebra kernels of GINKGO's CUDA backend, and compare the performance of the generated HIP code when being compiled for NVIDIA GPUs with the original kernel performance. We run our experiments on NVIDIA's V100 (SXM2 16 GB) [8] with cuda 9.2.148 and hip 3.1.20044–3684ef8 (which is the latest version on Jan. 31 2020). We compare the Sellp, Coo, and cuSPARSE/hipSPARSE (Splib_Csr) SpMV kernels, and the Conjugate Gradient Solver employing the Sellp SpMV kernel for the Krylov subspace generation using either CUDA and HIP on the same device. For result reproducibility, we archive all performance results in a public repository[2]. We evaluate the performance of the GINKGO SpMV for more than 2,800 matrices from the SuiteSparse Matrix Collection [10]. We run two iterations for warm-up and ten iterations to obtain average performance values.

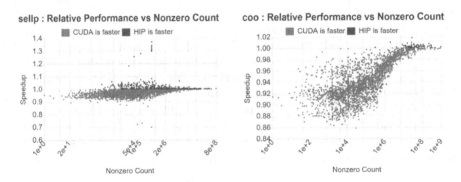

Fig. 4. Sellp SpMV (left) and Coo SpMV implemented in CUDA or HIP.

On the left-hand side of Fig. 4, we evaluate the performance for GINKGO's Sellp SpMV kernel, which does not use atomic operations. On the right-hand side of Fig. 4, we do the same comparison for GINKGO's Coo SpMV kernel which does rely on atomic operations. Running on NVIDIA's V100 GPU, one would expect to see small overhead of the HIP code interfacing CUDA code compared to native CUDA code. While this may prove true for most problems, we see some outliers where using the native CUDA implementation results in significant performance benefits. Surprisingly, for some test cases the HIP kernels achieve significantly better performance – even though HIP ultimately compiles with NVIDIA's nvcc compiler. The generated PTX code indicates that the differences may be attributed to slightly different types of load instructions being emitted, which in turn use different caches.

---

[2] https://github.com/ginkgo-project/ginkgo-data/tree/V100_cuda_hip.

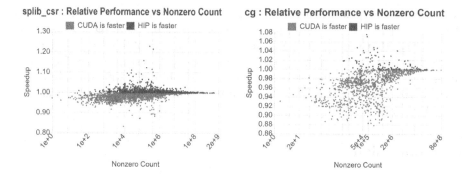

Fig. 5. Performance comparison for vendors' Csr SpMV (left) and 1,000 iterations of GINKGO's CG solver (right).

In Fig. 5 we do the same experiment for the vendors' Csr SpMV (left-hand side) and 1,000 iterations of GINKGO's Conjugate Gradient (CG) solver using GINKGO's Sellp SpMV (right-hand side). For the vendors' Csr SpMV comparison on the left, the performance differences reflect only the overhead of the invocation of cuSPARSE by hipSPARSE. In the CG performance comparison on the right, we observe up to 15% performance degradation coming from the aforementioned differences in code generation. This is in accordance with Philip C. Roth [9] who compares the performance of CUDA and HIP for the scalable heterogeneous computing (SHOC) benchmark [5].

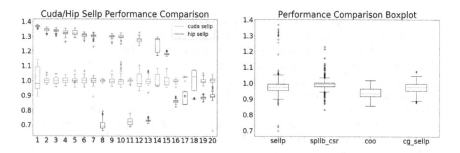

Fig. 6. Left: Performance variance for outliers in Sellp SpMV kernel analysis (Fig. 4). All performance is normalized to the mean performance of the CUDA backend, CUDA performance in red, (relative) performance of the HIP backend in blue. Right: Performance statistics for all test cases and all kernels/algorithms. (Color figure online)

As some of the performance differences in Fig. 4 are significant, we investigate in Fig. 6 (left) the mean and variance of the 20 most significant outliers in the Sellp SpMV analysis in Fig. 4 (left). These statistics are collected from over 20 runs, each averaging the kernel characteristics over 100 invocations. Acknowledging the reproducibility of these outliers, we emphasize that they are still almost negligible when considering the complete test suite of more than 2,800 test matrices: The performance ratio statistics on the right-hand side of Fig. 6 reveal that the performance means for all functionalities are just slightly below 1.0. Furthermore, 50% of the test cases show less than 3% performance difference, and 90% of the test cases show less than 10% performance difference. This reveals that HIP introduces only negligible overhead when comparing to CUDA-native code.

5   Conclusion

We elaborated how we extend the hardware scope of the GINKGO linear algebra package to feature a HIP backend for AMD GPUs. We discussed the porting effort, and how the use of a shared code base reduces to minimize code duplication in a library providing native backends for NVIDIA and AMD GPUs. We also detailed the addition of functionality currently lacking in the HIP ecosystem and evaluated the performance price of compiling HIP code for NVIDIA architectures. We found that a significant portion of sparse linear algebra kernels allows for good platform portability. In future, we will create a Intel GPU backend and compare the porting process with the HIP backend integration.

Acknowledgements. This research was supported by the Exascale Computing Project (17-SC-20-SC) and the Helmholtz Impuls und Vernetzungsfond VH-NG-1241.

References

1. The Top 500 List. https://www.top500.org/
2. The US Exascale Computing Project (ECP). https://www.exascaleproject.org/
3. AMD: HIP. https://github.com/ROCm-Developer-Tools/HIP
4. Anzt, H., Dongarra, J., Flegar, G., Higham, N.J., Quintana-Ortí, E.S.: Adaptive precision in block-Jacobi preconditioning for iterative sparse linear system solvers. Concurrency Comput. Pract. Exp. **31**(6), e4460 (2019)
5. Danalis, A., et al.: The scalable heterogeneous computing (SHOC) benchmark suite. In: Proceedings of the 3rd Workshop on General-Purpose Computation on Graphics Processing Units, pp. 63–74 (2010). https://doi.org/10.1145/1735688. 1735702. dl.acm.org
6. Google. https://github.com/google/googletest
7. Kuznetsov, E., Stegailov, V.: Porting CUDA-based molecular dynamics algorithms to AMD ROCm platform using hip framework: performance analysis. In: Voevodin, V., Sobolev, S. (eds.) RuSCDays 2019. CCIS, vol. 1129, pp. 121–130. Springer, Cham (2019). https://doi.org/10.1007/978-3-030-36592-9_11
8. NVIDIA Corp.: Whitepaper: NVIDIA TESLA V100 GPU Architecture (2017)
9. Roth, P.C.: Experiences with the Heterogeneouscompute Interface for Portability (HIP) on OLCF Summit, October 2019. https://www.olcf.ornl.gov/wp-content/ uploads/2019/10/Roth-HIP-on-Summit-20191009.pdf
10. SuiteSparse: Matrix Collection. https://sparse.tamu.edu. Accessed Jan 2020

11. Sun, Y., et al.: Evaluating performance tradeoffs on the radeon open compute platform. In: 2018 IEEE International Symposium on Performance Analysis of Systems and Software (ISPASS), pp. 209–218, April 2018. https://doi.org/10.1109/ISPASS.2018.00034

12. Zubair, M., Warner, J., Wagner, D.: Optimization of a solver for computational materials and structures problems on NVIDIA Volta and AMD Instinct GPUs. In: 2019 IEEE/ACM 10th Workshop on Latest Advances in Scalable Algorithms for Large-Scale Systems (ScalA), pp. 9–16, November 2019. https://doi.org/10.1109/ScalA49573.2019.00007

An Edge Attribute-Wise Partitioning and Distributed Processing of R-GCN Using GPUs

Tokio Kibata[✉], Mineto Tsukada, and Hiroki Matsutani

Keio University, 3-14-1, Hiyoshi, Yokohama 223-8522, Japan
{tokio,tsukada,matutani}@arc.ics.keio.ac.jp

Abstract. R-GCN (Relational Graph Convolutional Network) is one of GNNs (Graph Neural Networks). The model tries predicting latent information by considering directions and types of edges in graph-structured data, such as knowledge bases. The model builds weight matrices to each edge attribute. Thus, the size of the neural network increases linearly with the number of edge types. Although GPUs can be used for accelerating the R-GCN processing, there is a possibility that the size of weight matrices exceeds GPU device memory. To address this issue, in this paper, an edge attribute-wise partitioning is proposed for R-GCN. The proposed partitioning divides the model and graph data so that R-GCN can be accelerated by using multiple GPUs. Also, the proposed approach can be applied to sequential execution on a single GPU. Both the cases can accelerate the R-GCN processing with large graph data, where the original model cannot be fit into a device memory of a single GPU without partitioning. Experimental results demonstrate that our partitioning method accelerates R-GCN by up to 3.28 times using four GPUs compared to CPU execution for a dataset with more than 1.6 million nodes and 5 million edges. Also, the proposed approach can accelerate the execution even with a single GPU by 1.55 times compared to the CPU execution for a dataset with 0.8 million nodes and 2 million edges.

Keywords: GPU · R-GCN · GNN · Graph data · Knowledge base

1 Introduction

In recent years, it is expected that the next step of deep learning would be responding to the various structured data. Indeed, conventional deep learning models typically use data represented in Euclidean space. Meanwhile, one of new streams of deep learning is to use graph-structured data, which is represented in non-Euclidean space, such as GNNs (Graph Neural Networks) [7]. An algorithm applying CNN (Convolutional Neural Networks) for graph-structured data, called ConvGNNs (Convolutional GNNs), demonstrates practical results [3,4].

© Springer Nature Switzerland AG 2021
B. Balis et al. (Eds.): Euro-Par 2020 Workshops, LNCS 12480, pp. 122–134, 2021.
https://doi.org/10.1007/978-3-030-71593-9_10

R-GCN (Relational-Graph Convolutional Network) [6] is a derivative model of ConvGNNs and aims at filling in a lack of knowledge base. Missing data in a knowledge base can be classified into two types. One is a lack of attributes of nodes, and the other is a lack of links between nodes, called edges, on the graph. The edges have relational types of two nodes in some cases. Considering the edge types, R-GCN builds weight matrices for each type and direction (i.e., in and out of node) of edges. When predicting latent node attributes or edges on GNNs, the scalability problems always lie on. It is challenging to parallelize the model or graph processing of R-GCN using multiple GPUs for accelerating the execution. Particularly, R-GCN has a specific issue of scalability, because the size of weight matrices increases linearly with the number of edge types in addition to the number of nodes when these features are defined as one-hot vectors. There is a possibility that the size of weight matrices exceeds GPU device memory. To address this issue, in this paper, we propose a method to partition the graph-and-model simultaneously on R-GCN in order to accelerate the model training using one or more GPUs for large graph-structured datasets. More specifically, a node-wise partitioning was already used for [3,10], in this paper we propose an edge-wise partitioning method.

This paper is organized as follows. As related work, GNNs are overviewed, and especially R-GCN is detailed in Sect. 2. Section 3 describes the proposed method, and Sect. 4 shows its evaluation results. Conclusions and future work are discussed in Sect. 5.

2   Related Work

In this section, the overview of ConvGNNs is presented. R-GCN model is then described as a target of the proposed partitioning method.

2.1   ConvGNNs

GNNs are formulated by aggregation layer and combination layer [8]. The aggregation layer defines how to aggregate adjacent nodes' features. The combination layer defines a method to concatenate the result of the aggregation layer and a target node's feature. The l-th aggregation layer's output $a_v^{(l)}$, and the l-th combination layer's output $h_v^{(l)}$ for the target node v are defined as follows:

$$a_v^{(l)} = AGGREGATE^{(l)}\ (\{h_u^{(l-1)} : u \in \mathcal{N}_{(v)}\}), \tag{1}$$

$$h_v^{(l)} =\ COMBINE^{(l)}\ (h_v^{(l-1)}, a_v^{(l)}), \tag{2}$$

where $\mathcal{N}(v)$ is a set of adjacent nodes of node v, $a_v^{(l)}$ is an aggregated feature vector of adjacent nodes, and $h_v^{(l)}$ is a feature vector of the node v at l-th layer. In ConvGNNs, their weight matrices are updated with those multiplied by the adjacent node's feature vectors. For example, the l-th aggregation layer and the

l-th combination layer of GraphSage [5], one of ConvGNNs, are formulated as follows:

$$a_v^{(l)} = MAX(\{W_a^{(l)} \cdot h_u^{(l-1)}, \forall u \in \mathcal{N}(v)\}), \tag{3}$$

$$h_v^{(l)} = W_h^{(l)} \cdot [h_v^{(l-1)}, a_v^{(l)}], \tag{4}$$

where W_a and W_h are weight matrices for aggregation and combination layers, respectively. MAX is an element-wise max-pooling and the combination layer represents a linear mapping. Such approaches have a problem with the size of graph-structured data. Especially when GPUs are used for the acceleration of the model training, the graph-structured data are required to be partitioned into smaller batches. In GraphSage, a node-wise partitioning is applied to solve the problem. The technique to make batches is based on node sampling located around the target nodes, for example, by random walk. As a result, the graph is divided into batches so that each batch can be fit into a GPU device memory. Pinsage [10], an extension of GraphSage, is an item recommendation system for a web-scale graph-structured data, which is composed of three billion nodes and 18 billion edges with data-parallel processing using multiple GPUs, where these GPUs share the same parameters and operate different batches. The size of batches is determined based on the sampling range. GIN [8] is another GNN that has shown a stable and high prediction accuracy. Several ConvGNNs have been extended to make predictions in relational graphs [9].

2.2 R-GCN

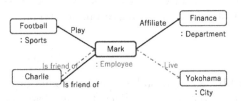

Fig. 1. Example of relational graph.

The R-GCN model aims to complete a lack of information on a knowledge base. Figure 1 illustrates an example of a knowledge base, composed by a triplet (subject, predicate, and object). In Fig. 1, the graph data contains information that "(Mark) (Play)s (Football)." Knowledge base requires two prediction tasks: entity clustering and link prediction. The entity clustering task corresponds to the prediction of Mark's occupation, "Employee." Completing the link "Live" from "Mark" to "Yokohama" is one of the link predictions. Note that it needs to consider edge directions and types. R-GCN introduces these edge attributes to conventional GCNs.

R-GCN models have weight matrices W_r, which are corresponding to each edge attribute r. A set of weight matrices takes edge types and directions into account. Also, W_0 is defined as self-loops' weight matrix that is a feed-forward from the previous layer. More specifically, a hidden vector h_v of a node v on an $(l+1)$-th layer can be calculated as follows [6]:

$$h_v^{(l+1)} = \sigma(\sum_{r \in \mathcal{R}} \sum_{u \in \mathcal{N}_v^r} \frac{1}{c_{v,r}} W_r^{(l)} h_u^{(l)} + W_0^{(l)} h_v^{(l)}), \tag{5}$$

where $\mathcal{N}_v^r$ is a set of adjacent nodes connected to node v with edge attribute r. $c_{v,r}$ is a normalization factor for normalizing the difference of node degree, and generally it is defined as $c_{v,r} = |\mathcal{N}_v^r|$. We here define two sublayers: matrix-operation layer and adding layer. The matrix-operation layer is in charge of the computation of $\frac{1}{c_{v,r}} W_r^{(l)} h_u^{(l)}$ and $W_0^{(l)} h_v^{(l)}$. The adding layer executes the other operations. The loss function for a model training is defined as follow:

$$\mathcal{L} = -\sum_{i \in \mathcal{Y}} \sum_{k=1}^{K} t_{v,k} \ln h_{v,k}^{(L)}, \tag{6}$$

where L is the number of hidden layers, $t_{v,k}$ is the k-th cluster's label on node v, and $h_{v,k}$ is the k-th entry of the network output for the node v. $\mathcal{Y}$ is a set of nodes that have labels. For the model training, there are two regularization methods to reduce the number of learnable parameters. With the regularization of *basis*-decomposition [6], weight matrices W_r are defined as follows:

$$W_r = \sum_{b=1}^{B} a_{r,b}^{(l)} V_b^{(l)}. \tag{7}$$

This regularization means that weight matrices are defined as a linear combination of basis transformations $V_b^{(l)} \in \mathbb{R}^{d^{(l+1)} \times d^{(l)}}$ with coefficients $a_{r,b}$ dependent on each edge attribute r. Also, weight matrices consume the memory only when the operation is executed on a layer that is related to the weight matrices. However, the size of weight matrices, used at the same time, increases proportionally to the number of edge attributes. Thus, the model has a scalability issue, especially under the condition where initial node features are set as one-hot vectors. As a result, it needs to partition both a graph and a model for acceleration with GPUs, as well as typical deep learning models.

3   Proposed Method

In this section, we introduce our edge attribute-wise graph partitioning method and a graph-and-model simultaneous parallel execution on R-GCN.

3.1 Edge Attribute-Wise Partitioning

In Sect. 2.2, we mentioned that the partitioning of both the graph and model is required to use GPUs for accelerating R-GCN execution with a large graph-structured data, because GPU device memory size is strictly limited. Generally, for executing deep learning on a GPU, the total size of a model and training data necessarily fits into the GPU device memory size. However, in the case of R-GCN model, the weight matrices W_r are required for each edge attribute r, which means that the model size increases proportionally to the number of edge attributes. This is an inherent scalability issue of R-GCN, which is different from other ConvGNNs. There are two ways of partitioning for fitting data and model sizes into GPU device memory: node-wise partitioning and edge attribute-wise partitioning. The node-wise graph partitioning is one of the existing solutions [3,10] to resolve the scalability problem on GNN models, making some batches by sampling adjacent nodes around target nodes. In this paper, on the other hand, we propose an edge attribute-wise partitioning to give a solution for the size of graph data as well as the size of the model. The benefit of the edge attribute-wise partitioning over the node-wise partitioning is as follows. Although the node-wise partitioning mainly aims at data-parallel computing, the partitioning results in an overlapping of weight matrices between submodels on R-GCN. In the worst case, the submodels' size is not reduced, and thus the scalability problem on R-GCN model would not always be solved. Meanwhile, the proposed edge attribute-wise partitioning aims at dividing a graph into some subgraphs in such a way that each edge attribute is exclusively divided. Here, each submodel should only have a weight matrix corresponding to the edge type that each subgraph has. Thus the size of the submodels is always scaled down. The memory space complexities of their weight matrices for input, hidden, and output layers are $O(|R_i||V_i||H|)$, $O(|R_i||H||H|)$, and $O(|R_i||H||O|)$, respectively, where $|R_i|$ is the number of edge attributes on the i-th subgraph, $|V_i|$ is the number of nodes on the i-th subgraph, $|H|$ is the number of hidden units, and $|O|$ is the dimension of output. We notice that there is no difference in the learning outcome between the division and the non-division implementations.

Figure 2 illustrates the concept of the graph partitioning, which is executed for a graph with four edge attributes. At first, a parent graph, i.e., the original graph data, is partitioned into portions, each having exactly one edge attribute. Subgraphs are finally constructed by assembling any of the portions. We propose two methods for grouping the portions into subgraphs. The first method that considers the number of edges in each subgraph and the second method that considers the number of edge attributes in each subgraph. In the first method, portions are distributed into subgraphs, minimizing the difference in the number of edges in subgraphs. In the second method, we sort portions in descending order by the number of edges. The sorted portions are assigned to one of the subgraphs in ascending order (subgraphs 1 to N) and then those in descending order (subgraphs N to 1) repeatedly. Here, we regard the portion including self-loops as a subgraph in distinction from others to reduce the size of submodels. The size of weight matrices depends on the number of nodes when initial node features are defined as one-hot vectors of local node IDs in each subgraph. Since the self-loop exists in all the nodes, the number of nodes in a self-loop subgraph is equal to that of the parent graph. A subgraph, including self-loops, increases the number of nodes in the subgraph, resulting in a larger submodel. To avoid this, we distinguish the self-loops from the others.

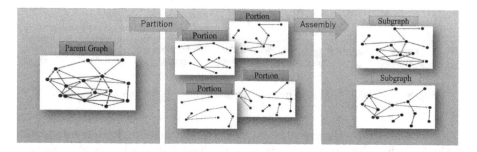

Fig. 2. Example of edge attribute-wise partitioning for graph with four edge attributes, making two subgraphs.

3.2 Graph-and-Model Simultaneous Partitioning

In this section, we propose the implementation of R-GCN using multiple GPUs. We note here that R-GCN has huge weight matrices when training a large graph data, especially on the input layer, because the scale grows proportionally with the numbers of nodes and the edge attributes. The edge attribute-wise partitioning can reduce not only batch sizes in the graph but also the size of weight matrices in each submodel. We introduce the following parallel and sequential implementations:

1. *CPU + MultiGPUs* setting: parallel execution using multiple GPUs, and
2. *CPU + 1GPU* setting: time-multiplexed sequential execution using a single GPU.

Figure 3 shows an execution flow on a matrix-operation layer of R-GCN under the CPU + MultiGPUs setting. In the execution, at first, subgraphs are generated by the edge attribute-wise partitioning. Then, the features of subgraphs are transferred to GPUs. In each GPU, weight matrices corresponding to the subgraph's edge attributes are set by computation of *basis*-decomposition regularization, and then the results are returned to a host CPU. In addition, the subgraph with only self-loops is operated on one of the GPUs by sharing this GPU with another subgraph. After that, the results are copied to the parent graph before executing. Then, the adding layer is executed for the parent graph.

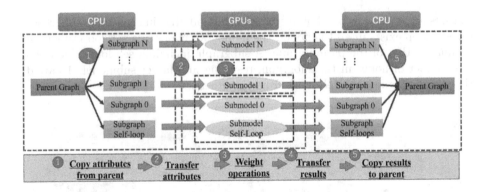

Fig. 3. Execution flow on a matrix-operation layer before an adding layer.

Figure 4 illustrates the execution to create weight matrices in each submodel. By the *basis*-decomposition regularization, the base matrices V should be shared with all the GPUs to make each set of weight matrices. That is a reason why basis transformations V is replicated to the other GPUs. Then, each GPU prepares the set of weight matrices corresponding to a transferred subgraph, by computing a replica of V and edge attribute coefficients a_r. CPU + 1GPU is also based on the edge attribute-wise partitioning. With this setting, each subgraph is transferred into a single GPU, and the submodel is executed on the GPU sequentially. We evaluate the execution time for the two implementations: CPU + MultiGPUs setting and CPU + 1GPU sequential execution setting.

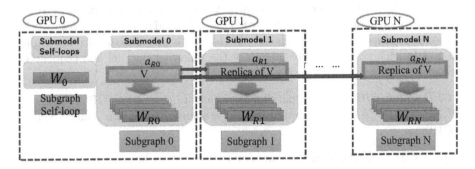

Fig. 4. Creating submodels on a matrix-operation layer under the *basis*-decomposition regularization condition, and distributing subgraphs on each GPU.

4   Evaluations

In this section, we evaluate the effectiveness of our proposal, the graph-and-model simultaneous partitioning on R-GCN. The evaluation environment is shown in Table 1.

Table 1. Execution environment.

OS	Ubuntu 16.04.6 LTS
CPU	Intel Core i7-6800K (6C) 3.40 GHz
GPU	NVIDIA GeForce GTX 1080Ti (11 GB GDDR5X)
DRAM	32 GB

4.1 Baseline

Implementation. We evaluate the execution time for model training by comparing three implementations with one or more GPUs to CPU only setting. Three implementations are as follows:

1. GPUonly where all the parameters and graph data are allocated on a single GPU without CPU,
2. CPU + MultiGPUs setting using 2–4 GPUs based on the model and graph simultaneously partitioning, and
3. CPU + 1GPU setting using a single GPU sequentially based on the model-and-graph simultaneous partitioning.

The second and third settings were introduced in Sect. 3.2. We use Pytorch as a deep learning framework. Also, DGL (Deep Graph library) [1] is used for operations on the graph-structured data, such as an aggregation of node information. As a baseline, we use a DGL's tutorial code for the implementations of CPU setting and GPUonly setting. In this paper, R-GCN model has two layers with 16 hidden units for BGS and 10 hidden units for AM and a random graph. Also, we set the number of basis transformations as 40, and we use SGD as the optimizer.

Datasets. We use three datasets: BGS, AM, and a random graph. BGS and AM are provided in Resource Description Framework format [5], and the random graph is generated with the Barabasi-Albert model [2]. Table 2 lists their parameters: the numbers of nodes, edge attributes, edges, labeled nodes, and classes. The datasets are preprocessed to fit DGL graph format and R-GCN model. Firstly, self-loops are added to graph data. In addition, the edges of the graph data are duplicated by considering edge directions. The number of edge attributes on the graph data becomes twice the original dataset by this preprocessing. In the graph, distant nodes which are more than three-hop away from the target node are pruned, because we assume a 2-layer model in which the three-hop away nodes do not affect outputs of the target nodes. We delete edges whose edge attributes are applied for less than 150 edges in the case of AM.

4.2 Result of Graph Partitioning

The proposed graph partitioning method is used to generate the subgraphs. Here, the number of nodes is related to the scale of the submodels in the input

Table 2. Datasets: BGS, AM, and random graph.

	BGS	AM	Random graph
# of nodes	333,845	1,666,764	800,000
# of edge attributes	103	120	100
# of edges	916,199	5,196,085	2,399,998
# of labeled nodes	146	1,000	400
# of classes	2	11	8

layer under the condition where the initial node features are defined as one-hot vectors. The number of edges determines the computation cost, and the number of edge attributes is proportional to the scale of the submodel. In this paper, we partition graphs and models into subgraphs in two ways as proposed in Sect. 3.1. In Sect. 4.3, the execution time of R-GCN is evaluated with GPUs while changing the number of subgraphs. Tables 3 and 4 show the results of partitioning each graph-structured data into four subgraphs and a subgraph that has only self-loops. We found that the way considering the number of edge attributes in each subgraph can minimize the size of weight matrices on each GPU. Thus, this approach is used in the following experiments.

Table 3. Parameters of subgraphs when applying edge attribute-wise partitioning, considering the number of edges in each subgraph.

(a) BGS

	Sub-0	Sub-1	Sub-2	Sub-3	Sub-self
# of nodes	205,111	279,072	171,265	84,573	333,017
# of edges	457,470	457,467	457,407	457,534	333,017
# of edge attributes	34	35	85	40	1

(b) AM

	Sub-0	Sub-1	Sub-2	Sub-3	Sub-self
# of nodes	1,013,531	1,073,744	1,118,582	915,739	1,203,676
# of edges	2,598,224	2,598,221	2,598,263	2,598,414	1,203,676
# of edge attributes	26	40	102	72	1

(c) Random graph

	Sub-0	Sub-1	Sub-2	Sub-3	Sub-self
# of nodes	656,908	651,308	656,959	663,528	800,000
# of edges	798,697	785,283	798,684	817,332	800,000
# of edge attributes	50	49	50	51	1

Table 4. Parameters of subgraphs when applying the edge-attributes partitioning, considering the number of edge attributes in each subgraph.

(a) BGS

	Sub-0	Sub-1	Sub-2	Sub-3	Sub-self
# of nodes	177,298	145,554	258,285	286,893	333,017
# of edges	460,080	460,080	454,859	454,859	333,017
# of edge attributes	49	49	48	48	1

(b) AM

	Sub-0	Sub-1	Sub-2	Sub-3	Sub-self
# of nodes	986,425	986,250	1,035,928	1,035,928	1,203,676
# of edges	2,901,669	2901,669	2,294,892	2,294,892	1,203,676
# of edge attributes	60	60	60	60	1

(c) Random graph

	Sub-0	Sub-1	Sub-2	Sub-3	Sub-self
# of nodes	657,309	644,850	650,788	657,179	800,000
# of edges	799,962	799,962	800,036	800,036	800,000
# of edge attributes	50	50	50	50	1

4.3 Execution Time

Table 5 shows a summary of the execution time. Although the datasets were also executed with GPUonly setting, the out of GPU memory occurred in the cases of AM and random graph. Especially for AM, the size of weight matrices on the input layer was over 17 GB, which explicitly demonstrates the necessity of the proposed model partitioning on R-GCN model with a large graph data. This motivates us the graph-and-model partitioning. Also, we remark that CPU + 4GPUs setting can accelerate the model training for all the datasets compared to CPU setting: 3.88 times for BGS, 3.28 times for AM, and 2.60 times for the random graph. We notice that in the backward phase for updating the parameters, CPU + 4GPUs setting is advantageous. On the other hand, in the forward phase, its advantage is not as much as in the backward phase, because the data transfer overhead becomes significant. Please note that, if a target graph data is small enough to execute GPUonly setting, this setting is the best choice.

Figure 5 shows the results of CPU + MultiGPUs setting and CPU + 1GPU setting while changing the number of GPUs and the number of graph divisions, respectively. Note that the out of memory occurred in the case of AM. We found firstly that the growth in the number of GPUs improves the performance. For BGS, the acceleration rate increases from 3.42 (CPU + 2GPUs) to 3.88 times (CPU + 4GPUs) compared to CPU setting. For the random graph, the acceleration rate increases from 2.48 (CPU + 3GPUs) to 2.60 times (CPU + 4GPUs) compared to CPU setting. The reason for the small increase in speed by increasing the number of GPUs is due to the processing of the aggregation layer on

Table 5. Mean training times (Forward, Backward, and Full) per epoch [sec] for executions on CPU, GPUonly, and CPU + 4GPU settings.

		BGS	AM	Random graph
Forward	CPU	1.26	4.86	1.94
	GPUonly	0.049	N/A	N/A
	CPU + 4GPU	0.80	3.68	1.34
Backward	CPU	7.78	37.07	9.92
	GPUonly	0.003	N/A	N/A
	CPU + 4GPU	1.53	9.11	3.21
Full	CPU	9.06	41.92	11.86
	GPUonly	0.052	N/A	N/A
	CPU + 4GPU	2.33	12.78	4.55

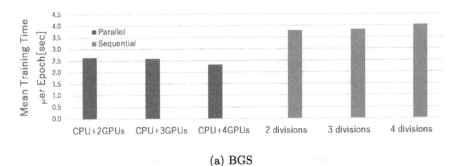

(a) BGS

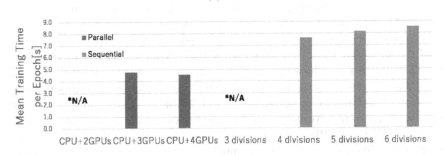

(b) Random Graph

Fig. 5. Execution time per epoch [sec] of BGS and random graph for CPU + MultiGPUs settings with 2–4 GPUs and CPU + 1GPU settings with 3–6 divisions. The number of divisions is defined as the number of subgraphs except for their self-loop subgraph, and *N/A indicates the out of memory occurred during execution.

CPU and feature exchange between the parent graph and subgraphs. Although the performance of the CPU + 1GPU is inferior to CPU + MultiGPUs setting, this setting accelerates the execution time by up to 2.38 and 1.55 times for BGS and the random graph, respectively, compared to CPU setting. We remark that our proposal can accelerate R-GCN even with a single GPU for training R-GCN model for a large graph. We also found here that the number of divisions is related to the performance, and minimizing the number of divisions can improve the performance. In the forward phase, the computation results are accumulated on a GPU and consume the memory capacity. As a result, CPU + 1GPU setting with three divisions for the random graph introduces the out of memory even though the execution on CPU + 3GPUs setting has been successfully done.

5   Conclusions

In this paper, we presented an edge attribute-wise graph partitioning and the graph-and-model simultaneous partitioning method on R-GCN to accelerate using one or more GPUs with large graph-structured data. Experimental results with CPU + MultiGPUs setting show that it can accelerate the model training of R-GCN with AM dataset with over 1.6 million nodes, 5 million edges, and 120 edge attributes. Besides, the CPU + 1GPU setting outperforms CPU setting by 1.55 times for a dataset with 0.8 million nodes, 2 million edges, and 100 edge attributes even with a single GPU. The result opens up possibilities to accelerate training R-GCN by using one or multiple GPUs, each having limited device memory capacity. As future work, we need to consider smaller batches with fine-grained mini-batch execution scheduling to release the memory allocation more frequently to utilize the GPU device memory more efficiently.

Acknowledgements. This work was partially supported by JSPS KAKENHI Grant Number JP19H04117.

References

1. Deep Graph Library. https://www.dgl.ai/pages/about.html
2. Albert, R., Barabasi, A.L.: Statistical Mechanics of Complex Networks. Rev. Mod. Phys. **74**, 47 (2002)
3. Hamilton, W., Ying, Z., Leskovec, J.: Inductive representation learning on large-graphs. In: Proceedings of the Neural Information Processing Systems (NeurIPS 2017), pp. 1024–1034 (2017)
4. Kipf, T.N., Welling, M.: Semi-supervised classification with graph convolutional networks. In: Proceedings of the International Conference on Learning Representations (ICLR 2017) (2017)
5. Ristoski, P., de Vries, G.K.D., Paulheim, H.: A collection of benchmark datasets for systematic evaluations of machine learning on the semantic web. In: Groth, P., et al. (eds.) ISWC 2016. LNCS, vol. 9982, pp. 186–194. Springer, Cham (2016). https://doi.org/10.1007/978-3-319-46547-0_20
6. Schlichtkrull, M., Kipf, T.N., Bloem, P., Berg, R.V.d., Titov, I., Welling, M.: Modeling relational data with graph convolutinal networks. arXiv preprint arXiv:1703.06103v4, October 2017
7. Wu, Z., Pan, S., Chen, F., Long, G., Zhang, C., Yu, P.S.: A comprehensive survey on graph neural networks. arXiv:1901.00596v4, March 2019

8. Xu, K., Hu, W., Leskovec, J., Jegelka, S.: How powerful are graph neural networks. In: Proceedings of the International Conference on Learning Representations (ICLR 2019) (2019)
9. Ye, R., Yujie Fang, H.Z., Wang, M.: A vectorized relational graph convolutional network for multi-relational network alignment. In: Proceedings of the International Joint Conference on Artificial Intelligence (IJCAI 2019), pp. 4135–4141 (2019)
10. Ying, R., He, R., Chen, K., Eksombatchai, P., Hamilton, W.L., Leskovec, J.: Graph convolutional neural networks for web-scale recommender systems. In: Proceedings of the International Conference on Knowledge Discovery & Data Mining (KDD 2018), pp. 974–983, August 2018

Parallelization of the k-means Algorithm in a Spectral Clustering Chain on CPU-GPU Platforms

Guanlin He[1(✉)], Stéphane Vialle[1], and Marc Baboulin[2]

[1] Université Paris-Saclay, CNRS, CentraleSupélec, Laboratoire de Recherche en Informatique, 91405 Orsay, France
guanlin.he@lri.fr, stephane.vialle@centralesupelec.fr
[2] Université Paris-Saclay, CNRS, Laboratoire de Recherche en Informatique, 91405 Orsay, France
baboulin@lri.fr

Abstract. k-means is a standard algorithm for clustering data. It constitutes generally the final step in a more complex chain of high quality spectral clustering. However this chain suffers from lack of scalability when addressing large datasets. This can be overcome by applying also the k-means algorithm as a pre-processing task to reduce the input data instances. We describe parallel optimization techniques for the k-means algorithm on CPU and GPU. Experimental results on synthetic dataset illustrate the numerical accuracy and performance of our implementations.

Keywords: k-means algorithm · Spectral clustering · Heterogeneous CPU-GPU computing

1 Introduction

Clustering refers to the process that aims at revealing the intrinsic structure of data by automatically grouping data instances into meaningful subsets called clusters. The intra-cluster similarity is supposed to be high while the inter-cluster similarity should be low. It is one of the most important tasks in machine learning and data mining and has numerous applications, such as image segmentation [16], video segmentation [17], document analysis [9], etc.

The k-means algorithm [13] is one of the most widely used clustering methods. It is a distance-based method that can efficiently find convex clusters, but it usually fails to discover non-convex clusters. It also relies on an appropriate selection of initial centroids to avoid being stuck in local minima solutions.

Spectral clustering [14] has gained popularity in the last two decades. Based on graph theory, it embeds data into the eigenspace of graph Laplacian and

G. He—Supported by the China Scholarship Council (No. 201807000143).

© Springer Nature Switzerland AG 2021
B. Balis et al. (Eds.): Euro-Par 2020 Workshops, LNCS 12480, pp. 135–147, 2021.
https://doi.org/10.1007/978-3-030-71593-9_11

then performs k-means clustering on the embedding representation. Compared to classical k-means, spectral clustering has many advantages. First, it is able to discover non-convex clusters. Then, it has no problem of initialization and can lead to a global solution. Furthermore, one can exploit the unique "eigengap heuristic" [12] to estimate the number of clusters if the clusters are distinctly separated. Finally, spectral clustering algorithms have the potential to be efficiently implemented on HPC platforms since they require substantial linear algebra computations that can be processed using existing HPC libraries. However, spectral clustering has in general a computational cost of $\mathcal{O}(N^3)$ where N is the number of data instances [20]. This can be a critical issue when dealing with large-scale applications where N can be of order 10^6 or even larger. To overcome this difficulty, some researchers reduce the computational complexity of spectral clustering through methodological changes, e.g., power iteration clustering [11]. It is also possible to use approximation or summarization techniques so that only a small subset of data is involved in the complex computation, e.g., sparsification [4], Nyström approximation [6], or representatives extraction (using a preliminary k-means step)[20]. Moreover, another powerful way is to accelerate spectral clustering on parallel and distributed architectures, where using CPU-GPU heterogeneous platforms is particularly attractive because it combines the strengths of both processors. Specifically, CPUs are efficient in performing traditional computation tasks and have much more memory space than GPUs, while GPUs provide high performance in mathematically intensive computations.

We are interested in proposing a general CPU-GPU-based implementation of spectral clustering that can address large problems. There are several related studies. Zheng et al. [22] present a parallelization of spectral clustering and implement it on CPU and on GPU separately, but the performance for calculating the affinity matrix remains to be improved and the situation is not considered when a matrix is too large to be loaded into the device memory. Sundaram and Keutzer [17] apply spectral clustering for long term video segmentation on a cluster of GPUs. However, their implementation is dedicated to video segmentation and there is no measurement of speedup. Jin and JaJa [8] present a hybrid implementation of spectral clustering on CPU-GPU platforms for problems with a large number of clusters, but the considered datasets are of medium size and the eigensolver performance appears limited.

In this paper, we consider the parallelization of the processing chain of large-scale spectral clustering by combining the use of representatives extraction with hybrid CPU-GPU computing. The main contributions of this paper are optimized implementations on CPU and GPU for the k-means algorithm, which are two steps of the global processing chain of spectral clustering. To our knowledge, most of the existing works related to parallel k-means algorithm on CPU (e.g., [3,10]) and on GPU (e.g., [3,5]) do not consider the issue of numerical accuracy that may occur in the update phase due to the propagation of round-off errors and that can lead to poor clustering quality. In this paper we address both high performance of the algorithm and numerical accuracy in the update phase of k-means clustering.

The remainder of this paper is organized as follows. Section 2 describes the computational chain for spectral clustering. In Sect. 3 we present our parallel implementations of k-means algorithm on CPU and GPU with the related optimizations. The experimental evaluation of our code is then presented in Sect. 4 and we conclude in Sect. 5.

2 A Computational Chain for Spectral Clustering

Spectral clustering has many slightly different algorithms. Here, we present the main steps of spectral clustering according to [12,14]. Given a set of N data instances of Dim dimensions: $x_1, ..., x_N$ in $\mathbb{R}^{Dim}$ that are supposed to be grouped into k_c clusters, the three main steps of spectral clustering are the following (see also the right part of Fig. 1):

1. **Construct the similarity matrix S.** The similarity graph, which can be represented by an $N \times N$ similarity matrix S, is used to model the similarity between data instances. ε-*neighborhood*, k-*nearest neighbors*, and *full connection* are three common ways to construct the similarity graph [12]. The first two ways yield typically sparse similarity matrix while the last one generates dense matrix. The degree matrix D is a diagonal matrix that can be easily derived from S with $d_i = \sum_{j=1}^{N} s_{ij}$. The unnormalized graph Laplacian is defined as $L = D - S$ and can be further normalized as the symmetrix matrix $L_{sym} = D^{-1/2}LD^{-1/2}$ [12]. Some other researchers define $L_{sym} = D^{-1/2}SD^{-1/2}$ that is normalized from S [14].
2. **Compute the first k_c eigenvectors $e_1, ..., e_{k_c}$ of graph Laplacian L_{sym}.** Here, by saying "the first k_c eigenvectors", we refer to the eigenvectors corresponding to the k_c smallest eigenvalues if graph Laplacian is normalized from L, or the k_c largest eigenvalues if normalized from S. Let E denote the $N \times k_c$ matrix containing the k_c eigenvectors as columns, then form the matrix T by normalizing each row of E to 1.
3. **Perform final k-means clustering.** Each row of T can be considered as the embedding representation in $\mathbb{R}^{k_c}$ of the original data instance with the same row number. Therefore, performing k-means clustering on the rows of T allows to obtain the k_c clusters of original data instances.

It can be seen that spectral clustering involves linear algebra computations, especially in the first two steps. This can be achieved using GPU computing and specifically some highly optimized CUDA libraries provided by NVIDIA, such as cuBLAS, cuSPARSE, cuSOLVER and nvGRAPH [15] or a public domain library like MAGMA [18]. If a matrix is sparse, e.g., the similarity matrix for ε-neighborhood graph or k-nearest neighbors graph, we can use the cuSPARSE library. The cuSOLVER library can be used for eigenvector computations in spectral clustering. Furthermore, the nvGRAPH, a library dedicated to graph analytics, contains an API for spectral clustering. However, the API has two important limits. First, it requires the number of clusters as an input in the configuration of spectral clustering (which, in practice, may be difficult to know

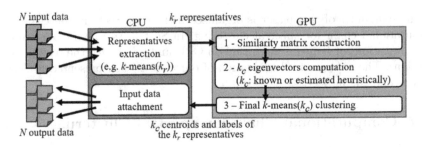

Fig. 1. Data flow for our complete spectral clustering chain

in advance). Second, it assumes that the similarity matrix (in CSR format) is already prepared, which can be computationally expensive for a general problem.

In view of the limits identified previously in related studies and in NVIDIA solutions, we propose a strategy for parallelizing the complete spectral clustering chain on CPU-GPU heterogeneous architectures as shown in Fig. 1: The first step of the data flow illustrated in Fig. 1 allows to reduce significantly the volume of N input data, extracting k_r *representatives* via k-means algorithm [20]. Typically, we have $k_c \ll k_r \ll N$. Each data instance is associated with the nearest representative. Then the k_r *representatives* are transferred from host to device and spectral clustering is performed on GPU on these representatives to find the k_c clusters, taking advantage of the CUDA libraries discussed earlier. In particular, it is possible to use either the cuSOLVER or the nvGRAPH Spectral Clustering API for the computation of eigenvectors. The latter also encapsulates the final k-means clustering step. The clustering result for the k_r representatives is transferred from device to host, and finally we obtain the cluster labels of N data instances according to the attachment relationships in the first step.

Moreover, some heuristic methods for the automatic estimation of k_c such as [12,19,21] can also be applied by using the eigenpairs calculated with or without the k_r *representatives* approach.

3   Optimizing Parallel k-means Algorithm

In this section, we present the standard k-means algorithm and then describe our parallel and optimized implementations on CPU and GPU, including the inherent bottlenecks and our optimization methods especially for the step of updating centroids.

3.1 k-means Algorithm

The k-means algorithm is a distance-based iterative clustering method. Algorithm 1 describes the main steps. The inputs are supposed to be a dataset containing N instances in Dim dimensions, and the desired number of clusters K. The first step consists in selecting K initial centroids from the dataset, either

---

Algorithm 1: k-means algorithm

Inputs: N data instances in Dim dimensions, K: nb of clusters
Outputs: Cluster labels of N data instances
1 Select K initial centroids;
2 **repeat**
3 | $ComputeAssign$ routine;
4 | $UpdateCentroids$ routine;
5 **until** *stopping criterion*;

---

randomly or in a heuristic way (see [1]). Then the algorithm repeats two routines, *ComputeAssign* and *UpdateCentroids*, until reaching the stopping criterion. The *ComputeAssign* routine computes the distance between each instance and each centroid, where the distances are measured using the Euclidean norm. For each instance, we compare the distances related to different centroids and assign the instance to the nearest centroid. In addition, we track the number of instances that have different assignments (i.e. cluster labels) over two consecutive iterations. The *UpdateCentroids* routine calculates the means of all instances that are assigned to the same centroid and updates the centroids. The stopping criterion can be either a maximal number of iterations, or a relatively stable result, i.e., when the proportion of data instances that change of label is lower that a predefined *tolerance*. The outputs are the cluster labels of all data instances.

3.2 Parallel Implementations

The parallelization of the k-means algorithm on CPU is achieved by using OpenMP and auto-vectorization and by minimizing cache misses. The GPU code is developed in CUDA. We minimize data transfers between CPU and GPU using pinned memory for fast transfers. Specifically, the data instances to be clustered are transferred from CPU to GPU at the beginning of program, then a series of CUDA kernels and library functions are launched from CPU to perform k-means clustering on GPU, finally the cluster labels are transferred to CPU. For the coalescence of memory access, we need to transfer the transposed matrix of data instances. We also transpose the matrix of centroids on GPU, but the overhead is insignificant since it is typically a small matrix. Moreover, in order to check the stopping criterion, at each iteration we need to transfer to CPU the number of instances that change of label, but the price of this transfer is negligible. Besides, we set the optimal sizes for grids and blocks of threads. The CPU code can be used for the preliminary step that extracts *representatives* while the GPU code can serve as the third step of the spectral clustering algorithm (see Fig. 1). In both codes, we minimize data storage and access by integrating distances computation and instances assignment into one routine (*ComputeAssign*).

This *ComputeAssign* routine exhibits a natural parallelism, leading to a straightforward parallel implementation, both on CPU and GPU, not detailed in this paper. Conversely, the *UpdateCentroids* routine appears more difficult to be efficiently parallelized and is a source of rounding errors due to reduction operations.

Effect of Rounding Errors. For implementations both on CPU and GPU, when using large datasets and floating-point numbers with single precision (*32-bits arithmetic*), we encountered the problem caused by rounding errors that derive from the finite representation capacity of floating-point numbers in particular when adding two numbers of very different magnitudes. In the *Update-Centroids* routine, the algorithm needs to calculate the sum of data instances in each cluster and then divide the sum by the number of instances in the cluster. Therefore, when a large number of instances are added together one by one naively, the accumulation of rounding errors that may occur finally deteriorates the clustering quality (see [7] for an illustration of the effect of rounding errors). On the other hand, using double precision (*64-bits arithmetic*) can reduce the effect of rounding errors to a satisfying level of accuracy in our use case, but the computational cost is higher (see e.g., [2]). To preserve the performance of computing in single precision while minimizing the effect of rounding errors, we developed a two-step method as follows.

Two-Step Method for *UpdateCentroids* Routine. We split data instances into a certain number of packages of similar size, then calculate the sum within each package (first step), and compute the sum of all packages (second step). By choosing an appropriate number of packages, we can avoid adding numbers of significantly different magnitudes and obtain satisfactory numerical accuracy. We illustrate hereafter how to efficiently parallelize this method on CPU and GPU.

```
1  #pragma omp parallel {
2      ... // Declare variables, reset count and cent to zeros
3      q = N / P;   r = N % P;                // Quotient & Remainder
4      // Sum the contributions to each cluster
5      #pragma omp for private(pack) reduction(+: count, cent)
6      for (int p = 0; p < P; p++) {          // Process by package
7          ...                                // Reset pack to zeros
8          ofs = (p < r ? ((q + 1) * p) : (q * p + r));  // Offset
9          len = (p < r ? (q + 1) : q);            // Length
10         for (int i = ofs; i < ofs + len; i++) { // 1st step reduction
11             int k = label[i];              // - Count nb of instances in
12             count[k]++;                    //   OpenMP reduction array
13             for (int d = 0; d < Dim; d++)  // - Reduction in thread
    private
14                 pack[k][d] += data[i*Dim + d];  //   array
15         }
16         for (int k = 0; k < K; k++)        // 2nd step reduction
17             for (int d = 0; d < Dim; d++)  // - Reduction in OpenMP
18                 cent[k][d] += pack[k][d];  //   reduction array
19     }
20     // Final averaging to get new centroids
21     #pragma omp for
22     for (int k = 0; k < K; k++)            // Process by cluster
23         for (int d = 0; d < Dim; d++)
24             cent[k][d] /= count[k];        // - Update global array
25 }
```

Listing 1.1. Two-step *UpdateCentroids* routine on CPU

Suppose that we divide N data instances into P packages and perform reductions in two steps, the CPU implementation code is displayed in Listing 1.1. We use both *private* and *reduction* clauses in OpenMP directive on line 5, to parallelize the outer loops of the 2 reduction steps, while inner loops are compliant with the main requirements of auto-vectorization (accessing contiguous array indexes and avoiding divergences) engaged with -O3 compilation flag.

For parallel implementation on GPU, we exploit shared memory, dynamic parallelism and multiple streams to achieve better performance. The *Update-Centroids* routine is split into two steps: `UpdateCent_S1` computing the sum of instance values within each package (step 1) and `UpdateCent_S2` computing the values of new centroids (step 2). As shown in Listing 1.2, by using dynamic parallelism (CUDA threads creating child threads), the host code is simplified to two parent kernel launches. Each parent grid is small and contains only *nb of streams* threads (one thread per stream).

```
1 cudaMemset(...);   // Reset G_count, G_pack to zeros
2 // nS1 & nS2 : nb of streams for Step1 & Step2
3 UpdateCent_S1_Parent<<<1,nS1>>>(G_label, G_pack, G_data_t, G_count);
4 UpdateCent_S2_Parent<<<1,nS2>>>(G_pack, G_cent_t, G_count);
```

Listing 1.2. Host code of the 2-step solution on GPU for *UpdateCentroids* routine

The parent kernel and child kernel of step 1 are exhibited in Listing 1.3. Each thread in `UpdateCent_S1_Parent` kernel processes several packages on its own stream (created on line 42), and launches one child grid per package of data instances (lines 47–57). Each child grid contains *nb of instances per package* × *nb of dimensions per instance* working threads, and child grids launched on different streams run concurrently as long as there are sufficient hardware resources in the GPU. This strategy allows to optimize the GPU usage independently of the number and size of packages. Thus, the number of packages is constrained only by the rounding error problem. The `cudaStreamDestroy` (line 58) ensures that this stream will not be reused to launch other threads, while the parent thread will only end when all of its child threads are finished.

In `UpdateCent_S1_Child` kernel, by using shared memory, the expensive *atomicAdd* operations are performed by every block instead of every thread, hence are reduced significantly (Listing 1.3, lines 31 and 33). Specifically, threads in the same block calculate the local sum by block size at first, then all the local sums are added together through a few *atomicAdd* operations.

```
1  // Child kernel of UpdateCentroids Step1
2  __global__ void UpdateCent_S1_Child(int pid, int ofs, int len, int *G_label
   ,
3                          T_real *G_pack, T_real *G_data_t, int *G_count
   ){
4    __shared__ T_real shTabV[BSYD][BSXP];      // Tab of instance values
5    __shared__ int shTabL[BSXP];               // Tab of labels(cluster
       Id)
6    // Index initialization
7    int baseRow = blockIdx.y * BSYD;           // Base row of the block
8    int row = baseRow + threadIdx.y;           // Row of child thread
9    int baseCol = blockIdx.x * BSXP + ofs;     // Base column of the
       block
10   int col = baseCol + threadIdx.x;           // Column of child thread
11   int cltIdx = threadIdx.y * BSXP + threadIdx.x; // 1D cluster index
```

```
12  // Load the values and cluster labels of instances into sh mem tables
13  if (col < (ofs + len) && row < Dim) {
14    shTabV[threadIdx.y][threadIdx.x] = G_data_t[row*N + col];
15    if (threadIdx.y == 0) shTabL[threadIdx.x] = G_label[col];
16  }
17  __syncthreads();           // Wait for all data loaded into the sh mem
18  // Compute partial evolution of centroid related to cluster number '
        cltIdx'
19  if (cltIdx < K) {
20    T_real Sv[Dim] = {0.0};   // Sum of values in each dimension
21    int count = 0;            // Counter of instances
22    // - Accumulate contributions to cluster number 'cltIdx'
23    for (int x = 0; x < BSXP && (baseCol + x) < (ofs + len); x++) {
24      if (shTabL[x] == cltIdx) {
25        count++;
26        for (int y = 0; y < BSYD && (baseRow + y) < Dim; y++)
27          Sv[baseRow + y] += shTabV[y][x];
28      }
29    }
30    // - Save the contrib. of block into global contrib. of the package
31    if (blockIdx.y == 0 && count != 0) atomicAdd(&G_count[cltIdx], count);
32    for (int d = 0; d < Dim; d++)
33      if (Sv[d] != 0.0) atomicAdd(&G_pack[d*K*P + K*pid + cltIdx], Sv[d]);
34  }
35 }
36
37 // Parent kernel of UpdateCentroids Step1
38 __global__ void UpdateCent_S1_Parent(...) {
39   int tid = threadIdx.x;                     // Thread id
40   if (tid < P) {
41     ...                                      // Declare variables and stream
42     cudaStreamCreateWithFlags(&s, cudaStreamDefault);
43     q = N / P;  r = N % P;                    // Quotient & remainder
44     np = (P - 1) / nS1 + 1;                   // Nb of packages for each
          stream
45     Db.x = BSXP;  Db.y = BSYD;  Db.z = 1;    // BSXP: Block X-size for
          package
46     Dg.y = (D - 1) / BSYD + 1;  Dg.z = 1;    // BSYD: Block Y-size for dim
47     for (int i = 0; i < np; i++) {
48       pid = i * nS1 + tid;                   // Package id
49       if (pid < P) {
50         ofs = (pid < r ? ((q + 1) * pid) : (q * pid + r));  // Offset
51         len = (pid < r ? (q + 1) : q);                      // Length
52         Dg.x = (len - 1) / BSXP + 1;
53         // Launch a child kernel on a stream to process a package
54         UpdateCent_S1_Child<<<Dg,Db,0,s>>>(pid, ofs, len, G_label, G_pack,
55                                            G_data_t, G_count);
56       }
57     }
58     cudaStreamDestroy(s);
59   }
60 }
```

Listing 1.3. Device code on GPU for step 1 of *UpdateCentroids* routine

A similar strategy is used to implement step 2 of our complete solution on GPU. Each thread of the parent grid processes several packages, and creates child grids on its own stream. Each child grid is in charge to update the $K \times Dim$ centroid values with the contribution of its package. So, it contains $K \times Dim$ threads, each one executing only few operations and one *atomicAdd* (shared memory is not adapted to and not used in step 2 computations). Again, using dynamic parallelism and multiple streams has allowed to speedup the execution.

4   Experimental Evaluation

The experiments have been carried out on a server located at CentraleSup-elec (Metz campus). This server has two 10-core Intel(R) Xeon(R) Silver 4114 processors at 2.2 GHz, and a NVIDIA GeForce RTX 2080 Ti containing 4352 CUDA cores. The CPU code is compiled with gcc version 7.4.0 (with -O3 flag) to have parallelization with OpenMP, vectorization on AVX units and various optimizations. The GPU code is compiled with CUDA version 10.2. Moreover, to use dynamic parallelism in CUDA (see Sect. 3.2) we need to adopt the *separate compilation mode*: generating and embedding relocatable device code into the host object, before calling the device linker.

As benchmark, we use a synthetic 4D dataset created in Python. It contains 50 million instances uniformly distributed in 4 convex clusters (12.5 million instances in each cluster). Each cluster has a radius of 9 and the centroids are supposed to be (40, 40, 60, 60), (40, 60, 60, 40), (60, 40, 40, 60) and (60, 60, 40, 40), respectively, in the way that the k-means algorithm would not be sensitive to the initialization of centroids and would not be trapped in local minimum solutions. However, due to the intrinsic errors of generating pseudo-random numbers and the rounding errors of floating-point numbers, it appears the calculated centroids could have a deviation of order 10^{-4} from the ideal ones.

In our benchmark, we iterate the algorithm while any data instance is attached to a new centroid (*tolerance* = 0, see Sect. 3.1). Since the number of iterations on CPU and GPU can vary depending on independent selections of initial centroids and on the numerical precision, we are more interested here in the elapsed time per iteration than the overall execution time. The most important results in our tables are highlighted in boldface.

In Table 1, we evaluate the k-**means clustering on CPU** by comparing the average numerical error of final centroids and the elapsed time per iteration by varying the number of threads, the arithmetic precision, and the number of packages. The column "Loop" represents the whole of two k-means routines. We

Table 1. k-means clustering on CPU (synthetic dataset)

Threads	Precision	Nb of packages	Numerical error	Init time (ms)	Time per iteration (ms)			Nb of iterations	Overall time (ms)
					Compute-Assign	Update	Loop		
1 thread	Single	1	3.009794	0.009	591.47	152.31	743.78	12	8925.37
		10	0.244048	0.012	616.94	151.19	768.12	5	3840.61
		100	**0.000745**	0.008	594.13	152.36	**746.49**	6	4478.95
		1000	**0.000746**	0.018	588.39	153.88	**742.27**	6	4453.64
	Double	1	0.000741	0.009	631.58	171.11	802.69	6	4816.15
40 threads (40 logical cores)	Single	1[a]	3.009794	0.194	67.47	165.96[a]	233.43	6	1400.77
		10[b]	0.244047	0.178	72.50	27.96[b]	100.46	5	502.48
		100	**0.000746**	0.197	63.06	21.13	**84.19**	6	505.34
		1000	**0.000746**	0.201	61.62	13.90	**75.52**	6	453.32
	Double	1	0.000741	0.139	76.55	208.04	284.59	6	1707.68

[a] 1 package ⟶ 1 task during main computations ⟶ only 1 working thread

[b] 10 packages ⟶ 10 tasks during main computations ⟶ only 10 working threads

observe that using a certain number of packages in the *UpdataCentroids* routine reduces the numerical error in single precision. In our case, using 100 packages is enough for achieving the same numerical accuracy as in double precision. Using single precision instead of double precision decreases the elapsed time.

We give in Table 2 the accuracy and performance results of k-**means clustering on GPU**. Using packages reduces the effect of rounding errors, and this reduction is enhanced by using the shared memory that allows initial local reductions. The routine *UpdateCentroids* is the most time-consuming routine on GPU while *ComputeAssign* represents a small proportion of the runtime. In our GPU implementation, we optimize the configuration of grids and blocks of threads. Table 3 shows an example of how block configuration affects the performance where we set BLOCK_SIZE_Y (BSYD in listings) to 4 (the number of dimensions of the synthetic data). Note that the centroids initialization and most of data transfers are performed only one time, hence their impact on the whole runtime decreases with the number of iterations. The elapsed time for regular transpositions of some small data appears negligible (Table 2).

Table 2. k-means clustering on GPU (synthetic dataset)

Precision	Nb of pack-ages	Numerical error	Overhead time (ms)		Init time (ms)	Time per iteration (ms)			Nb of itera-tions	Overall time (ms)
			Transfer	Transpose		Compute-Assign	Update	Loop		
Single	1	0.000992	81.15	0.15	2.64	1.96	13.77	15.73	5	162.59
	10	0.000760	81.13	0.12	2.75	1.96	13.58	15.54	5	161.70
	100	**0.000739**	81.18	0.19	2.74	1.97	13.29	**15.26**	5	160.41
	1000	0.000741	81.11	0.29	2.65	1.98	14.07	16.05	5	164.30
Double	1	0.000741	81.13	0.14	2.65	8.98	32.05	41.03	5	289.07

Table 3. Influence of block size on performance

BLOCK_SIZE_X for packages (BSXP in listings)	Time of Update per iteration (ms)	
	100 packages	1000 packages
16	15.65	18.36
32	**13.29**	**14.07**
64	17.62	18.92

Table 4 demonstrates the impact of GPU optimization on the running time of *UpdateCentroids*. Compared to the naïve implementation with many *atomicAdd* operations, using shared memory reduces significantly the execution time for different number of packages. The dynamic parallelism also improves the performance in the case of 100 packages and 1000 packages but it degrades the performance for 10000 packages. This is because the GPU hardware resources are not fully concurrently exploited when there are a large number of small packages to be processed on the default stream. Therefore, introducing multiple streams could contribute to the concurrent use of hardware resources and consequently reduce the execution time, which is clearly demonstrated in the case of 10000 packages. The combined use of dynamic parallelism, shared memory and streams achieves very good performances for a general number of packages.

The speedups for the two routines of k-means and the resulting full iteration are displayed in Table 5. For the k-means loop, the best speedup obtained (compared with the sequential implementation) is about $\times10$ on CPU using 40 logical cores and almost $\times50$ on GPU (which is 5 times faster than on CPU using 40 logical cores). For the *ComputeAssign* routine we achieve much higher speedups (around $\times300$) on GPU than on CPU while the speedups for the *UpdateCentroids* routine are similar on CPU and GPU.

Table 4. Impact of GPU optimization on the execution time of *UpdateCentroids*

Optimization on GPU	Time of Update per iteration (ms)		
	100 packages	1000 packages	10000 packages
Naïve	241.15	261.72	513.37
Dynamic parallelism	94.52	97.63	3155.18
Shared memory	17.05	23.47	88.14
Dynamic parallelism & Shared memory	13.39	14.13	2368.82
Shared memory & Streams	15.28	19.71	70.42
Dynamic parallelism & Shared memory & Streams	**13.29**	**14.07**	**29.19**

Table 5. Speedups of k-means routines on synthetic dataset (single precision)

Speedup	CPU 40 threads vs. 1 thread		GPU vs. CPU 1 thread		GPU vs. CPU 40 threads	
	100 packages	1000 packages	100 packages	1000 packages	100 packages	1000 packages
ComputeAssign	$\times9.42$	$\times9.55$	$\times302.06$	$\times297.42$	$\times30.06$	$\times31.15$
Update	$\times7.21$	$\times11.07$	$\times11.46$	$\times10.94$	$\times1.59$	$\times0.99$
Loop	$\times\mathbf{8.87}$	$\times\mathbf{9.83}$	$\times\mathbf{48.93}$	$\times\mathbf{46.25}$	$\times\mathbf{5.52}$	$\times\mathbf{4.71}$

5   Conclusion and Future Work

We have proposed parallel implementations on CPU and GPU for the k-means algorithm, which is a key component of the computational chain for spectral clustering on CPU-GPU heterogeneous platforms. We have addressed via a two-step reduction the numerical accuracy issue that may occur in the phase of updating centroids due to the effect of rounding errors. Our GPU implementation employs dynamic parallelism, shared memory and streams to achieve optimal performance for updating centroids. Experiments on a synthetic dataset demonstrate both numerical accuracy and parallelization efficiency of our implementations.

In this paper we have used only a synthetic dataset but as future work we plan to evaluate our parallel k-means algorithms on real-world datasets and compare our implementation with other existing ones. In particular we expect to obtain higher speedups in high-dimensional datasets or those containing a large number of clusters, where the phase of computing the distances is more significant.

References

1. Arthur, D., Vassilvitskii, S.: k-means++: the advantages of careful seeding. In: Proceedings of the Eighteenth Annual ACM-SIAM Symposium on Discrete Algorithms, SODA 2007, New Orleans, Louisiana, USA (2007)
2. Baboulin, M., et al.: Accelerating scientific computations with mixed precision algorithms. Comput. Phys. Commun. **180**(12), 2526–2533 (2009)
3. Bhimani, J., Leeser, M., Mi, N.: Accelerating k-means clustering with parallel implementations and GPU computing. In: 2015 IEEE High Performance Extreme Computing Conference, HPEC 2015, Waltham, MA, USA (2015)
4. Chen, W., Song, Y., Bai, H., Lin, C., Chang, E.Y.: Parallel spectral clustering in distributed systems. IEEE Trans. Pattern Anal. Mach. Intell. **33**(3) 568–586 (2011)
5. Cuomo, S., De Angelis, V., Farina, G., Marcellino, L., Toraldo, G.: A GPU-accelerated parallel K-means algorithm. Comput. Electric. Eng. **75**, 262–274 (2019)
6. Fowlkes, C.C., Belongie, S.J., Chung, F.R.K., Malik, J.: Spectral grouping using the Nyström method. IEEE Trans. Pattern Anal. Mach. Intell. **26**(2), 214-225 (2004)
7. Jézéquel, F., Graillat, S., Mukunoki, D., Imamura, T., Iakymchuk, R.: Can we avoid rounding-error estimation in HPC codes and still get trustful results? working paper or preprint (2020). https://hal.archives-ouvertes.fr/hal-02486753
8. Jin, Y., JáJá, J.F.: A high performance implementation of spectral clustering on CPU-GPU platforms. In: 2016 IEEE International Parallel and Distributed Processing Symposium Workshops, IPDPS Workshops 2016, Chicago, IL, USA, 23–27 May 2016, pp. 825–834. IEEE Computer Society (2016)
9. Karypis, M.S.G., Kumar, V., Steinbach, M.: A comparison of document clustering techniques. In: Text Mining Workshop at KDD2000 (2000)
10. Laccetti, G., Lapegna, M., Mele, V., Romano, D., Szustak, L.: Performance enhancement of a dynamic K-means algorithm through a parallel adaptive strategy on multicore CPUs. J. Parallel Distrib. Comput. **145**, 34–41 (2020)
11. Lin, F., Cohen, W.W.: Power iteration clustering. In: Proceedings of the 27th International Conference on Machine Learning (ICML 2010), 21–24 June 2010, Haifa, Israel, pp. 655–662 (2010)
12. von Luxburg, U.: A tutorial on spectral clustering. Stat. Comput. **17**(4), 395–416 (2007)
13. MacQueen, J., et al.: Some methods for classification and analysis of multivariate observations. In: Proceedings of the Fifth Berkeley Symposium on Mathematical Statistics and Probability, vol. 1(14), pp. 281–297 (1967)
14. Ng, A.Y., Jordan, M.I., Weiss, Y.: On spectral clustering: analysis and an algorithm. In: Advances in Neural Information Processing Systems 14 (Neural Information Processing Systems: Natural and Synthetic, NIPS 2001, 3–8 December 2001, Vancouver, British Columbia, Canada), pp. 849–856 (2001)
15. NVIDIA: nvGRAPH Library User's Guide (2019). https://docs.nvidia.com/cuda/pdf/nvGRAPH_Library.pdf
16. Shi, J., Malik, J.: Normalized cuts and image segmentation. IEEE Trans. Pattern Anal. Mach. Intell. **22**(8), 888–905 (2000)
17. Sundaram, N., Keutzer, K.: Long term video segmentation through pixel level spectral clustering on GPUs. In: IEEE International Conference on Computer Vision Workshops, ICCV 2011 Workshops, Barcelona, Spain (2011)
18. Tomov, S., Dongarra, J., Baboulin, M.: Towards dense linear algebra for hybrid GPU accelerated manycore systems. Parallel Comput. **36**(5&6), 232–240 (2010)

19. Xiang, T., Gong, S.: Spectral clustering with eigenvector selection. Pattern Recognit. **41**(3), 1012–1029 (2008)
20. Yan, D., Huang, L., Jordan, M.I.: Fast approximate spectral clustering. In: Proceedings of the 15th ACM International Conference on Knowledge Discovery and Data Mining, Paris, France, 2009 (2009)
21. Zelnik-Manor, L., Perona, P.: Self-tuning spectral clustering. In: Advances in Neural Information Processing Systems 17 (Neural Information Processing Systems, NIPS 2004, 13–18 December 2004, Vancouver, Canada), pp. 1601–1608 (2004)
22. Zheng, J., Chen, W., Chen, Y., Zhang, Y., Zhao, Y., Zheng, W.: Parallelization of spectral clustering algorithm on multi-core processors and GPGPU. In: 13th Asia-Pacific Computer Systems Architecture Conference, pp. 1–8. IEEE (2008)

Management of Heterogeneous Cloud Resources with Use of the PPO

Włodzimierz Funika[1]($\boxtimes$)(iD), Paweł Koperek[1](iD), and Jacek Kitowski[1,2](iD)

[1] Faculty of Computer Science, Electronics and Telecommunication, Department of Computer Science, AGH, al. Mickiewicza 30, 30-059 Kraków, Poland
{funika,kito}@agh.edu.pl, pkoperek@gmail.com
[2] AGH, ACC CYFRONET AGH, ul. Nawojki 11, 30-950 Kraków, Poland

Abstract. Reinforcement learning has been recently a very active field of research. Thanks to combining it with Deep Learning, many newly designed algorithms improve the state of the art. In this paper we present the results of our attempt to use the recent advancements in Reinforcement Learning to automate the management of heterogeneous resources in an environment which hosts a compute-intensive evolutionary process. We describe the architecture of our system and present evaluation results. The experiments include autonomous management of a sample workload and a comparison of its performance to the traditional automatic management approach. We also provide the details of training of the management policy using the Proximal Policy Optimization algorithm. Finally, we discuss the feasibility to extend the presented approach to other scenarios.

Keywords: Reinforcement learning · Heterogeneous cloud resources · Automatic management · Proximal policy optimization

1 Introduction

Many software systems designed nowadays exploit the cloud computing infrastructures which offer high availability, security and the flexibility to allocate the resources on-demand. The last factor often drives the decision to implement a specific system using cloud resources as it allows to greatly reduce the costs of running a distributed application. Such elasticity unfortunately requires paying the price of designing the application to handle scaling events, e.g. changing the number of virtual machines (*horizontal scaling*) or adding or removing RAM, CPU or storage (*vertical scaling*). Deploying the application requires also creating a policy which will define the conditions under which the system should be scaled and which resources should be utilized in such a case. It might be possible to create a configuration which will work correctly over a long period of time if the environment shows stable seasonal usage patterns. Unfortunately, in many cases such patterns do not exist, what calls for using an automatic scaling policy. We can define it as *a dynamic process [...] that adapts software configurations [...] and hardware resources provisioning [...] on-demand, according to the time-varying environmental conditions* [6].

© Springer Nature Switzerland AG 2021
B. Balis et al. (Eds.): Euro-Par 2020 Workshops, LNCS 12480, pp. 148–159, 2021.
https://doi.org/10.1007/978-3-030-71593-9_12

The area of the Reinforcement Learning (*RL*) techniques has been explored for a long time [12,22]. Initially the techniques and algorithms from this category could be only used in relatively simple problems. Handling more complex domains became possible with recent advancements in, e.g. computer games [18], robot control [11] or the game of Go [21]. One of the main drivers of progress has been the application of Deep Learning in various forms: Deep Q Learning [17], Asynchronous Actor-Critic Agents (A3C) [19], Proximal Policy Optimization [20]. One of the main advantages of the mentioned methods is the ability to learn through observing and interacting with an environment which is similar to or the same as the one the agent is going to operate in. Such an approach allowed to achieve results which have surpassed the performance of humans.

Such successes suggest that applying Deep Reinforcement Learning (*DRL*) in other domains can also render good results. One such area is the automatic scaling of distributed applications deployed to heterogeneous cloud resources. The cloud infrastructure becomes the environment where an automatic agent operates, its state becomes the state which is subject to change. Cloud vendor API calls become the actions the agent can potentially execute. Measurements and metrics which can be used to determine the mentioned state are driven by the technologies used to implement the application and thanks to that are well defined. The goals of the system are also clear (e.g. reducing RAM consumption, CPU load, request latency, cost of resources) what helps to translate them into a reward function. Such a reward function becomes the feedback mechanism for the agent and allows to evaluate the impact of executed actions. Thanks to that, the agent does not need to rely on any prior knowledge and can use a process of trial-and-error experiments to discover the optimal management policy.

In our previous work [10] we have demonstrated how to leverage the described ideas to create a system capable of automatic scaling of homogeneous cloud infrastructure hosting a CPU-intensive workload. In this paper we extend this approach to heterogeneous cloud resources: the system can adjust not only the amount of resources but can also decide on the features of the added resources. The training does not require providing any additional information about the managed system or specifying resources capabilities. All decisions are derived from the experience gained from simulations. The system has been implemented as an extension to Semantic-Based Automatic Monitoring and Management (SAMM) monitoring software [9].

The paper is organized as follows: in Sect. 2 we overview related work, Sect. 3 describes the design and architecture of the environment and Sect. 4 explains the policy training procedure. Section 5 discusses the design of the experiment and description of the environment it was executed in. Section 6 provides the experiment results and discussion. Section 7 summarizes our research and outlines further work.

2   Related Work

Minimizing the monetary cost of cloud resources while maintaining business requirements (sometimes defined through Quality-of-Service metrics) is a very complex task and has been an active research area for years. There are many different approaches that can be used depending on the conditions of the environment which should be managed. The most distinctive approaches include: *rule-based control* [7,14] (action execution occurs when a condition defined a priori is met, *search based optimization* [16,24] (decisions form a large, finite search space and choosing among them is treated as a search problem), *control theory-based* [4] (control theory mechanisms are used to make a decision).

There have been a number of attempts to apply Reinforcement Learning techniques, which can be classified as *search based optimization*. In [23] authors explore applying variants of the Q-learning algorithm to provisioning cloud resources. They focus on a horizontally scaling infrastructure used to handle a stream of requests defined in a benchmark dataset. They demonstrate that a policy can be first trained using a simulator and then applied to a real cloud environment. In [6] a system for automatic traffic optimization (*AuTO*) is presented. Authors implement it with the use of the Deep Deterministic Policy Gradient (DDPG) training algorithm, which utilizes two neural networks: the *actor* (responsible for making decisions) and the *critic* (used to evaluate the actor's decisions). The first one consists of two fully-connected hidden layers with 600 neurons each. The second one reuses those and adds an additional layer on top. Such a model is used to demonstrate the performance and adaptiveness of the discussed approach to the control of dynamic traffic. In [10] we demonstrated how a similar algorithm, the Proximal Policy Optimization (PPO) [20], can be used to horizontally scale cloud resources. The implementation has been limited to control resources of a single type.

Reinforcement Learning

One of the more active areas of research in machine learning is the Reinforcement Learning (*RL*) [13,22]. Its primary focus is to discover a policy for agents which autonomously take actions within a specific environment. The policy maximizes a reward whose value is returned to the agent. The process of training an agent relies on executing a series of actions. After each of them the agent observes their consequences and builds up its own knowledge. The knowledge of the agent is built from observing the consequences of its actions. There is no *supervising entity* providing feedback on how taking a certain action is better than taking others. This distinguishes this approach from *supervised learning*. RL is also different than *unsupervised learning* which focuses on discovering the internal structure of a collection of unlabeled data.

Over the years many different approaches to RL were proposed. We can broadly categorize them as:

- *Online* and *offline* which differ in when the agent's policy is changed. In case of the *online* approach, an update happens after every step, in the *offline* case - after the full *episode* (i.e. when the training scenario is finished, the environment needs to restart and the reward is presented to the agent).

- *Model-based* and *model-free* which differ in how the environment is modeled by the agent. In the former approach an explicit model is created (e.g. through reward estimations or specification of state transitions), in the latter one - creating such a model is not necessary (the decision making process assumes that it is sufficient to have a sample of information about state transitions).

Combining Deep Learning techniques with the *model-free* approach became popular recently and resulted in creating so called *Deep Reinforcement Learning* (DRL). In this approach, neural networks can be used to create an approximation of a function which is a part of an algorithm (e.g. the Q-function in [17]). Alternatively, in case of policy gradient methods, neural networks can be used directly as the policy functions. The training process adjusts their weights (Θ) based on the gradient of an estimated scalar performance objective function $J(\Theta)$ in respect to those policy parameters:

$$\Theta_{k+1} = \Theta_k + \alpha \nabla_\Theta J(\Theta_k) \tag{1}$$

where Θ_k denotes policy's parameters in the k-th iteration of the training process. The performance is usually understood as the reward returned from environment. There are multiple versions of policy gradient optimization. In our research we focus on the *Proximal Policy Optimization* (PPO) [20].

The aim of the algorithm is to calculate the parameter update in such a way, that it ensures that the difference to the previous version of the policy is relatively small. This goal is achieved through modification of the objective function. It is defined as follows:

$$J(\Theta) = L^{CLIP}(\Theta) = \mathbb{E}_t \left[min(r_t(\Theta)A_t, clip(r_t(\Theta), 1 - \epsilon, 1 + \epsilon)A_t) \right] \tag{2}$$

where $\mathbb{E}_t$ denotes calculating average over a batch of samples at timestamp t, A_t is an estimator of the advantage function which helps to evaluate which action is the most beneficial in a given state. r_t marks probability ratio $r_t(\Theta) = \frac{\pi_\Theta(a_t|s_t)}{\pi_{\Theta_{old}}(a_t|s_t)}$ in which $\pi_\Theta(a_t|s_t)$ denotes the probability of taking an action a in state s by a stochastic policy and Θ_{old} are the policy parameters before the update. The $clip(r_t(\Theta), 1 - \epsilon, 1 + \epsilon)$ function keeps the value of $r_t(\Theta)$ within some specified limits (*clips* it at the end of the range) and ϵ is a hyperparameter with a typical value between 0.1 and 0.3.

In our previous research [10] we experimented with a number of policy gradient methods (Vanilla Policy Gradient, Proximal Policy Optimization, Trust-Region Policy Optimization) out of which the PPO rendered the best empirical results in the automated resources management.

3   Architecture

From a high-level perspective, the system under discussion creates a feedback loop in which the policy interacts with the environment under management. Its complete architecture is presented in Fig. 1.

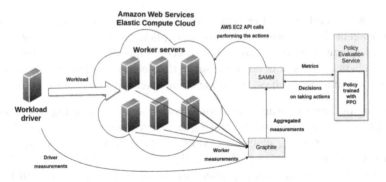

Fig. 1. Components of the discussed system. Arrows denote interactions between them.

The loop starts with collecting measurements about the resources which take part in executing the workload. Each of them is configured to start reporting relevant measurements as soon as it becomes online. The measurements often differ in their nature what influences how often their values are provided, e.g. the amount of free RAM and CPU usage is reported every 10 s while the virtual machine (VM) count - once per minute. To simplify the implementation of collecting of those raw measurements, we introduced the Graphite monitoring tool [2]. Graphite aggregates all the collected values into a single interval to create a consistent snapshot of the environment. This interval in our case is set to one minute.

Next, the measurements are collected by the SAMM experimental monitoring and management system [9]. SAMM enables experimenting with new approaches to management automation. It allows to easily add support for new types of resources, integrate new algorithms and technologies and observe their impact on the observed system. In our case, after retrieving raw data points, SAMM calculates values of the following metrics: *ratio of allocated cores, average CPU utilization, 90th percentile of CPU utilization, average RAM utilization, 90th percentile of RAM utilization, ratio of jobs waiting for processing to the number of jobs submitted, ratio of jobs waiting for processing to the number of jobs submitted in the last monitoring interval.* They are being used to describe the current state of the cloud environment and are further passed to the *Policy Evaluation Service.* After a decision is taken, SAMM uses cloud vendor's API to implement it. It takes into the account the constraints of the environment (e.g. resource changes are adjusted to adhere to the warm-up and cool-down restrictions).

The *Policy Evaluation Service* provides decisions on how to change the allocation of resources based on the results of evaluation of the observed system state. The decisions are made according to the policy trained with the use of the PPO algorithm. The results of the evaluation may include: *starting a new small, medium or large VM* (deficient resources are used to handle the workload given the current system state), *removing resources - shutting down a small, medium, large VM* (excessive resources is used given the current state of the system), *doing nothing* (a proper amount of resources is allocated).

One should remember that not always it is possible to immediately execute an action. This process is always subject to environment constraints. We might need to wait for a while because: the system is in a *warm-up* or *cool-down* (a period of inactivity to allow to stabilize the metrics after the previous action has been executed), the previous request might still be being fulfilled, the request failed and needs to be retried in some time. In order to be able to train a policy which can cope with such limitations, those factors need to be involved in the simulation used for training.

The described system makes a few assumptions about the workload it helps to manage:

- processing is organized into many independent tasks,
- the number of tasks which are yet to be executed can be monitored,
- the tasks which have been interrupted before finishing (e.g. in case the processing VMs are shutdown) are rescheduled,
- the tasks are considered idempotent, i.e. executing them multiple times does not change the end result,
- resources used to generate the workload are not under automatic management (prevents from accidental termination of the workload).

Fulfilling the monitoring requirements may require introducing extensions to the software which generates the workloads and instrumenting resources which are used to create tasks.

4 Policy Training

One of the main challenges in the design of an autonomous management system is organization of the training process. Using an environment with real cloud resources would be the best solution. Unfortunately, with this approach the cost of creating a DRL policy becomes a major disadvantage. The training algorithm needs to go through multiple iterations of interacting with the managed system and observing its responses. Especially at the beginning the actions chosen for execution might be quite random, what can easily destabilize the observed application, even make it completely unusable for the end users. Since such a situation is unacceptable in a production system, the training requires a separate, duplicate environment. This increases the overall cost of running the system. To avoid this issue, we decided to use a simulation as an isolated, safe training environment. Regardless of the decisions made, their consequences are not applied to any production system. This allows experimenting even with the actions that may lead to catastrophic events. Using a simulator allows to significantly cut the computational monetary cost of training resources compared with the actual system. Since a simulation is isolated, the process can be replicated and parallelized to allow for evaluation of multiple agents at the same time. The flow of time in a simulation can be changed what allows to reduce the time required to conduct training. The behavior of the environment and the workload are fully deterministic and can be easily repeated if needed.

The policy training process has been implemented using a separate environment depicted in Fig. 2.

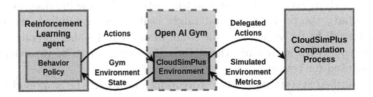

Fig. 2. Components of the training system; arrows denote interactions between them.

The simulator has been implemented following the results of our prior research [10]. The main process utilizes the CloudSim Plus simulation framework [8]. To decouple it from other components and allow for easy reuse, it is additionally wrapped with the interface provided by the Open AI Gym framework [5]. This helps to easily launch experiments with various RL algorithms independently of the presented architecture.

We simulated a single datacenter capable of hosting Virtual Machines (VMs) of three types: small, medium and large. Their specification followed the configuration of Amazon's *large* (2 core CPU and 8 GB of RAM), *xlarge* (4 core CPU and 16 GB of RAM) and *2xlarge* (8 core CPU and 32 GB of RAM) EC2 instances. Each simulation started with 1 virtual machine of each type active and run until all the scheduled tasks were completed (there was an artificial deadline). We attempted to use a few different workloads. The best results in training were achieved by using a set of 1551 jobs generated specifically for the purpose of our experiment. The jobs were organized into 21 batches (10 batches of 100 and 11 batches of 50 jobs) submitted every 8 min. Every job requested 360 s on a single CPU core. The final job has been added 30 min after the final batch what ensured that there is always a cool-down period of time at the end. We considered such workload typical in our sample environment.

The training objective was defined as maximizing the following reward function: $F(T_S, T_M, T_L, T_Q) = -(T_S * 0.2 + T_M * 0.4 + T_L * 0.8 + 0.036 * T_Q)$ which was the negative cost of resources used for processing. T_S, T_M, T_L denote the number of hours of running *small*, *medium* or *large* VMs (with an hourly cost respectively \$0.2, \$0.4 and \$0.8). The reward included paying penalties for missing SLA targets, \$0.036 for each of T_Q hours spent by tasks waiting for execution. Waiting time or waiting queue size was not limited. In order to reduce the training time, the simulation time was speeded up sixty times. The training algorithm followed the *Proximal Policy Optimization* procedure described in Sect. 2. The progress of training (reward obtained in the subsequent simulations) is depicted in Fig. 3.

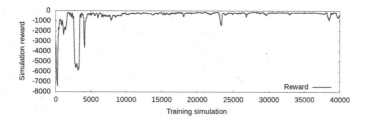

Fig. 3. Policy training progress - reward obtained in subsequent simulations.

5   Experiment Design

In order to evaluate our approach, we designed an experiment in which we wanted to compare our policy to another algorithm. The overall objective was to perform sample computations while limiting the cost of the used cloud resources.

As a sample workload, we have used the *pytorch-dnn-evolution* tool [3]. This is a tool which attempts to discover an optimal structure of a Deep Neural Network (*DNN*) to solve a given problem (e.g. categorize images in a given set) using a co-evolutionary algorithm. Such an approach can be used for domains where supervised learning techniques can be used, i.e. there are well defined training and test datasets. Unfortunately, due to the size of those datasets, in many such problems, evolution-based methods are costly and time consuming. The evaluation of individuals (complete DNNs), which is required for the evolution process to progress, includes training them over the mentioned large datasets. To mitigate this issue, the co-evolutionary algorithm interleaves two evolutionary processes: the first one which attempts to find the hardest to solve small subset of the large training dataset, the second one which evolves the DNNs and uses the small subset in the individual evaluation. Reducing the amount of data required to conduct the evaluation allows to greatly speed up the comparison between individuals and enables using the evolutionary approach.

This algorithm produces a high number of relatively small tasks. They are independent from each other and can be easily processed in parallel on a cluster of machines. Workload scheduling is resilient to task failures and reschedules tasks in case processing them have not succeeded. The capacity of the job queue is in practice infinite thanks to small size of a single job description. Those features help to implement support for scaling events: each virtual machine used to conduct training can be safely shut down at any time. New machines can be added and start processing the evaluation tasks without additional configuration. The number of tasks varies over time, which allows to potentially reduce the cost of running the evolutionary process by reducing the amount of the used resources (VMs) when the demand for resources drops. In our case, the evolutionary process tries to find an optimal architecture of neural network which recognizes hand written digits. We have ran 20 iterations of evolution over a population of 32 individuals and 16 fitness predictors (subsets of 2000 images from the large training set). The evaluation of a single neural network comprised the training over 10 iterations of a given fitness predictor. The MNIST dataset [15] has been used as the training set from which subsets are selected.

As a compute infrastructure we have used the Amazon Web Services Elastic Compute Cloud (AWS EC2) [1]. The managed environment consisted of three Auto Scaling Groups groups of *m5a.large*, *m5a.xlarge* and *m5a.2xlarge* virtual machines which could have up to 10 instances each. All VMs were running in the US North Virginia region and in the same availability zone to avoid the problems with network latency added by multi-zone setups. The workload driver, together with SAMM and Graphite, have been running on a separate VM.

To provide a reference point for the results obtained with the use of the presented policy, we also attempted to manage the *pytorch-dnnevo* workload with the use of a rule-based policy configured within the Auto Scaling Group. This cloud vendor feature starts and stops virtual machines based on the CPU usage or currently running machines. A new machine is started whenever the metric value is higher than a pre-defined threshold. If the value drops below the threshold, one of the running machines is terminated. We found empirically that a threshold value of 75% average CPU usage renders the best results.

6   Experiment Results

In Fig. 4 we present the course of the experiment. We show how many virtual machines of different types were active at a given point in time compared to what was the actual number of jobs waiting for processing. The shape of the charts (the *steps*) is caused by an artificial delay introduced after executing an action (the *cool-down* period).

The overall results of the experiment are as follows: the experiment runtime was 173 min with the cost of resources equal to $8,67 for the PPO-trained policy, and respectively 149 min and $9,95 for the threshold-based approach. The first policy had a slower execution (by 16,1% - 24 min) but a lower resources cost (by 12,9% - $1.28). The cost of the additional infrastructure is the same in both cases (an additional VM to host other elements of the system). The main objective of the policy was to conduct the computations while minimizing costs. In that context, the PPO-trained policy rendered better results. It traded additional processing time for lowering the overall cost or resources.

The PPO-trained policy maintained a similar number of VMs of all types running most of the time. Occasionally it would attempt to reduce the amount of *small* VMs what seemed to be a result of pauses between submitting jobs of subsequent evolution iterations. However, those drops would get quickly compensated. The number of *medium* and *large* machines was relatively stable. The threshold-based policy was more eager to introduce changes and was able to launch machines of different types in the same time. As soon as the processing load was decreasing, it started to reduce the amount of used resources. It seemed that most of the time all resource types were treated similarly (the number of *small, medium and large* VMs was increased and decreased in the same time).

We acknowledge that this might not be a fully fair comparison, e.g. it might be possible to fine tune the threshold to avoid the described initial slow-down.

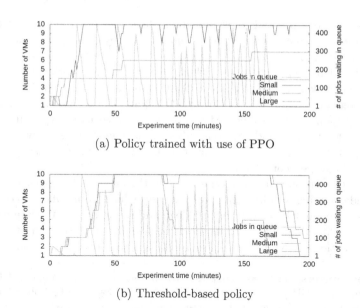

(a) Policy trained with use of PPO

(b) Threshold-based policy

Fig. 4. Number of started VMs in context of jobs waiting in the queue.

Alternatively, using multiple rules and thresholds might achieve even better results. This experiment shows, however, that the use of a PPO-trained policy renders results which are on-par with a well established approach. Using a RL-based policy has an advantage of being able to take into account multiple factors without having to specify some special parameters for each of them, e.g. the thresholds. The training process was flexible and can be easily reused to create policies for other, similar workloads.

7   Conclusions and Further Research

In this paper we have presented a novel approach to automating heterogeneous resource allocation. We proposed an architecture of a monitoring system which exploits recent advancements in the Deep Reinforcement Learning field. Through an experiment the AWS Elastic Compute Cloud, we explained how to train a policy with use of the PPO algorithm and deploy it to a real-world cloud infrastructure. We demonstrated that using such a policy can render better results comparing with a traditional threshold-based one. However, depending on the amount of the managed resources due to the additional cost of the additional VM, the overall improvement might be reduced. The DRL based approach also had other advantages (no manually set thresholds, easy including multiple decision factors, easy reuse in context of similar applications).

The approach we have used to train the policy delivered good results. The resulting policy could manage a sample AWS-based infrastructure. Using a simulator allowed to run many more interactions with a simulated environment than it would be possible in a real environment. In the same time the cost of training has been greatly reduced comparing to running a copy of a production version of the managed application.

We have identified some issues which require further work. Our resource allocation policy was unable to react to changes in the environment fast enough. It was limited by having to wait through the grace period and was capable of starting or stopping only a single VM at a time. In line with our expectations, the policy was able to make good decisions only in situations, to which it was exposed in the prior training (e.g. was very slow to shutdown the unused resources after the workload stopped completely).

We plan to continue the work on extending the described approach. Further work includes adding a policy improvement loop which would allow to dynamically adjust the policy to a changing workload and would remove the requirement of training the policy prior to the deployment. We also aim to extend the range of available actions to enable adding or removing more resources at once.

Acknowledgements. The research presented in this paper was supported by the funds assigned to AGH University of Science and Technology by the Polish Ministry of Science and Higher Education. The experiments have been carried out on the PL-Grid infrastructure resources of ACC Cyfronet AGH and on the Amazon Web Services Elastic Compute Cloud.

References

1. Amazon Web Services Elastic Compute Cloud. https://aws.amazon.com/ec2/. Accessed 30 Dec 2019
2. Graphite Project. https://graphiteapp.org/. Accessed 28 Nov 2019
3. PyTorch DNN Evolution. https://gitlab.com/pkoperek/pytorch-dnn-evolution. Accessed 01 Dec 2019
4. Ashraf, A., et al.: CRAMP: cost-efficient resource allocation for multiple web applications with proactive scaling. In: 4th IEEE International Conference on Cloud Computing Technology and Science Proceedings, pp. 581–586, December 2012
5. Brockman, G., et al.: OpenAI Gym (2016). http://arxiv.org/abs/1606.01540
6. Chen, L., et al.: AuTO: scaling deep reinforcement learning for datacenter-scale automatic traffic optimization. In: SIGCOMM 2018, New York, USA, pp. 191–205 (2018)
7. Ferretti, S., et al.: Qos-aware clouds. In: 2010 IEEE 3rd International Conference on Cloud Computing, pp. 321–328, July 2010
8. Filho, M.C.S., et al.: Cloudsim plus: a cloud computing simulation framework pursuing software engineering principles for improved modularity, extensibility and correctness. In: IFIP/IEEE Symposium on Integrated Network and Service Management, pp. 400–406, May 2017
9. Funika, W., et al.: Towards autonomic semantic-based management of distributed applications. Comput. Sci. **11**, 51–64 (2010)
10. Funika, W., Koperek, P.: Evaluating the use of policy gradient optimization approach for automatic cloud resource provisioning. In: Wyrzykowski, R., Deelman, E., Dongarra, J., Karczewski, K. (eds.) PPAM 2019. LNCS, vol. 12043, pp. 467–478. Springer, Cham (2020). https://doi.org/10.1007/978-3-030-43229-4_40

11. Gu, S., et al.: Deep reinforcement learning for robotic manipulation with asynchronous off-policy updates. In: Proceedings 2017 IEEE International Conference on Robotics and Automation (ICRA), Piscataway, NJ, USA. IEEE, May 2017
12. Kaelbling, L.P., et al.: Reinforcement learning: a survey. CoRR cs.AI/9605103 (1996). http://arxiv.org/abs/cs.AI/9605103
13. Kitowski, J., et al.: Computer simulation of heuristic reinforcement learning system for nuclear plant load changes control. Comput. Phys. Commun. **18**, 339–352 (1979)
14. Koperek, P., Funika, W.: Dynamic business metrics-driven resource provisioning in cloud environments. In: Wyrzykowski, R., Dongarra, J., Karczewski, K., Waśniewski, J. (eds.) PPAM 2011. LNCS, vol. 7204, pp. 171–180. Springer, Heidelberg (2012). https://doi.org/10.1007/978-3-642-31500-8_18
15. LeCun, Y., Cortes, C.: MNIST handwritten digit database (2010). http://yann.lecun.com/exdb/mnist/
16. Minarolli, D., Freisleben, B.: Distributed resource allocation to virtual machines via artificial neural networks. In: 2014 Proceedings of the 22nd Euromicro International Conference on Parallel, Distributed, and Network-Based Processing, PDP 2014, pp. 490–499. IEEE Computer Society, Washington, DC (2014)
17. Mnih, V., et al.: Playing Atari with deep reinforcement learning (2013). http://arxiv.org/abs/1312.5602
18. Mnih, V., et al.: Human-level control through deep reinforcement learning. Nature **518**(7540), 529–533 (2015)
19. Mnih, V., et al.: Asynchronous methods for deep reinforcement learning. In: Balcan, M.F., Weinberger, K.Q. (eds.) Proceedings of the 33rd International Conference on Machine Learning, vol. 48, pp. 1928–1937. PMLR, 20–22 June 2016
20. Schulman, J., et al.: Proximal policy optimization algorithms. CoRR abs/1707.06347 (2017). http://arxiv.org/abs/1707.06347
21. Silver, D., et al.: Mastering the game of go without human knowledge. Nature **550**, 354–359 (2017)
22. Sutton, R.S.: Temporal credit assignment in reinforcement learning. Ph.D. thesis (1984)
23. Wang, Z., et al.: Automated cloud provisioning on AWS using deep reinforcement learning. CoRR abs/1709.04305 (2017). http://arxiv.org/abs/1709.04305
24. Xiong, P., et al.: SmartSLA: cost-sensitive management of virtualized resources for CPU-bound database services. IEEE Trans. Parallel Distrib. Syst. **26**, 1441–1451 (2014)

An Open-Source Virtualization Layer for CUDA Applications

Niklas Eiling$^{(\boxtimes)}$, Stefan Lankes, and Antonello Monti

E.ON Energy Research Center, Institute for Automation of Complex Power Systems,
RWTH Aachen University, Aachen, Germany
{niklas.eiling,slankes,amonti}@eonerc.rwth-aachen.de
http://www.acs.eonerc.rwth-aachen.de

Abstract. GPUs have achieved widespread adoption for High-Performance Computing and Cloud applications. However, the closed-source nature of CUDA has hindered the development of otherwise commonly used virtualization techniques. In this paper, we evaluate the feasibility of building a GPU virtualization layer that isolates the GPU and CPU parts of CUDA applications to achieve better control of the interactions between applications and the CUDA libraries. We present our open-source tool that transparently intercepts CUDA library calls and executes them in a separate process using remote procedure calls. This allows the execution of CUDA applications on machines without a GPU and provides a basis for the development of tools that require fine-grained control of the GPU resources, such as checkpoint/restore and job schedulers.

Keywords: GPU · Virtualization · CUDA · Remote execution

1 Introduction

Hardware accelerators continue to attract significant interest in the cloud- and High-Performance-Computing (HPC) fields. Today, a growing number of clusters employ GPUs as hardware accelerators, because of the high peak performance and efficiency they offer at a reasonable cost [1,6]. The reason for these advantages is the optimization of GPUs for application profiles that are common in many computing applications: Highly parallel programs that use similarly executing threads to process large amounts of data. This leads to clusters with GPUs having better energy efficiency and a higher performance/price ratio than those without GPUs [6]. As power efficiency is increasingly becoming a limiting factor for performance [4,18], GPUs will certainly play an even more important role in future high performance systems. Despite this, they are rarely integrated into otherwise commonly used virtualization techniques that have the ability to improve availability and utilization of resources by allowing dynamic allocation and/or restriction of computing resources [5,8].

© Springer Nature Switzerland AG 2021
B. Balis et al. (Eds.): Euro-Par 2020 Workshops, LNCS 12480, pp. 160–171, 2021.
https://doi.org/10.1007/978-3-030-71593-9_13

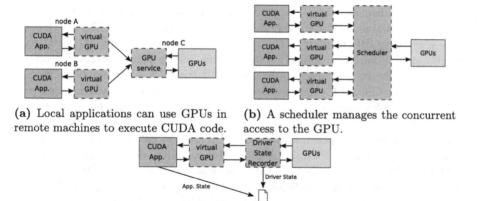

(a) Local applications can use GPUs in remote machines to execute CUDA code.

(b) A scheduler manages the concurrent access to the GPU.

(c) Recording driver interactions of CUDA applications enables checkpoint/restart.

Fig. 1. A GPU virtualization layer (in gray) is an enabler for several techniques that increase flexibility, utilization, or fault tolerance of clusters.

GPU virtualization is challenging because of the tight integration between user-level code and the device driver that manages the interaction between CPU and GPU. As accelerator devices, GPUs are able to execute programs similarly to CPUs, but require to be controlled by CPU code. Thus, a GPU application consists of a CPU part and a GPU part. The CPU part consists of a process that interacts with the GPU driver to provide the GPU part with input data, to launch the GPU code and to collect the computation results. Furthermore, GPUs have on-board memory that is separate from the main memory accessible by the CPU. To distinguish the two memory types, we stick to the CUDA terminology of calling the GPU memory *device memory* and the CPU memory *host memory*. While there are several frameworks that developers might use to create GPU applications [12], CUDA is most commonly used for the implementation of computing applications. CUDA consists of several software layers with multiple APIs, that provide different abstraction levels for the interaction with the GPU, most notable the CUDA runtime library and the lower-level driver library. NVIDIA keeps the implementation of these libraries proprietary. This significantly hinders the research on novel GPU virtualization techniques for which the interaction of applications with the GPU devices has to be manipulated. Nevertheless, this paper focuses on NVIDIA GPUs and CUDA, as these products are the most commonly used for computing tasks[1].

---

[1] The Top500 list (https://www.top500.org/) from November 2019 that ranks the fastest HPC clusters contains no cluster that uses GPUs from different vendors.

The virtualization of GPUs involves inserting a virtualization layer between CUDA applications and the GPU device. Conceptually, the CUDA application uses a virtual GPU instead of the real device, thus decoupling the CPU part of the application from the GPU part. This allows complete control of the interactions between CUDA applications and the GPU, thus enabling several usage scenarios for GPUs that are not possible with standard NVIDIA tools (see Fig. 1). GPU virtualization enables remote execution, i.e., the sharing of GPUs by multiple CUDA applications, which may be located on different systems. This makes a cluster setup possible, where GPUs are concentrated on a few nodes, instead of being homogeneously distributed across all nodes. With such a setup, a higher GPU utilization is achievable because the amount of GPU and CPU resources assigned to jobs is flexible [16]. Furthermore, the fine-grained control of the computing resources assigned to individual CUDA applications allows the implementation of custom schedulers that can balance, limit and track the use of GPU resources. Different CUDA applications may then be isolated from the influence of other processes on the system, in respect of performance and resources. GPU virtualization is also a requirement for the implementation of checkpoint/restart schemes for CUDA applications, where the execution state is saved and may be restored later. Checkpoint/restart requires virtualization for the ability to record the interactions with the GPU driver. During the execution of GPU code, the NVIDIA driver exhibits a changing internal state, which cannot be trivially reconstructed without knowledge of past driver interactions. Checkpoint/restart may be used to increase the flexibility and fault tolerance of clusters and to facilitate task migration thereby enabling dynamic load balancing [8].

This paper presents a virtualization layer that enables the realization of these scenarios. It is able to fully control the usage of GPU resources of CUDA applications, thus allowing redirection, manipulation and recording of device interactions, while CUDA applications stay unaware of the virtualization. The rest of the paper is structured as follows: In Sect. 2, we provide an overview of the current state of research into GPU virtualization. Section 3 presents the implementation of our virtualization layer. We evaluate our solution in Sect. 4 and finally draw a conclusion in Sect. 5.

2   Related Work

There has been some previous work on the virtualization for CUDA applications. However, for most virtualization solutions no source code is available and others support only outdated CUDA versions.

rCUDA allows CUDA application to use GPUs installed in a remote system [3], as shown in Fig. 1a. This is achieved by replacing the CUDA APIs with alternatives that forward CUDA API calls of local applications to a remote machine either via a TCP connection or via Infiniband verbs. rCUDA supports the driver API and the runtime API as well as several higher-level CUDA APIs, such as cuDNN, cuSOLVER and cuBLAS. The runtime API is re-implemented using the driver API, making the implementation of new API functions work-intensive as there is not always a clear driver API counterpart to runtime API functions. The tool achieves memory bandwidths that are comparable with native CUDA executions, when a sufficiently fast interconnect is used [14]. The most recent release does only support CUDA 9.0 and may therefore not be used with GPUs from the Turing generation. rCuda is not open-source and the authors make only a small amount of implementation details available, making detailed evaluation of the approach and code reuse impossible. The authors target users who want to remotely execute existing applications and therefore do not require source code access. However, not being open-source makes rCuda impossible to use for research into advanced virtualization strategies such as those shown in Fig. 1.

Another GPU virtualization approach is DS-CUDA [13], which targets a scenario where a cloud provides the GPU resources for local CUDA applications. Similarly to rCuda, DS-CUDA uses a client-server architecture, where API calls in a CUDA application are forwarded to a server that interacts with the GPU devices. For the communication DS-CUDA can use RPC or Infiniband verbs. The authors increase the reliability of GPU calculations by allowing redundant calculations, where API calls are performed on multiple GPUs and repeated if they have different results. DS-CUDA is licensed under a GPLv3 license and supports version 6 of the CUDA toolkit. This means GPUs newer than from the Pascal generation are not supported by DS-CUDA. Furthermore, the tool is not actively developed anymore.

vCUDA uses runtime API interception and redirection to provide GPU access to virtual machines [15]. Similarly to the previous tools, vCUDA redirects API calls of CUDA applications in the virtual machine to a server process running on the host which in turn forwards them to the CUDA driver. However, vCUDA only supports CUDA version 1.1, which predates support for any data center grade GPU from the Tesla line of products. Additionally, the source code of vCUDA is not available anymore.

The CUDA Multi-Process Service (MPS) enables multiple GPU jobs to be executed concurrently, thus increasing GPU utilization compared to the case where only a single application may occupy a GPU at any given time [11]. MPS achieves this by replacing the CUDA APIs with a client-server structure, where client processes send GPU tasks to a server who manages the concurrent access to the GPUs. MPS uses named pipes and domain sockets for this communication. Limitations of MPS include incomplete support for all CUDA features, a limited amount of client-server connections and only a simple job scheduler. Furthermore, MPS is not open-source thus making customizations and reuse impossible.

None of the previously discussed solutions represents an open-source virtualization solution for GPUs that supports the latest GPU generation. In this paper, we present a novel tool that offers all the benefits of previous work, while supporting the latest GPUs and being released under an open-source license.[2]

---

[2] The code is available at https://github.com/RWTH-ACS/cricket.

3 GPU Virtualization for CUDA Applications

The goal of our virtualization solution for GPUs is to offer a basis for the development of resource management strategies that require control over how applications use computing resources. A key requirement is that the code has to be published under an open-source license to allow researchers to reuse and build on top of the existing code. Furthermore, many scenarios require transparency or binary compatibility, that is, original CUDA application code cannot be required to be modified, as their source code might not be available. A transparent solution also means that applications remain unaware of the virtual nature of the execution environment. The improved flexibility and control introduced by virtualization is not allowed to come at the cost of large performance overheads. Another requirement is support for the latest GPU generation and CUDA toolkit[3].

GPU virtualization requires the insertion of a virtualization layer in the GPU software stack. The task of this virtualization layer is to separate the CUDA application from the real device and manage the interactions between both. The virtual device used by applications may differ from the real device, e.g., they may be located on different machines or the computing resources of the virtual device may be limited. We achieve the separation by splitting the GPU and CPU parts of CUDA applications into separate processes. Instead of directly accessing GPU resources, CUDA applications use Remote Procedure Calls (RPC) to send requests to an RPC server that is responsible for the management of the available GPUs.

The remaining chapter introduces details about our implementation and the rationale behind design choices that had to be made.

3.1 The CUDA Software Stack

CUDA offers multiple ways of interfacing applications with the GPU driver: High-level primitives, the runtime API and the lower level driver API. At which level the virtualization layer is inserted requires careful consideration. The ideal point for this would be between driver API and NVIDIA driver, as this way all software layers above the driver would be unaware of the virtualization, thus achieving full transparency to any GPU application (Fig. 2). However, due to the closed-source nature of the NVIDIA driver and the API implementations, there is not enough information available to implement this approach.

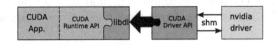

Fig. 2. With default setting the CUDA runtime API is linked statically. It loads the driver API dynamically during startup using `dlopen` and `dlsym`.

---

[3] As of writing the latest GPU generation and CUDA version are Turing and CUDA 10.2.

Going one layer up the software stack, the next possible point of separation is at the CUDA driver API. However, as a result of undocumented interactions, the driver API cannot be cleanly separated from the runtime API. Consequently, a virtualization layer at the driver API level does not allow the use of the original runtime API on top of it. Because of these complications, we opted to implement a virtualization layer that may be inserted at the levels of either the runtime API or the driver API. CUDA applications may use one of the virtualization layer positions depending on whether they use the runtime API or the driver API. While involving more work, this has the benefit of completely isolating the user code of the CUDA application from any internal state of the CUDA APIs, as interactions between the APIs are hidden behind the virtualization layer. For applications that use the runtime API, one API call often necessitates multiple driver API calls. Therefore, virtualization at the position of the runtime API requires less communication, making it beneficial for performance.

A prerequisite for the insertion of the virtualization layer is that the replaced CUDA API library is linked dynamically to the CUDA application. This is because with dynamically linked libraries the library code is loaded during the startup of the application, making the replacement of the library code possible. With statically linked libraries the library code is inserted into the application binary at compile time. The replacement of statically linked code requires techniques such as instrumentation, which introduce significant performance degradation [7, 10].

With dynamic linking, we can intercept the calls to library functions and replace them with our own code by replacing the linked object with a different one that exports the same symbols. Using this technique, we achieve the insertion of our virtualization layer by loading a replacement library that overwrites the function symbols of the original CUDA API libraries.

3.2 Isolation with Remote Procedure Calls (RPCs)

After library calls have been intercepted, they have to be forwarded to the real GPU. For this, an RPC server process waits for incoming GPU resource request from CUDA applications, executes them and passes the results back to the original application. Unlike other approaches, such as rCUDA, we execute the original API function even for the runtime API and do not re-implement the runtime API using the driver API. We use the Transport Independent Remote Procedure Calls (TI-RPC) implementation of the Remote Procedure Call Protocol Specification Version 2 [17] as a basis for this communication.

The replacement library that inserts the virtualization layer, uses a library constructor to set up the connection to the RPC server process. Our virtualization layer supports connections via either a domain socket or a TCP socket. A TCP connection enables the use of a GPU that is installed in a different system than where the CUDA application runs. The RPC server process is also realized by launching the CUDA application binary and loading a dynamic library at startup. The library constructor for the RPC server only waits for incoming RPC requests and never launches the original main function. By using a

Fig. 3. Replacing the runtime API with RPC code allows separating the CUDA application from the internal state of both runtime and driver APIs.

dynamic library instead of building a standalone server application, the server process has access to the GPU code, the code for launching kernels, and the CUDA initialization functions, which the CUDA compiler inserts into the application binary. Because the management of these resources is not documented, using the original binary enables us to initialize CUDA and launch kernels as if writing a normal CUDA application.

Some CUDA API functions return pointers to internal resources, e.g., pointers to device memory and internal data structures. These pointers are only intended for passing to the CUDA APIs and user programs should not dereference them directly. Instead of collecting and copying the internal data structures from the RPC server process to the CUDA application, we pass only the raw pointer values, ignoring the fact that they reference address spaces in a different process. This way, for most API functions the virtualization layer needs to transfer only a small amount of data for parameter and return values. In contrast, the `cudaMemcpy` class of API functions is often used to transfer large amounts of application data between host and device memories. Using our RPC approach, we have to first copy this data from the CUDA application to the RPC server, which copies it to the GPU memory. When the CUDA application is launched on the same system as the RPC server, we can avoid this additional copy operation by using shared memory. Using Infiniband IBverbs, our virtualization layer is able to use RDMA in case the CUDA application and the RPC server execute on different systems. However, these optimizations require setting up the shared memory or RDMA memory segments during the allocation of the host memory from which a transfer originates. Therefore, increasing the transfer performance using shared memory or IBverbs only works for applications that allocate host memory using the `cudaHostAlloc` function, which is originally intended to request pinned memory from which CUDA can perform faster copy operations to device memory.

Figure 3 summarizes how requests to a virtual GPU occur. A CUDA API call in the CUDA application is redirected to our replacement library. The library implements all CUDA API functions with procedures that execute a remote procedure call to the server process. There, the request is executed using the original API function of either the runtime or driver APIs. The server collects the results and sends them back to the CUDA application, where they are returned to the original program.

4   Evaluation

For the evaluation we use one system equipped with two Intel Xeon Gold 6128 CPUs and Tesla P40 and Tesla T4 GPUs and one node with two AMD Epyc 7301 CPUs and no GPUs. Both nodes are connected via a Gigabit Ethernet and an Infiniband 100 Gb/s link using Mellanox MCX556A-ECAT ConnectX-5 Adapter Cards. Unless otherwise noted, we are using the Infiniband Link with IP over Infiniband (IPoIB) for the communication between the nodes. While we confirmed the compatibility of our virtualization layer with the previously mentioned GPUs, the performance impact of virtualization is independent of the specific GPU. Therefore, this section presents results only for the Tesla T4, as it is from the latest generation. All measurements have been performed using version 10.2 of the CUDA toolkit. We compare the execution time of several applications when using our virtualization solution to the case where no virtualization is employed. Additionally, we performed several micro benchmarks to assess potential sources of overhead.

4.1   Benchmarks

The virtualization layer introduces overhead as a result of the communication between CUDA applications and the RPC server. To analyze the impact of this overhead on CUDA applications, we evaluate our virtualization layer with two of the example applications distributed with the CUDA Toolkit and two third-party application. The *matrixMul* application performs a series of densely filled matrix-matrix multiplications without repeatedly copying the data between host and device. The *nbody* application is a physics simulation that computes the gravitational interaction between a configurable amount of bodies. *hotspot* from the Rodinia Benchmark Suite [2] is a thermal simulation application that solves differential equations. *DPsim* is a real-time capable power system simulator for

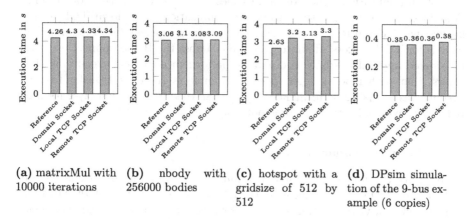

(a) matrixMul with 10000 iterations   **(b)** nbody with 256000 bodies   **(c)** hotspot with a gridsize of 512 by 512   **(d)** DPsim simulation of the 9-bus example (6 copies)

Fig. 4. Execution time overhead based on 25 averaged runs on a Tesla T4.

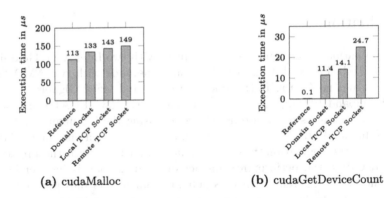

(a) cudaMalloc   (b) cudaGetDeviceCount

Fig. 5. CUDA API overhead based on 100 averaged runs on a Tesla T4.

dynamic phasor and electromagnetic transient simulations [9]. The variety of considered applications shows our virtualization layer supports a set of CUDA features is sufficient for productive use.

Figure 4 compares the reference execution time of the applications without virtualization with our virtualization layer using a domain socket connection, a local loopback TCP connection and a remote TCP connection between two systems. It shows a low overhead due to the virtualization layer for matrixMul, nbody and dpsim. For hotspot, the remote execution introduces an overhead of approx 25%. This is because of all applications hotspot transfers the largest amount of memory between host and device memories, resulting in the transfer bandwidth reduction of the virtualization layer having a higher impact on the execution time. The matrixMul applications mostly launches kernels and performs only a few other calls to the CUDA API. The low overhead for this application thus shows that kernel dispatches are not significantly slowed down by the virtualization layer.

For all applications, the execution times when communicating locally via a domain socket are larger than when communication via a local TCP socket, suggesting that the RPC implementation is not as efficient for domain sockets as it is for TCP sockets. Remote executions across the IPoIB connection of the considered applications have comparable performance to local executions. This shows, that with modern high speed interconnects the data transfer between systems has a smaller performance impact than the virtualization layer itself for data-intensive applications such as hotspot.

4.2   Micro Benchmarks

To quantify the impact the virtualization layer has on the execution time of calls to the CUDA API, we measure the latency of two typical CUDA API functions in different virtualization scenarios. cudaMalloc allocates a region of device memory and represents a commonly used API function. cudaGetDeviceCount returns the number of GPUs available to the CUDA API. As such, this function requires the transfer of only a single integer, resulting in almost all latency being due to communication delays.

For both API functions we measure an overhead between 11.4 to 36 μs when using the virtualization layer. This increase is due to the execution of additional code and copying of parameters and results that is necessary for the redirection of API calls. While the impact of the virtualization layer on individual functions is comparatively large, most applications do not perform a high number of CUDA API calls. For example, the previously considered applications nbody, hostpot and DPsim perform 72, 10 and 72 API calls, respectively. Only matrixMul performs a higher amount of 10033, while still showing only a small overhead due to the virtualization layer (see Fig. 4a). Instead of performing more calls to CUDA functions with increasing problem sizes, most applications require the transfer of more data between host and device memory. Therefore, the CUDA API functions responsible for transferring data between host and device memories also require an analysis.

Figure 6 shows the achieved memory transfer bandwidth for the reference case and with our virtualization layer using local and remote communication. The virtualization layer decreases the bandwidth for transfers from and to the GPU, as a result of the additional data transfer between CUDA application and RPC server. The previous observation that the RPC implementation is not able to fully utilize the bandwidth of domain sockets is here again visible. When the pinned memory API is used on local data transfers, our virtualization layer avoids the additional transfer by instead using shared memory. Therefore, the performance for this case is comparable to the reference case of using the pinned memory API without virtualization (see Fig. 6a and Fig. 6b).

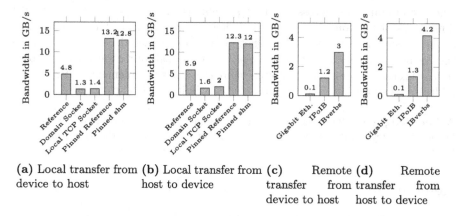

(a) Local transfer from device to host   (b) Local transfer from host to device   (c) Remote transfer from device to host   (d) Remote transfer from host to device

Fig. 6. Memory transfer bandwidth based on 100 averaged runs of `bandwidthTest` application from the CUDA toolkit.

When client and server reside on different computing nodes the interconnect bandwidth limits the overall transfer bandwidth up to approx. 1.2 GB/s (see Fig. 6c and Fig. 6d). Using Gigabit Ethernet we measure a bandwidth of approximately 112 MB/s for device to host transfers and 114 MB/s for host to device transfers, which is close to the maximum bandwidth of Gigabit Ethernet. However, using the IPoIB interconnect the virtualization layer does not fully utilize the available interconnect bandwidth. Even when using IBverbs for the transfer, the achieved bandwidth is below the interconnect capacity and lower than in the reference case without virtualization. While further optimization efforts into increasing the achieved bandwidth seem promising, the application evaluation showed already low additional overhead on the overall execution time for remote execution compared to local execution.

5   Conclusion

The virtualization solution for GPU devices presented in this paper provides a basis for future research on advanced task management techniques, which may increase flexibility, utilization, and fault tolerance. Our virtualization layer is fully transparent to CUDA applications, i.e., requires no source code modifications or recompilation. This is despite the closed-source nature of the CUDA software that makes the development of virtualization solutions for GPUs difficult. By intercepting CUDA API calls and redirecting them to a separate process, we achieve isolation and full control of GPU resources used by applications. Even though the virtualization layer increases the individual CUDA API functions latency and reduces memory transfer bandwidths, this incurs only a small overhead to the overall execution time of CUDA applications. The overhead when communicating across different systems is mainly due to the bandwidth limitations of the considered Gigabit Ethernet interconnect. Thus, faster interconnects, such as 10 Gigabit Ethernet or Infiniband should be able to increase the memory transfer bandwidth. Because we publish our code under an open source license, others may customize and reuse it to implement software that addresses the growing need for increased flexibility in HPC clusters.

Acknowledgment. This research and development was supported by the German Federal Ministry of Education and Research under Grant 01IH16010C (Project ENVE-LOPE).

References

1. Baker, Z.K., Gokhale, M.B., Tripp, J.L.: Matched filter computation on FPGA, cell and GPU. In: 15th Annual IEEE Symposium on Field-Programmable Custom Computing Machines (FCCM 2007), pp. 207–218, April 2007. https://doi.org/10.1109/FCCM.2007.52
2. Che, S., et al.: Rodinia: a benchmark suite for heterogeneous computing. In: 2009 IEEE International Symposium on Workload Characterization (IISWC), pp. 44–54. IEEE (2009)

3. Duato, J., Peña, A.J., Silla, F., Mayo, R., Quintana-Ortí, E.S.: rCUDA: reducing the number of GPU-based accelerators in high performance clusters. In: 2010 International Conference on High Performance Computing Simulation, pp. 224–231, June 2010. https://doi.org/10.1109/HPCS.2010.5547126

4. Esmaeilzadeh, H., Blem, E., Amant, R.S., Sankaralingam, K., Burger, D.: Dark silicon and the end of multicore scaling. IEEE Micro **32**(3), 122–134 (2012). https://doi.org/10.1109/MM.2012.17

5. Gavrilovska, A., et al.: High-performance hypervisor architectures: virtualization in HPC systems. In: Workshop on System-Level Virtualization for HPC (HPCVirt). Citeseer (2007)

6. Kutzner, C., Páll, S., Fechner, M., Esztermann, A., de Groot, B.L., Grubmüller, H.: More bang for your buck: improved use of GPU nodes for GROMACS 2018. J. Comput. Chem. **40**(27), 2418–2431 (2019). https://doi.org/10.1002/jcc.26011

7. Laurenzano, M.A., Tikir, M.M., Carrington, L., Snavely, A.: PEBIL: efficient static binary instrumentation for Linux. In: 2010 IEEE International Symposium on Performance Analysis of Systems Software (ISPASS), pp. 175–183 (2010)

8. Milojičić, D.S., Douglis, F., Paindaveine, Y., Wheeler, R., Zhou, S.: Process migration. ACM Comput. Surv. **32**(3), 241–299 (2000). https://doi.org/10.1145/367701.367728

9. Mirz, M., Vogel, S., Reinke, G., Monti, A.: DPsim–a dynamic phasor real-time simulator for power systems. SoftwareX **10**, 100253 (2019). https://doi.org/10.1016/j.softx.2019.100253

10. Nethercote, N., Seward, J.: Valgrind: a framework for heavyweight dynamic binary instrumentation. In: Proceedings of the 28th ACM SIGPLAN Conference on Programming Language Design and Implementation, PLDI 2007, pp. 89–100. Association for Computing Machinery, New York (2007). https://doi.org/10.1145/1250734.1250746

11. NVIDIA Corporation: Multi-process service. Technical report. https://docs.nvidia.com/deploy/pdf/CUDA_Multi_Process_Service_Overview.pdf. Accessed 04 May 2020

12. NVIDIA Corporation: NVIDIA(R) CUDA(TM) architecture. Technical report. http://developer.download.nvidia.com/compute/cuda/docs/CUDA_Architecture_Overview.pdf. Accessed 10 May 2020

13. Oikawa, M., Kawai, A., Nomura, K., Yasuoka, K., Yoshikawa, K., Narumi, T.: DS-CUDA: a middleware to use many GPUs in the cloud environment. In: 2012 SC Companion: High Performance Computing, Networking Storage and Analysis, pp. 1207–1214 (2012)

14. Reaño, C., Silla, F.: A performance comparison of CUDA remote GPU virtualization frameworks. In: Proceedings of the 2015 IEEE International Conference on Cluster Computing, CLUSTER 2015, pp. 488–489. IEEE Computer Society (2015). https://doi.org/10.1109/CLUSTER.2015.76

15. Shi, L., Chen, H., Sun, J., Li, K.: vCUDA: GPU-accelerated high-performance computing in virtual machines. IEEE Trans. Comput. **61**(6), 804–816 (2012)

16. Silla, F., Prades, J., Iserte, S., Reaño, C.: Remote GPU virtualization: is it useful? In: 2016 2nd IEEE International Workshop on High-Performance Interconnection Networks in the Exascale and Big-Data Era (HiPINEB), pp. 41–48 (2016)

17. Srinivasan, R.: RPC: remote procedure call protocol specification version 2 (1995)

18. Villa, O., et al.: Scaling the power wall: a path to exascale. In: SC 2014: International Conference for High Performance Computing, Networking, Storage and Analysis, pp. 830–841, November 2014. https://doi.org/10.1109/SC.2014.73

High Performance Portable Solver for Tridiagonal Toeplitz Systems of Linear Equations

Beata Dmitruk[⊠] and Przemysław Stpiczyński

Institute of Computer Science, Maria Curie-Skłodowska University,
ul. Akademicka 9, 20-033 Lublin, Poland
beata.dmitruk@umcs.pl, przem@hektor.umcs.lublin.pl

Abstract. We show that recently developed *divide and conquer* parallel algorithm for solving tridiagonal Toeplitz systems of linear equations can be easily and efficiently implemented for a variety of modern multicore and GPU architectures, as well as hybrid systems. Our new portable implementation that uses OpenACC can be executed on both CPU-based and GPU-accelerated systems. More sophisticated variants of the implementation are suitable for systems with multiple GPUs and it can use CPU and GPU cores. We consider the use of both *column-wise* and *row-wise* storage formats for two dimensional double precision arrays and show how to efficiently convert between these two formats using cache memory. Numerical experiments performed on Intel CPUs and Nvidia GPUs show that our new implementation achieves relatively good performance.

Keywords: Tridiagonal Toeplitz systems · Parallel algorithms · Vectorization · Portability · OpenACC · Hybrid systems

1 Introduction

Tridiagonal Toeplitz systems of linear equations appear in many theoretical and practical applications. For example, numerical algorithms for solving boundary value problems for ordinary and partial differential equations reduce to such systems [13,15]. They also play an important role in piecewise cubic interpolation and spline algorithms [4,14]. There are several methods for solving such systems (the review of the literature can be found in [5]). Rojo [10] proposed a method for solving symmetric tridiagonal Toeplitz systems using LU decomposition of a system with almost Toeplitz structure together with Sherman-Morrison's formula and this approach was modified to obtain new solvers for a possible parallel execution [7,9].

In [5] we proposed a new divide and conquer parallel algorithm for solving such systems using the splitting $T = LR + P$, where L, R are bidiagonal and P has only one non-zero entry. We showed how to reduce the number of necessary

© Springer Nature Switzerland AG 2021
B. Balis et al. (Eds.): Euro-Par 2020 Workshops, LNCS 12480, pp. 172–184, 2021.
https://doi.org/10.1007/978-3-030-71593-9_14

synchronizations and use SIMD extensions of modern processors. Our OpenMP (version 3.1) implementation of this method achieved very good speedup on Intel Xeon CPUs (up to 5.06) and Intel Xeon Phi (up to 29.45). While this approach can be further improved using more sophisticated vectorization techniques such as the use of intrinsics [1,8,11], it will result in a loss of portability between different architectures. OpenACC is a standard for accelerated computing [2,6]. It offers compiler directives for offloading C/C++ and Fortran programs from host to attached accelerator devices. Such simple directives allow marking regions of source code for automatic acceleration in a portable vendor-independent manner. However, sometimes it is desired to apply some high-level transformations of source codes to achieve better performance [2,6,12]. Marked sources can be compiled for a variety of accelerators and parallel computers based on multicore CPUs. It is also possible to use OpenACC and OpenMP together to utilize CPU and GPU cores at the same time.

In this paper, we present a new portable OpenACC-based implementation of the algorithm that can be used on both CPUs and GPU accelerators without any changes in the source code. We also show how to use both OpenACC and OpenMP to utilize multiple GPUs, as well as implement the algorithm for hybrid systems. We study its performance on Intel Xeon CPUs and three Nvidia GPUs architectures: Kepler, Turing, and Volta. We consider both *column-wise* and *row-wise* storage formats for two dimensional arrays and show how to efficiently convert arrays between these two formats using cache memory to ensure coalesced access to device's global memory. We also discuss which format is more suitable for CPU-based and GPU-accelerated architectures.

2   Parallel Algorithm

Let us consider a tridiagonal Toeplitz system of linear equations $T\mathbf{x} = \mathbf{f}$ of the following form

$$
\begin{bmatrix}
t_2 & t_3 & & & \\
t_1 & t_2 & t_3 & & \\
& \ddots & \ddots & \ddots & \\
& & t_1 & t_2 & t_3 \\
& & & t_1 & t_2
\end{bmatrix}
\begin{bmatrix}
x_0 \\ x_1 \\ \vdots \\ \vdots \\ x_{n-1}
\end{bmatrix}
=
\begin{bmatrix}
f_0 \\ f_1 \\ \vdots \\ \vdots \\ f_{n-1}
\end{bmatrix}.
\tag{1}
$$

For the sake of simplicity we assume that $n = 2^k$, $k \in \mathbb{N}$. The matrix T can be decomposed as

$$
T = \underbrace{\begin{bmatrix}
1 & & & \\
\alpha & 1 & & \\
& \ddots & \ddots & \\
& & \alpha & 1 \\
& & & \alpha & 1
\end{bmatrix}}_{L}
\underbrace{\begin{bmatrix}
\beta & t_3 & & \\
& \beta & t_3 & \\
& & \ddots & \ddots \\
& & & \beta & t_3 \\
& & & & \beta
\end{bmatrix}}_{R}
+
\underbrace{\begin{bmatrix}
t_3\alpha & 0 & \dots & 0 \\
0 & 0 & & \vdots \\
\vdots & & \ddots & \vdots \\
0 & \dots & \dots & 0
\end{bmatrix}}_{P},
\tag{2}
$$

where $\alpha = (t_2 + \text{sign}(t_2)\sqrt{(t_2)^2 - 4t_1t_3})/(2t_3)$ and $\beta = t_2 - t_3\alpha$. Using (2) we can rewrite the Eq. (1) as follows

$$\begin{bmatrix} x_0 \\ x_1 \\ \vdots \\ x_{n-1} \end{bmatrix} = \underbrace{(LR)^{-1} \begin{bmatrix} f_0 \\ f_1 \\ \vdots \\ f_{n-1} \end{bmatrix}}_{\mathbf{v}} - \underbrace{t_3\alpha x_0 \, (LR)^{-1} \begin{bmatrix} 1 \\ 0 \\ \vdots \\ 0 \end{bmatrix}}_{\mathbf{u}} \tag{3}$$

or simply $\mathbf{x} = \mathbf{v} - t_3\alpha x_0\mathbf{u}$. Then the solution to (1) can be found using:

$$\begin{cases} x_0 = \frac{v_0}{1+t_3\alpha u_0} \\ x_i = v_i - t_3\alpha x_0 u_i, \quad i = 1,\ldots,n-1. \end{cases} \tag{4}$$

In order to solve (1) we have to find two vectors $\mathbf{v}$ and $\mathbf{u}$, solving two systems of linear equations with the same coefficient matrix, namely LR. The solution to a system of linear equations $LR\mathbf{y} = \mathbf{d}$ can be found in two stages. First, we solve $L\mathbf{z} = \mathbf{d}$, and then $R\mathbf{y} = \mathbf{z}$. This can be easily done using the following simple sequential algorithm based on the two recurrence relations:

$$\begin{cases} z_0 = d_0 \\ z_i = d_i - \alpha z_{i-1}, \quad i = 1,\ldots,n-1, \end{cases} \tag{5}$$

and

$$\begin{cases} y_{n-1} = z_{n-1}/\beta \\ y_i = (z_i - t_3 y_{i+1})/\beta, \quad i = n-2,\ldots,0. \end{cases} \tag{6}$$

This simple sequential algorithm can be efficient only for small values of n because it does not utilize the underlying hardware of modern processors, namely multiple cores and vector units. In order to obtain an efficient parallel algorithm for solving (5) let us consider the following *divide and conquer* method. First, we choose two integers $r, s > 1$, $rs = n$, and rewrite L in the following block form:

$$L = \begin{bmatrix} L_s & & & \\ B & L_s & & \\ & \ddots & \ddots & \\ & & B & L_s \end{bmatrix}, \quad L_s = \begin{bmatrix} 1 & & & \\ \alpha & 1 & & \\ & \ddots & \ddots & \\ & & \alpha & 1 \end{bmatrix}, \quad B = \begin{bmatrix} 0 \cdots & 0 & \alpha \\ \vdots & & 0 & 0 \\ \vdots & \ddots & & \vdots \\ 0 \cdots & \cdots & 0 \end{bmatrix}. \tag{7}$$

Let us define:

$$\mathbf{e}_k = (0,\ldots,\underbrace{0,1,0}_{k},\ldots,0)^T \in \mathbb{R}^s, \ k = 0,\ldots,s-1,$$

and split $\mathbf{d}, \mathbf{z}$ into vectors $\mathbf{d}_i = (d_{is},\ldots,d_{(i+1)s-1})^T$, $\mathbf{z}_i = (z_{is},\ldots,z_{(i+1)s-1})^T \in \mathbb{R}^s$, for $i = 0,\ldots,r-1$. Then $L\mathbf{z} = \mathbf{d}$ can be rewritten as follows:

$$\begin{cases} \mathbf{z}_0 = L_s^{-1}\mathbf{d}_0 \\ \mathbf{z}_i = L_s^{-1}\mathbf{d}_i - \alpha z_{is-1}L_s^{-1}\mathbf{e}_0, \quad i = 1,\ldots,r-1. \end{cases} \tag{8}$$

Similarly, in case of the upper bidiagonal system $R\mathbf{y} = \mathbf{z}$, assuming the same as previously, we get the following block form of R:

$$R = \begin{bmatrix} R_s & C & & \\ & R_s & \ddots & \\ & & \ddots & C \\ & & & R_s \end{bmatrix}, \quad R_s = \begin{bmatrix} \beta & t_3 & & \\ & \beta & \ddots & \\ & & \ddots & t_3 \\ & & & \beta \end{bmatrix}, \quad C = \begin{bmatrix} 0 & \cdots\cdots & 0 \\ \vdots & & \ddots & \vdots \\ 0 & 0 & & \vdots \\ t_3 & 0 & \cdots & 0 \end{bmatrix}. \quad (9)$$

Analogously to (8), we get the following formula to find $\mathbf{y}$:

$$\begin{cases} \mathbf{y}_{r-1} = R_s^{-1}\mathbf{z}_{r-1} \\ \mathbf{y}_i = R_s^{-1}\mathbf{z}_i - t_3 y_{(i+1)s}R_s^{-1}\mathbf{e}_{s-1}, \quad i = r-2,\ldots,0. \end{cases} \quad (10)$$

The algorithm for solving $LR\mathbf{y} = \mathbf{d}$ based on (8) and (10) comprises two main stages (A and B), each consisting of three steps, has a lot of potential parallelisms. All vectors $L_s^{-1}\mathbf{d}_i$, $i = 0,\ldots,r-1$, can be found in parallel (Step A1). Indeed, when we form the matrix $D = [\mathbf{d}_0,\ldots,\mathbf{d}_{r-1}]$, all columns of $X = L_s^{-1}D$ can be found using the following vector-recursive formula:

$$X_{i,*} \leftarrow D_{i,*} - \alpha * X_{i-1,*}, \quad i = 1,\ldots,s-1, \quad (11)$$

where $X_{i,*}$ and $D_{i,*}$ denote i-th rows of X and D, respectively. Then we can find the last entry of each vector $\mathbf{z}_i$, $i = 1,\ldots,r-1$, sequentially (Step A2) applying (8). Finally, again in parallel, we calculate $s-1$ remaining entries of $\mathbf{z}_1,\ldots,\mathbf{z}_{r-1}$ (Step A3). In the case of (10) we proceed similarly. If $Z = [\mathbf{z}_0,\ldots,\mathbf{z}_{r-1}]$, then $Z \leftarrow R_s^{-1}Z$ can be found (Step B1) using:

$$Z_{i,*} \leftarrow (Z_{i,*} - t_3 * Z_{i+1,*})/\beta, \quad i = s-2,\ldots,0. \quad (12)$$

Then during the sequential part (Step B2) we find first entries of each $\mathbf{y}_i$, $i = r-2,\ldots,0$, and finally (Step B3) we use (10) to calculate in parallel all remaining entries of $Y = [\mathbf{y}_0,\ldots,\mathbf{y}_{r-1}]$. The algorithm should be applied twice to find vectors $\mathbf{v}$ and $\mathbf{u}$, respectively. Then we use (4) to find the solution to (2). Note that (4) can be easily vectorized and parallelized.

3   OpenACC-Based and Hybrid OpenMP+OpenACC Implementations

The algorithm for solving (2) presented in Sect. 2 can be easily implemented using OpenACC. Parallel steps A1, A3, B1, B3 can be vectorized and parallelized using **parallel loop** constructs. It means that the execution of the independent loops will be distributed among gangs that work in SIMD mode utilizing available hardware. The steps A2 and B2 are sequential and should be executed by a single gang. Figure 1 (left) shows our OpenACC implementation of the steps A1, A2, A3 using the *column-wise storage* format for the matrix X stored as a double precision array. This format is the most natural because there is no need to do

```
1   // column-wise storage
2   // Step A1
3   #pragma acc parallel present(x)
4   {
5     #pragma acc loop  independent
6     for(int j=0;j<r;j++){
7       for(int i=1;i<s;i++)
8         x[j*s+i]-=x[j*s+i-1]*alpha;
9     }
10  }
11  // Step A2
12  #pragma acc parallel num_gangs(1)
13                      present(x)
14  {
15    for(int j=1;j<r;j++)
16      x[(j+1)*s-1]-=x[j*s-1]*e0_last*alpha;
17  }
18  // Step A3
19  #pragma acc parallel deviceptr(e0)
20                      present(x)
21  {
22    #pragma acc loop independent
23    for(int j=1;j<r;j++){
24      last1=x[j*s-1]*alpha;
25      #pragma acc loop  independent
26      for(int i=0;i<s-1;i++)
27        x[j*s+i]-=last1*e0[i];
28    }
29  }
```

```
// row-wise storage
// Step A1
#pragma acc parallel present(x)
{
  for(int i=1;i<s;i++){
    #pragma acc loop  independent
    for(int j=0;j<r;j++)
      x[i*r+j]-=x[(i-1)*r+j]*alpha;
  }
}
// Step A2
#pragma acc parallel num_gangs(1)
                    present(x)
{
  for(int j=1;j<r;j++)
    x[n-r+j]-=x[n-r+j-1]*e0_last*alpha;
}
// Step A3
#pragma acc parallel deviceptr(e0)
                    present(x)
{
  #pragma acc loop independent
  for(int i=0;i<s-1;i++){
    last1=e0[i]*alpha;
    #pragma acc loop independent
    for(int j=1;j<r;j++)
      x[i*r+j]-=x[(s-1)*r+j-1]*last1;
  }
}
```

Fig. 1. OpenACC implementations of the parallel algorithm based on (8) using *column-wise storage* (left) and *row-wise storage* (right)

any data transfers after choosing specific values of r, s. Unfortunately, this format does not allow to use of coalesced memory access to global memory of devices [3] during the steps A1 and B1. Thus, one can expect that the performance of the implementation using such storage format can be much worse compared to the implementation using the *row-wise storage* format (Fig. 1, right). In this case, all references to global memory are coalesced. Figure 2 shows simple parallel loops that can be used to convert between *column-wise storage* and *row-wise storage*. Unfortunately, such conversion between formats can significantly reduce the overall performance because of non-coalesced memory access.

```
1   // from column-wise to row-wise
2   #pragma acc parallel loop independent present(b,x)
3       for(int i=0;i<n;i++)
4         x[i]=b[i/r+(i%r)*s];
5     ...
6   // from row-wise to column-wise
7   #pragma acc parallel loop independent present(b,x)
8       for(int i=0;i<n;i++)
9         b[i]=x[i/s+(i%s)*r];
```

Fig. 2. Simple conversion between considered *column-wise* and *row-wise* array storage formats using OpenACC **parallel** construct

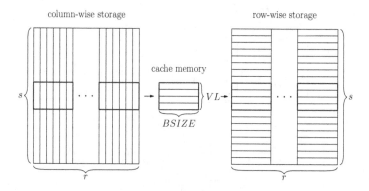

Fig. 3. Conversion from *column-wise* to *row-wise* array storage using device cache memory

In order to improve the performance of the implementation let us consider a more sophisticated method for conversion between *column-wise* and *row-wise* storage formats that uses cache memory to ensure coalesced memory access (Fig. 5). Each gang of $BSIZE$ threads is responsible for reading a block of $VL \times BSIZE$ elements from the array stored *column-wise* using coalesced memory access and writing it to the cache memory. Then such a block is moved to a new array stored *row-wise*. Figures 3 and 4 explain how to do it. A gang of threads operates on a sequence of VL blocks of $VL \times NC$ elements, where $VL \times NC = BSIZE$. Each column of such a block is loaded by VL threads, where VL is the size of a warp [3]. As soon as all blocks are in the cache memory, all threads within a gang write rows of $BSIZE$ elements into global memory. Devices coalesce such global memory access issued a warp into as few transactions as possible to minimize DRAM bandwidth [3]. Finally, it should be noted that in both cases (i.e. *column-wise* and *row-wise* storage formats) the steps B1, B2, B3 have been implemented similarly to excerpts of the source code shown in Fig. 1. Computations according to (4) have been implemented using `acc parallel loop` construct.

Figure 6 shows how to use OpenMP and OpenACC to utilize two GPUs. Two halves of the arrays are stored *row-wise* in global memories of GPUs. We create two OpenMP threads, each responsible for controlling one GPU. GPUs share data via host memory. The array `shared_data` is allocated on the host and each GPU has its copy of this array. The `update self` construct is used to update data on the host, while `update device` updates device memory. It is necessary to synchronize threads using the `omp barrier` construct. This approach can also be applied to utilize GPU and CPU cores at the same time. Figure 7 shows the idea of hybrid implementation using OpenMP and OpenACC. CPU is responsible for finding r_1 first columns, while GPU is used to find further r_2 columns, where $r_1 + r_2 = r$. Note that in this case, OpenMP nested parallelism should be enabled [8].

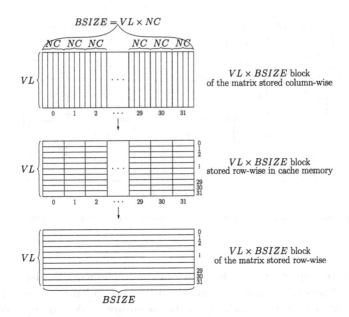

Fig. 4. Conversion of a $VL \times BSIZE$ block stored *column-wise* to *row-wise* storage performed by a single gang of threads ($VL = 32$, $BSIZE = 256$)

```
1   #pragma acc parallel  present(b) deviceptr(x) vector_length(BSIZE)
2   {
3       float xc[VL][BSIZE];
4       #pragma acc cache(xc)
5
6       for(int k=0;k<s;k+=VL){
7           // each gang reads VL x BSIZE block from column-wise format to cache
8           #pragma acc loop gang
9           for(int j=0;j<r;j+=BSIZE){
10              #pragma acc loop seq
11              for(int l=0;l<BSIZE;l+=NW)
12              #pragma acc loop vector
13              for(int i=0;i<BSIZE;i++)
14                  xc[i%VL][l+i/VL]= x[(j+l+i/VL)*s+k+i%VL];
15          }
16          // each gang writes VL x BSIZE block from cache to row-wise format
17          #pragma acc loop  gang vector
18          for(int j=0;j<r;j++){
19              #pragma acc loop seq
20              for(int i=0;i<VL;i++)
21                  b[(k+i)*r+j]=xc[i][j%BSIZE];
22          }
23      }
24  }
```

Fig. 5. OpenACC implementation of the conversion from *column-wise* to *row-wise* using device cache memory

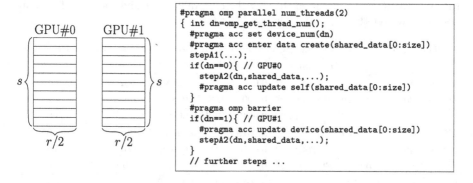

Fig. 6. Data distribution and general processing scheme for two GPUs

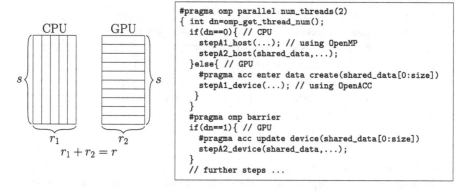

Fig. 7. Hybrid implementation for host (OpenMP) and GPU (OpenACC)

4   Results of Experiments

All experiments have been carried out on four different target architectures which are modern accelerated systems allowing OpenACC and OpenMP programming models. **Multicore** is a server with two Intel Xeon E5-2670 v3 (totally 24 cores with hyper-threading, 2.3 GHz), 128 GB RAM, running under Linux with CUDA 10.0 and Portland Group PGI compilers and tools version 19.4 with OpenMP and OpenACC support. **Kepler** is just like **multicore**, with NVIDIA Tesla K40m GPU (2880 cores, 12 GB RAM). Similarly, **Volta** is just like **multicore**, but with NVIDIA Tesla V100 GPU (5120 cores, 32 GB RAM). Finally, **Turing** is a server with Intel Core i7 (totally 4 cores with hyper-threading, 3.0 GHz), 24 GB RAM, NVIDIA GEFORCE RTX 2080 SUPER GPU (3072 cores, 8 GB RAM) running under Linux with CUDA 10.0 and PGI compilers.

We have tested three versions of our OpenACC-based implementation. The first one uses *column-wise* storage. The next two implementations rely on *row-wise* storage using the simple conversion between formats (Fig. 2) and the more sophisticated method (Fig. 5) that utilizes cache memory, respectively.

Table 1. Multicore: execution time for the best values of r and speedup of column-wise method over the sequential Thomas algorithm

n	Thomas alg.	Seq. alg.	OpenMP		Column-wise		Row-wise		Row-wise with cache		Speedup
			r	Time	r	Time	r	Time	r	Time	
2^{15}	0.0011	0.0016	2^6	0.0005	2^5	0.0007	2^9	0.0084	2^8	0.0026	1.55
2^{16}	0.0020	0.0029	2^7	0.0008	2^6	0.0009	2^{10}	0.0085	2^8	0.0043	2.18
2^{17}	0.0039	0.0054	2^8	0.0014	2^6	0.0013	2^{10}	0.0089	2^{10}	0.0057	3.04
2^{18}	0.0077	0.0104	2^4	0.0025	2^7	0.0019	2^{11}	0.0096	2^{11}	0.0076	4.05
2^{19}	0.0148	0.0186	2^6	0.0032	2^8	0.0026	2^{11}	0.0102	2^{11}	0.0077	5.68
2^{20}	0.0284	0.0362	2^6	0.0048	2^8	0.0040	2^{11}	0.0133	2^{11}	0.0108	7.03
2^{21}	0.0564	0.0741	2^6	0.0092	2^9	0.0076	2^{11}	0.0177	2^{11}	0.0160	7.39
2^{22}	0.1134	0.1528	2^8	0.0199	2^{10}	0.0179	2^{11}	0.0411	2^{11}	0.0308	6.34
2^{23}	0.2249	0.3030	2^8	0.0431	2^{10}	0.0405	2^{12}	0.0968	2^{12}	0.0671	5.55
2^{24}	0.4478	0.6055	2^8	0.0879	2^{10}	0.0865	2^{14}	0.1859	2^{12}	0.1368	5.18
2^{25}	0.8939	1.2097	2^6	0.1512	2^{11}	0.1728	2^{14}	0.3629	2^{11}	0.2754	5.17
2^{26}	1.7859	2.4179	2^6	0.2809	2^{13}	0.3480	2^{14}	0.7270	2^{11}	0.5540	5.13
2^{27}	3.5695	4.8255	2^6	0.5385	2^{14}	0.6983	2^{13}	1.4673	2^{15}	1.0915	5.11
2^{28}	7.1368	9.6747	2^8	1.0314	2^{14}	1.4021	2^{14}	2.9030	2^{12}	2.1780	5.09
2^{29}	14.2987	19.3526	2^8	2.0027	2^{15}	2.8156	2^{15}	5.8509	2^{12}	4.3571	5.08
2^{30}	28.5449	38.7018	2^9	3.9222	2^{15}	5.6348	2^{15}	11.6869	2^{16}	8.8644	5.07

On **multicore** (Table 1) we have also tested the OpenMP version of *column-wise* implementation compiled with the PGI compiler, the sequential Thomas algorithm, the algorithm based on sequential formulas (5), (6) and the simple automatic parallelization of (4).

Tests have been performed for various problem sizes and values of the parameter r. Because of global memory limitations, in case of **Kepler** and **Turing**, the biggest problem size is $n = 2^{28}$. We have observed that the best performance is achieved when r is $O(\sqrt{n})$, and then the performance differs slightly. Tables 1, 2, and 3 show the results obtained for the best value of r. Table 2 also contains the results obtained for

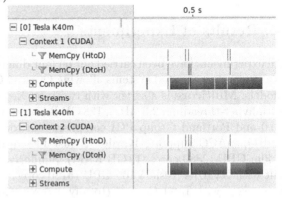

Fig. 8. NVIDIA Visual Profiler result for two GPUs implementation

our OpenMP+OpenACC implementations (i.e. for two GPUs and hybrid one utilizing GPU and CPU cores). Moreover, it shows the order of the relative error

Table 2. Kepler: relative error and the execution time for the best values of r. * - results obtained using the hybrid implementation

n	Error	Kepler						2 × Kepler	
		Column-wise		Row-wise		Row-wise with cache		Row-wise with cache	
		r	Time	r	Time	r	Time	r	Time
2^{15}	10^{-14}	2^9	0.0012	2^9	0.0012	2^8	0.0011	2^8	0.0013
2^{16}	10^{-14}	2^9	0.0018	2^{10}	0.0016	2^9	0.0016	2^9	0.0016
2^{17}	10^{-14}	2^{10}	0.0023	2^{10}	0.0018	2^{10}	0.0022	2^{10}	0.0025
2^{18}	10^{-15}	2^{10}	0.0032	2^{11}	0.0025	2^{10}	0.0030	2^{10}	0.0031
2^{19}	10^{-15}	2^{10}	0.0045	2^{11}	0.0034	2^{10}	0.0040	2^{10}	0.0044
2^{20}	10^{-16}	2^{11}	0.0062	2^{11}	0.0047	2^{11}	0.0054	2^{11}	0.0056
2^{21}	10^{-16}	2^{11}	0.0095	2^{12}	0.0069	2^{11}	0.0079	2^{12}	0.0082
2^{22}	10^{-16}	2^{12}	0.0152	2^{12}	0.0108	2^{12}	0.0115	2^{12}	0.0112
2^{23}	10^{-16}	2^{12}	0.0249	2^{13}	0.0180	2^{12}	0.0181	2^{12}	0.0173
2^{24}	10^{-15}	2^{12}	0.0481	2^{13}	0.0334	2^{13}	0.0296	2^{13}	0.0241
2^{25}	10^{-14}	2^{12}	0.0926	2^{14}	0.0715	2^{13}	0.0511	2^{13}	0.0384
2^{26}	10^{-14}	2^{12}	0.1938	2^{14}	0.1636	2^{13}	0.0950	2^{14}	0.0607
2^{27}	10^{-13}	2^{15}	0.4599	2^{14}	0.3276	2^{14}	0.1802	2^{14}	0.1029
2^{28}	10^{-13}	2^{16}	0.9259	2^{14}	0.6757	2^{14}	0.3614	2^{15}	0.1856
2^{29}	10^{-12}	–	–	–	–	2^{16}	1.2689*	2^{15}	0.3491
2^{30}	10^{-11}	–	–	–	–	2^{16}	2.7807*	–	–

achieved when solving the system of linear equations that arises for second order ordinary differential equations $y''(x) - py'(x) - qy(x) = g(x)$, where $x \in [a, b]$ and $y(a) = A$, $y(b) = B$.

We can observe that *column-wise* storage is the best for **multicore** and in this case, there is no need to perform conversion to *row-wise* storage. Thus, such conversion should be performed only if any GPU device is present. It can be easily checked using the acc_get_num_devices() function from OpenACC Runtime Library. It means that the source code will work properly on GPU-accelerated and non-accelerated systems without any changes.

Our OpenACC implementation compiled for non-accelerated multicore systems achieves good speedup over the sequential Thomas algorithm (up to 7.39) and its performance is about 65% of the performance achieved by our OpenMP-based implementation [5]. Thus, if we only consider CPU as the target architecture, the use of OpenMP is a better choice. In most cases for all tested GPUs, the implementation using *row-wise* storage achieves much better performance than the version using *column-wise* storage. We can also observe that the use of cache memory allows to speedup conversion between considered storage formats, especially on **Kepler**. In this case, the version using *row-wise* storage is more than 50% faster for bigger problem sizes. In the case of **Turing** and **Volta**, the use of

Table 3. Turing and Volta: the execution time for the best values of r.

n	Turing						Volta					
	Column-wise		Row-wise		Row-wise with cache		Column-wise		Row-wise		Row-wise with cache	
	r	Time	r	Time	r	Time	r	Time	r	Time	r	Time
2^{15}	2^8	0.0007	2^9	0.0007	2^9	0.0007	2^8	0.0007	2^9	0.0006	2^9	0.0006
2^{16}	2^9	0.0009	2^9	0.0009	2^9	0.0009	2^8	0.0010	2^9	0.0009	2^9	0.0010
2^{17}	2^9	0.0010	2^{10}	0.0009	2^9	0.0010	2^9	0.0010	2^{10}	0.0008	2^{10}	0.0009
2^{18}	2^{10}	0.0014	2^{10}	0.0012	2^{10}	0.0014	2^9	0.0013	2^{10}	0.0010	2^{10}	0.0012
2^{19}	2^{10}	0.0019	2^{11}	0.0016	2^{11}	0.0021	2^{10}	0.0017	2^{10}	0.0014	2^{11}	0.0017
2^{20}	2^{11}	0.0027	2^{12}	0.0023	2^{11}	0.0027	2^{10}	0.0023	2^{10}	0.0018	2^{11}	0.0022
2^{21}	2^{11}	0.0037	2^{12}	0.0032	2^{12}	0.0040	2^{11}	0.0031	2^{10}	0.0025	2^{12}	0.0030
2^{22}	2^{11}	0.0057	2^{13}	0.0050	2^{12}	0.0057	2^{11}	0.0043	2^{10}	0.0034	2^{12}	0.0043
2^{23}	2^{12}	0.0090	2^{13}	0.0085	2^{12}	0.0090	2^{12}	0.0061	2^{10}	0.0052	2^{13}	0.0061
2^{24}	2^{12}	0.0147	2^{14}	0.0154	2^{13}	0.0150	2^{12}	0.0090	2^{10}	0.0087	2^{13}	0.0095
2^{25}	2^{12}	0.0260	2^{13}	0.0322	2^{13}	0.0264	2^{12}	0.0152	2^{10}	0.0169	2^{14}	0.0155
2^{26}	2^{12}	0.0460	2^{14}	0.0700	2^{14}	0.0447	2^{12}	0.0274	2^{10}	0.0387	2^{14}	0.0260
2^{27}	2^{13}	0.0846	2^{15}	0.1938	2^{14}	0.0801	2^{13}	0.0463	2^{10}	0.0850	2^{15}	0.0455
2^{28}	2^{13}	0.1653	2^{16}	0.3927	2^{14}	0.1569	2^{14}	0.0995	2^{10}	0.1804	2^{15}	0.0799
2^{29}	-	-	-	-	-	-	2^{14}	0.2622	2^{15}	0.3973	2^{15}	0.1793
2^{30}	-	-	-	-	-	-	2^{15}	0.5849	2^{16}	0.7926	2^{16}	0.3454

cache memory is profitable for bigger problem sizes. It should be noticed that the performance on all considered GPUs significantly outperforms the performance achieved on **multicore**. Thus, the use of our hybrid implementation is profitable for bigger problem sizes, i.e. when the GPU memory capacity is exceeded (see Table 2, the results marked with "*"). Our implementation for two GPUs scales very well (see Table 2, **2 × Kepler**) without significant performance overheads (Fig. 8). It should be noticed that the timing results do not take into account the time needed to copy data between host and GPUs. However, solving considered systems is, in most cases, a part of a larger problem. The implementation achieves the performance of 6.6 GFLOPS on **multicore** and 68.4 GFLOPS on **Volta** what is far from the peak performances of those architectures, but is normal for problems where the ratio of the number of memory references to the number of arithmetic operations is $O(1)$. Finally, let us observe that the relative error of the solution obtained by the parallel algorithm is acceptable.

5   Conclusions and Future Work

We have presented the new portable OpenACC-based implementation of the solver for tridiagonal Toeplitz systems of linear equations. Numerical experiments show that *column-wise* storage is the best for CPU-based architectures and it achieves good speedup (up to 7.39) over the sequential Thomas algorithm. In most cases for all tested GPUs, the implementation using *row-wise* storage achieves much better performance than the version using *column-wise* storage and the use of cache memory allows to improve its performance. Moreover, all considered GPUs outperform CPU-based systems. We have also shown how to use OpenMP and OpenACC together in order to obtain the implementation suitable for systems with multiple GPUs or hybrid systems. In the future, we plan to study the numerical properties of the method, especially its stability.

References

1. Amiri, H., Shahbahrami, A.: SIMD programming using intel vector extensions. J. Parallel Distrib. Comput. **135**, 83–100 (2020). https://doi.org/10.1016/j.jpdc.2019.09.012. http://www.sciencedirect.com/science/article/pii/S074373151830813X

2. Chandrasekaran, S., Juckeland, G. (eds.): OpenACC for Programmers: Concepts and Strategies. Addison-Wesley, Boston (2018)

3. Cheng, J., Grossman, M., McKercher, T. (eds.): Professional CUDA C Programming. Wiley, Indianapolis (2014)

4. Chung, K.L., Yan, W.M.: Parallel B-spline surface fitting on mesh-connected computers. J. Parallel Distrib. Comput. **35**, 205–210 (1996). https://doi.org/10.1006/jpdc.1996.0082

5. Dmitruk, B., Stpiczyński, P.: Vectorized parallel solver for tridiagonal Toeplitz systems of linear equations. In: Wyrzykowski, R., Deelman, E., Dongarra, J., Karczewski, K. (eds.) PPAM 2019. LNCS, vol. 12043, pp. 93–103. Springer, Cham (2020). https://doi.org/10.1007/978-3-030-43229-4_9

6. Farber, R. (ed.): Parallel Programming with OpenACC. Morgan Kaufmann, Cambridge (2017)

7. Garey, L., Shaw, R.: A parallel method for linear equations with tridiagonal Toeplitz coefficient matrices. Comput. Math. Appl. **42**(1), 1–11 (2001). https://doi.org/10.1016/S0898-1221(01)00125-0

8. Jeffers, J., Reinders, J., Sodani, A.: Intel Xeon Phi Processor High-Performance Programming: Knights Landing edition. Morgan Kaufman, Cambridge (2016)

9. McNally, J.M., Garey, L., Shaw, R.: A communication-less parallel algorithm for tridiagonal Toeplitz systems. J. Comput. Appl. Math. **212**, 260–271 (2008). https://doi.org/10.1016/j.cam.2006.12.001

10. Rojo, O.: A new method for solving symmetric circulant tridiagonal systems of linear equations. Comput. Math. Appl. **20**, 61–67 (1990). https://doi.org/10.1016/0898-1221(90)90165-G

11. Stpiczyński, P.: Language-based vectorization and parallelization using intrinsics, OpenMP, TBB and Cilk Plus. J. Supercomput. **74**(4), 1461–1472 (2018). https://doi.org/10.1007/s11227-017-2231-3

12. Stpiczyński, P.: Algorithmic and language-based optimization of Marsa-LFIB4 pseudorandom number generator using OpenMP, OpenACC and CUDA. J. Parallel Distrib. Comput. **137**, 238–245 (2020). https://doi.org/10.1016/j.jpdc.2019.12.004

13. Stpiczyński, P., Potiopa, J.: Solving a kind of boundary-value problem for ordinary differential equations using Fermi - the next generation CUDA computing architecture. J. Comput. Appl. Math. **236**(3), 384–393 (2011). https://doi.org/10.1016/j.cam.2011.07.028

14. Terekhov, A.V.: A highly scalable parallel algorithm for solving Toeplitz tridiagonal systems of linear equations. J. Parallel Distrib. Comput. **87**, 102–108 (2016). https://doi.org/10.1016/j.jpdc.2015.10.004
15. Vidal, A.M., Alonso, P.: Solving systems of symmetric Toeplitz tridiagonal equations: Rojo's algorithm revisited. Appl. Math. Comput. **219**, 1874–1889 (2012). https://doi.org/10.1016/j.amc.2012.08.030

HighPerMeshes – A Domain-Specific Language for Numerical Algorithms on Unstructured Grids

Samer Alhaddad[1], Jens Förstner[1], Stefan Groth[2], Daniel Grünewald[3], Yevgen Grynko[1], Frank Hannig[2(✉)], Tobias Kenter[1], Franz-Josef Pfreundt[3], Christian Plessl[1], Merlind Schotte[4], Thomas Steinke[4], Jürgen Teich[2], Martin Weiser[4], and Florian Wende[4]

[1] Paderborn Center for Parallel Computing and Department of Computer Science and Department of Electrical Engineering, Paderborn University, Paderborn, Germany
[2] Hardware/Software Co-Design, Department of Computer Science, Friedrich-Alexander University Erlangen-Nürnberg (FAU), Erlangen, Germany
{frank.hannig,stefan.groth}@fau.de
[3] Fraunhofer Institut für Techno- und Wirtschaftsmathematik, Kaiserslautern, Germany
[4] Zuse Institute Berlin, Berlin, Germany

Abstract. Solving partial differential equations on unstructured grids is a cornerstone of engineering and scientific computing. Nowadays, heterogeneous parallel platforms with CPUs, GPUs, and FPGAs enable energy-efficient and computationally demanding simulations. We developed the HighPerMeshes C++-embedded Domain-Specific Language (DSL) for bridging the abstraction gap between the mathematical and algorithmic formulation of mesh-based algorithms for PDE problems on the one hand and an increasing number of heterogeneous platforms with their different parallel programming and runtime models on the other hand. Thus, the HighPerMeshes DSL aims at higher productivity in the code development process for multiple target platforms. We introduce the concepts as well as the basic structure of the HighPerMeshes DSL, and demonstrate its usage with three examples, a Poisson and monodomain problem, respectively, solved by the continuous finite element method, and the discontinuous Galerkin method for Maxwell's equation. The mapping of the abstract algorithmic description onto parallel hardware, including distributed memory compute clusters, is presented. Finally, the achievable performance and scalability are demonstrated for a typical example problem on a multi-core CPU cluster.

Keywords: Domain-specific language · Numerical algorithms · Unstructured grids · Parallel computing

© Springer Nature Switzerland AG 2021
B. Balis et al. (Eds.): Euro-Par 2020 Workshops, LNCS 12480, pp. 185–196, 2021.
https://doi.org/10.1007/978-3-030-71593-9_15

1   Introduction

Simulations of physical systems described by partial differential equations (PDEs) are the cornerstone of computational science and engineering. The ever-growing need for computational performance due to the increasing number and scale of simulations has led to the rise of different and heterogeneous parallel computing platforms, ranging from multi-core CPUs to massively parallel distributed systems and from SIMD vector units to GPUs and FPGAs. Adapting complex simulation algorithms to and implementing them efficiently on these different architectures is a demanding task requiring in-depth computer science knowledge that is usually not directly available to numerical mathematicians and computational engineers. Consequently, many large scale simulation codes address only a narrow and often traditional range of computing environments, missing the performance opportunities offered by new architectures.

In this paper, we present the HighPerMeshes embedded DSL that provides an abstraction layer to C++ application developers to implement efficient mesh-based algorithms for PDE problems on unstructured grids. The focus of the DSL is on finite element (FE) and discontinuous Galerkin (DG) or finite volume (FV) discretizations to address iterative and matrix-free solvers as well as time-stepping schemes. Large parts of PDE simulation problems thus can be covered. HighPerMeshes draws heavily on the C++17 standard and template metaprogramming for genericity and extensibility. Additionally, compile-time information through template parameters can benefit the code generation for specific target architectures.

The following other software projects address PDE computations on unstructured grids: Traditional library approaches such as deal.II [1], DUNE [3], or Kaskade 7 [7] focus on application building blocks and usually provide a rather explicit parallelization based on threads or MPI, providing one or a few selected back ends such as PETSc [2]. High-level DSLs such as FEniCS [16] or FreeFEM [10] on the other hand, allow to specify PDE problems in very abstract notation and use code generation techniques to create efficient simulation programs. The projects closest in scope and intention are the OP2 [17]/PyOP2 [20] and Liszt [6] DSLs, by providing interfaces to execute local compute kernels on unstructured meshes and to access data associated with different mesh entities. These approaches depend on C++, Python, and Scala code transformation and compilation techniques [19]. In contrast, we rely on template metaprogramming methods.

2   The HighPerMeshes Domain-Specific Language

Picking the right abstraction level is central for every DSL or library interface targeting mesh-based algorithms for PDEs. It needs to provide idioms for specifying the algorithmic building blocks on an abstraction level that is high enough to be mapped efficiently to different computing environments. Furthermore, it should be detailed enough to allow implementing a wide range of established or yet to be developed discretizations schemes and numerical algorithms. The HighPerMeshes DSL aims at providing abstractions on a level that is just high enough to allow for an efficient mapping to sequential and multithreaded CPU execution, distributed memory systems, and accelerators. On this level, the core components of mesh-based PDE algorithms include mesh data structures, the association of Degrees of Freedom (DoFs) to mesh entities such as cells and vertices, and the definition of kernel functions that encapsulate local computations with shape functions defined on single mesh cells or faces.

2.1   Mesh Interface

Computational meshes decompose the computational domain $\Omega \subset \mathbb{R}^d$ into simple shapes such as triangles or tetrahedra by which PDE solutions can be represented. Unstructured meshes do so in an irregular pattern that can be adapted to complex geometries or local solution features in a flexible way. Unlike for structured meshes, neighborhood relations between these cells are not implied by the storage arrangement of their constituting vertices, but are usually defined through connectivity lists that specify how they are made up of vertices. Therefore, the storage efficiency of unstructured meshes can be very low if the specifics of the hardware architecture are not taken into account. Similarly, when accessing or iterating over mesh entities (cells, faces, edges, and vertices for $d = 3$), the memory structuring and arrangement of, e.g., geometrically neighboring entities can be critical to performance and present optimization targets on the mesh implementation for different architectures.

The construction of a mesh in the HighPerMeshes DSL starts from a set of vertices $V = \{v_m \in \mathbb{R}^d\}$ and a set $C = \{i_n | n = 0, \ldots, \#\text{cells} - 1\}$ of connectivity lists $i_n \subset \{0, \ldots, |V| - 1\}$ representing the cells in the mesh.

Users can create meshes by providing V and C directly or by using one of the available import parsers for common mesh data files. Each $i \in C$ references into the vertex set V to encode an entity of the cell dimensionality $d_{\text{cell}} \leq d$. Sub-entities or constituting entities like edges and faces correspond to index sets $j \subset i \in C$ that are deduced according to a particular scheme that is specific to the entity type. All entities are stored in a $(d_{\text{cell}} + 1)$-dimensional set data-structure using their index sets. The mesh manages a lookup table which for each entity holds the IDs of all its constituting entities with one dimension lower, and another with the IDs of all incident super-entities, if present.

Users of the DSL can define their own entity types by implementing the interfaces EntityTopology and EntityGeometry. The two interfaces define the base functionality that is needed by the DSL, e.g., to navigate through all the different entities in the mesh or provide face normals. Entity-specific extensions can be added easily, which enhances the usability of the DSL.

For the hierarchical definition of entities as an affiliation of sub-entities, EntityTopology and EntityGeometry must know the actual type of their implementation for explicit instantiations, e.g., requesting or providing information about entities of different dimensionality.

On top of the mesh implementation is the mesh partitioning, which is needed for work distribution in the parallel context. The PartitionedMesh type inherits all functionality and state from the Mesh type. It selects from C a subset of the entities in the mesh and redirects this subset to the Mesh base type.

Iterator ranges over entities of any valid dimension can be created by the mesh and any valid entity through

```
template<int Dimension>
EntityRange<Dimension> GetEntities(){..}.
```

Both `EntityT` and `(Partitioned)Mesh` extend this functionality in different ways, thereby enabling the user of the DSL to query topological and geometrical information inside and outside of the kernel functions.

2.2 Buffer Types for Storing Coefficient Vectors

PDE solutions are generally discretized using finite-dimensional ansatz spaces and are represented by coefficient vectors with respect to a certain basis. In FE, FV, and DG methods, the basis functions are associated with mesh entities and have a support contained in the union of the cells incident to their entity. The mapping of coefficients, or Degrees of Freedom (DoFs) to storage locations and access to them depends on the target architecture and may involve nontrivial communication. Therefore, the DSL provides buffer types for coefficient vector storage to relieve the user from these considerations.

Depending on the ansatz space, a particular number of basis functions is associated with mesh entities of different dimensions. Therefore, the number of coefficients $\eta_{\tilde{d}}$ associated to entities of dimension $\tilde{d} \in \{0, \ldots, d_{\text{cell}}\}$ has to be specified when constructing a buffer. Additionally, global values as coefficients of the constant basis function can be stored, e.g.,

```
Runtime hpm{..};
auto dofs = MakeDofs<1,1,1,1,2>(); /* η = {η_d̃, 2} = {1,1,1,1,2} */
auto buffer = hpm.GetBuffer<float>(mesh,dofs);
```

for $d_{\text{cell}} = d = 3$. The buffer holds one value of type `float` for each node, edge, face, and the cell itself. Two additional entries are provided for global values.

DoFs are accessed through a "local-view object" (`lv` in Listing 1, line 7) inside kernel functions. These local views are a tuple of implementation-defined objects that are accessible with the `GetDof` function, which requests DoFs of a certain dimension. This is necessary because access patterns may provide DoFs associated with mesh entities of different dimensions.

Given a data access pattern (Sect. 2.3) and a specific entity—typical program executions loop over all or a subset of the entities in the mesh, one after the other—the corresponding local view makes for a linearly indexable type inside the kernel function, thereby hiding data layout and storage internals.

2.3 Iterating over the Mesh with Local Kernels

In the PDE solver algorithms that we target, a significant part of PDE computation on meshes involves the evaluation of values, derivatives, or integrals on cells or faces, and is therefore local. This allows for various kinds of parallelization, depending on the target architecture. Typically, these local calculations in space are embedded into time-stepping loops or iterative algorithms, which imply dependencies based on the data access patterns of the kernels. With a scheduler that suitably resolves these dependencies, additional parallelism can be exploited by partially overlapping subsequent time steps.

In HighPerMeshes, the application developer specifies the calculations as local kernels at entity granularity and invokes a dispatcher to take care of their parallel execution and scheduling. Line 1 of Listing 1 shows the definition of a distributed dispatcher that uses the command line arguments to set up its environment. The advantage of using this dispatcher model is a complete separation of parallelization techniques and kernel definitions. The interface is technology-agnostic and does not require knowledge about parallel programming.

The dispatcher's `Execute` method takes a number of kernels to be executed as its arguments. If required, those arguments might be supplemented by a range of time steps, as shown in line 3 of Listing 1, in order to iterate the defined sequence of kernels more than once in the specified range. Each kernel must define a range of entities to iterate over. To enable flexible parallelization strategies, the DSL does not guarantee a processing order for these entities. For example, the function call `mesh.GetEntityRange<CellDimension>()` in line 5 specifies that the dispatcher iterates over all cells. `ForEachEntity` in line 4 defines an iteration over all entities in that range. Here, HighPerMeshes provides another option: `ForEachIncidence<D>` iterates over all sub-entities of a certain dimension D for the entities in the given range.

The kernel requires a tuple of access definitions, as seen in line 6. Access definitions specify the mode (any of `Read`, `Write`, and `ReadWrite`) and the access pattern for the DoF access. This allows the scheduler to calculate dependencies between kernels, thereby avoiding conflicting DoF accesses in scatter operations despite parallelization. Access patterns determine the DoFs relevant for the calculation by specifying a set of mesh entities incident or adjacent to the local entity. `Cell` in line 6 means that the kernel requires access to the DoFs from the given `buffer` that are associated with the local cell, as frequently used in DG methods. Other common access patterns involve a local cell and all of its incident sub-entities, usually encountered in FE methods, or the two cells incident to a face for flux computations in DG or FV methods. While HighPerMeshes aims at providing all access patterns necessary for common kernel descriptions in FE or DG methods, they can be easily extended by providing the required neighborhood relationship in the mesh interface.

Lastly, the user must define a kernel to be executed (line 7). It must be a callable that takes the specified entities, time steps, and a local-view object `lv` as its arguments. The latter allows access to the requested DoFs.

```
1  DistributedDispatcher dispatcher{argc,argv};
2  dispatcher.Execute(
3    Range{100},
4    ForEachEntity(
5      mesh.GetEntityRange<CellDimension>(),
6      tuple(Write(Cell(buffer))),
7      [](const auto& cell,auto step,auto& lv) { /*kernel body*/ }));
```

Listing 1. Example of a dispatcher definition and kernel execution.

3   Using the DSL

In this section, examples and code segments are presented to illustrate the methods described in Sect. 2 and to explain their use. Further information about the algorithms and examples can be found in the public repositories[1,2].

3.1   Matrix-Free Solver for the Poisson Equation

For illustrating the usage of the DSL, the elliptic Poisson problem

$$-\Delta u = f \quad \text{in } \Omega \subset \mathbb{R}^3, \qquad u = 0 \quad \text{on } \Gamma \subset \mathbb{R}^3 \tag{1}$$

with homogeneous Dirichlet boundary conditions is solved by a matrix-free conjugate gradient (CG) method [11,21]. By discretizing (1) with linear finite elements on a tetrahedralization of Ω, i.e. with one DoF per vertex, a system $Ax = b$ of linear equations is obtained [5]. Since A is symmetric and positive definite, its solution is the minimizer of the convex minimization problem $F(x) = \frac{1}{2}x^T A x - b^T x \to \min$.

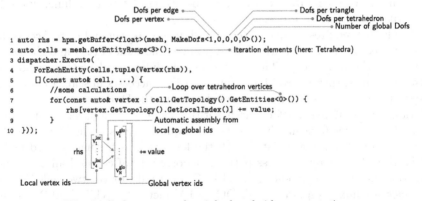

Fig. 1. Code segment for right-hand side computation.

In order to solve this equation system, the right-hand side (*rhs*) b must be assembled. This is done using the buffer datatype and the loop *ForEachEntity*, which iterates over the vertices of each cell (in this case, tetrahedra) and stores the corresponding value in the buffer (Fig. 1 code line 8). The homogeneous Dirichlet boundary conditions can be built into the rhs here as well. To solve the system, a matrix-free CG iteration is used. Its main algorithmic building block is the computation of matrix-vector products Ax. Instead of assembling A and

---

[1] https://github.com/HighPerMeshes/highpermeshes-dsl.
[2] https://github.com/HighPerMeshes/highpermeshes-drts-gaspi.

performing linear algebra operations, we assemble the product Ax directly by evaluating

$$s_j = \underbrace{\int_C \nabla\phi_i \nabla\phi_j \, dC}_{A(i,j)_{cell}} \cdot x_j \tag{2}$$

per cell and with ϕ_* as shape functions (see line 9 of Listing 2). The same procedure is used for all further matrix-vector products. Finally, the result can be saved into a file and visualized using, for example, *ParaView*.

```
1  auto AssembleMatrixVecProduct =
2      ForEachEntity(cells, tuple(Vertex(s)),
3      [](const auto& cell) {
4          auto& indices = cell.GetTopology().GetVertexIndices();
5          for (int col = 0; col < ncols; ++col) {
6              for (int row = 0; row < nrows; ++row) {
7                  float a_ij = .. //set a_ij using shape functions
8                  s[indices[col]] += a_ij * x[indices[row]];
9      }}
10     });
```

Listing 2. Example of a matrix-free computation.

3.2 Discontinuous Galerkin Time Domain (DGTD) Maxwell Solver

Here we sketch an implementation of a Maxwell solver based on the DGTD numerical scheme [9,12]. An initial value problem is solved in the time domain in a free space mesh with perfect electric conductor (PEC) boundary conditions. The user can modify the code accordingly if field sources, materials, or absorbing boundaries are needed. The simulation domain is discretized in a triangular or tetrahedral mesh, which is used as an input. Then, DoFs or calculation points are created within the cells, depending on the ansatz order specified by the user. For example, a three-dimensional simulation with third-order accuracy requires 20 DoFs in each cell to represent the unknown fields. The right-hand sides of Maxwell's equations are evaluated during Runge-Kutta time integration at each time step according to the DGTD method formulation

$$\dot{\mathbf{E}} = \mathbf{D} \times \mathbf{H} + (\mathcal{M})^{-1}\mathcal{F}\left(\Delta\mathbf{E} - \hat{n} \cdot (\hat{n} \cdot \Delta\mathbf{E}) + \hat{n} \times \Delta\mathbf{H}\right) \tag{3}$$

$$\dot{\mathbf{H}} = -\mathbf{D} \times \mathbf{E} + (\mathcal{M})^{-1}\mathcal{F}\left(\Delta\mathbf{H} - \hat{n} \cdot (\hat{n} \cdot \Delta\mathbf{H}) + \hat{n} \times \Delta\mathbf{E}\right) \tag{4}$$

Here $\mathbf{D} \times \mathbf{H}$ and $\mathbf{D} \times \mathbf{E}$ are the curls of the magnetic and electric fields. Correspondingly, $\mathcal{M}$ is the mass matrix, $\mathcal{F}$ the face matrix, $\Delta\mathbf{E}, \Delta\mathbf{H}$ are field differences between the neighboring cells at the interfaces, and $\hat{n}$ the face normal [9]. The first term (the curls) involves only cell-local DoFs and is therefore called "volume kernel" (see Listing 3).

```
 1  auto volumeKernelLoop = ForEachEntity(cells,
 2      tuple(Read(Cell(H)),Cell(rhsE),..),
 3      [&](const auto& cell,..,auto& lv){
 4          Mat3D D = cell.GetGeometry().GetInverseJacobian()*2.0;
 5          ForEach(numVolumeNodes,[&](const int n){
 6              const auto& H = GetDofs<3>(get<0>(lv));
 7              Mat3D dH;
 8              ForEach(numVolumeNodes,[&](const int m) {
 9                  dH += DyadicProduct(derivative[n][m],H[m]);
10              });
11              auto& rhsE = GetDofs<3>(get<1>(lv));
12              rhsE[n] += Curl(D,dH);
13              // code for rhsH: analogue to rhsE
14          });
15      });
```

Listing 3. Code segment for the Maxwell volume kernel.

The second term in (3, 4), the "surface kernel," (see Listing 4) stems from a surface integral over the cell's faces, and involves those DoFs from within the two incident cells located on these faces. Calculating the surface kernel requires some operations provided directly by the DSL, e.g., `GetNormal()`. The implementation complexity of DG on unstructured meshes comes from the access or mapping to the neighboring cells DoFs in order to calculate fluxes across faces as described in (3, 4). This access is performed with the data structure `NeighboringNodeMap` (line 12 in Listing 4), which provides the corresponding index for the DoFs in the local view.

```
 1  auto surfaceKernelLoop = ForEachIncidence<2>(cells,
 2      tuple(Read(ContainingMeshElement(H)),
 3          Read(ContainingMeshElement(E)),
 4          Read(NeighboringMeshElementOrSelf(H)),
 5          Read(NeighboringMeshElementOrSelf(E)),
 6          Write(ContainingMeshElement(rhsE))),
 7      [&](const auto& cell, const auto& face,..,auto& lv){
 8          const auto& H = GetDofs<3>(get<0>(lv));
 9          // buffer access to E, nH, n, E, rhsE is analogous
10          auto& NeighboringNodeMap {DgNodeMap.Get(cell,face)};
11          int faceIndex = face.GetTopology().GetLocalIndex();
12          auto faceUnitNormal = face.GetGeometry().GetUnitNormal();
13          auto edg = (face.GetGeometry().GetNormal()*2.0/
14          cell.GetGeometry().GetAbsJacobianDeterminant()).Norm()
                *0.5;
15          ForEach(numSurfaceNodes,[&](const int m){
16              const auto dH = edg*Delta(H,nH,m,NeighboringNodeMap);
17              const auto dE =
18              edg*DirectionalDelta(E,nE,face,m,NeighboringNodeMap);
19              const auto fluxE = (dE-(dE*faceUnitNormal)*
                    faceUnitNormal+CrossProduct(faceUnitNormal,dH));
20              ForEach(numVolumeNodes,[&](const int n){
21                  rhsE[n] += LIFT[face_index][m][n]*fluxE;
22              });
23          });
24      });
```

Listing 4. Code segment for the Maxwell surface kernel.

3.3   Finite Elements for Cardiac Electrophysiology

The excitation of cardiac muscle tissue is described by electrophysiology models such as the monodomain model

$$\dot{u} = \nabla \cdot (\sigma \nabla u) + I_{\text{ion}}(u, w), \tag{5}$$
$$\dot{w} = f(u, w),$$

where σ is the conductivity, I_{ion} is the ion current that forms together with the gating dynamics $f(u, w)$ the membrane model. The simplest FitzHugh-Nagumo membrane model defines $I_{\text{ion}}(u, w) = u(1-u)(u-a) - w$ and $f(u, w) = \epsilon(u - bw)$ with $0 < a, b, \epsilon < 1$ [4, 15, 23].

The method of lines [22] discretizes the monodomain model (5) first in space and then in time. For the discretization of space, we use linear finite elements again, leading to the system

$$M\dot{u} = \sigma A u + M \cdot I_{\text{ion}}(u, w)$$
$$\dot{w} = f(u, w)$$

with mass matrix M and stiffness matrix A. For time discretization, the forward Euler method

$$u_{t+1} = u_t + \tau \underbrace{\left(M^{-1}\sigma A u_t + I_{\text{ion}}(u_t, w_t)\right)}_{\dot{u} := u_d}, \quad w_{t+1} = w_t + \tau f(u_t, w_t) \tag{6}$$

is widely used in cardiac electrophysiology due to its simplicity and its stability for reasonable step sizes τ [18].

In order to avoid inverting the globally coupled mass matrix, the row-sum mass lumping technique is applied to M [13]. This yields a diagonal approximation M_l of M and allows for efficient, explicit formation of M_l^{-1} to be used in (6) instead of M^{-1}, and matrix-free storage in vector form. The right-hand side u_t including the matrix-vector product $A u_t$ is assembled directly as in (2) without forming A:

```
1  auto fwEuler = ForEachEntity(
2      mesh.GetEntityRange<0>(),
3      tuple(Vertex(u), Vertex(Read(u_d))),
4      [&](const auto& vertex, auto step, auto& lv) {
5          auto& u = GetDofs<0>(get<0>(lv));
6          auto& u_d = GetDofs<0>(get<1>(lv));
7          u[0] += tau * u_d[0];
8      });
```

Listing 5. Code example of an implementation of a first-order solver (forward Euler).

3.4   Distributed Scalability Experiments

In this section, we analyze the distributed scalability of the matrix-vector product (Listing 2), the volume kernel (Listing 3), and the surface kernel (Listing 4).

The experiments were executed on a cluster, where each compute node consists of two sockets. Each socket contains an Intel Xeon Gold 6148 "Skylake" CPU, which has 20 cores and a base frequency of 2.4 GHz. Hyper-threading is deactivated. The nodes are connected on a 100 Gb/s Intel Omni Path network. All experiments were executed with 20 threads per socket, as the scalability of our threading approach on a single compute node has already been shown [8].

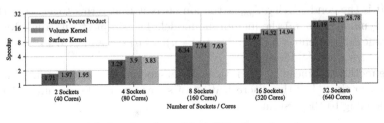

(a) Acceleration with ACE's thread pool

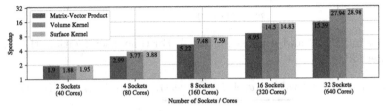

(b) Acceleration with OpenMP

Fig. 2. Speedup for iterating over the specified kernels on a mesh with 400,000 tetrahedra and 1000 time steps on an increasing amount of sockets compared to executing the same kernels on one socket. The evaluated back ends use ACE's thread pool (a) or OpenMP (b).

We conducted the experiments for 1000 time steps on a synthetic mesh of 400,000 tetrahedra. Such a setup represents a typical problem size targeted by the distributed dispatcher. For mesh partitioning, we use the Metis library [14].

Figure 2 shows the speedup over a single node for the distributed dispatcher when either scheduling tasks to ACE's thread pool or accelerating tasks with OpenMP for an increasing amount of compute nodes. As a baseline for each experiment, we measure the execution time with both back ends on a single socket, i.e., 20 cores, and use the faster one. For 640 cores, the back end feeding threads to ACE's thread pool achieves better speedups for the matrix-vector product with a speedup of 21.19. The volume and surface kernels achieve a better speedup in the case of OpenMP acceleration, with a speedup of 27.94 and 28.98, respectively. Furthermore, the volume and surface kernels scale better than the matrix-vector multiplication because they are more compute-intensive. They iterate over 20 DoFs instead of just one. To achieve this kind of scalability, the dispatcher requires a sufficient workload.

The results show that HighPerMeshes allows an efficient distribution of matrix-free algorithms. They also show that the provided abstractions are not tailored to a specific back end. Instead, both reference implementations achieve similar speedups, thus showing that the language is portable to different technologies.

Conclusion

HighPerMeshes is an embedded DSL that provides high-level abstractions for iterative, matrix-free algorithms on unstructured grids. It is a powerful tool enabling users to run simulations and implement their own modifications for complex multi-scale problems from a broad range of application domains.

The data structures and procedures provided by HighPerMeshes allow efficient parallelization and distribution as shown by our implementation of a dispatcher that distributes kernels with the help of GASPI, ACE, and OpenMP. This gives the user the opportunity to take advantage of complex parallelization techniques and task scheduling without being an expert on parallelization, saving implementation time and effort on one side, and offering flexibility for different computing platforms without the need for code modification on the other side.

Acknowledgments. This work was partially funded by the German Federal Ministry of Education and Research (BMBF) within the collaborative research project "HighPer-Meshes" (01IH16005). The authors gratefully acknowledge the funding of this project by computing time provided by the Paderborn Center for Parallel Computing (PC^2).

References

1. Arndt, D., et al.: The `deal.II` library, version 9.1. J. Numer. Math. **27**(4), 203–213 (2019)
2. Balay, S., et al.: PETSc (2019). https://www.mcs.anl.gov/petsc
3. Bastian, P., et al.: A generic grid interface for parallel and adaptive scientific computing. Part II: implementation and tests in DUNE. Computing **82**(2), 121–138 (2008). https://doi.org/10.1007/s00607-008-0004-9
4. Dauby, P., Desaive, T., Croisier, H., Kolh, P.: Standing waves in the FitzHugh-Nagumo model of cardiac electrical activity. Phys. Rev. E **73**(2), 021908 (2006)
5. Deuflhard, P., Weiser, M.: Adaptive Numerical Solution of PDEs. Walter de Gruyter, Berlin (2012)
6. DeVito, Z., et al.: Liszt: a domain specific language for building portable mesh-based PDE solvers. In: Proceedings of Conference on High Performance Computing Networking, Storage and Analysis (SC 2011), p. paper 9. ACM (2011)
7. Götschel, S., Schiela, A., Weiser, M.: Kaskade 7 - a flexible finite element toolbox. Comp. Math. Appl. **81**, 444–458 (2020)
8. Groth, S., Grünewald, D., Teich, J., Hannig, F.: A runtime system for finite element methods in a partitioned global address space. In: CF 2020: Proceedings of the 17th ACM International Conference on Computing Frontiers. ACM (2020). https://doi.org/10.1145/3387902.3392628

9. Grynko, Y., Förstner, J.: Simulation of second harmonic generation from photonic nanostructures using the discontinuous Galerkin time domain method. In: Agrawal, A., Benson, T., De La Rue, R.M., Wurtz, G.A. (eds.) Recent Trends in Computational Photonics. SSOS, vol. 204, pp. 261–284. Springer, Cham (2017). https://doi.org/10.1007/978-3-319-55438-9_9
10. Hecht, F.: New development in FreeFem++. J. Numer. Math. **20**(3–4), 251–265 (2012). https://freefem.org/
11. Hestenes, M.R., Stiefel, E., et al.: Methods of conjugate gradients for solving linear systems. J. Res. Natl. Bur. Stand. **49**(6), 409–436 (1952)
12. Hesthaven, J.S., Warburton, T.: Nodal Discontinuous Galerkin Methods: Algorithms, Analysis, and Applications. Springer, New York (2008). https://doi.org/10.1007/978-0-387-72067-8
13. Hughes, T.J.: The Finite Element Method: Linear Static and Dynamic Finite Element Analysis. Courier Corporation (2012)
14. Karypis, G., Kumar, V.: A fast and high quality multilevel scheme for partitioning irregular graphs. SIAM J. Sci. Comput. (SISC) **20**(1), 359–392 (1998)
15. Liu, F., Zhuang, P., Turner, I., Anh, V., Burrage, K.: A semi-alternating direction method for a 2-D fractional FitzHugh-Nagumo monodomain model on an approximate irregular domain. J. Comput. Phys. **293**, 252–263 (2015)
16. Logg, A., Mardal, K.A., Wells, G.N., et al.: Automated Solution of Differential Equations by the Finite Element Method. Springer, Heidelberg (2012). https://doi.org/10.1007/978-3-642-23099-8
17. Mudalige, G.R., Giles, M.B., Reguly, I., Bertolli, C., Kelly, P.H.J.: OP2: an active library framework for solving unstructured mesh-based applications on multi-core and many-core architectures. In: Proceedings of Innovative Parallel Computing (InPar), pp. 1–12 (2012)
18. Puwal, S., Roth, B.J.: Forward Euler stability of the bidomain model of cardiac tissue. IEEE Trans. Biomed. Eng. **54**(5), 951–953 (2007)
19. Rathgeber, F., et al.: Firedrake: automating the finite element method by composing abstractions. ACM Trans. Math. Softw. (TOMS) **43**(3), 24:1–24:27 (2016)
20. Rathgeber, F., et al.: PyOP2: a high-level framework for performance-portable simulations on unstructured meshes. In: Proceedings of the 2nd International Workshop on Domain-Specific Languages and High-Level Frameworks for High Performance Computing (WOLFHPC), pp. 1116–1123. ACM, November 2012
21. Saad, Y.: Iterative Methods for Sparse Linear Systems, vol. 82. SIAM (2003)
22. Schiesser, W.E., Griffiths, G.W.: A Compendium of Partial Differential Equation Models: Method of Lines Analysis with Matlab. Cambridge University Press, Cambridge (2009)
23. Sermesant, M., Coudière, Y., Delingette, H., Ayache, N., Désidéri, J.A.: An electromechanical model of the heart for cardiac image analysis. In: Niessen, W.J., Viergever, M.A. (eds.) MICCAI 2001. LNCS, vol. 2208, pp. 224–231. Springer, Heidelberg (2001). https://doi.org/10.1007/3-540-45468-3_27

Implementation and Evaluation
of CUDA-Unified Memory in Numba

Lena Oden$^{(\boxtimes)}$ and Tarek Saidi

Fernuniversität in Hagen, Lehrstuhl Technische Informatik, Hagen, Germany
`lena.oden@fernuni-hagen.de`

Abstract. Python as a programming language is increasingly gaining importance, especially in data science, scientific, and parallel programming. With the Numba-CUDA, it is even possible to program GPUs with Python using a CUDA like programming style. However, Numba is missing support for CUDA-unified memory, which can help to simplify programming even more and allows dynamic work distribution between GPUs and CPUs. In this work, we implement and evaluate the support for unified memory in Numba. As expected, the performance of unified memory is worse than using explicit data transfers, but can outperform the performance of the implicit methods provided by Numba. Additionally, using unified memory can help to reduce the Python interpreter overhead and therefore help to improve the performance of small problem sizes. The use of system-wide atomic can help to improve the work distribution between GPU and CPU, but when using more CPU threads the performance suffers under the Python global interpreter lock (GIL).

Keywords: GPU · Python · Unified memory · Numba

1 Introduction

In the early days of information technology, the exorbitant costs of machines eclipsed all other accompanying costs, especially for programming these machines. However, the exponential growth in computing speed and the increasing complexity of software systems ensured that the circumstances were reversed. Many organizations found that their software development costs began to exceed the hardware costs.

A sign of this development is the continuing trend towards the use of dynamic scripting languages. Although these are not compatible with compiled languages and considerably slower, but the development costs can be reduced [14]. One language that is popular in this context is Python.

To compensate for the speed disadvantages of the scripting language, performance critical numerical calculations are written in compiled languages, either by using pre-compiled libraries like numpy or scipy, or by using bridge technologies like cython. However, the desire to carry out mathematical calculations directly in Python is obvious [2]. They enable the rapid development of prototypes and their iterative improvement on an algorithmic level. In fact, the greatest and

© Springer Nature Switzerland AG 2021
B. Balis et al. (Eds.): Euro-Par 2020 Workshops, LNCS 12480, pp. 197–208, 2021.
https://doi.org/10.1007/978-3-030-71593-9_16

most efficiently exploitable optimization potential is usually to be found in the higher-level algorithms of a calculation, whereas low-level optimizations often do not yield a profit in relation to the effort involved [16].

A possibility to create high-performance code for numerical calculations directly in Python is provided by the Python extension module Numba [9]. Numba is a just-in-time compiler that allows the translation of selected computationally intensive Python functions into optimized machine code. The execution speed of these functions is similar to pre-compiled code of other languages [1]. Numba supports the parallelization of Python code and often requires only minor code changes. In addition, Numba-CUDA can also be used to program NVIDIA GPUs.

Since GPUs have their own local memory, data must be exchanged between the system memory and the device memory. Numba-CUDA uses a very simple implicit mechanism by default. It copies all data used before a calculation into the device memory and back after completion of a kernel. If this is done explicitly in the program code, however, the complexity of the programs and the porting effort for existing algorithms increase. If, on the other hand, the data transfer is implicitly performed, the speed can suffer depending on the efficiency of the transfer.

With unified memory, the CUDA platform offers a technology that allows avoiding unnecessary data transfers and explicit memory management [7]. Unified memory provides a uniform virtual address space between system and device memory. On newer GPUs, the data transfer between the physical storage is completely transparent due to a demand paging mechanism implemented at driver and hardware level.

However, unified memory currently is not supported in Numba. In this work, we extend Numba-CUDA to support unified memory, in order to allow efficient implicit memory management. We evaluate our implementation in terms of performance and compared with other memory management provided by Numba-CUDA.

2 Background

In this section, we will give a short overview of the technical background of unified memory and Numba.

2.1 Numba

Numba is a just-in-time compiler working at the level of individual functions in Python. The primarily intention is to accelerate numerical calculations. Unlike other JIT compilers for interpreted languages, Numba is not designed to produce machine code that necessarily works in the same way as the interpreter. Instead, Numba uses knowledge about the internals of data types to compile the Python code into simpler machine code. As a result, Numba only supports a subset of Python that is tailored to the scope of numerical calculations. However, thanks to this, Numba achieves execution speeds similar to compiled C code.

The compilation starts by converting the Python byte code into an immediate representation, called Numba IR. On this, the type interference is performed. If the type of each value can be inferred, the code is lowered to LLVM, which is then used to create the final machine code. In addition to the generation of JIT compiled CPU functions, Numba supports, in similar way, the generation of CUDA kernels for execution on the GPU. Because of the highly parallel programming model of CUDA, CUDA kernels under Numba differ in some aspects of CPU functions. For example, when calling a kernel, the thread grid must be explicitly specified, similar to C-CUDA.

The compilation process for CUDA kernels is essentially the same as for CPU-functions. The generated NVVM-IR is a modification of the of the LLVM IR code [4]. This intermediate code is translated by the LLVM-based proprietary library libNVVM to CUDA PTX-assembly code. When using NumPy arrays for CUDA-kernel input and output, Numba will implicitly transfer data between the host and the device without additional instructions. To allow explicit control over the memory, Numba provides so-called device arrays and functions. This is similar to regular C-CUDA programming using CUDA-copy functions.

2.2 Unified Memory in CUDA

CUDA integrates allocated device memory into the virtual address space of the host system, whereby each memory address is unique [3]. However, this alone does not yet allow every processor (or GPU) to access every memory region, but only local memory. One way to overcome this limitation is to use CUDA with *mapped memory*. This allows the GPU to access areas of host memory directly, but does not allow the CPU to access GPU memory.

With CUDA 6.0 and Kepler-generation GPUs, the CUDA memory model has been extended to include *managed memory* or *unified memory*, which allows all processors equal access to all data in an uniform virtual address space, regardless of the physical location. The advantage of this technology is primarily simplified programming, since explicit data transfer between host and device are omitted. On older GPUs, explicit data transfer was handled in the background.

Unified memory on newer GPUs is based on the demand paging mechanism. If a memory page is accessed, which is not currently in main memory, a page fault occurs and the operating system takes the necessary actions to make the page available. The unified memory works in a similar way. If the GPU accesses a memory page that is physically located in the host memory, a page fault occurs, which is handled by the GPU by transferring the respective page to host memory On Power9 systems, the same mechanism also works in the opposite direction, when the CPU accesses GPU memory. Such CPU-side page faults are hardware technically only possible since the introduction of the Pascal on architecture on Power9 system and also require operating system support, which is currently only available on Linux.

On systems that do not support GPU page faults, pages owned by the CPU are instead written to the respective GPU pages when a kernel is started and written back, if the kernel is completed.

With newer GPU-architectures, the system has been further refined so that, for example, pages are not necessarily transferred from one memory to the other during the first access, but only when a certain number of accesses has been exceeded.

3   Related Work

Unified memory was evaluated by different groups. In [10], the speed of unified memory with CUDA 6 and GPUs of the Kepler generation is examined. In almost all cases unified memory leads to significant performance losses. The authors consider the simplifications achieved by unified memory as marginal and only saw a benefit when using more complex data structures.

In [11] a consistent speed disadvantage of around 10% is found in the use of unified memory with GPUs of the Kepler generation. They attribute the performance losses on the one hand to the redundant transfer of data by the unified memory runtime system and on the other hand to the overhead of handling page faults.

Since its introduction with CUDA 6 and the Kepler architecture, unified memory has experienced some improvements. In [8] unified memory was evaluated on modern Pascal- and Volta-GPUs. This work also came to the conclusion that the use of unified memory is generally associated with significant performance losses. However, for memory oversubscribing use cases, unified memory allows a strong reduction of complexity in the memory management.

In [6] a benchmark suite, Chai, designed for heterogeneous computations, is introduced. Using these benchmarks, the workload distribution between CPUs and GPU generally shows a speed gain compared to a CPU-only or GPU-only calculations. Furthermore, it was found that the use of unified memory in conjunction with system-wide atomic operations for synchronisation has a clearly positive effect on performance.

As Python is widely used in scientific programming, different papers deal with the performance for parallel applications written in Python, including the use of GPUs. In [15] the same application is evaluated in Python/Numba and CUDA/Fortran. In [12] a detailed analysis of Numba is provided, but the authors do not provide a detailed comparison to C-CUDA. In [13] we compared the performance of C-CUDA and Numba-CUDA, but mainly focus on the performance of the compute kernels. The memory transfer between GPUs and CPUs was not considered.

4   Implementation of Unified Memory in Numba-Cuda

Unified memory simplifies programming by eliminating the need for explicit memory transfers between different physical memories. This means, the distinction between host arrays (i.e. normal NumPy arrays) and device arrays should be repealed. Additional, System-wide atomic operations should be made available in Numba, on both sides, CPU and GPU to allow work distribution. The implementation should fit well into the programming interface of Numba and make as few adjustments as possible to port existing programs. The current version of the patch is available as gist on github.[1]

4.1 Managed Memory Arrays

The CUDA driver provides the function cuMemAllocManaged() to allocate managed memory. CPython allows a program-wide exchange of the used memory allocation functions through user-defined variants [17]. A simple solution could simply replace any memory request in Python with cuMemAllocManaged(). This would mean that each newly created NumPy array is automatically allocated in managed memory. This approach has a certain elegance at first glance, but also has a large number of problems.

Access to the CUDA driver API is only possible after loading a corresponding extension module, unless you modify the Python interpreter itself. This means, memory blocks from different systems must be managed, which is a time- consuming task. Additionally, this approach is not compatible with non-Linux systems or GPUs of the pre-Pascal era. Therefore, we introduce a new array class, which allocates and stores data in a unified memory block instead of host memory (normal numpy array) or GPU memory (device memory class). This avoids the problems listed above and only used data are stored in managed memory.

To ensure universal usability, we implemented a new array class, called *ManagedArray*, as a derived class of *numpy.ndarray*. This allows the usage like a *normal* NumPy array without further effort. In particular, managed arrays can be used directly in Numba and Numpy CPU functions.

When a new instance is initialized, the required memory for the data is allocated using cuMemAllocManaged() and passed as a buffer object to the superclass. The buffer object automatically frees the memory with `cuMemFree()` when the last reference to the object is removed. Besides of this modifications, all other functions can be inherited from the original numpy array superclass and no further modifications are needed. In an application, the allocation of a memory array must be replaced with the new class. To prevent Numba from making a automatic copy of the data to the GPU when a kernel is called, the class is marked the with `__cuda_memory__`. Listing 1.1 shows how the new class can be used to created manged device arrays.

Listing 1.1. Example of unified memory allocationd in Numba

```
numba.cuda.managed_array(shape, dtype=np.float, order='C')
numba.cuda.managed_array_like(ary)
numba.cuda.to_managed(ary)
```

4.2 Global Atomic Functions

Numba supports some atomic operations for CUDA kernels, such as atomic *fetch_and_add* by using `numba.cuda.atomic.add()`. The analysis of the IR and PTX (cuda assembly) code generated by Numba shows that these atomic operations have a GPU-wide validity rang. This means the atomicity is guaranteed for all other threads of the same GPU, but not with the host or other GPUs. To enable system-wide atomic operations, a PTX command like `atom.sys.op.type` has to be generated. The current, official version of LLVM supports system-wide atomic operations by special IR commands of the form llvm.nvvm.atom.gen.sys.*. Since Numba uses the non-open source LLVM based library libNVVM for PTX code generation, we investigated the support of these commands. We learned that the LLVM system wide atomics used with CUDA version 10.1 were not recognized.

As an alternative we identified the use of inline assembler expressions in the intermediate code. This means that instead of an NVVM IR command, the appropriate PTX code is embedded directly The IR code thus loses abstraction, but there are no disadvantages in practical application.

The newly introduced system-wide atomic operations are oriented to the already existing operations. For CPU functions, Numba does not support any user-addressable atomic operations or other synchronization mechanisms at all, as Numba primarily relies on semi to fully automatic parallelization of loops. The implementation of atomic operations for CPU code turned out to be simple. Numba simply needed to be extended to generate the LLVM IR command `atomicrmw`. The semantics of the CPU functions correspond to those of the GPU variants (see Listing 1.2).

Listing 1.2. Example of atomic usage on the CPU and GPU

```
numba.cuda.atomic.system.add(ary, idx, val)
numba.atomic.add(ary, idx, val)
```

5 Evaluation

In this section, we evaluate the performance of our unified memory implementation in CUDA-Numba. All benchmarks were executed on an NVIDIA Tesla V100 GPU, which is equipped to a node with two IBM POWER9 processors (8 cores per core). We used CUDA 10.1.105. This system has full support for all unified memory features. We evaluate the performance of Unified Memory in Numba and explain the behavior compared to the same methods in C-CUDA applications.

5.1 Micro-Benchmarks

In the first step, we implemented three *synthetic* benchmarks. These benchmarks do not perform any usefull computation, but serve the purpose of transferring data between host and device. The tests emulate the memory access patterns of typical application scenarios.

– *data transfer full* - In this benchmark, we first initialize an array on the host. A GPU kernel performs a simple calculation on this array and writes the result back. The CPU verifies the result. For this test, all data must first be copied into GPU memory and transferred back after the computation is completed for verification. The data volume, that is transferred is independent of the memory management method, as all used data is modified on the GPU.

– *data transfer partial* - This benchmark uses three arrays. Two provide input data and are initialized on the host side. The GPU reads data from input vectors and writes the result to the output vector. The hosts requires these data to verify the result.

– *data transfer multikernel* - In this test, two GPU kernels are executed successively. It uses one array. The second kernel uses the results of the first as input. The result of the second kernel is written to this array and the result is evaluated on the CPU. A suitable memory management avoids the data transfer between the execution of the two kernels.

For these benchmarks, five different memory management variants implemented and compared for Numba-CUDA

– *Implicit*: Only ordinary NumPy arrays are used. The data transfer is carried out automatically by Numba.

– *Explicit*: Device arrays are used and copy operations between Host and device explicitly triggered. Data is only copied when it is required.

– *Explicit pinned*: Similar to *explicit*, but the host arrays are allocated on pinned memory

– *Smart*: Numba Smart arrays are used, which perform the data transfer automatically as in the implicit case, but should use more intelligent mechanism to avoid unnecessary copying.

– *Managed*: Unified memory arrays are used.

Note that *smart arrays* are deprecated, but we still use them here to compare the performance. We also implemented C-CUDA versions of the benchmarks, using the explicit, pinned and managed memory.

5.2   Micro-benchmark-Performance

Figures 1, 2 and 3 show the performance of these benchmarks in Numba. For small array sizes, up to around 64 kByte, the managed array class shows quite good performance compared to the other methods. For the partial and multi-kernel benchmark, the performance is almost comparable to the pinned memory and much better than for smart arrays or the implicit variant.

For larger arrays, however, this changes. For the full data transfer benchmark, our managed array class performs significantly worse than all other variants. For the partial- and multi-kernel benchmark, only the implicit variant is worse than the manged class. This is as expected, since for the partial and multi kernel benchmark the implicit version copies unnecessary data.

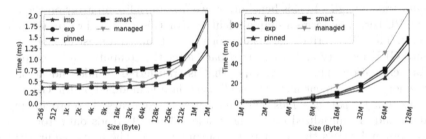

Fig. 1. Full data transfer Numba performance

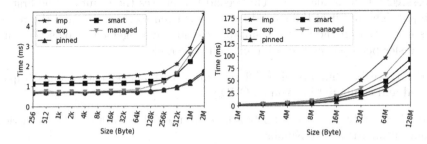

Fig. 2. Partial data transfer Numba performance

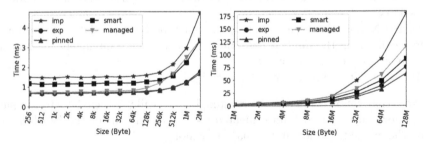

Fig. 3. Multikernel data transfer Numba performance

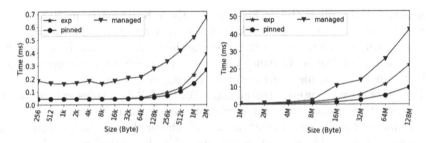

Fig. 4. Full data transfer C performance

The performance of the managed class for large arrays is worse than using explicit copies/This is the expected behavior from previous work evaluating managed memory. Still, there are some results that are surprising, especially when comparing the results of the Numba benchmarks with the C-CUDA benchmarks.

The results of the full data transfer benchmark for C-CUDA are shown in Fig. 4. The differences between the managed memory and the explicit variants are larger than for Numba, even for smaller arrays. Furthermore, the runtime of the C-CUDA variants is significantly shorter than the Numba version, especially for small arrays.

It is surprising that the smart array variant performs significantly worse than the explicit variant, since the number of copy operations performed should be the same We used the Nvidia profiling tool nvprof to understand this behavior better. For the partial benchmark, three copy operations are required: The two input vectors are copied to the device and the output vector is copied back. The implicit class requires six copy operations, since always all vectors are copied in and out. The smart class requires four copy operations: all vectors are copied in, but only the result is copied back. The additional copy explains the performance difference for the smart array class. For the multi-kernel benchmark, the same applies: the smart array class copies the data from GPU to host between the two kernel calls, although the data are not required on the host.

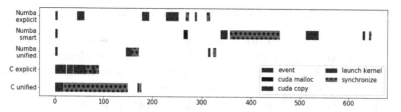

Fig. 5. Timeline of the CUDA-API calls for the different versions of the full-data transfer benchmarks (4 kByte array)

Figure 5 shows the timing of CUDA API-function calls for different versions of the full data transfer benchmark. This allows us to better understand the differences between the Numba version and the C versions. For this size, there is only a small difference between pinned and unpinned memory. Additional, the smart class behaves similarly to the implicit case. Therefore and, due to lack of space, we refrain from the presentation of these. We use CUDA-events to measure the timing, so we show the API calls starting with the recording of the first event and synchronising the second event.

By using implicit or smart data transfer, a cudaMalloc operation is required before the kernel is started. Using smart or Numpy arrays, only the host memory is allocated when a new array is created. Numba has a lazy deallocation policy, so these vectors are not freed when the function ends (instead there is a garbage collection that regularly releases all vectors together). Still, there is no reuse of allocated memory beyond the lifetime of an array.

The runtime of the calls to actual CUDA-API are similar for the C-Cuda and Numba versions, and the kernel have a similar runtime. However Numba versions have much more time passing between calls. The C-Cuda version usually has less than a microsecond between two API calls, while the Numba version sometimes requires more than 100 ms.

One reasons for this is the Python interpreter overhead. Although the same compiled CUDA-functions and kernels are called, using python everything in between is handled by the interpreter. Especially with small array sizes this overhead is much higher than the actual runtime of the kernel and the data transfer.

This shows one advantage of unified memory in Numba: Because fewer function calls are needed (no copy functions), the interpreter overhead is much smaller. Therefore we see a comparable performance for the whole benchmark for small sizes compared to the explicit case and a better performance than using implicit or smart copies. For larger arrays, however, this advantage increasingly fades into the background. The Python overhead remains constant, while the copy times and kernel runt times increase. Since the kernel runtime increases significantly when using unified memory (as every access to a new memory page triggers a page fault), the performance of unified memory is also significantly worse in our Numba benchmarks.

5.3   Work Distribution Using Atomic Operations

In order to use the new possibilities for work-sharing between several process units (PU), we transferred a benchmark from the Chai Benchmark Suite [6] to Numba. The Chai benchmarks are particularly suitable for computations based on the division of work in heterogeneous systems.

We selected the RSCD benchmark as an example. It calculates the RANSAC algorithm [5], which is an iterative method for estimating mathematical models on the basis of incorrect measured values. The benchmark distributes the work between PUs by dividing the input data. We implemented two the variants of the benchmark in Python/Numba:

– *rscd_d*. Uses discrete memory and explicit data transfer. The partitioning of the input data is carried out static, according to a specified CPU-to-GPU ratio α.
– *rscd_u*. All PUs use the same memory for input and output, using manged memory. The workload is distributed dynamically, using atomic operations.

The use of unified memory the elimination of initial data partitioning, multiple keeping of variables and the final merging of results reduces the code complexity. The code of the variant rscd_u is significantly simpler than the variant rscd_d. We increased the size of the problem from the original vector by about factor 10 to generate more computational effort. Figure 6 shows the results. The problem with the Chai benchmark is that it was developed primarily for embedded systems. On our high performance GPUs, splitting the work between GPU and host always leads to a worse result than if the calculation is done on the GPU only (this is also true for the C-CUDA version of the benchmark). We have used a small alpha of 0.01 for the static distribution. Even with this distribution, in which the CPUs only do 1% of the work, the performance is worse than when the job is only run on the GPU. This is similar to the distribution achieved when using dynamic distribution.

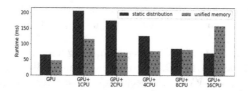

Fig. 6. Results of the Chai benchmark

The benchmark benefits in most configurations clearly from the use of unified memory. Using only GPU the runtime of variant rscd_u is 31% lower than that of the variant rscd_d. One of the reasons for this is certainly also that the problem size of the Chai benchmark is comparatively small, and many of the effects explained in the previous chapter play a role here. However, the use of atomic operation reduces the number of kernel invocations and thus the Python interpreter overhead.

The runtime of the unified memory benchmark increases, if more CPUs are used. One reason is CPython is not able to execute Python code in parallel in several threads simultaneously. The Global Interpreter Lock (GIL) ensures that only one thread of Python code is executed at a time. All other threads can execute only external non-Python code at the same time. As a result, the overhead of calling a JIT-compiled Numba function for the CPU threads are summed up, since the GIL is not unlocked until the JIT compiled machine code is called up. This requires further optimazation in future work.

6 Conclusion

In this work we have implemented and evaluated the support of unified memory in Numba. Unlike the use of C-CUDA, there are cases where unified memory can help to improve performance by reducing the number of function calls and thus the overhead of the Python interpreter. However, this is only true for small problem sizes and if many context switches between GPU and Python are required. This is especially true for work sharing benchmarks between GPU and CPU, where the use of atomic operations allow a simple work distribution between CPU and GPU.

In a next step we want to evaluate the performance on embedded devices like the Jetson series. Although there is less support for unified memory here, we believe that they benefit even more from unified memory and the reduced overhead. We also want to implement more features in Numba to improve the use of GPU memory, like the memory hints.

References

1. Anaconda, I., et al.: Numba user manual: overview. http://numba.pydata.org/numba-doc/latest/user/overview.html
2. Cai, X., Langtangen, H.P., Moe, H.: On the performance of the Python programming language for serial and parallel scientific computations. Sci. Program. **13**(1), 31–56 (2005)
3. NVIDIA cooperation: CUDA C programming guide. https://docs.nvidia.com/cuda/archive/9.1/pdf/CUDA_C_Programming_Guide.pdf
4. NVIDIA cooperation: NVVM IR specification 1.4: reference guide. https://docs.nvidia.com/pdf/NVVM_IR_Specification.pdf
5. Fischler, M.A., Bolles, R.C.: Random sample consensus: a paradigm for model fitting with applications to image analysis and automated cartography. Commun. ACM **24**(6), 381–395 (1981)
6. Gómez-Luna, J., et al.: Chai: collaborative heterogeneous applications for integrated-architectures. In: 2017 IEEE International Symposium on Performance Analysis of Systems and Software (ISPASS), pp. 43–54. IEEE (2017)
7. Harris, M.: Unified memory for CUDA beginners. https://devblogs.nvidia.com/unified-memory-cuda-beginners/
8. Knap, M., Czarnul, P.: Performance evaluation of unified memory with prefetching and oversubscription for selected parallel CUDA applications on NVIDIA Pascal and Volta GPUs. J. Supercomput. **75**(11), 7625–7645 (2019). https://doi.org/10.1007/s11227-019-02966-8
9. Lam, S.K., Pitrou, A., Seibert, S.: Numba: a LLVM-based python JIT compiler. In: Proceedings of the Second Workshop on the LLVM Compiler Infrastructure in HPC, p. 7. ACM (2015)
10. Landaverde, R., Zhang, T., Coskun, A.K., Herbordt, M.: An investigation of unified memory access performance in CUDA. In: 2014 IEEE High Performance Extreme Computing Conference (HPEC), pp. 1–6. IEEE (2014)
11. Li, W., Jin, G., Cui, X., See, S.: An evaluation of unified memory technology on NVIDIA GPUs. In: 2015 15th IEEE/ACM International Symposium on Cluster, Cloud and Grid Computing, pp. 1092–1098. IEEE (2015)
12. Marowka, A.: Python accelerators for high-performance computing. J. Supercomput. **74**(4), 1449–1460 (2017). https://doi.org/10.1007/s11227-017-2213-5
13. Oden, L.: Lessons learned from comparing C-CUDA and Python-Numba for GPU-computing. In: 2020 28th Euromicro International Conference on Parallel, Distributed and Network-Based Processing (PDP), pp. 216–223 (2020)
14. Ousterhout, J.K.: Scripting: higher level programming for the 21st century. Computer **31**(3), 23–30 (1998)
15. Pierro, V., Troiano, L., Mejuto, E., Filatrella, G.: Stochastic first passage time accelerated with CUDA. J. Comput. Phys. **361**, 136–149 (2018)
16. Smaalders, B.: Performance anti-patterns. Queue **4**(1), 44–50 (2006)
17. Van Rossum, G., Drake Jr, F.L.: Python/C API reference manual. Python Software Foundation (2002)

ParaMo - Workshop on Parallel Programming Models in High-Performance Cloud

Workshop on Parallel Programming Models in High-Performance Cloud (ParaMo)

Workshop Description

ParaMo is a forum for researchers working on programming models, networking, resource management, and runtime to solve the problems on parallel computing in high-performance cloud. The notion of cloud computing has changed the way we utilize computing resources. Since High-Performance Computing (HPC) has long suffered from under- or over-utilization of resources, many HPC researchers are trying to adapt HPC applications to the cloud environment. With proper adaptation, HPC applications are able to enhance their resource utilization ratio and scalability by using virtualized and on-demand resources in clouds. When we discuss HPC in clouds, we should discuss the parallel programming models as well. Various parallel programming models and their frameworks (e.g., MPI, OpenMP, OpenCL, CUDA, and MapReduce) have been proposed for parallel computing. For example, the MapReduce programming model has been used for various big data processing applications since it helps to reduce the complexity of problem parallelization such as decomposition, communication, and scheduling. However, a parallel programming model should be carefully selected for HPC applications to achieve high performance and efficient resource usage because their target hardware architectures (e.g., many-core, GPU, InfiniBand, etc.) are different as well as the abstraction levels. For example, MapReduce may not be a suitable choice of parallel programming model for a large-scale graph data processing problem. In addition, since traditional parallel programming models, such as MPI, are implemented for a single-tenant cluster environment, applying these models to HPC applications in the cloud is challenging in terms of resource management.

The second International Workshop on Parallel Computing Models in High-Performance Cloud (ParaMo 2020) was held as a virtual event in Warsaw, Poland. The workshop was organized in conjunction with the Euro-Par annual international conference. The format of the workshop was the technical presentation of research papers. Around twenty people attended the online sessions.

This year, we received ten articles for review, from European and Asian countries. After a thorough peer-reviewing process, we selected five articles for presentation at the workshop (50% acceptance ratio). The review process focused on the quality of the papers, their innovative ideas, and the soundness of the presentation.

We would like to thank the ParaMo Advisory Committee, the Program Committee, and the sub-reviewers, who made the workshop possible. We would also like to thank Euro-Par for hosting our community, and the Euro-Par workshop chairs, Prof. Bartosz Baliś and Prof. Dora Blanco Heras, for their help and support.

Organization

Program Co-chairs

Hyun-Wook Jin   Konkuk University, South Korea
Sangyoon Oh   Ajou University, South Korea

Advisory Committee

Geoffrey C. Fox   Indiana University, USA
Dhabaleswar K. Panda   Ohio State University, USA

Publicity Chair

Yin-Goo Yim   Konkuk University, South Korea

Program Committee

Seung-Hee Bae   Intel, USA
Jee Choi   University of Oregon, USA
Jong Choi   Oak Ridge National Lab., USA
Cheol-Ho Hong   Chung-Ang University, South Korea
Xiaoyi Lu   Ohio State University, USA
Blesson Varghese   Queen's University Belfast, UK
Wenjun Wu   Beihang University, China
Beytullah Yildiz   Atılım University, Turkey
Weikuan Yu   Florida State University, USA

Performance Evaluation of Java/PCJ Implementation of Parallel Algorithms on the Cloud

Marek Nowicki[1]([⊠]) , Łukasz Górski[2] , and Piotr Bała[2]

[1] Faculty of Mathematics and Computer Science,
Nicolaus Copernicus University in Toruń, Torun, Poland
`faramir@mat.umk.pl`
[2] Interdisciplinary Centre for Mathematical and Computational Modeling,
University of Warsaw, Warsaw, Poland
`{lgorski,bala}@icm.edu.pl`

Abstract. Cloud resources are more often used for large scale computing and data processing. However, the usage of the cloud is different than traditional High-Performance Computing (HPC) systems and both algorithms and codes have to be adjusted. This work is often time-consuming and performance is not guaranteed. To address this problem we have developed the PCJ library (Parallel Computing in Java), a novel tool for scalable high-performance computing and big data processing in Java. In this paper, we present a performance evaluation of parallel applications implemented in Java using the PCJ library. The performance evaluation is based on the examples of highly scalable applications that run on the traditional HPC system and Amazon AWS Cloud. For the cloud, we have used Intel x86 and ARM processors running Java codes without changing any line of the program code and without the need for time-consuming recompilation. Presented applications have been parallelized using the PGAS programming model and its realization in the PCJ library. Our results prove that the PCJ library, due to its performance and ability to create simple portable code, has great promise to be successful for the parallelization of various applications and run them on the cloud with a similar performance as for HPC systems.

Keywords: Cloud computing · Parallel computing · Performance evaluation · Java · PCJ · HPC · Cloud

1 Introduction

Cloud computing, despite its quite long presence and stable position on the market differs from High Performance Computing (HPC). While both target large scale workloads with scalability being the main factor, this target is achieved differently.

© Springer Nature Switzerland AG 2021
B. Balis et al. (Eds.): Euro-Par 2020 Workshops, LNCS 12480, pp. 213–224, 2021.
https://doi.org/10.1007/978-3-030-71593-9_17

HPC is concerned with the vertical scalability. Typical workflow may be conceived as a single application processing extremely large datasets in parallel, with data being shared by the compute nodes. Therefore network performance becomes a limiting factor, with advancements in the networking technology being crucial for the successful parallelization of workloads [38]. Cloud computing can be connected with horizontal scalability. Here a problem can be effortlessly divided into a number of independent sub-problems, each susceptible to being solved in a self-contained manner. Multiple instances of a given application run in concert, with their number being dynamically adjusted to account for the current system's load [38].

HPC and cloud computing, therefore, try to achieve a different type of scalability. To achieve their aim, both techniques use their types of optimized hardware. The feasibility of choosing one or the other depends on the particular application's requirements. However, there is increasing interest in finding solutions that bridge HPC and cloud computing. New solutions have to be open to new programming languages utilized, *inter alia*, by Big Data and Artificial Intelligence communities as well. To address this problem, we have focused on the usability of Java for HPC applications. Usage of well-established industrial language opens the field for easy integration of both workload types. The PCJ library (Parallel Computing in Java) [25] fully complies with core Java standards, therefore, the programmer does not have to use additional libraries, which are not part of the standard Java distribution. Thus user is free from the burden of installing (properly versioned) dependencies, as the library is a single self-contained *jar* file, which can be easily dropped into the *classpath*.

In the previous works, we have shown that the PCJ library allows for the easy and feasible development of computational applications as well as Big Data and AI processing running on supercomputers or clusters. The performance comparison with the C/MPI based codes has been presented in previous papers [22,26]. The extensive comparison with Java-based solutions including APGAS (Java implementation of X10 language) has been also performed [27,31].

In this paper, we contribute by focusing on the performance of selected applications run on the Amazon Web Services (AWS) Elastic Compute Cloud (EC2) using both Intel and ARM architectures. The ultimate aim is to show the feasibility of using Java and the PCJ library for the development of parallel applications run on the cloud. The results have been compared to the state of the art HPC system, namely Cray XC40 equipped with the Intel processors.

Intel architecture is available at AWS since the beginning, the ARM architecture has been added at the end of 2018 [2]. In this case dedicated processors designed for AWS are used, called AWS Graviton, that are modified ARM Cortex-A72 processor [42]. AWS continues to develop its own ARM processors and recently announced AWS Graviton2 processors to be available in new instance types [3].

2   Related Work

The interest in joining the traditional HPC computing and exploiting the potential of the cloud has already been growing for some time. It has been noted that while the HPC paradigm offers great computing capabilities, the cloud offers elasticity and dynamic allocation of resources on a scale unseen before. There is a growing influx of competent engineers that specialize in DevOps and are well-acquainted with microservices, virtualization, and the contenerization of software (with tools like Kubernetes or Docker). On the other hand, traditional HPC was concerned mainly with languages like C or Fortran, which are now decreasing in popularity. Moreover, the divergence between traditional HPC workloads and emerging new ones could already have been observed in the case of Big Data processing or Artificial Intelligence applications. They are implemented in languages like Java or Scala which, up to now, were out of interest of the HPC community.

MPI, which is the basic parallelization library, is also criticized because of the complicated API and difficulty in programming. Users are looking for easy to learn, yet feasible and scalable tools more aligned with popular programming languages such as Java or Python. They would like to develop applications using workstations or laptops and then easily move them to large systems including HPC-based peta- and exascale ones or to deploy them on a cloud.

Cloud has been already recognized as a way for provisioning tailored-to-fit computational resources for medium-sized HPC workloads [15]. It was found that it is especially well-suited for communication-intensive applications (up to low processor count) and embarrassingly parallel ones (up to high processor count) [14].

PCJ library deviates from the standard scientific message-passing paradigm and instead opts to use the PGAS model. The model aims to present the programmer with an abstraction of unified memory view, even when in fact it is distributed among the computer nodes. The PGAS model is supported by libraries such as SHMEM [10], or Global Arrays [20] as well as by specialized languages or dialects, such as UPC [6] (C-based), Fortran [33], X10 [9] or Chapel [8]. PGAS systems differ in the way the global namespace is organized.

The perspective language is, amongst others, Java due to its popularity and portability. Java has good support of threads since the beginning. The parallelization tools available for Java include threads and Java Concurrency which have been introduced in Java SE 5 and improved in Java SE 6 [29]. There are also solutions based on various implementations of the MPI library [7,40], distributed Java Virtual Machine [4] and solutions based on Remote Method Invocation (RMI) [19]. We should also mention solutions motivated by the PGAS approach represented by Titanium [41]. Titanium defines new language constructs and has to use a dedicated compiler which makes it difficult to follow recent changes in Java language.

The APGAS library for Java [37] adds asynchronism to the PGAS model by adopting a task-based approach. The parallelization and distribution concepts are the same as those of IBM's parallel language X10. Program execution starts with a single task. Later, any task can spawn any number of child tasks dynamically synchronously or asynchronously. In either case, the programmer must specify an execution place for each task. Inside each place, tasks are automatically scheduled to workers. The place-internal scheduler is implemented with Java's Fork/Join-Pool [30].

Yet another solution for writing high-performance HPC applications, that incorporates the PGAS programming paradigm is PCJ library described in next section.

3   The PCJ Library

PCJ [1, 25] is an open-source Java library that does not require any language extensions or special compiler. The user has to download the single jar file (or use build automation tool with dependency resolvers like Maven or Gradle) on any system with Java installed.

The PCJ library is designed to support the application running on the multi-core, multinode systems. The programmers are provided with the PCJ class with a set of methods to implement necessary parallel constructs. All technical details like threads administration, communication, and network programming are hidden from the programmers. The intranode communication is implemented using the Java Concurrency mechanism. The object sent from one thread to another has to be serialized, and then deserialized on the other thread and stored in memory. This way of cloning data is safe, as the data is deeply copied – the other thread has its copy of data and can use it independently. The communication between nodes uses standard network communication with sockets. The network communication is performed using Java New IO classes (i.e. `java.nio.*`). The details of the algorithms used to implement PCJ communication are described in the [25].

The PCJ library provides necessary tools for PGAS programming including threads numbering, data transfer and threads synchronization. The communication is one-sided and asynchronous which makes programming easy and less error-prone. With a relatively simple set of methods, programmers can easily implement data and work partitioning best suited to the problem they are solving. Instead of modifying the problem to fit the given programming model, the user optimally implements his algorithm using the PCJ library as a tool to expose parallelism.

The PCJ library has won the HPC Challenge award in 2014 and has already been used for the parallelization of multiple applications. A good example is a communication-intensive graph search from the Graph500 test suite. The PCJ implementation scales well and outperforms Hadoop implementation by the factor of 100 [28,34]. PCJ library was also used to develop code for the evolutionary algorithm which has been used to find a minimum of a simple function as defined in the CEC'14 Benchmark Suite [17]. Recent examples of PCJ usage include parallelization of the sequence alignment [23,24]. PCJ library allowed for the easy implementation of the dynamic load balancing for multiple NCBI-BLAST instances spanned over multiple nodes. The obtained performance was at least 2 times higher than for the implementations based on the static work distribution. Another example that uses the PCJ library is an application for calculating the parameters of *C. Elegans* connectome model [13,32] that uses differential evolution algorithm.

4   Experimental Setup

The cloud used is the Amazon AWS EC2. We have used the instances in the Europe (Frankfurt) region (*eu-central-1*).

We have used *t2.xlarge* instances equipped with Intel(R) Xeon(R) CPU E5-2686 v4 processors (2.3 GHz). Each instance consists of 4 vCPUs, 16 GB RAM. The network performance is described as *moderate*, what translates into about 1 Gbps network bandwidth. The instances' operating system is Amazon Linux 2 AMI 2.0.20200207.1 x86_64 HVM gp2 with additionally installed OpenJDK Runtime Environment Corretto-11.0.6.10.1 implementation of JVM.

Due to the increasing popularity of ARM processors, we have also used *a1.xlarge* instances equipped with AWS Graviton Processors (2.3 GHz) featuring 64-bit ARM Neoverse cores designed by AWS and optimized for performance and cost. Each instance consists of 4 vCPUs, 8 GB RAM with EBS disk storage. The network bandwidth is up to 10 Gbps. The instances' operating system is Amazon Linux 2 LTS Arm64 AMI 2.0.20200207.1 arm64 HVM gp2 with OpenJDK Runtime Environment Corretto-11.0.6.10.1 implementation of JVM.

The next two AWS EC2 instance types are: *a1.4xlarge* and *a1.metal*. Both instances are almost identical to *a1.xlarge* instance types, but each instance consists of 16 vCPUs (or 16 CPUs in *bare metal* type, where the physical cores are directly used) and 32 GB RAM. All other setups have been the same as for *a1.xlarge* instances.

For the reference, we have used the performance results obtained using a typical HPC system such as the Cray XC40 system at ICM (University of Warsaw, Poland). The computing nodes are homogenous. Each node is equipped with the two 12-core Intel Xeon E5-2690 v3 processors (2.60 GHz) with hyperthreading available (2 threads per core) and 128 GB RAM. Cray Aries interconnect is used for communication. The operating system on nodes of Cray XC40 was SUSE Linux Enterprise Server 12. The Oracle Java 1.8.0_51 implementation of Java Virtual Machine was used. The choice of Cray XC40 systems is motivated by the recent announcement of the first exascale systems which will be a continuation of such architecture [39].

All systems use the PCJ library in version 5.0.8 for parallel execution. The source code was compiled into *bytecode* on the local machine, and the compiled version was transferred to computing systems. The applications were run on the systems without any modification.

5   Performance Results

This section describes three applications with performance evaluation made on different hardware systems. Selected applications have various execution profile: CPU bound (DES decryption, Subsect. 5.1), communication bound (FFT, Subsect. 5.2) and Big Data type (WordCount, Subsect. 5.3). Such selection allows us to test different aspects of application performance including computation, communication, and I/O.

5.1   DES Decryption

Hidden text decryption is an example of the CPU intensive, trivially parallel problem which can be solved in different ways. The DES encryption can be decrypted using a brute force algorithm, therefore we have used implementation based on the analysis of all possible encryption keys. In our example, the hidden text is decoded with usage of the various keys using the DES algorithm. If the decoded text contains a given pattern, the text is treated as properly decoded. The keys are generated to cover all possible combinations of a given key length and the workload is divided equally between available processors. For the encryption key of length n there are 2^n possible combinations. Usually, the search is stopped while matching key is found, but for our performance tests, we have tested a whole range of keys.

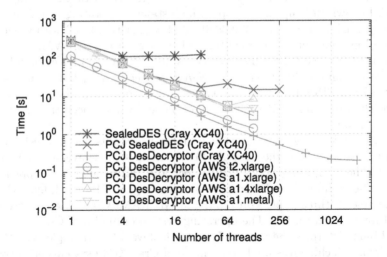

Fig. 1. The performance of the parallel decryption run on the Cray XC40 and AWS Cloud (x86 and ARM processors). The PCJ and thread based implementations are presented. The 26-bit key was used.

The decryption algorithm has been implemented in Java using different parallelization tools and methods. In all cases `SealedObject` from `javax.crypto` package has been used to store keys and to perform decryption of the hidden text.

Different implementations have been tested:

SealedDES – Java threads implementation. The work is distributed among vanilla Java threads and each thread is processing a subset of keys. At each loop iteration new `SealedObject` is created. This implementation is limited to the single node (i.e. single JVM). Full source code is available on GitHub at [5].

PCJ SealedDES – PCJ implementation developed based on the Java threads implementation. The work is distributed among PCJ threads in the same manner as for the SealedDES. Full source code is available on GitHub at [16].

PCJ DesDecryptor – modified PCJ implementation. The single `SealedObject` is created for each PCJ thread and is reused for all iterations of the main loop. Full source code is available on GitHub at [21].

The performance results are presented in Fig. 1. The limited scalability of Java threads implementation is visible. The PCJ SealedDES implementation scales much better, up to thousands of cores, depending on the key size. The improved PCJ implementation removes multiple `SealedObject` creation performed in each iteration of the main loop. This significantly reduces memory operations as well as Garbage Collector invocations. As a result, code performs about 3.5 times faster and scales to the larger number of cores.

The best performing implementation (i.a. PCJ DesDecryptor) has been run on the AWS cloud. Scalability is very good, but, as presented in Fig. 1, overall performance for the AWS cloud is lower than for Cray XC40. The difference is higher for *a1* instances which reflects performance difference between x86 and ARM processors.

5.2   Fast Fourier Transform

Fast Fourier Transform (FFT) is used as a benchmark for communication-intensive parallel algorithms. The most widely used implementation is based on the algorithm published by Takahashi and Kanada [36]. The PCJ implementation is based on the Coarray Fortran 2.0 [18]. It uses a radix 2 binary exchange algorithm that aims to reduce interprocess communication: firstly, a local FFT calculation is performed based on the bit-reversing permutation of input data; after this step all threads perform data transposition from block to cyclic layout, thus allowing for subsequent local FFT computations; finally, a reverse transposition restores data to is original block layout [18]. The communication is localized in the all-to-all routine that is used for a global conversion of data layout, from block to cyclic and *vice verse*. The implementation details are described in [26]. Full source code is available on GitHub at [11].

The PCJ implementation of FFT has been run on a Cray XC40 system and AWS cloud using a different number of threads. Because of the exchange algorithm, the number of threads was a power of 2 which, in the case of Cray XC40, resulted in partial utilization of the computing nodes. In the Fig. 2 we have presented application speed (i.e. number of floating-point operations per second) which is a standard performance measure used for FFT. The FFT code runs faster on Cray XC40 and scales up to several PCJ threads. The scalability is better for larger arrays as it was presented in the [26]. The AWS cloud shows also good scalability. The results obtained with 16 threads running on each processor are similar for ARM (Graviton) and x86 processors. For a smaller number of threads (4 per processor) the code runs faster on x86 architecture. However, with the increase of the number of nodes, the performance becomes similar for both ARM and x86 processors. One should note, that performance of the AWS cloud (x86 processors) and Cray XC40 are almost the same for the small number of threads (up to 4). In this case, code is running on a single node and is not using interconnect. This reflects the nature of the FFT application which is communication bound and therefore performance is limited by the bandwidth of communication channel rather than by CPU speed. Cray XC40 is equipped with faster interconnect which results in better performance of communication bound applications.

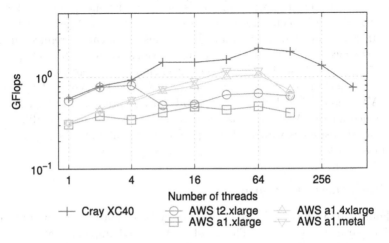

Fig. 2. The performance of the parallel FFT run on Cray XC40 and Amazon EC2 cloud for both x86 and arm64 (AWS Graviton) processors. The length of the array used for FFT is 2^{20}. The performance is plotted in GFlops (higher value means better performance).

5.3   WordCount

WordCount is traditionally used to showcase the basics of the map-reduce programming paradigm. It works by reading an input file line-by-line and counting individual word occurrences (map phase). The reduction is performed by summing the partial results calculated by worker threads.

In the PCJ code, each line of input text is divided into words and each thread saves partial results to its shareable global variable. For simplicity, the code does not perform any further preprocessing (like stemming or lemmatization). After this phase, a reduction occurs with thread 0 as root. No overlap between the two phases is facilitated. The results presented hereinafter use a simple serial reduction scheme. For better results, a hypercube-based reduction can be used, as presented in our other works [28]. Full source code and sample input data are available on GitHub at [12].

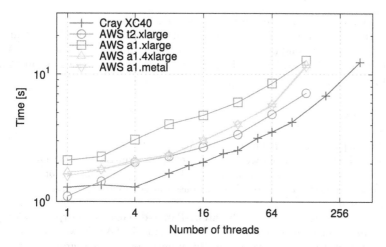

Fig. 3. The performance (execution time) of the WordCount benchmark run on AWS cloud and Cray XC40 in the weak scalability mode.

For the performance tests, we have used ISO 8859-1 encoded text of the original French version of Georges de Scudéry's *Artamène ou le Grand Cyrus* [35]. The tests were performed in a weak scalability regime resulting in the processing 10 MB file by each thread.

Results presented in Fig. 3 show similar scalability for the code run on both Intel and ARM processors. Once more, the code executed on the Cray XC40 runs 2 times faster compared to the AWS cloud. Good performance of ARM instances compare to the x86 comes mainly form EBS disk storage.

6   Conclusions

Results presented here show the feasibility of Java language to implement parallel applications running on the AWS cloud. The performance results, compare to state of the art HPC system (Cray XC40) are good, especially that code used is, due to the portability of Java, exactly the same. The PGAS programming model implemented by PCJ library allowed for easy implementation of a various parallel schema to run both on the HPC and cloud resources.

This was possible due to the PCJ library which brings parallel capabilities of the PGAS programming model to Java. The PGAS model, available mainly for C and Fortran, has been successfully used to implement many HPC applications, but it has not been widely used for Java. As presented in the paper, the PCJ library fills this gap and allows for easy development of scalable parallel applications for both Cloud and HPC architectures without the need for recompilation.

Moreover, the presented performance of the ARM processors, shows that they become a feasible alternative to x86 architecture.

Acknowledgment. This research was carried out with the support of the Interdisciplinary Centre for Mathematical and Computational Modelling (ICM) the University of Warsaw providing computational resources under grants no GB65-15, GA69-19. The authors would like to thank CHIST-ERA consortium for financial support under HPDCJ project.

References

1. PCJ homepage. http://pcj.icm.edu.pl. Accessed 12 Feb 2020
2. Barr, J.: New – EC2 Instances (A1) Powered by Arm-Based AWS Graviton Processors. AWS News Blog, 26 November 2018. https://aws.amazon.com/blogs/aws/new-ec2-instances-a1-powered-by-arm-based-aws-graviton-processors/. Accessed 18 Feb 2020
3. Barr, J.: Coming Soon – Graviton2-Powered General Purpose, Compute-Optimized and Memory-Optimized EC2 Instances. AWS News Blog, 3 December 2019. https://aws.amazon.com/blogs/aws/coming-soon-graviton2-powered-general-purpose-compute-optimized-memory-optimized-ec2-instances/. Accessed 18 Feb 2020
4. Bonér, J., Kuleshov, E.: Clustering the Java virtual machine using aspect-oriented programming. In: AOSD 2007 Proceedings of the 6th International Conference on Aspect-Oriented Software Development (2007)
5. Carey, N.: Parallel DES Key Cracker Benchmark: SealedDES implementation - source code. https://github.com/ncarey/Parallel-DES-Key-Cracker-Benchmark/blob/a760f6412495eb186a6dea53fa0aab1ed3546732/source/SealedDES.java. Accessed 12 Feb 2020
6. Carlson, W.W., Draper, J.M., Culler, D.E., Yelick, K., Brooks, E., Warren, K.: Introduction to UPC and language specification. Technical Report CCS-TR-99-157, IDA Center for Computing Sciences (1999)
7. Carpenter, B., Getov, V., Judd, G., Skjellum, A., Fox, G.: MPJ: MPI-like message passing for Java. Concurrency: Pract. Experience **12**(11), 1019–1038 (2000)
8. Chamberlain, B.L., Callahan, D., Zima, H.P.: Parallel programmability and the chapel language. Int. J. High Perform. Comput. Appl. **21**(3), 291–312 (2007)
9. Charles, P., et al.: X10: an object-oriented approach to non-uniform cluster computing. In: ACM SIGPLAN Notices, vol. 40, pp. 519–538. ACM (2005)
10. Feind, K.: Shared memory access (SHMEM) routines. Cray Research (1995)
11. Górski, Ł.: PCJ Fast Fourier Transform - source code. https://github.com/hpdcj/hpc-challenge-fft/tree/ebd557e40ad50f614a869000321ee822b67d2623. Accessed 12 Feb 2020
12. Górski, Ł.: PCJ WordCount - source code. https://github.com/hpdcj/wordcount/tree/6a265bc92147a89c37176692ccae8dcf8d97df72. Accessed 12 Feb 2020
13. Górski, Ł., Rakowski, F., Bała, P.: Parallel differential evolution in the pgas programming model implemented with PCJ Java library. In: Wyrzykowski, R., Deelman, E., Dongarra, J., Karczewski, K., Kitowski, J., Wiatr, K. (eds.) PPAM 2015. LNCS, vol. 9573, pp. 448–458. Springer, Cham (2016). https://doi.org/10.1007/978-3-319-32149-3_42
14. Gupta, A., Milojicic, D.: Evaluation of HPC applications on cloud. In: 2011 Sixth Open Cirrus Summit, pp. 22–26. IEEE (2011)
15. He, Q., Zhou, S., Kobler, B., Duffy, D., McGlynn, T.: Case study for running HPC applications in public clouds. In: Proceedings of the 19th ACM International Symposium on High Performance Distributed Computing, pp. 395–401 (2010)

16. Korona, M.: PCJ SealedDES - source code. https://github.com/hpdcj/PCJ-tests/blob/96907dd4f0b0165cdd1a807005294c5cb84012c2/src/org/pcj/tests/app/des/PCJSealedDES.java. Accessed 12 Feb 2020
17. Liang, J., Qu, B., Suganthan, P.: Problem definitions and evaluation criteria for the CEC 2014 special session and competition on single objective real-parameter numerical optimization. Zhengzhou University, Zhengzhou China and Technical Report, Nanyang Technological University, Singapore, Computational Intelligence Laboratory (2013)
18. Mellor-Crummey, J., et al.: Class ii submission to the hpc challenge award competition coarray fortran 2.0. http://www.hpcchallenge.org/presentations/sc2011/hpcc11_report_caf2_0.pdf
19. Nester, C., Philippsen, M., Haumacher, B.: A more efficient RMI for Java. Java Grande **99**, 152–159 (1999)
20. Nieplocha, J., Harrison, R.J., Littlefield, R.J.: Global arrays: a non-uniform-memory-access programming model for high-performance computers. J. Supercomputing **10**(2), 169–189 (1996)
21. Nowicki, M.: PCJ DesDecryptor - source code. https://github.com/hpdcj/PCJ-tests/blob/12c407d24c57442d8fac1395dd44bd8e4d6021cc/src/org/pcj/tests/app/des/DesDecryption.java. Accessed 12 Feb 2020
22. Nowicki, M., Bała, P.: Parallel computations in Java with PCJ library. In: 2012 International Conference on High Performance Computing and Simulation (HPCS), pp. 381–387. IEEE (2012)
23. Nowicki, M., Bzhalava, D., Bała, P.: Massively parallel sequence alignment with BLAST through work distribution implemented using PCJ library. In: Ibrahim, S., Choo, K.-K.R., Yan, Z., Pedrycz, W. (eds.) ICA3PP 2017. LNCS, vol. 10393, pp. 503–512. Springer, Cham (2017). https://doi.org/10.1007/978-3-319-65482-9_36
24. Nowicki, M., Bzhalava, D., Bała, P.: Massively parallel implementation of sequence alignment with basic local alignment search tool using parallel computing in Java library. J. Comput. Biol. **25**(8), 871–881 (2018)
25. Nowicki, M., Górski, Ł., Bała, P.: PCJ - Java library for highly scalable HPC and big data processing. In: 2018 International Conference on High Performance Computing and Simulation (HPCS), pp. 12–20. IEEE (2018)
26. Nowicki, M., Górski, Ł., Bała, P.: Performance evaluation of parallel computing and Big Data processing with Java and PCJ library. Cray Users Group (2018). https://cug.org/proceedings/cug2018_proceedings/includes/files/pap139s2-file1.pdf. Accessed 12 Feb 2020
27. Nowicki, M., Górski, Ł., Bała, P.: PCJ Java Library as a solution to integrate HPC. In: Big Data and Artificial Intelligence Workloads (in review)
28. Nowicki, M., Ryczkowska, M., Górski, Ł., Bala, P.: Big data analytics in Java with PCJ library: performance comparison with Hadoop. In: Wyrzykowski, R., Dongarra, J., Deelman, E., Karczewski, K. (eds.) PPAM 2017. LNCS, vol. 10778, pp. 318–327. Springer, Cham (2018). https://doi.org/10.1007/978-3-319-78054-2_30
29. Oracle: Java Platform, Standard Edition 6, Features and Enhancements (2006). http://www.oracle.com/technetwork/java/javase/features-141434.html. Accessed 12 Feb 2020
30. Oracle: Class ForkJoinPool (2018). https://docs.oracle.com/javase/10/docs/api/java/util/concurrent/ForkJoinPool.html
31. Posner, J., Reitz, L., Fohry, C.: Comparison of the HPC and big data Java libraries spark, PCJ and APGAS. In: 2018 IEEE/ACM Parallel Applications Workshop, Alternatives To MPI (PAW-ATM), pp. 11–22. IEEE (2018)

32. Rakowski, F., Karbowski, J.: Optimal synaptic signaling connectome for locomotory behavior in Caenorhabditis elegans: design minimizing energy cost. PLoS Comput. Biol. **13**(11), e1005834 (2017)
33. Reid, J.: The new features of Fortran 2008. In: ACM SIGPLAN Fortran Forum, vol. 27, pp. 8–21. ACM (2008)
34. Ryczkowska, M., Nowicki, M., Bała, P.: Level-synchronous BFS algorithm implemented in Java using PCJ library. In: 2016 International Conference on Computational Science and Computational Intelligence (CSCI), pp. 596–601. IEEE (2016)
35. Scudéry, M.D.: Artamène ou le grand Cyrus (1972)
36. Takahashi, D., Kanada, Y.: High-performance radix-2, 3 and 5 parallel 1-d complex FFT algorithms for distributed-memory parallel computers. J. Supercomputing **15**(2), 207–228 (2000)
37. Tardieu, O.: The apgas library: resilient parallel and distributed programming in java 8. In: Proceedings of the ACM SIGPLAN Workshop on X10, pp. 25–26. ACM (2015)
38. Thirunavukkarasu, S.: Foundation of learning structure infusion for high execution processing in the cloud. Int. J. Pure Appl. Math. **119**(12), 5253–5264 (2018)
39. Trader, T.: It's Official: Aurora on Track to Be First US Exascale Computer in 2021. HPC Wire, 18 March 2019. https://www.hpcwire.com/2019/03/18/its-official-aurora-on-track-to-be-first-u-s-exascale-computer-in-2021/. Accessed 18 Feb 2020
40. Vega-Gisbert, O., Roman, J.E., Squyres, J.M.: Design and implementation of Java bindings in Open MPI. Parallel Comput. **59**, 1–20 (2016)
41. Yelick, K., et al.: Titanium: a high-performance Java dialect. Concurrency Comput. Pract. Experience **10**(11–13), 825–836 (1998)
42. Yokoyama, D., Schulze, B., Borges, F., Mc Evoy, G.: The survey on ARM processors for HPC. J. Supercomputing **75**(10), 7003–7036 (2019). https://doi.org/10.1007/s11227-019-02911-9

Parallelizing Automatic Temporal Cognitive Tool for Large-Scale Online Learning Analytics

Tianrui Jiang$^{(\boxtimes)}$, Wenjun Wu, and Yanjun Pu

State Key Laboratory of Software Development Environment,
Beihang University, Beijing, China
{jiangtianrui,wwj,puyanjun}@nlsde.buaa.edu.cn

Abstract. With the advent of Massive Online Open Courses (MOOCs), the data scale of student learning behavior has significantly increased. In order to analyze these datasets efficiently and present on-the-fly intelligent tutoring to online learners, it is necessary to improve existing learning analytics tools in a parallel and automatic way. We introduce Automatic Temporal Cognitive (ATC) model to describe temporal progress of online learners and evaluate their mastery of course knowledge. As a complex dynamic Bayesian network model, it often causes high computational overhead of training the ATC model via Probabilistic Programming tools. The time-consuming Monte Carlo sampling adopted by the mainstream implementations renders parameter fitting for the model a slow execution process. To address the issue, this paper proposes to transform the ATC model into the form of nonlinear Kalman filter and presents a new parallel ATC tool based on the Spark framework with the method of Unscented Kalman Filter (UKF). This tool improves the ATC model by using a parallel UKF method with the capability of automatically estimating the parameters in the whole sequential process. Experimental results demonstrate that this tool can achieve the fast execution speed and greatly improve the robustness of training parameters on different sizes of real educational data sets.

Keywords: Learning analytic · Nonlinear state-space model · Kalman filter · Spark framework · Probabilistic programming

1 Introduction

With the development of Internet, online education has greatly increased in both scale and quality. Therefore, more and more students take part in MOOCs courses, which leads to large scale learning behavior data. Learning analytics tools are widely used to estimate the students' knowledge state through mining their learning behavior data in online educational systems. There are plenty of tools for learning analytics such as Cognitive Diagnosis Model [1,2] and Knowledge Tracing Model [3]. Among them, Automatic Temporal Cognitive Model

© Springer Nature Switzerland AG 2021
B. Balis et al. (Eds.): Euro-Par 2020 Workshops, LNCS 12480, pp. 225–236, 2021.
https://doi.org/10.1007/978-3-030-71593-9_18

(ATC) [4] can accurately trace a student's latent knowledge state during his skill acquisition process. Based on the ATC model, developers can build intelligent tutoring services to provide students instant feedbacks or recommendations for their study, and generate assessment reports daily to enable class instructors to quickly evaluate study process. Given the significant increase in the scale of students and dynamics of in-class enrollment, it is important to design an efficient and robust ATC-based intelligent tutoring algorithm for online education systems.

ATC model is a unified and integrated framework that can automatically discover a multiple-dimensional cognitive model and formulate a dynamic learning process over longitudinal student data. This framework enables us to trace the nonlinear dynamic change of multi-dimensional skills including skill improvement and forgetting during a student's learning process. Moreover, based on it, we can automatically build the cognitive model through student performance data to describe the latent skill vector (Q-matrix [5]) for educational content.

Currently, there are two main problems regarding the ATC parameter tuning and execution efficiency. The first one is how to configure the parameters with their proper probability distribution. Generally, the training result of parameters may have some noise which is probably caused by slip and guessing during the assessment-taking process of students. Because the ATC is essentially a dynamic Bayesian network, it is necessary to adopt Probabilistic Programming [6,7] to infer its parameters. The second problem is how to improve the execution efficiency. The increase in the amount of data often results in longer fitting time for the ATC model. When the data scale reaches tens of thousands of students, the training process can last for several hours or even days. In the field of learning analytics, there are some tools available for speeding up the training process of cognitive learner models, such as Parallelizing Bayesian Knowledge Tracing Tool [8]. Unfortunately, none of them can be applied to the ATC model because their approaches are constrained in the linear state-space framework of Hidden Markov Process, which cannot model nonlinear dynamics in dynamic cognitive skills. As a result, this computation problem for the ATC model hinders the on-the-fly learning analytics in online education platforms that often must handle many learning behavior event records on daily basis.

In this paper, we introduce a Kalman-Filter-based Automatic Parallel (KFAP) tool for parameter estimation of the ATC model. This new tool regards the ATC model as a nonlinear random process and thus uses Singular Value Decomposition-Unscented Kalman Filter (SVD-UKF) to estimate its parameters. Based on the Spark framework, KFAP parallelizes the execution of SVD-UKF computation. The major contributions of KFAP tool in our paper include: (1) Improvement in speed and stability: Using Unscented Kalman Filter to fit parameters of dynamic Bayesian network instead of MCMC (Markov Chain Monte Carlo) sampling, which makes the EM (Expectation Maximization) algorithm applicable. Thanks to it, ATC model has a huge acceleration.
(2) Improvement in scale of data: Parallelizing the implementation of SVD-UKF for ATC based on the Spark framework, which makes big data analysis possible.

2   Related Work

2.1   Automatic Temporal Cognitive Model

Automatic Temporal Cognitive Model (ATC) [4] is a new cognitive learner model by integrating essential psychometric components of Cognitive Diagnosis Model (CDM) and Knowledge Tracing (KT) Model.

CDM is a kind of cognitive diagnosis techniques that aims to predict student performance by discovering student states from the response of their exercises. It contains Item Response Theory (IRT) [9], Deterministic Inputs, Noisy-and gate model, and so on. IRT describes the basic relation between the probability that a student can correctly answer an exercise and his mastery of relevant knowledge. It provides a logistic function to model the probability of getting a correct answer using the parameters including proficiency, difficulty, and discrimination, which is defined as formula:

$$p_{sq} = f\left(\alpha_q\left(\theta_s - \beta_q\right)\right) \tag{1}$$

where α_q means the question discrimination, β_q is the question difficulty, θ_s is the student proficiency and f denotes the sigmoidal function mapping the calculation result of the student skill and question parameters to 0 and 1.

KT is proposed by AT Corbett and JR Anderson [3]. It detects an individualized sequence of exercises to the student based on the probability estimates. Based on this approach, they introduced Bayesian Knowledge Tracing (BKT) using the hidden Markov chain. The classic BKT framework can only describe temporal learning process centered around single-dimensional knowledge concepts.

To overcome the limitation of CDM and BKT, we propose ATC model as a general dynamic Bayesian network in [4]. ATC is a unified and integrated framework to automatically discover a multiple-dimensional cognitive model and formulate a student model over longitudinal student data. This framework enables us to trace the dynamic change of multi-dimensional skills including skill improvement and forgetting for the student learning process. Moreover, based on the framework, we can automatically build the cognitive model through student performance data to describe the latent skill vector for educational content. Although the complexity of the ATC model ensures better performance in analyzing student learning process, it brings a new challenge in the aspect of model training. The nonlinearity in the ATC model makes it impossible to adopt Expectant Maximization in parameter estimation in the same way as Hidden Markov Model based BKT. Instead, it must rely upon the slow MCMC sampling of probabilistic programming for dynamic Bayesian network. As a result, Stan [10] is used to train the ATC model by sampling different combination of parameters and selecting the best optimal result.

2.2   Parallel Algorithm in Model Optimization

Expectation-Maximization (EM) algorithm is an iterative algorithm used for maximum likelihood estimation containing hidden variables. Many parallel algorithms for EM computation have been proposed, such as a generic parallel implementation of the EM algorithm for computer vision in parallel distributed memory environments [11] and the fast parallel implementation of EM on NVIDIA GPUs using CUDA [12]. Based on the work of Pedro, Cui [8] applied the parallel algorithm in three distributed frameworks including Graph Lab [13], Piccolo and Spark [14]. Hunter implemented a large-scale online Expectation Maximization with Spark Streaming for low-latency applications [15,16]. Davier et.al introduced the parallel EM algorithm without improvement for Generalized Latent Variable Models and evaluated the overall gain in different CPU environments [17]. In the field of Probabilistic Programming Language (PPL), Masegosa et al. implemented a toolbox for scalable probabilistic machine learning with a special focus on massive streaming data [18]. Within PPL, most research efforts mainly focus on the majorization design during the sampling process. However, the way of sampling has an inborn property of instability that its performance heavily depends on the initial point. There is no clear standard to guarantee the convergence of sampling results delivered by the algorithms.

Among knowledge-related models, DJ Cook, LB Holder, G Galal, R Maglothin proposed an algorithm in parallel graph-based knowledge discovery [19]. Robert J. Hilderman suggested the method of parallel knowledge discovery using domain generalization graphs [20]. Unfortunately, to the best of our knowledge, none of the above publications are suitable for ATC. These researchers didn't present good solution to the problem of optimizing parameters in ATC, which is a nonlinear probabilistic programming model, with large number of data sets.

2.3 Kalman Filter and Its Extension for Nonlinear Dynamic Systems

Kalman Filter (KF) is a general algorithm for state-space models, which is able to infer latent variables by using a series of observations and estimating a joint probability distribution over the variables for each timeframe. KF can cope with the circumstance when the observation sequence contains statistical noises and other inaccuracies. The typical KF assumes the Gaussian distribution and linear system in target models. When the transmission function becomes nonlinear, modified KF solutions such as Extended Kalman Filter (EKF), Unscented Kalman Filter (UKF), Particle Filter (PF) and Deep KF method [21], have to be applied for nonlinear transformation.

UKF uses a series of samples to approximate the probability density function. It takes several key points to express one state and gives a weight to every point. During the calculation, it transforms these key points and determines the new distribution with them. UKF has a stability issue where a covariance matrix is non-positive definite matrix. Influenced by conditions and model disturbances, when the variance matrix loses the property of positive definition, the Cholesky decomposition algorithm in the traditional UT transform cannot sample the Sigma point, resulting in program interruption and poor stability. To solve this problem, a method named Singular Value Decomposition (SVD) can be integrated into the UKF as SVD-UKF [22]. The new algorithm ensures the positive property of the variance matrix via SVD and deliver more robust results.

3   Kalman-Filter-Based Automatic Parallel Tool for ATC Model

The ATC model is a nonlinear state-space model that consists of two main parts: skill embedding for item response and temporal change in skill level.

(1) Skill embedding for item response: Given the ability of student s and the difficulty of an exercise i, the model can decide the probability $p_{s,i}$ that present the probability of s has a correct response on i. We combine latent skill embedding for personalized lesson sequence recommendation [23] and IRT [24] to construct its item response function as formula (2, 3):

$$q_{s,i} = \frac{\overrightarrow{\theta}_s \cdot \overrightarrow{a}_i}{\|\overrightarrow{a}_i\|} - \|\overrightarrow{a}_i\| \tag{2}$$

$$p_{s,i} = Pr\left(R_{s,i} = 1 \mid \overrightarrow{\theta}_s, \overrightarrow{a}_i\right) = \phi\left(q_{s,i}\right) \tag{3}$$

ϕ is the logistic function convert the possibility between 0 and 1. θ_s is the vector which represents the ability of each skill of student s. Vector a_i represents the required skill level of exercise i , $R_{s,i}$ is the result of the response of s on i.

(2) Temporal change in skill level: Given the ability $\theta_{s,t}$ of student s at time t and the improvement l_i that the exercise i can offer, we can calculate the ability $\theta_{s,t+1})$ of student s at time $t+1$, which can be expressed as formula (4, 5):

$$\theta_{s,(t+1),n} \sim N\left(\mu_{s(t+1),n}, \sigma^2\right) \tag{4}$$

$$\mu_{s(t+1),n} = (\theta_{s,t,n} + l_{i,n} * \phi\left(q_{s,i}\right)) * f(\Delta t) \tag{5}$$

where $\theta_{s,t,n}$ means the able of the $n-th$ skill in the dimension of $\theta_{s,t}$. $l_{i,n}$ means the value of the $n-th$ dimension of the vector l_i. The forget coefficient $f(\Delta t)$ is relevant to Δt where Δt is the interval between timestep t and timestep $t+1$. Because the transmission function (Eq. 4) represents a Wiener process, KF can be used to estimate the parameters of the ATC model. In order to accelerate the calculation of KF, many methods have been proposed, such as Parallelized sigma-point KF [25] and decentralized structures for parallel KF [26]. However, due to the fact that KF is a matrix-based operation, these methods mainly focus on the acceleration of matrix optimization, which gives little benefit to the improvement of the overall efficiency of model training. In our case, the improvement with pure parallelization in the matrix operation is much less significant compared with the effect of KF parallelization over the large scale of students.

Since the ATC model contains a non-linear transition function, UKF should be applied to process the process of parameter estimation. We choose SVD-UKF to avoid the non-positive definite matrix. Given the inherent independent learning behavior of online students, we decide to build Kalman-Filter-based Automatic Parallel (KFAP) tool containing the method SVD-UKF based on the Spark framework. With the help of it, EM algorithm can be used instead of slow MCMC sampling in STAN. The KFAP structure is illustrated as Fig. 1.

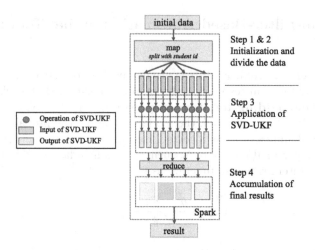

Fig. 1. Sketch map of parallelizing method

The total training process in the KFAP tool is divided into four stages, including sequence extraction, initialization and distribution of data, calculation with SVD-UKF, collection of results and EM calculation. The original learning sequence data comes from the online data collection system regularly. The original sequence usually contains useless information and needs to be cleaned. The detailed steps are shown as following:

Step1: Extract the answer sequence from the original sequence data. Then, divide the data by student ID. In each student's answer sequence, sort it by chronological order. Finally, Step 1 provides plenty of answer sequences and each sequence represents the time series data of answers of one student.

Step2: After getting the time series data, random values are assigned to the initial capacity of learners and the coefficient of difficulty of assessments. Spark can be used and answer sequences will be distributed to computational nodes. Each node receives only a small part of sequence set. Thus, there is no need to worry about how large the scale of online data is because they are divided into little portion marked with learner.

Step3: With the initial capacities of learners and the coefficient of difficulty of assessments, the model can use the recursion formula that depicts the transformation of the capacity of learner with his answer sequence. KF needs two parts to calculate: the formula of transition and the formula of emission. After some transformation of ATC, here comes the formula that is suitable for SVD-UKF:

$$\theta_t = g\left(\theta_{t-1}\right) + \eta, \eta \sim \mathcal{N}(0, Q) \tag{6}$$

$$y_t = h\left(\theta_t\right) + \varepsilon, \epsilon \sim \mathcal{N}(0, R) \tag{7}$$

$$g\left(\theta_t\right) = \left(\theta_t + l_t\right) * f_t \tag{8}$$

$$h\left(\theta_t\right) = \Phi\left(\frac{\theta_t \cdot a_i^T}{\|a_i\|} - \|a_i\|\right) \tag{9}$$

Among formula (6, 7, 8, 9), ϕ is logistic function. Vector $\boldsymbol{\theta}_t \in \mathbb{R}^k$ represents the ability of each skill of student s at the timestep t. Vector $a_i \in \mathbb{R}^k$ represents the required skill level of exercise i. The value y_t is the predicted value at the timestep t. The coefficient f_t is the effect on forgetting of student s from timestep t to timestep t + 1. The model uses SVD-UKF [22] in this step for the nonlinearity of transition and the robust process. With its help, the model can trace the transformation data of each learner during his whole learning process. Finally, KFAP gives the cross-entropy value of each answer sequence.

Step4: After step3, this model accumulates all cross-entropy and regard this sum as the loss function. With the help of this function, the Expectation Maximization Algorithm (EM), which was introduced by T.K. Moon [27] for more than 20 years is applied. The final procedure is to estimate the model parameters by maximizing the following objective function:

$$L(\omega) = LogLikelihood = \sum_{S} \sum_{L_s} \log P\left(R \mid \theta_0, D, G, Q, R\right) \qquad (10)$$

4   Experiments

4.1   Datasets

The experiments run two real datasets to test KFAP. OLI Biology dataset[1] was collected from Open Learning Initiative online course of biology from 2012 to 2014 include 5186 learners and 4831 unique assessments, with different learning modules such as Lipids, Meiosis, Proteins and so on. Our experiment datasets take each module as an independent input. Students' correct rates of responses range from 70% to 95%. Tsinghua University Web Learning dataset is acquired from Tsinghua University MOOC platform. It contains both global and university open learning classes. There are many types of data, including classroom lectures, classroom assessments, interaction with multimedia, and after-school assessments. So far, a total of millions of pieces of learning behavior data have been collected. In the experiment, its data has been divided into different courses.

4.2   Improvement During Fitting Process

In the experiment, the model can get the estimation of a student whether he or she can give a correct response to certain assessment. In Fig. 2, one can observe AUC[2] and Log-Likelihood (loglike) at each iteration of gradient descent. Figure 2 shows that after about 10 times of iterations, the rising trend of the loglike curve slows down. Then, the AUC curve keeps up with the loglike curve and stabilizes at about 0.82, which represents a favorable performance of estimation.

---

[1] https://pslcdatashop.web.cmu.edu/Project?id=115.
[2] Area Under Curve: a value between 0 and 1 that measures the discriminative ability of a binary classifier.

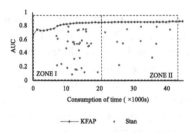
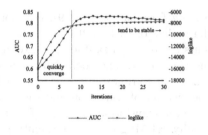

Fig. 2. AUC and loglike performance during the ATC parameter fitting process

Fig. 3. Comparison of the AUC performance of KFAP and Stan Sampling

4.3 Execution Time and Robustness

Stan is a state-of-the-art tool for statistical modeling and high-performance statistical computation. Because of the stochastic nature of sampling, Stan is instable and its result has plenty of randomness. Application of Kalman Filter can effectively reduce the execution time consumed during the period of optimizing. Figure 3 compares the AUC performance between the sampling in Stan and KFAP for ATC model training. In order to get AUC values during different execution moments, we set the break points between several gradient descent processes and export AUC values in KFAP. In the case of running Stan, we repeat the experiments for multiple times with different iteration sampling durations. The increase in sampling time will extend execution time. With the testing data, AUC acquired by KFAP quickly achieves a satisfactory performance and becomes stable after 2–3 h. In contrast, Stan performs in a very unstable way with the initial iterations. One can see that the AUC of Stan sampling ranges from 0.1 to 0.7 during 10000–20000 s. With such a high uncertainty, it takes much longer time for Stan to prepare and optimize its performance. In Zone I of 3, before Stan has run sufficient rounds of sampling, its performance heavily depends on the initial sampling point, which has more uncertainty than Zone II. When the sampling points are accumulated in Zone II, AUC tends to reach a better status than Zone I and generate a probability to express a rough estimation of the optimal parameters. As a contrast, with the KF and gradient descent, KFAP can quickly converge to the local optimal result since the first few of iterations.

4.4 Acceleration with Spark Framework

Spark can distribute a big volume of operations to many executors. Figure 4 shows the variation tendency of execution time with increasing number of executors. In this experiment, a dataset (9k rows) of 445 students is chosen and execution time is sampled by 10 iterations during the fitting process. The curve shows clearly that KFAP can significantly reduce the execution time with the increase in the number of executors. Figure 5 displays the time consumption with different sizes of datasets (with 4k, 8k, 12k and 16k rows) in different number of executors (iteration time $= 5$). KFAP keeps achieving a good performance when the scale of datasets become larger. As each executor can work more efficiently with the increase in datasets, KFAP is suitable to be extended to large-scale datasets.

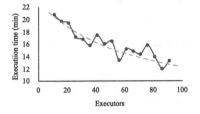

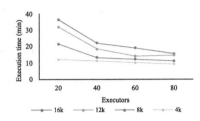

Fig. 4. Execution time with different clusters

Fig. 5. Execution time with different datasets

Another comparison is made between the efficiency of the model training running on a single machine and on a Spark framework. The single machine contains a CPU of Intel E3-1246, with 8 GB allocated memory. The Spark cluster has 10 machines, 71 cores (with 1 core of master), 372 GB memory (with 20 GB of master). Because of sufficient memory in Spark framework, the algorithm can design more intermediate variables in order to reduce the execution time. The detailed parameters are shows in the Table 1:

Table 1. The specification of computing node of two methods

Method	CPU	Process speed	Cores	Processor	Memory
Single machine	E3-1246 v3	3.5 GHz	1	1	8 GB
Spark framework	Spark with E3-1246 v3	3.5 GHz	71	71	372 GB

We trained the ATC model with the datasets both on the single machine and parallel implementation with Spark. Figure 6 shows the improvement of execution time with/without Spark boost. In fact, the model with the Spark framework can utilize more CPU cores and larger memory, thus resulting in significant improvement in terms of running speed especially with the large-scale datasets.

Table 2 chooses 4 different modules (A: Mitosis, B: Carbohydrates, C: Meiosis, D: Lipids) from OLI Biology and shows the final result and its execution time of KFAP, indicating that the KFAP tool can ensure the excellent AUC performance for the ATC model. With the increase in the scale of learning datasets increases, we can correspondingly add more computing cores in the Spark framework to speed up the model training process.

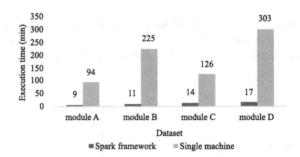

Fig. 6. Improvement of execution time with Spark

Table 2. Performance with different datasets

Dataset size	N:student	N:assessment	Log-likelihood	AUC	Iteration	Execution time(s)
8541	445	12	−3159.69	0.94	87	5933
18547	436	45	−7859.17	0.82	31	5316
2878	71	18	−1015.50	0.82	69	4523
2904	65	45	−1214.04	0.75	41	4256

5   Conclusion

In this paper, we propose a Kalman-Filter-based Automatic Parallel (KFAP) tool for the ATC, which is implemented on the Spark framework and adopts Singular Value Decomposition-Unscented Kalman Filter. The two major improvements of KFAP includes: (1) Using Unscented Kalman Filter to substitute for Stan, which makes the EM algorithm to fit parameters possible. (2) Paralleling implementation of SVD-Unscented Kalman Filter tool for the ATC model based on the Spark framework. Experimental results confirm that our system achieves performance improvements in both execution time and the robustness of the model training process. Our future work includes generalization of the KFAP to other nonlinear state-space models and investigation into deep Kalman filters.

Acknowledgements. This work was supported by Development Program of China (Funding No. 2018YFB1004502), NSFC (Grant No. 61532004) and State Key Laboratory of Software Development Environment (Funding No. SKLSDE-2020ZX-01). This work is partially funded by Beijing Advanced Innovation Center for Big Data and Brain Computing, Beihang University, Beijing, 100191.

References

1. De La Torre, J.: A cognitive diagnosis model for cognitively based multiple-choice options. Appl. Psychol. Meas. **33**(3), 163–183 (2009)
2. Hartz, S.M.C.: A Bayesian framework for the unified model for assessing cognitive abilities: Blending theory with practicality. PhD thesis, ProQuest Information and Learning (2002)

3. Corbett, A.T., Anderson, J.R.: Knowledge tracing: modeling the acquisition of procedural knowledge. User Model. User-adapted Interaction **4**(4), 253–278 (1994). https://doi.org/10.1007/BF01099821
4. Pu, Y., Wu, W., Jiang, T.: Atc framework: a fully automatic cognitive tracing model for student and educational contents. In: EDM (2019)
5. Barnes, T.: The q-matrix method: mining student response data for knowledge. In: American Association for Artificial Intelligence 2005 Educational Data Mining Workshop, pp. 1–8, AAAI Press, Pittsburgh (2005)
6. Prékopa, A.: Probabilistic programming. Handb. Oper. Res. Manag. Sci. **10**, 267–351 (2003)
7. van de Meent, J.-W., Paige, B., Yang, H., Wood, F.: An introduction to probabilistic programming. arXiv preprint arXiv:1809.10756 (2018)
8. Pu, Y., Wu, W., Han, Y., Chen, D.: Parallelizing Bayesian knowledge tracing tool for large-scale online learning analytics. In: 2018 IEEE International Conference on Big Data (Big Data), pp. 3245–3254. IEEE (2018)
9. Embretson, S.E., Reise, S.P.: Item response theory. Psychology Press, London (2013)
10. Montes-Restrepo, V., Strobbe, G., van Mierlo, P., Vandenberghe, S.: Effects of conductivity perturbations of the tri-layered skull on EEG source analysis. J. Clim. **26**(22), 8895–8915 (2013)
11. López-de Teruel, P.E., García, J.M., Acacio, M.E.: The parallel EM algorithm and its applications in computer vision. In: PDPTA, pp. 571–578 (1999)
12. Kumar, N.S.L.P., Satoor, S., Buck, I.: Fast parallel expectation maximization for Gaussian mixture models on GPUs using CUDA. In: 2009 11th IEEE International Conference on High Performance Computing and Communications, pp. 103–109. IEEE (2009)
13. Gonzalez, J.E., Low, Y., Gu, H., Bickson, D., Guestrin, C.: Powergraph: distributed graph-parallel computation on natural graphs. In: Presented as part of the 10th {USENIX} Symposium on Operating Systems Design and Implementation ({OSDI} 12), pp. 17–30 (2012)
14. Zaharia, M., Chowdhury, M., Franklin, M.J., Shenker, S., Stoica, I., et al.: Spark: cluster computing with working sets. HotCloud, **10**(10-10), 95 (2010)
15. Zaharia, T.H.T.D.M., Bayen, A., Abbeel, P., Hunter, T.: Large-scale online expectation maximization with spark streaming. In: EECS, Berkeley.edu, pp. 1–5 (2012)
16. Zaharia, M., et al.: Resilient distributed datasets: a fault-tolerant abstraction for in-memory cluster computing. In: Presented as part of the 9th {USENIX} Symposium on Networked Systems Design and Implementation ({NSDI} 12), pp. 15–28 (2012)
17. von Davier, M.: High-performance psychometrics: the parallel-e parallel-m algorithm for generalized latent variable models. ETS Res. Rep. Ser. **2016**(2), 1–11 (2016)
18. Masegosa, A.R., et al.: Amidst: a java toolbox for scalable probabilistic machine learning. arXiv preprint arXiv:1704.01427 (2017)
19. Cook, D.J., Holder, L.B., Galal, G., Maglothin, R.: Approaches to parallel graph-based knowledge discovery. J. Parallel Distrib. Comput. **61**(3), 427–446 (2001)
20. Hilderman, R.J., Hamilton, H.J., Kowalchuk, R.J., Cercone, N.: Parallel knowledge discovery using domain generalization graphs. In: Komorowski, J., Zytkow, J. (eds.) PKDD 1997. LNCS, vol. 1263, pp. 25–35. Springer, Heidelberg (1997). https://doi.org/10.1007/3-540-63223-9_103
21. Krishnan, R.G., Shalit, U., Sontag, D.: Deep kalman filters. arXiv preprint arXiv:1511.05121 (2015)

22. Ma, Y., Wang, Z., Zhao, X., Han, J., He, Y.: A UKF algorithm based on the singular value decomposition of state covariance. In: 2010 8th World Congress on Intelligent Control and Automation, pp. 5830–5835. IEEE (2010)
23. Reddy, S., Labutov, I., Joachims, T.: Latent skill embedding for personalized lesson sequence recommendation. arXiv preprint arXiv:1602.07029 (2016)
24. Sheng, Y., et al.: Markov chain Monte Carlo estimation of normal ogive IRT models in matlab. J. Stat. Softw. **25**(8), 1–15 (2008)
25. Azam, S.E., Ghisi, A., Mariani, S.: Parallelized sigma-point kalman filtering for structural dynamics. Comput. Struct. **92**, 193–205 (2012)
26. Hashemipour, H.R., Roy, S., Laub, A.J.: Decentralized structures for parallel kalman filtering. IEEE Trans. Autom. Control **33**(1), 88–94 (1988)
27. Moon, T.K.: The expectation-maximization algorithm. IEEE Sig. Process. Mag. **13**(6), 47–60 (1996)

Experiments Using a Software-Distributed Shared Memory, MPI and 0MQ over Heterogeneous Computing Resources

Loïc Cudennec[1,2][ID] and Kods Trabelsi[1]

[1] CEA, LIST, PC 172, 91191 Gif-sur-Yvette, France
kods.trabelsi@cea.fr
[2] Department of Artificial Intelligence, DGA MI, BP 7, 35998 Rennes Armées, France
loic.cudennec@intradef.gouv.fr

Abstract. Distributed heterogeneous computing systems escalate the problem of choosing the appropriate programming model. Programming models such as message passing are efficient but require low-level management of communications. Higher level of programming such as shared memory are convenient for the application design but they usually have performance issues. With the recent development of distributed heterogeneous systems and new protocols to access remote memories, there is an opportunity for distributed shared memory systems to offer a satisfying level of abstraction while not giving up on performance. In this paper a video processing application is written using MPI, 0MQ and an in-house software-distributed shared memory (S-DSM) backend and deployed over a set of heterogeneous computing boards. Results show that 0MQ implementation is the most efficient but at the price of writing the application with the targeted platform in mind. The S-DSM implementation runs up to 2 times faster than the pure OpenMPI implementation and competes with 0MQ when the data granularity is small.

Keywords: Heterogeneous computing · Distributed computing · Distributed shared memory · Message passing

1 Introduction

Heterogeneous systems are now prevalent in everyday technology including embedded devices, autonomous vehicles, high-performance computing architectures and cloud infrastructures. They offer the possibility to build a specific platform for specific needs in terms of functionality, power processing and energy consumption. However such architectures are complex to program because they escalate the classical problem of hybrid computing in which each resource type exhibits a specific programming interface. Some of these heterogeneous systems are distributed, composed by a mix of heterogeneous computing nodes interconnected by a network, without physical shared memory. For example, microservers

© Springer Nature Switzerland AG 2021
B. Balis et al. (Eds.): Euro-Par 2020 Workshops, LNCS 12480, pp. 237–248, 2021.
https://doi.org/10.1007/978-3-030-71593-9_19

are built upon a backplane that provides networking capabilities, power supply and extension slots to host heterogeneous boards such as high-end processors, low-power processors, many-core processors, GPU and FPGA. A common way of programming such platforms is to rely on the message passing paradigm, using popular libraries like MPI and ZeroMQ. With message passing the developer has to manually manage shared data, keep track of their location and initiate the transfers. Another possibility is to use computing frameworks, mainly based on dataflow and workflow programming paradigms such as StarPU. Finally, it is possible to deploy a software-distributed shared memory (S-DSM) that aggregates remote physical memories into a global logical space. The system is in charge of transparently managing shared data and is a step towards single system image (SSI). Using S-DSM allows to conveniently design the application as a regular Posix-like parallel application. S-DSM have been studied from the late eighties with networks of workstations [12], clusters [1], computing grids and clouds [8] and more recently with heterogeneous platforms [6,7]. However it is a common understanding that S-DSM offers poor performances in comparison to message passing, because of the abstraction layer that comes with a price. This explains why S-DSM has never really been used in HPC systems, except for DSM implemented using cache-coherent hardware such as in the Tilera/Mellanox Tile GX many-core processor and further developments in cache coherent interconnects. However these hardware DSM are static by design, usually limited to processors or small homogeneous clusters with dedicated high-performance networks and not prone to be deployed on distributed heterogeneous architectures. Software-DSM are more portable than hardware DSM, they can cope with dynamicity and reconfiguration of the platform and they offer a higher level of abstraction for the application. A few work in the literature evaluate the performance of using a S-DSM compared to message passing. In 1997, Scales and Gharachorloo [17] provide some benchmarks between the Oracle 7.3 distributed database running on 2 DEC AlphaServer 4100 SMP (4 processors) and the Oracle database running on top of the Shasta S-DSM. Results show that using the S-DSM is 2 to 4 times slower than the baseline version. In the late nineties, Bader and Jaja [2] compare the CVM [10] S-DSM to MPICH over the DEC AlphaServer 2100 system, using up to 8 nodes. Results show that MPICH outperforms CVM by a factor of 10. In the early 2000, Werstein et al. [19] evaluate the Tread-Marks [1] DSM together with the PVM and MPI message passing frameworks over a Beowulf cluster composed by 32 Intel Pentium III nodes. Results show that the performance of DSM is poorer than PVM and MPI especially when scaling up. However, using the Mandelbrot computing kernel the DSM competes with PVM and MPI. In 2011, Dimakopoulos [18] compares data transfer overheads between MPI and the MOME [8] and MOCHA [11] S-DSM over a 16-node Sun Fire x4100 cluster. Results show that MPI is faster by a factor of 6 to 8 compared to S-DSM. All these results instigate a cold reception whenever a *Yet Another* S-DSM is submitted to the HPC community. Furthermore, S-DSM systems presented in the literature rarely compare the performance of applications running over the S-DSM with the same application running over a message passing framework. With the recent development of high-performance networks, the specification of new remote access protocols such as one-sided communications, RDMA, RoCE, PGAS, OpenCAPI, CCIX, Gen-Z, CXL, there is a renewal of interest in shared memory systems [5,13,16] to unify memory accesses between CPU, GPU, general-purpose accelerators, FPGA and non-volatile memories. Unlike homogeneous computing clusters, such distributed heterogeneous systems require more complex development and tight optimizations to obtain performances. With classical MP-based implementations this complexity is directly exposed to the user. Today S-DSM can play a role not only by offering an abstraction layer, but also by bringing optimization and smart decision for data management directly in the runtime. In the Grappa [14] S-DSM proposed in 2015 the authors show that porting over the S-DSM several computing frameworks such as MapReduce and GraphLab can run up to 1.33 faster than the baseline implementations on a 128-node AMD Interlagos cluster using a Mellanox Infiniband interconnect. In this momentum of renewal, the Argo [9] DSM proposes new coherence mechanisms that allow to match or exceed MPI implementations of some SPLASH and NAS benchmarks running onto a cluster of 128 AMD Opteron NUMA nodes. Note that Argo is implemented on top of MPI to manage remote connections. These are promising results, being the demonstration that a S-DSM can perform better than other MP-based implementations. It also advocates for the use of high-level programming models without giving up on performance. The main contribution of this paper is to report on the ins and outs of writing an application using message-passing and S-DSM. We start from an application specification and we elaborate different implementations to compare performance over a distributed heterogeneous computing platform. These implementations include the well-established message-passing OpenMPI runtime, the lightweight ZeroMQ (0MQ) message-passing runtime and an in-house S-DSM [3,4] built upon OpenMPI and designed to study data management over heterogeneous architectures. Results show that the S-DSM implementation outperforms the pure OpenMPI implementation by a factor 2 and get close to the ZeroMQ implementation performance for data-sets with smaller granularity.

2   Implementations of a Video Processing Application

In this work we consider a video processing application that has been used to experiment and showcase several distributed heterogeneous computing platforms such as the Christmann RECS|Box microserver [15]. This application opens a video stream, either from a file or a camera, decodes the frames, distributes the frames to remote processing tasks and encodes the processed frames back to a file or a live display. The computing kernel is a 3×3 convolution used for edge detection. From this specification we have implemented three versions based on MPI, ZeroMQ and the S-DSM. These versions share the exact same code in C, except for data management. Figure 1 illustrates the communication sequences between the input task, the processing tasks and the output task for the different implementations. MPI and ZeroMQ implementations are quite straightforward and

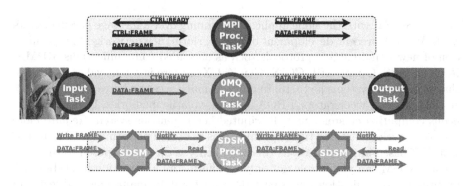

Fig. 1. Transferring and accessing frames in MPI, 0MQ and S-DSM.

are similar to a *split-join* dataflow, using multiple producer-consumer patterns. The S-DSM implementation is more complex (inner communications occurring between S-DSM servers are not represented here) because each access to a shared data triggers multiple communications between S-DSM servers and applications tasks, according to the data coherence protocol. The MPI implementation generates around twice as much messages as ZeroMQ, and the S-DSM generates 10 times more messages than ZeroMQ.

MPI. The global behavior of the MPI implementation is as follows: 1) the processing task sends a control message to the input task to indicate they are ready to take a job, 2) the input task sends a control message with job information followed by the input frame to the processing task and 3) once the frame has been processed, the processing task sends a control message followed by the processed frame to the output task. When deploying more than one processing task, it implements an eager scheduling in which tasks that run faster are whiling to process more frames than the others. This implementation is based on simple MPI concepts including synchronous and asynchronous version of `Send` for sending messages, `Probe` and `Wait` for checking if a message is available and a communication is completed and `Recv` to receive a message. We do not use collective primitives nor advanced group communication operations. There are three variants of the code: 1) *Synchronous single buffer* means that a single buffer is used on the input task to send frames to the processing tasks. *Synchronous* means that the input process waits for the completion of the `Send` operation before decoding and sending the next frame. 2) *Asynchronous single buffer* allows the input task and the processing tasks to not wait for the completion of the `Send` operation, allowing local parallelism between the user code and the MPI runtime (e.g. decode next frame, process next frame while sending the previous one). 3) *Asynchronous multiple buffers* means that one buffer is allocated on the input task per processing task, allowing to drastically increase the parallelism between frame decoding and the management of communications in the MPI runtime. In these experiments we use the OpenMPI 3.x runtime because of its popularity and the possibility to compile the source code without a glitch onto different

Linux distributions (Ubuntu, Debian, Raspbian, Lebian) and processors (Intel Core i7, Arm Cortex) deployed in our heterogeneous platform.

ZeroMQ (0MQ). ZeroMQ is a lightweight message passing framework released around 2010. It offers a low-latency implementation of sockets based on communication patterns instead of basic message passing. There is no logical process overlay built on top of the communication sockets such as *communicators* and *ranks* for MPI. Therefore, when connecting to a distant node, the IP address or hostname must be known, which is platform-dependent and less elegant. ZeroMQ is expected to be more efficient than MPI notably because there is no node bootstrapping, peer discovery and group communication overlay management. In this implementation of the video processing application, a request-reply *REQ-REP* communication pattern is used between the input task (acting as a server, *REP*) and the processing tasks (acting as clients, *REQ*). The resulting interaction makes the processing tasks ask the input task for the next frame to compute. As for the MPI implementation, it implements an eager scheduling of frames onto processing tasks. The *PUSH-PULL* communication pattern is used between the processing tasks (*PUSH*) and the output task (*PULL*) in order to collect the results. Note that this pattern implements *fair-queuing* which explains it cannot be used between input and processing tasks because it would evenly distribute frames onto processing tasks, hence not implementing an eager scheduling.

S-DSM. The shared memory implementation is based on the S-DSM presented in 2017 in Cudennec [3]. This S-DSM relies on the OpenMPI 3.x runtime in order to manage the underlying peer network and message delivery. It is organized as a super-peer topology made of a peer-to-peer network of S-DSM servers for cache and metadata management, and a set of clients to run the user code. The coherence protocol is a 4-state (MESI) home-based protocol. Shared data are stored into atomic pieces of data called *chunks*. The S-DSM provides a regular interface for accessing chunks and performing distributed synchronizations. It also introduces an event-based programming language in which it is possible to subscribe to chunks in order to be notified whenever the chunk has been modified, as in a publish-subscribe communication pattern [4]. In this implementation of the video processing application, frames are stored in the shared memory: for each processing task a shared input buffer and a shared output buffer are allocated in the S-DSM. The input task writes incoming frames into the input buffer of a ready task. The processing task gets notified, reads the frame from its input buffer and write the processed frame into its output buffer. The output task gets notified that a new result is available, it reads the frame and checks for frame reordering before sending to the output. The resulting application layout is close to a dataflow, which is indeed a common way of implementing dataflow runtimes over shared memory.

Table 1. Platform description and number of nodes (#) used in the experiments.

Node	Processor	Cores	RAM	Storage	Network	#
Gateway	Intel Core i7 6800K	6	64GB	SSD	Gb Ethernet	1
Raspberry Pi 3B+	ARM Cortex A53	4	1GB	SD	USB 2.0	2
Odroid XU4	ARM Cortex A15/A7	4/4	2GB	SD	USB 3.0	1
Odroid XU3	ARM Cortex A15/A7	4/4	2GB	SD	USB 2.0	1
HiKey Kirin 970	ARM Cortex A73/A53	4/4	6GB	UFS	USB 3.0	2
Nvidia Jetson TX2	Denver/ARM Cortex A57	2/4	8GB	eMMC	Gb Ethernet	1
Adapteva Parallella	ARM Cortex A9/Epiphany	2/16	1GB	SD	Gb Ethernet	0

Table 2. Calculating the *ideal* number of processed frames per node type using the Pthread implementation (theory, no communications). Note that we use two RPI and two Kirin boards in our experiments, which is taken into account when calculating the *ideal* number of processed frames. The effective number of processed frames observed in the experiments are given for MPI, S-DSM and 0MQ for each node type. *Deviation* is the cumulative distance with the *ideal* number of processed frames (smaller is better).

		Core i7	TX2	XU3	XU4	Kirin 970	RPI 3B+	Deviation
HD	Time per frame (s)	0.041	0.131	0.145	0.219	0.153	0.341	
	Normalized to RPI	8.317	2.603	2.351	1.557	2.228	1	
	Ideal (nb of frames)	506	158	143	95	136	61	0
	MPI (nb of frames)	178	180	131	152	175	153	680
	S-DSM (nb of frames)	490	226	65	92	119	92	262
	0-MQ (nb of frames)	196	166	147	151	160	158	620
UHD-1	Time per frame (s)	0.103	0.353	0.597	0.864	0.463	1.202	
	Normalized to RPI	11.669	3.405	2.013	1.391	2.596	1	
	Ideal nb of frames	590	172	102	70	131	51	0
	MPI (nb of frames)	173	179	127	158	172	159	834
	S-DSM (nb of frames)	475	228	66	94	124	93	330
	0-MQ (nb of frames)	196	166	146	157	160	157	800
UHD-2	Time per frame (s)	0.342	1.363	2.091	3.478	4.260	4.625	
	Normalized to RPI	13.523	3.393	2.211	1.329	1.085	1	
	Ideal nb of frames	717	180	117	70	58	53	0
	MPI (nb of frames)	355	237	118	118	120	119	724
	S-DSM (nb of frames)	453	234	70	98	126	99	622
	0-MQ (nb of frames)	752	123	40	79	99	58	268

3   Results

The hardware platform is a small cluster of heterogeneous computers and development boards connected to a Gigabit Ethernet switch. Table 1 describes the node types of the platform and the number of nodes that are used in the following experiments. These nodes are representative of the hardware that can be integrated within HPC microservers, cloud infrastructures and platforms for autonomous vehicles, albeit the form-factor of the resulting setup and the poor network performance for some of the nodes connected via Ethernet over USB. In all experiments, a processing task is deployed on each node and the two input and output tasks are co-located on the Core i7 Gateway node. In the specific case of a S-DSM deployment, a S-DSM data server is deployed on the Core i7 node. When deploying the configuration with 4 servers, 3 additional servers are deployed on the Nvidia TX2 and the two Odroid XU3 and XU4 nodes.

Ideal Computation Time. It is possible to evaluate the *ideal* computation time of the application by measuring the time it takes to run the computational kernel on each node. This information is used to calculate the contribution of each node in the global computation, without considering network communications and other input-output operations. Table 2 presents the processing times measured on each node type to run a convolution (stencil 3 × 3). The frame size follows the HD, UHD-1 and UHD-2 standards and the corresponding frame representation sizes are 2 MB, 8 MB and 33 MB (as for a 256 bits, greyscale frame). Processing times do not include input and output operations on local storage to read and write the frame. The *ideal* computation time of the application when running on the whole platform can be calculated because the convolution kernel is not data-dependent, which means that its complexity does not depend on the input data, therefore making the convolution processing deterministic. Table 2 presents the results step-by-step. The first step is to calculate the normalized performance of the node, taking the Raspberry Pi 3B+ as reference (RPI performance is set to 1). For example, the normalized performance of the Core i7 for UHD-2 indicates that the Core i7 computes more than 13 times faster than the RPI. The second step is to calculate the workload coefficient per input data-set. This can be done using the following equation (note that we do not use the Adapteva Parallella board and that there are two RPI and two Kirin boards in the setup):

$$\alpha * (P_{i7} + P_{TX2} + P_{XU3} + P_{XU4} + 2 * P_{Kirin} + 2 * P_{RPI}) = NB\_FRAMES$$

With P_n the normalized performance of node type n, NB_FRAMES the number of frames in the input video and α the unknown workload coefficient. In the following experiments, the HD, UHD-1 and UHD-2 video samples are taken from the '3DMark Port Royal Demo' benchmark, with a total of 1296 frames for HD, 1298 for UHD-1 and 1306 for UHD-2. The α workload coefficient is therefore 60.9 for HD, 50.6 for UHD-1 and 53.0 for UHD-2. The last step is to calculate the *ideal* number of processed frames per node type using the following formula: $NB\_Frames_n = \alpha * P_n$. From this result it is possible to calculate the *ideal* global processing time using the following formula: $GLOBAL\_TIME = max(NB\_Frames_n * TIME\_PER\_FRAME_n)$. This gives 20.8 s for HD, 61.3 s for UHD-1 and 247.0 s for UHD-2. This *ideal* processing time does not include overheads such as distributing the computation over a network, managing the communication buffers and processor caches.

Comparing Implementations Performance. The three main implementations of the video processing application (OpenMPI 3.x, S-DSM and ZeroMQ 4.x) have been deployed on the heterogeneous platform and evaluated using the three video samples (HD, UHD-1 and UHD-2). Results are given in Fig. 2 and can be compared to the *ideal* computation time. The S-DSM implementation generates around 39000 messages at the MPI level, the MPI implementation generates around 6500 messages and the ZeroMQ implementation generates around 3900 messages. The ZeroMQ implementation is the fastest for each data-set, and even more when dealing with bigger data: the global computing time is smaller when processing UHD-2 frames (568 s) than UHD-1 frames (731 s). While being a counter-intuitive result, it is usually explained by the adequacy between data granularity and the management of network and processor caches. By default, the ZeroMQ runtime sets the capacity of communication pipes, also called *High-Water Mark*, to 1000 messages (or even no limit for early versions of the runtime) which leads to memory overflow and a `segfault` on nodes with limited physical memory such as the Raspberry Pi. In these experiments, the *High-Water Mark* is set to 10 which allows the proper termination of the application with all data-sets. It also prevents from cache pollution that acts as a performance killer on several nodes. The latter point being one of the main reason why ZeroMQ performs significantly better than the other MPI-based implementations. A second counter-intuitive result is that the S-DSM implementation (over MPI) is performing better than the regular MPI implementation. For HD and UHD-1 it even gives results close to the ZeroMQ implementation. Four configurations of the S-DSM are used, as a combination of enabling or not the logging of events (stats logging) and deploying a single or 4 metadata and cache servers. Stats logging generates around 240000 events per run that are stored in the physical memories of the nodes before being dumped into files at the end of the computation. This implies a significant overhead, while mandatory to finely analyze the S-DSM behavior. Using 4 metadata and cache servers let the S-DSM system balance access requests to shared data among different nodes, hence being more responsive. One of the main reason the S-DSM performs better than MPI is because of the parallelism of data it introduces, similar to a pipeline: each time a shared data is modified, it is sent to the S-DSM servers, and not to the input buffer of another processing task. Therefore, processing nodes do not have to undergo all incoming data, but rather ask for them in a on-demand basis thanks to the S-DSM programming model. For small data-sets (HD and UHD-1), the best MPI implementation computation time is more than 2 times slower than the best S-DSM configuration computation time. For UHD-2, the *async multiple buffers* implementations performances are close to the S-DSM, revealing the importance of manually managing the communication buffers to increase the parallelism degree. However, it is very far from the ZeroMQ performance, which is quite a surprise as it relies on the same programming model.

Influence on User Code. The user code can be split into two parts: the processing time which is the time spent in the computing kernel, and the waiting time which is the time spent between the end of a kernel call and the beginning

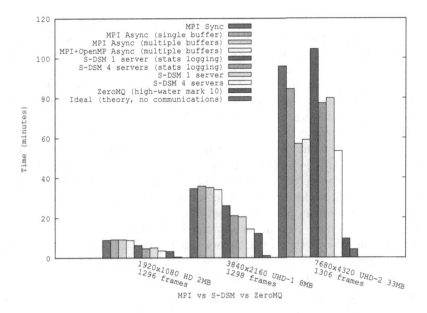

Fig. 2. Comparing the different application implementations.

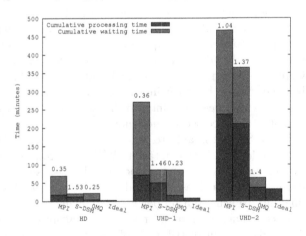

Fig. 3. Cumulative processing and waiting times using the best implementations.

of the next call. This waiting time includes operations to asynchronously send the previously processed frame to the output task and to synchronously retrieve the next incoming frame. This is a relevant indicator to know if frames are delivered just in time and to identify a data starvation crisis. Figure 3 presents the cumulative processing and waiting times for the best MPI, S-DSM and ZeroMQ implementations. Labels on top of bars represent processing times divided by waiting times. Beware of this representation: the global processing time of the application as shown in Fig. 2 is the consequence of particular intricacies of individual processing and waiting times, and cannot be compared to a simple sum of processing and waiting times. There are several conclusions based on this figure. First, the cumulative processing time of ZeroMQ is close to the *ideal* cumulative processing time which means that the frames have been wisely dispatched to the computing nodes and that the ZeroMQ runtime does not interfere with the computing capabilities. Second, the S-DSM performance is close to ZeroMQ for HD and UHD-1 data-sets despite a higher cumulative processing time. As a counterpart, the cumulative waiting time is smaller which indicates that the S-DSM runtime was able to deliver data in a more efficient way than ZeroMQ. In that case, increasing the size of communication pipes (*High-Water Mark*, HWM) for ZeroMQ might decrease the cumulative waiting time but at the price of increasing the memory footprint, degrading the processing performance and even getting a memory overflow as discussed previously. Therefore, there is a trade-off to find when setting an arbitrary value for HWM, which is not acceptable for a regular user. Finally, the pure MPI implementation reveals important processing and waiting times with the three data-sets.

Load Balancing. One of the main reason the cumulative processing times and waiting times are increasing comes from a poor load balancing of frames onto computing resources. The three implementations are all based on eager scheduling of frames onto computing resources. Therefore, the effective load balancing of frames is a direct consequence of the underlying communications and data management runtime. It is possible to compare the effective scheduling of frames in the experiments with the *ideal* number of processed frames as presented in Table 2. The Core i7 node is the most powerful node and should process more frames than the other nodes. However in all the experiments the Core i7 node is far from processing the expected number of frames. The cumulative distance from the *ideal* number of processed frames shows that for the smaller data-sets (HD and UHD-1) the S-DSM is able to manage a better load balancing than MPI and ZeroMQ while for a larger data-set (UHD-2) ZeroMQ offers the best load balancing which finally explains why processing UHD-2 is faster than UHD-1. Communication runtimes such as MPI and ZeroMQ are complex distributed software. The inability to achieve a proper load balancing for the smaller data-sets might be the consequence of smart mechanisms against message delivery starvation, which leads to a fair distribution of frames among the nodes instead of favoring the Core i7 node as expected. Note that this underlying behavior is hidden to the application developer. Despite being implemented over MPI, the S-DSM has better load balancing, which can be explained by the important mix of control and data messages exchanged between several nodes whenever accessing a frame in the shared memory. Therefore the communication pattern to access a frame is more complex and more resilient to specific runtime arbitration.

4   Conclusion

Software-distributed shared memory adoption in high-performance computing systems is conditioned upon reaching acceptable performances. In this work, a distributed application has been written over message passing and S-DSM frameworks and deployed over an heterogeneous platform. Results show that the S-DSM implementation is faster than the pure MPI implementation and competes with the lightweight ZeroMQ implementation for small granularity data sets. It appears that the MPI runtime is designed and optimized for super-computing architectures with strong assumption on hardware capabilities (processor speed, amount of physical memory and networking performance). With the development of distributed heterogeneous architectures, these assumptions are not reliable, especially with low-power processors and embedded devices. In such a context, the S-DSM is able to introduce intermediate storage places which prevents from the overload of communication buffers on processing nodes. The management of such intermediate storage places is transparent for the application, which is inherent to the S-DSM approach compared to message passing frameworks. Several conclusions come with this work: 1) lightweight message passing (0MQ) is faster but at the price of specializing the application to the platform, 2) the OpenMPI runtime is not optimized for running onto low-power processing boards, and 3) S-DSM overhead is getting smaller compared to message passing, as the hardware is becoming more complex to deal with. Therefore, while probably still not being fully adapted to large-scale homogeneous clusters, this work shows that S-DSM is a serious contender to leverage the computing capabilities of distributed heterogeneous architectures and their applications.

Acknowledgments. This work has received funding from the European Union's Horizon 2020 research and innovation action under grant agreement No 688201.

References

1. Amza, C., et al.: TreadMarks: shared memory computing on networks of workstations. IEEE Comput. **29**(2), 18–28 (1996)
2. Bader, D., Jaja, J.: Simple: a methodology for programming high-performance algorithms on clusters of symmetric multiprocessors (SMPS). J. Parallel Distrib. Comput. **58**, 92–108 (1999). https://doi.org/10.1006/jpdc.1999.1541
3. Cudennec, L.: Software-distributed shared memory over heterogeneous micro-server architecture. In: Heras, D.B., Bougé, L. (eds.) Euro-Par 2017. LNCS, vol. 10659, pp. 366–377. Springer, Cham (2018). https://doi.org/10.1007/978-3-319-75178-8_30
4. Cudennec, L.: Merging the publish-subscribe pattern with the shared memory paradigm. In: Mencagli, G., et al. (eds.) Euro-Par 2018. LNCS, vol. 11339, pp. 469–480. Springer, Cham (2019). https://doi.org/10.1007/978-3-030-10549-5_37
5. Dragojevic, A., Narayanan, D., Hodson, O., Castro, M.: FaRM: fast remote memory. In: Proceedings of the 11th USENIX Conference on Networked Systems Design and Implementation, pp. 401–414 (2014). https://doi.org/10.5555/2616448.2616486

6. Gelado, I., Stone, J.E., Cabezas, J., Patel, S., Navarro, N., Hwu, W.M.W.: An asymmetric distributed shared memory model for heterogeneous parallel systems. In: Proceedings of the Fifteenth Edition of ASPLOS on Architectural Support for Programming Languages and Operating Systems, ASPLOS XV, ACM, New York, NY, USA, pp. 347–358 (2010)

7. Ghane, M., Chandrasekaran, S., Cheung, M.S.: Towards a portable hierarchical view of distributed shared memory systems: challenges and solutions. In: Proceedings of the 11th International Workshop on Programming Models and Applications for Multicores and Manycores. PMAM 2020 (2020)

8. Jegou, Y.: Implementation of page management in MOME, a user-level DSM. In: CCGrid 2003, 3rd IEEE/ACM International Symposium on Cluster Computing and the Grid, pp. 479–486 (2003). https://doi.org/10.1109/CCGRID.2003.1199404

9. Kaxiras, S., Klaftenegger, D., Norgren, M., Ros, A., Sagonas, K.: Turning centralized coherence and distributed critical-section execution on their head: a new approach for scalable distributed shared memory. In: Proceedings of the 24th International Symposium on High-Performance Parallel and Distributed Computing, pp. 3–14 (2015)

10. Keleher, P.: CVM: The coherent virtual machine TR93-215 (1995)

11. Kise, K., Katagiri, T., Honda, H., Yuba, T.: Evaluation of the acknowledgment reduction in a software-DSM system. In: Proceedings of the 6th International Conference on parallel Processing and Applied Mathematics, pp. 17–25 (2005)

12. Li, K.: IVY: a shared virtual memory system for parallel computing. In: Proceedings 1988 International Conference on Parallel Processing, pp. 94–101. University Park, PA, USA, August 1988

13. Mitchell, C., Geng, Y., Li, J.: Using one-sided RDMA reads to build a fast, CPU-efficient key-value store. In: Proceedings of the 2013 USENIX Conference on Annual Technical Conference, pp. 103–114 (2013). https://doi.org/10.5555/2535461.2535475

14. Nelson, J., et al.: Latency-tolerant software distributed shared memory. In: 2015 USENIX Annual Technical Conference (USENIX ATC 2015), pp. 291–305. USENIX Association, Santa Clara, CA (2015)

15. Oleksiak, A., et al.: M2DC - modular microserver datacentre with heterogeneous hardware. In: Microprocessors and Microsystems, vol. 52, pp. 117–130 (2017). https://doi.org/10.1016/j.micpro.2017.05.019

16. Ross, J.A., Richie, D.A.: Implementing openshmem for the adapteva epiphany risc array processor. In: Procedia Computer Science, International Conference on Computational Science, ICCS 2016, San Diego, California, USA, vol. 80, pp. 2353–2356, 6–8 June 2016

17. Scales, D.J., Gharachorloo, K.: Towards transparent and efficient software distributed shared memory. ACM SIGOPS Oper. Syst. Rev. **31**(5), 157–169 (1997). https://doi.org/10.1145/269005.266673

18. Dimakopoulos, V.V., Hadjidoukas, P.E.: HOMPI: a hybrid programming framework for expressing and deploying task-based parallelism, pp. 14–26 (2011)

19. Werstein, P., Pethick, M., Huang, Z.: A performance comparison of DSM, PVM and MPI, pp. 476–482 (2003). https://doi.org/10.1109/PDCAT.2003.1236348

On the Provenance Extraction Techniques from Large Scale Log Files: A Case Study for the Numerical Weather Prediction Models

Alper Tufek$^{(\boxtimes)}$ ⓘ and Mehmet S. Aktas ⓘ

Yildiz Technical University, Istanbul, Turkey
alper.tufek@std.yildiz.edu.tr, aktas@yildiz.edu.tr

Abstract. Day by day, severe meteorological events increasingly highlight the importance of fast and accurate weather forecasting. There are various Numerical Weather Prediction (NWP) models worldwide that are run on either a local or a global scale to predict future weather. NWP models typically take hours to finish a complete run, however, depending on the input parameters and the size of the forecast domain. Provenance information is of central importance for detecting unexpected events that may develop during model execution, and also for taking necessary action as early as possible. Besides, the need to share scientific data and results between researchers or scientists also highlights the importance of data quality and reliability. In this study, we develop a framework for tracking The Weather Research and Forecasting (WRF) model and for generating, storing, and analyzing provenance data. We develop a machine-learning-based log parser to enable the proposed system to be dynamic and adaptive so that it can adapt to different data and rules. The proposed system enables easy management and understanding of numerical weather forecast workflows by providing provenance graphs. By analyzing these graphs, potential faulty situations that may occur during the execution of WRF can be traced to their root causes. Our proposed system has been evaluated and has been shown to perform well even in a high-frequency provenance information flow.

Keywords: Machine learning-based provenance extraction · Numerical weather prediction models · Provenance · Provenance analysis · Weather forecast models

1 Introduction

The importance of fast and reliable weather forecasting in today's world continues to increase. Today, we almost always take weather conditions into account before we decide on a journey or any other kind of activity. Because of global warming, there is a significant increase in the number of extraordinary weather events. Weather events such as hurricanes, floods, high winds, etc. can cause large-scale loss of property and life if the necessary measures are not taken. In this context, faster and more accurate weather prediction becomes more crucial. This makes it necessary for meteorologists, scientists, and researchers to work together, share the input/output data they use, and exchange the results obtained.

© Springer Nature Switzerland AG 2021
B. Balis et al. (Eds.): Euro-Par 2020 Workshops, LNCS 12480, pp. 249–260, 2021.
https://doi.org/10.1007/978-3-030-71593-9_20

Various Numerical Weather Prediction (NWP) models are run each day in different meteorology organizations across the world to make weather forecasts. These models mathematically simulate the atmosphere and the oceans and calculate such parameters as temperature, pressure, wind speed, etc. by processing data primarily used for meteorological purposes, such as radar/satellite data and/or observation data gathered from weather observation stations. NWP models are usually run more than once every day at regular intervals. However, data collected from the aforementioned scientific measurement devices are very diverse, both in format and in size. Therefore, the management of data quality, reusability, and reliability become more complex and difficult. In this respect, the need for systematic provenance is gaining importance, especially in scientific studies [1].

Provenance is defined by the W3C consortium in its PROV specification [2] as all of the entities, events, and persons that have some impact on the process of generating a data product, which can be used to assess the quality and reliability of the data. Modifications to the data, the methods used in the production process, and metadata for reproducing the same data can be included in the definition of provenance.

In this study, the Weather Research and Forecasting (WRF) model, one of the widely used NWP models, is used. WRF is an open-source NWP model widely used worldwide by meteorologists and researchers. Being open-source and having large community support can be considered as the advantages of the model. The WRF model is used for weather forecasts by meteorological organizations in many countries across the world, including Turkey.

The WRF model, as well as other NWP models, take input parameters such as the boundary information of the prediction domain, and the resolution at which the predicted values are to be calculated. When the model starts to run it usually takes hours to produce its results, depending on the input parameters. Most of the time, it is not possible to intervene in the course of model execution. To be able to evaluate the correctness of the model outputs after its completion, it is of great importance to track the processing steps that took place during the generation process. In this way, whether an error occurred in the prediction phase and, if so, the location of the cause can be easily detected.

The main motivation for this study is to address the lack of capability for provenance support in WRF model software, a widely used numerical weather prediction model. The WRF model is composed of several executable programs, each of which generates some particular log outputs. Other than that, there is no structured provenance generation or storage in any phase of a complete execution cycle. These raw log outputs are just free-form text lines containing various levels of information about the execution details. The contents of a log file that a specific WRF program produces can change, even from one version of the program to the next.

The main contribution of this study is to address the aforementioned motivating points and provide methodologies for machine learning-based ways of provenance collection for WRF model software. We investigate WRF, and we analyze the log files generated in the course of its execution. We develop a machine learning-based parser, which utilizes classification algorithms and eliminates the need for a rule database to be present as a prerequisite.

Log analysis is one of the commonly used methods to obtain provenance information. However, the quality of the provenance information produced in this method is both highly dependent on the level of detail of the log files and on what percentage of log lines containing provenance it can capture. In our previous work [3], we developed a rule-based log parser to extract provenance information from WRF logs. This approach was based on a rule database that utilized a list of special keywords, which helps the log parser distinguish those lines containing provenance information. These keywords were predetermined manually. In this study, we propose a novel approach to provenance extraction from log files, which is based on machine-learning techniques. In this approach, a classification model is constructed by training on various log files before deployment. Here, the machine learning-based parser eliminates the need for a rule database at the expense of a small percentage of provenance loss.

The paper is organized as follows. Section 2 provides a literature review. Section 3 presents a brief overview of the Weather Research and Forecasting (WRF) model. Section 4 briefly mentions the PROV specification. Section 5 explains detailed information about the proposed methodology for machine learning-based provenance parser. In Sect. 6, the implementation details of the prototype system are explained. In Sect. 7, the performance tests on the proposed framework are mentioned and the test results and evaluations are discussed. Finally, in Sect. 8, the results obtained in the study are summarized.

2 Literature Review

Both storage and computing capacities of computer systems are increasing day by day, so computer systems are being used more frequently by all scientific disciplines to solve problems that require complex calculations and/or require the processing of large volumes of data. The scientific programs developed within the scope of these scientific studies are generally developed by scientists from their own disciplines, so the priority of the developers is to produce algorithmically correct solutions to scientific problems. For this reason, scientific programs generally do not have an integrated provenance infrastructure.

Simmhan et al. propose a general-purpose framework in their work in 2006, which allows provenance information to be compiled from data-driven scientific workflows [4]. They try to define the requirements for systems that collect data and workflow provenance. They also develop a standalone tool, Karma [5], as a prototype for the collection, representation, and storage of provenance data. Karma then evolves into the PROV compliant Komadu [6] framework that is used in this study as the provenance storage backend. This provenance framework is tested on the Linked Environments for Atmospheric Discovery (LEAD) project by Droegemeier et al. [7]. LEAD is a meteorological research and training project that is Service-Oriented Architecture-SOA based and designed to enable operations such as access, pre-processing, assimilation, management, analysis, data mining, visualization, etc. to be easily applied, independent of the format and the location of the data. Karma is workflow-oriented and needs a workflow orchestrator. Therefore, it needs each discrete event (workflow step) to be defined and implemented as an SOA-service. SOA-based architectures have been studied in detail in different studies such as [8–10]. In our study, we focus on numerical weather forecast models, particularly WRF, and make no modifications to the scientific source code. Our approach does not require a workflow orchestrator. We analyze log outputs and make inferences about the internal steps of the execution.

In 2013, Jensen et al. proposed a provenance framework to be used in the processing of satellite data [11]. NOAA and NASA instrument data from satellites are beamed down to locations where they are gathered and then sent for processing. Jensen et al. used the Karma tool as the backend provenance storage and retrieval in their proposed framework and developed an adaptor to extract provenance-related activities from application log files. The Karma provenance system uses an extension of version 1.1 of the Open Provenance Model (OPM) [12] for its data model for external communication. Shu et al. conducted a similar case study on the modeling and analysis of provenance data in hydrological models [13]. They present a provenance model for the representation of provenance information in streamflow forecasting. For this purpose, they extend the Open Provenance Model to satisfy the requirements for their case. There exist various other provenance-based systems utilizing the Karma tool [21–23]. In our study, the provenance representation and data model are fully compatible with the W3C consortium's PROV specification, which defines a common provenance framework that is independent of a specific domain.

However, to the best of our knowledge, weather prediction/atmosphere modeling systems that are run either on a global or a regional scale by meteorological organizations or by universities or research institutions within the scope of scientific research or weather forecasting are not capable of producing, storing and analyzing systematic provenance records. The Global Forecast System (GFS)[1] is a non-open source numerical weather prediction system that includes a global model run by the United States' National Weather Service (NWS). It is workflow-based and composed of multiple workflow components (data assimilation, forecast model, post-processing, etc.). Bernardet et al. proposed an infrastructure, NWP Information Technology Environment – NITE, for scientists to configure, launch, and track experiments with various NWP models including GFS. The main goal is to record the provenance of codes, scripts, and configuration files, and inputs related to an experiment, so that it can be reviewed and reproduced [14]. ECMWF's Integrated Forecasting System (IFS)[2] has its own workflow management system, ecFlow. Each workflow must be defined as task suites.

In this study, we have designed a provenance/tracking system for the open-source WRF model that is used by most meteorological organizations in different countries across the world. The log files produced during the execution of the WRF model are analyzed, and lines containing provenance information are filtered in the first stage. In the second stage, the corresponding provenance notifications are generated and recorded in a provenance database in the background according to the information in the filtered lines. In our earlier work [3], we proposed a rule-based log parser to extract provenance information from these log files. The parser utilized a rule database that consists of a list of special keywords to distinguish lines containing provenance information. In this

---

[1] https://www.ncdc.noaa.gov/data-access/model-data/model-datasets/global-forcast-system-gfs.
[2] https://www.ecmwf.int/en/research/modelling-and-prediction.

study, we introduce a novel approach to filtering log files. In this approach, line filtering is achieved by machine-learning methods.

Text classification by machine-learning algorithms has been used in countless areas such as search engines [15, 16], social media platforms [17], indexing, and emotion analysis in texts [18, 19]. We utilize various text classification algorithms inside the machine learning-based log parser. This way, our tracking and provenance analysis tool can run on different log files when filtering the lines containing provenance in WRF log files without the need for a rule base.

3   The Weather Research and Forecasting Model Components and Data Products

The WRF model is an open-source software package consisting of various sub-modules and used for atmosphere modeling and weather forecasting. These sub-modules are broadly divided into four groups: 1-WRF Pre-processing System (WPS), 2-WRF Model Core, 3-WRF Data Assimilation (WRFDA), 4-Post-Processing Tools.

The input/output files used, and the temporary/intermediate/final files created throughout an execution cycle of the Weather Research and Forecasting Model are shown in Fig. 1. More detailed information about each phase can be found in Section III of our previous paper [3].

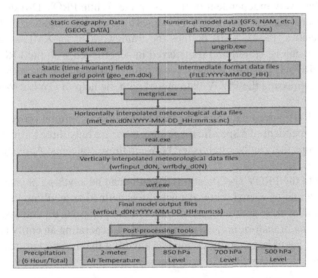

Fig. 1. WRF components and data products pipeline

The final results file contains various meteorological parameter values (temperature, humidity, pressure, wind speed and direction, precipitation, etc.) calculated for each horizontal and vertical grid point, depending on the resolution of the forecast region.

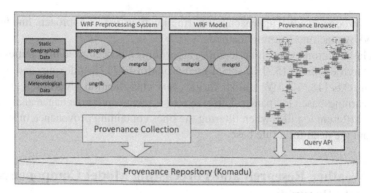

Fig. 2. The general architecture of the proposed system and basic data flow

Figure 2 illustrates the main components of the WRF model and the overall architecture of the provenance collection and presentation modules.

4   PROV-O Provenance Standard

The PROV specification [20] is a family of general-purpose documents recommended by the W3C consortium for modeling, representing, storing, and transferring of provenance data in a standard way independent of the discipline. While PROV-DM defines a basic data model for provenance data, PROV-N defines a provenance notation that people can understand. Besides, PROV-XML defines the framework of an XML schema so that provenance data can be stored and transferred in accordance with the PROV-DM data model, while PROV-O provides the necessary definitions to be able to create provenance ontologies by expressing the PROV data model with the help of OWL 2 Web Ontology Language.

Since the PROV specification is intended to provide a common provenance framework that is independent of a specific discipline, there are only three basic concepts and basic relationships that can be established between those concepts: Activity, Entity, and Agent.

According to the PROV specification, an entity can be anything physical, digital or conceptual, or a real or virtual thing. An activity is defined as anything that takes place in a given period of time and that carries out certain operations on entities. Operations such as processing, transforming, changing, using, or generating an entity are examples of activities. An agent is generally defined as anything that has certain responsibilities concerning entities or activities. An agent may be an entity or an activity.

5   Proposed Methodology

There are various approaches to obtaining provenance information. The first is the manual labeling approach. This method is not effective since it requires a high amount of labor and time. It is also error-prone because it is human-handled.

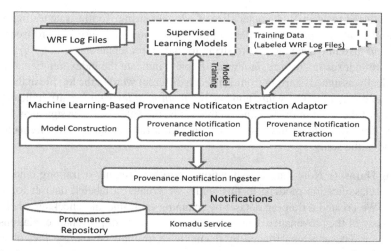

Fig. 3. Machine learning-based approach to provenance collection from WRF modules

The second approach is to modify the source code to make it produce provenance records automatically. However, the disadvantages of this method are the lack of access to the source code of the software at hand, the need to recompile the code after the changes to the source code, as well as the additional errors this may cause.

A third method sometimes referred to as scavenging, is to examine sources such as various log files that are generated during the execution of programs and to extract provenance information from these sources. Even if it may lack a configurable debug level setting or enough information for a complete provenance, this approach is more applicable to most use cases than the other two methods.

In our previous work [3], we introduced an alternative approach that utilized both the scavenging method and the instrumentation of the shell script files. These are external shell scripts that are not part of the WRF software. They just invoke the required WRF components and insert the related provenance information into the log file. In that previous work, we proposed a rule-based provenance extraction method where the rules must be maintained manually by the programmer to adapt the parser to different log files. In this study, we investigate the use of supervised learning algorithms to model the provenance data and predict the type of provenance notifications. Here, machine-learning algorithms are employed during the analysis of log lines produced by the WRF model. In other words, lines containing provenance information are predicted by using text classification methods.

Figure 3 shows the component diagram of the machine learning-based provenance collection methodology that we have developed. To illustrate the testing of the machine learning algorithms, the following supervised learning algorithms are used to classify lines containing provenance information: Logistic Regression, Naive Bayes, Random Forest, and Multilayer Perceptron.

Data Pre-processing: Using N-gram frequency profiles, one can provide a simple data representation to categorize text files for a wide range of classification tasks. N-gram frequency profiles are a commonly used approach in text classification. An N-gram is usually referred to as an N-character slice of a longer string. To illustrate testing of the text classification for provenance data, in this study, we simply use N-word frequency profiles and take into account 1-word string for data representation.

Feature indexes in *"feature_index:value"* pairs indicate the index numbers that are automatically assigned, starting from 1, to each different word in the log file in the order they are encountered. The *value* number in *"feature_index:value"* pairs indicates the frequency of the word in the log line. In this study, the value part is assigned as 1 in all samples, since only the term existence is considered rather than the term frequency in the scope of the study.

Training Dataset: Note that, classification algorithms require a training data set to construct classification models. In this study, we created a labeled dataset for WRF log files. We created a training dataset by scanning each line and checking whether it contains any of the provenance data and determine the type of provenance relationship. The training dataset is constructed by manually examining sample log files obtained from the WRF scientific program modules.

In the pre-processed log files after N-gram conversion, the first value in each row represents the label of the class to which that row is assigned. The class labels that start from zero, indicating an irrelevant line, and will go up to the total number of different types of provenance relationships, incrementing by one. We use the following possible provenance relationships as labels according to the PROV-O Specification: used, *wasGeneratedBy, wasAssociatedWith, wasInformedBy, wasAttributedTo, wasDrivedFrom, actedOnBehalfOf*.

Model Construction: Model construction is performed with a training set of log files before the system is deployed. The log file is given as input to the machine learning algorithms to train a classification model. In the scope of the study, we constructed various machine-learning models by using Logistic Regression, Naive Bayes, Random Forest, and Multilayer Perceptron algorithms.

Provenance Notification Prediction: The classification process for the new WRF log lines is performed based on the constructed models. Each model predicts one class label from the available multi-class labels. After the prediction phase, the Adaptor constructs a provenance notification with the appropriate provenance relationship and sends it to the provenance repository. We discuss the evaluation of the prediction tasks in Sect. 7.

The proposed approach can be used in the same way to analyze the log files of different Numerical Weather Prediction models other than the WRF model, without requiring software development.

6 Prototype Implementation

To illustrate the testing of the proposed system, we developed a prototype. The machine learning-based provenance parser is designed as a middle layer software between the WRF software and the provenance repository software. For the repository, we used a PROV-O compatible provenance storage technology, Komadu Service.

In this study, Turkish State Meteorological Service[3] provided the computational facilities and input atmospheric data for running the WRF model. We obtained the log files from various runs of the WRF model and used them in the testing of the proposed provenance extraction methodologies. The WRF model is run with the highest possible *debug_level* to minimize any possible missing provenance information.

PROV-DM, an XML-based W3C PROV specification, is used for modeling provenance information obtained from provenance extraction software.

The implementation of the machine-learning algorithms used in this study is done by using the MLlib (Machine Learning Library) library of Apache Spark[4], an open-source cluster-computing engine developed within the Apache Software Foundation. The classification algorithms in the MLlib library accept files of LIBSVM format as input. LIBSVM is a sparse feature vector notation, a file format with rows representing a feature vector that is composed of "*attribute_index:value*" pairs separated by a space character. We investigated the performance of the prototype and discussed the results in the next section.

7 Performance Evaluation

To evaluate the performance of the proposed system, various experiments are conducted. All of the system components are implemented in Java language. A working prototype of the system is deployed on two virtual machines running on top of a computer with a Windows 10 operating system, Intel Core i7 4720HQ CPU, and 8 GB RAM. One of the virtual machines features Ubuntu 12.04 as the guest operating system, where the Komadu Service runs stable. The other virtual machine uses Ubuntu 16.04, where the WRF runs smoothly. Both virtual machines have 4 GB of RAM and two CPU cores. The Java version used is JDK 1.8.0.

The proposed system's classification performance in terms of accuracy and precision/recall metrics is evaluated. To illustrate the testing of the parser, various classification algorithms are picked up from different categories. The Logistic Regression algorithm is selected among regression-based classifiers. Naive Bayes is picked up among Bayesian classifiers. The random forest algorithm is selected as a representative of tree-based classifiers. Finally, multilayer perceptron is picked up from neural network-based classifiers.

Three different versions of log files are used in the experiments for the evaluation of classification performance. One of these files is generated by the WRF model executed with *debug_level* 100 while the other two are generated with *debug_level* 150. The summary statistics of these log files are given in Table 1. 'Dictionary size' in the table refers to the total number of distinct words in the corresponding log file.

Raw log files must first be converted to LIBSVM format to be input to the classification algorithms. For this purpose, log lines are converted to feature vectors by using the Apache Spark machine-learning library's CountVectorizer and CountVectorizerModel classes. Then, static class labels are determined for multi-class classification. Afterward,

---

[3] https://www.mgm.gov.tr.

[4] https://spark.apache.org/mllib.

Table 1. Summary statistics of log files used in experiments

File name	log_100	log_100_v1	log_100_v2
debug_level	100	150	150
Total number of rows	28,159	83,444	141,831
Total number of words	121,246	898,786	1,716,024
The average number of words per line	4.30	10.77	12.10
Dictionary size	842	3,235	3,283

data in LIBSVM format are input to Logistic Regression, Naive Bayes, Random Forest, and multilayer perceptron algorithms, and classification models are trained.

To evaluate the performance of the classification process, the classification accuracies of the algorithms are examined. Each test procedure is repeated 100 times for each algorithm-log file combination, and the average with the standard deviation of classification accuracy is calculated. A 10-fold cross-validation approach is chosen for the evaluation methodology. Each log file is randomly split into 10 subsets of approximately equal size. Each time, a different subset is selected as the test set, and the remaining subsets are used for training. The overall performance metric for a specific log file is calculated by taking the average of the results calculated for each one of the 10 subsets.

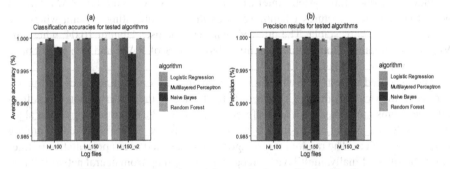

Fig. 4. Accuracy and precision results for multi-classification

We evaluated all the algorithms' multi-class classification performance in terms of accuracy and precision metrics and the results can be seen in Fig. 4a and Fig. 4b, respectively. We notice that all algorithms seem to have achieved very high classification accuracies and performed with high precision and high recall. Therefore, we argue that successful provenance extraction can be conducted without the need for a ruleset.

As a last note, the size and the contents of the log files produced by the WRF model may show some variations depending on the parameters, such as the size of the region to be predicted or the length of the prediction period. However, when different log files are examined, it can be seen that they generally have a common pattern and a high degree of similarity. For this reason, it is observed that the machine-learning models achieve very high performance on various log files obtained after running the WRF model with different initial parameters, such as time periods or prediction regions.

8 Conclusion

In this study, we investigate a machine learning-based approach to provenance extraction from log files of scientific applications. In this approach, supervised learning algorithms are used to model the provenance data and predict the type of provenance relationships. Here, machine-learning algorithms are employed during the analysis of log lines produced by the WRF model. To obtain different provenance relationships from the log lines, multi-classification is utilized. The results indicate that successful provenance extraction can also be conducted by utilizing machine-learning algorithms without the need for a ruleset. Hence, the use of machine-learning algorithms for log parsing for provenance can eliminate the need for a rule database.

To facilitate testing of the system, we developed a prototype implementation and made it available as open-source software at the GitHub repository. The system is implemented with Apache Spark's MLLIB library, from which the Logistic Regression, Naive Bayes, Random Forest, and multilayer perceptron algorithms are applied for multi-class classification. The trained models are run on the sample log files, and it is observed that they perform well even on log files containing a large number of lines.

References

1. Simmhan, Y.L., Plale, B., Gannon, D.: A survey of data provenance in e-science. ACM SIGMOD Rec. **34**(3), 31–36 (2005). https://doi.org/10.1145/1084805.1084812
2. Missier, P., Belhajjame, K., Cheney, J.: The W3C PROV family of specifications for modelling provenance metadata. In: Proceedings of the 16th International Conference on Extending Database Technology, pp. 773–776 (2013). https://doi.org/10.1145/2452376.2452478
3. Tufek, A., Gurbuz, A., Ekuklu, O.F., Aktas, M. S.: Provenance collection platform for the Weather Research and Forecasting Model. In: 2018 14th International Conference on Semantics, Knowledge and Grids (SKG), pp. 17–24 (2018). https://doi.org/10.1109/skg.2018.00009
4. Simmhan, Y.L., Plale, B., Gannon, D.: A framework for collecting provenance in data-centric scientific workflows. In: 2006 IEEE International Conference on Web Services (ICWS06), pp. 427–436 (2006). https://doi.org/10.1109/icws.2006.5
5. Indiana University, Pervasive Technology Institute. (n.d.). Karma. Pervasive Technology Institute website: https://pti.iu.edu/impact/open-source/karma.html. 12 Apr 2020
6. Indiana University, Data To Insight Center (D2I). (n.d.). Komadu: Provenance collection and visualization tool based on W3C PROV standard, GitHub website: https://github.com/Data-to-Insight-Center/komadu. 12 Apr 2020
7. Droegemeier, K.K., et al.: Linked environments for atmospheric discovery (LEAD): architecture, technology roadmap and deployment strategy. In: 21st Conference on Interactive Information Processing Systems for Meteorology, Oceanography, and Hydrology, January 2005
8. Aktas, M.S., Fox, G.C., Pierce, M., Oh, S.: XML metadata services. Concurrency Comput. Pract. Experience **20**(7), 801–823 (2008). https://doi.org/10.1002/cpe.1276

9. Aktas, M.S., Pierce, M.: High-performance hybrid information service architecture. Concurrency Comput. Pract. Experience **22**(15), 2095–2123 (2010). https://doi.org/10.1002/cpe.1557

10. Aktas, M.S., Fox, G.C., Pierce, M.: Information services for dynamically assembled semantic grids. In: 2005 First International Conference on Semantics, Knowledge and Grid, pp. 10–10 (2005). https://doi.org/10.1109/skg.2005.83

11. Jensen, S., Plale, B., Aktas, M.S., Luo, Y., Chen, P., Conover, H.: Provenance capture and use in a satellite data processing pipeline. IEEE Trans. Geosci. Remote Sens. **51**(11), 5090–5097 (2013). https://doi.org/10.1109/TGRS.2013.2266929

12. Moreau, L., et al.: The open provenance model core specification (v1.1). Future Gener. Comput. Syst. **27**(6), 743–756 (2011). https://doi.org/10.1016/j.future.2010.07.005

13. Shu, Y., Taylor, K., Hapuarachchi, P., Peters, C.: Modelling provenance in hydrologic science: a case study on streamflow forecasting. J. Hydroinformatics **14**(4), 944–959 (2012). https://doi.org/10.2166/hydro.2012.134

14. Bernardet, L., Carson, L., Tallapragada, V.: The design of a modern information technology infrastructure to facilitate research-to-operations transition for NCEP's modeling suites. Bull. Am. Meteor. Soc. **98**(5), 899–904 (2017). https://doi.org/10.1175/bams-d-15-00139.1

15. McCallumzy, A., Nigamy, K., Renniey, J., Seymorey, K.: Building domain-specific search engines with machine learning techniques. In: Proceedings of the AAAI Spring Symposium on Intelligent Agents in Cyberspace, pp. 28–39 (1999). http://citeseerx.ist.psu.edu/viewdoc/summary?doi=10.1.1.14.4717

16. Boyan, J., Freitag, D., Joachims, T.: A machine learning architecture for optimizing web search engines. In: AAAI Workshop on Internet Based Information Systems, pp. 1–8 (1996). http://citeseerx.ist.psu.edu/viewdoc/summary?doi=10.1.1.41.9172

17. Agichtein, E., Castillo, C., Donato, D., Gionis, A., Mishne, G.: Finding high-quality content in social media. In: Proceedings of the 2008 International Conference on Web Search and Data Mining, pp. 183–194 (2008). https://doi.org/10.1145/1341531.1341557

18. Neethu, M.S., Rajasree, R.: Sentiment analysis in Twitter using machine learning techniques. In: 2013 Fourth International Conference on Computing, Communications and Networking Technologies (ICCCNT), pp. 1–5 (2013). https://doi.org/10.1109/ICCCNT.2013.6726818

19. Pang, B., Lee, L., Vaithyanathan, S.: Thumbs up?: Sentiment classification using machine learning techniques. In: Proceedings of the ACL-02 Conference on Empirical Methods in Natural Language Processing, vol. 10, pp. 79–86 (2002). https://doi.org/10.3115/1118693.1118704

20. Groth, P., Moreau, L. (Eds.). (n.d.). PROV-Overview: An Overview of the PROV Family of Documents. https://www.w3.org/TR/prov-overview. 12 Apr 2020

21. Baeth, M., Aktas, M.: Detecting misinformation in social networks using provenance data. Concurrency Comput. Pract. Experience **31**(3), e4793 (2019)

22. Baeth, M., Aktas, M.: An approach to custom privacy policy violation detection problems using big social provenance data. Concurrency Comput. Pract. Experience **30**(21), e4690 (2018)

23. Riveni, M., Nguyen, T., Aktas, M.S., Dustdar, S.: Application of provenance in social computing: a case study. Concurrency Comput. Pract. Experience **31**(3), e4894 (2019)

Improving Existing WMS for Reduced Makespan of Workflows with Lambda

Ali Al-Haboobi[1(✉)] and Gabor Kecskemeti[1,2(✉)]

[1] Institute of Information Technology, University of Miskolc, Miskolc, Hungary
{al-haboobi,kecskemeti}@iit.uni-miskolc.hu
[2] Department of Computer Sceince, Liverpool John Moores University,
Liverpool, UK
g.kecskemeti@ljmu.ac.uk

Abstract. Scientific workflows are increasingly important for complex scientific applications. Recently, Function as a Service (FaaS) has emerged as a platform for processing non-interactive tasks. FaaS (such as AWS Lambda and Google Cloud Functions) can play an important role in processing scientific workflows. A number of works have demonstrated their ability to process these workflows. However, some issues were identified when workflows executed on cloud functions due to their limits (e.g., stateless behaviour). A major issue is the additional data transfer during the execution between object storage and the FaaS invocation environment. This leads to increased communication costs. DEWE v3 is one of the Workflow Management Systems (WMSs) that already had foundations for processing workflows with cloud functions. In this paper, we have modified the job dispatch algorithm of DEWE v3 on a function environment to reduce data dependency transfers. Our modified algorithm schedules jobs with precedence constraints to be executed in a single function invocation. Therefore, later jobs can utilise output files generated from their predecessor job in the same invocation. This reduces the makespan of workflow execution. We have evaluated the improved scheduling algorithm and the original with small- and large-scale Montage workflows. The experimental results show that our algorithm can reduce the overall makespan in contrast to the original DEWE v3 by about 10%.

Keywords: Scientific workflows · Cloud functions · Serverless architectures · Makespan

1 Introduction

A scientific workflow application consists of a large number of dependent jobs with complex precedence constrains between them, e.g. Montage [5], CyberShake [4], and LIGO [1]. These applications need large resources for processing such as cloud computing. Moreover, they require Workflow Management Systems (WMS) such as Pegasus [3] and Kepler [2] for handling the jobs. These

© Springer Nature Switzerland AG 2021
B. Balis et al. (Eds.): Euro-Par 2020 Workshops, LNCS 12480, pp. 261–272, 2021.
https://doi.org/10.1007/978-3-030-71593-9_21

WMSs help to keep the applications constraints by following a specific order of processing and ensuring the availability of data dependencies.

Function as a Service (FaaS) is a commercial cloud platform (e.g. AWS Lambda) for running distributed applications with highly scalable processing capabilities. FaaS platforms often have significant limitations on individual invocations e.g., temporary storage and memory. Several studies (e.g., [6,13]) have investigated whether large-scale scientific workflows can be executed on function platforms in spite of their limitations. They execute scientific workflows in functions by sending a set of jobs to be run in each function invocation. When invocations complete successfully, FaaS services remove all temporary files due to their storage space limits (e.g., 500 MB in case of Lambda). Thus, output files (which can act as data dependencies for other jobs) resulting from the invocations need to be transferred to an object storage. Unfortunately, this leads to increased communication costs. As a result, the total workflow execution time (makespan) will be longer due to more dependency movement than on non-function based platforms.

[11] presented a prototype for workflows on cloud functions. In [6] the DEWE v3 is introduced that is also able to process scientific workflows using AWS Lambda and Google Cloud Functions (GCF). DEWE can process scientific workflows in three different execution modes: traditional cluster, cloud functions, and hybrid mode (combining the other two modes). Both mentioned WMS solutions were evaluated with the Montage workflow (which is a compute- and data-intensive, astronomy focused scientific application). Testing with smaller Montage workflows does not show significant differences with regards to makespan. Larger scale ones show the deficiency of these previous approaches though: their scheduling algorithm sends jobs to functions without considering job precedence requirements. Jobs with precedence could be sent as a single set for their corresponding function invocation. Thus large scale montage exhibits the problem of increased makespan due to more frequent dependency transfers.

We have changed the scheduling algorithm of DEWE v3 to reduce data dependency transfers. Our improved algorithm schedules jobs with precedence requirements to be executed in a single function invocation. It schedules a predecessor job with its successor jobs that have no other predecessor jobs to the same shard to run in the same function invocation. As a result, we moved some workflow management behaviour inside the functions, as these functions now need to assure the job ordering when they process them. Consequently, successor jobs can utilise the output files generated from their predecessor job in the same function invocation. This will ensure we don't need to transfer the dependencies to the object store prematurely. We can schedule jobs with precedence constraints in a single shard. Because they will be captured in order by the shard and Lambda. Subsequently, Lambda will be immediately getting these jobs in a single batch.

We have evaluated our approach with AWS Lambda as our target platform. AWS offers Kinesis for queueing tasks to particular functions. Function instances have their own queues (called shards). When a function completes its current task, Lambda will pull all or some of the jobs with precedence requirements based on its batch size and the sequence of the jobs on a shard. Consequently, the remaining jobs will be waiting on the shard for the next Lambda invocation.

In our experiment, we have evaluated our improved approach and the original DEWE v3 with the 0.10° and 6.0° Montage workflows. The 6.0° workflow can be considered large-scale as it has a total of 8,586 jobs with a data dependency size of 38 GB. In addition, DEWE has already shown a large amount of re-transfer data behaviour. We used the small 0.1° workflow to show that our approach does not alter the performance. Due to Lambda's limitations, some files cannot be processed in functions, for these we used one sufficiently sized VM.

The experimental results show that our improved system can outperform DEWE v3 in most cases. At best, in contrast to the original, we have 10% shorter makespan. This demonstrates that our improved scheduling algorithm can reduce the execution time of scientific workflows on the Lambda platform.

The remainder of this paper is structured as follows. In Sect. 2, we will present background knowledge and related works. In Sect. 3, we will explain the improved algorithm and how we changed DEWE v3. We evaluated our improvements and contrasted it to the original algorithm in Sect. 4. Finally, Sect. 5 concludes the paper and suggests some future works.

2   Background Knowledge and Related Works

2.1   Background Knowledge

A workflow can be modelled as a Directed Acyclic Graph (DAG) that consists of a set of jobs which follow a specific order in processing. The vertices represent the workflow jobs and the edges represent data dependencies between these jobs.

Executing workflows on IaaSs leads to the challenge of determining the number of VMs to back the workflow's jobs. There are different numbers of jobs in each phase of the workflow which all could require different levels of computing resources. In order to speed up the workflow execution, we can add more VMs for processing the jobs in a certain phase. However, this may lead to a resource under-utilization issue for other phases. Unless the workflow management system is capable of dynamically reducing the number of backing VMs.

AWS presented Lambda[1] in 2014 while Google introduced cloud functions (GCF[2]) in 2016. The advantage of using cloud functions is the dynamic automation of resource provisioning by scaling up or down based on the workflow execution requirements. Moreover, the billing interval for cloud functions is based on 100 ms while recently Amazon and Google have changed the interval billing of virtual machines from per-hour to per-second. The function is stateless and its runtime environment is instantiated and terminated for each function invocation. Additionally, Microsoft and IBM have presented their own versions of FaaS that are Microsoft Azure Functions[3] and IBM OpenWhisk Functions[4].

---

[1] https://aws.amazon.com/lambda/.

[2] https://cloud.google.com/functions/.

[3] https://docs.microsoft.com/en-us/azure/azure-functions/functions-overview.

[4] https://cloud.ibm.com/docs/openwhisk?topic=openwhisk-getting-started.

If workflows are executed on one of the above FaaS systems, the dynamic management of backing VMs becomes unnecessary by WMSs as FaaS systems include automated resource management in the background. Therefore, the number of concurrent invocations into the infrastructure can more closely follow the actual workflow's demands.

[10] presented an evaluation for the following serverless computing providers: Amazon, Microsoft, Google, and IBM. They tested the function platforms by invoking CPU, memory, and disk-intensive functions. They found that at the time of writing, Amazon's was better. In addition, they also pointed out that computing with cloud functions is more cost-effective than virtual machines due to zero delay in booting up new resources. In addition, they also pointed out that costs only get charged for the function's actual execution time rather than paying for the idle periods as well for virtual machines. As a result, we have chosen Lambda to run workflows due to its efficiency and effectiveness comparing with other platforms.

2.2   Related Works

[11] suggested five different architectures for executing scientific workflows on the cloud. It presented a prototype for serverless computing that integrated the HyperFlow engine with GCFs and AWS Lambda. It designed to investigate the feasibility of executing compute- and data-intensive scientific workflows on cloud functions. It was tested with 0.25° and 0.4° Montage workflows and they found the approach highly promising. In addition, in [12] they presented the same prototype and tested it with the same previous montage workflows as well as a 0.6° Montage workflow. They run 0.6° as the largest workflow due to Lambda limits for the temporary storage 500 MB. Their approaches also manifest the deficiency with large-scale workflows that causes increased data dependency transfers.

[6] developed a more advanced system called DEWE v3 that is able to process scientific workflows on three different modes: traditional cluster, cloud functions, and a hybrid mode that combines the two. They evaluated it with small- and large-scale Montage workflows. The system has demonstrated the ability of cloud functions to run large-scale scientific workflows with complex precedence constrains. However, it uses a scheduling algorithm that batches jobs to Lambda without considering jobs with precedence requirements to run in a single Lambda invocation. As a result, more data dependency transfers can occur during execution between storage service and the Lambda invocation execution environment. Thus, this leads to increased communication costs.

[9] outlined the challenges for executing scientific workflows on a serverless computing platform. They proposed a Serverless Deadline-Budget Workflow Scheduling (SDBWS) algorithm that was modified to be applicable for function platforms. It was tested with the small-scale 0.25° Montage workflow on AWS Lambda. The algorithm used different memory sizes for Lambda based on the deadline and budget constraints assigned by the user. In addition, the function

resource is selected depending on the combined factors: cost and time. Their approach also exhibits the deficiency with large-scale workflows that causes increased data dependency transfers.

[13] presented work for evaluating three cloud function platforms which are Lambda, GCF, and OpenWhisk (from IBM). They evaluated the platforms with a large-scale (over 5000 jobs in parallel) bag-of-tasks style workflow. The experimental results showed that Lambda and GCF can provide more computing power if one requests more memory, while OpenWhisk is not offering an important difference. Consequently, cloud functions can provide a high level of parallelism for workflows with a large number of parallel tasks at the same time. However, they experimented with a bag-of-tasks approach where they did not consider data dependency transfers.

3   Improving an Existing Workflow Management System

DEWE v3 has three different execution modes including a cloud functions mode that we targeted to implement our approach on it. The functions mode runs workflows on FaaS platforms such as AWS Lambda. Inside this mode, we modified the AWS Lambda specific job dispatch algorithm to reduce data dependencies transfer. In the next paragraphs, we will put our modifications in context, then we will discuss our approach in detail.

The DEWE v3 system reads the workflow definition from an XML file. After the definition is loaded, the job binaries and input files are uploaded to Amazon S3. In the beginning, all jobs that have no predecessor jobs are scheduled to Amazon Kinesis stream into a common job queue. The scheduling algorithm works by predecessor jobs triggering their successor jobs when they are completed. Moreover, the Lambda function pulls a set of jobs from the Kinesis shards based on the Lambda's batch size. Therefore, the maximum amount of jobs in a single function invocation will be limited by the batch size. Depending on configuration, Kinesis can have one or more shards. Each shard acts as an independent queue for a particular function instance. Therefore, the number of parallel Lambda invocations is equal to the number of shards in Kinesis. By increasing the number of shards, DEWE v3 can speed up the execution time of scientific workflows. Figure 1 shows the original algorithm of DEWE v3 that we will compare it with our improved algorithm.

Many challenges are exposed when workflows executed on cloud functions due to different constraints. Firstly, functions have some limits such as the amount of compute, memory, and storage resources that can use them to run and store functions. For instance, Lambda needs to delete all the temporary files when a set of jobs are successfully executed due to its storage space limit 500 MB. Therefore, more data dependencies transfer occur during the execution between object storage and the function invocation environment, leading to more communication costs. Secondly, functions are stateless leading to the requirement that the output data files must be stored on an external service.

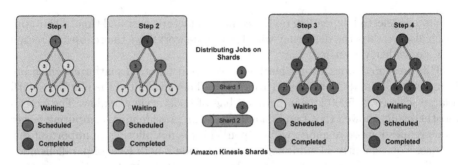

Fig. 1. The scheduling steps of the original algorithm with a sample workflow example.

3.1   Proposed Approach

We started to implement our approach in DEWE v3 to lessen data dependency transfers and to reduce the makespan of the workflow execution. We choose DEWE v3 as the foundation because it was the closest existing open source WMS to our goals. We changed its job dispatch algorithm to improve its data dependency transfers. We moved the following workflow management behaviour inside shards and the Lambdas. Jobs with precedence constraints will be sent to the same Kinesis shard (in the order they need to be executed). Subsequently, each shard will assure the sequence of the jobs in processing by Lambda. To guarantee strictly increasing ordering, we have sent jobs serially to a shard. Additionally, we used the SequenceNumberForOrdering parameter that guarantees the order of jobs on a shard[5]. Next, Lambda will receive a batch of jobs based on its batch size to run them sequentially in a single invocation. But before starting any job on the Lambda, each job will read its data dependencies from the S3 storage and then storing again the output files to it. Moreover, running jobs sequentially in a single Lambda invocation will benefit our improved algorithm that it must preserve the dependence constraints. Finally, if there are remaining jobs on the shard, they will wait for the next Lambda invocation for executing.

We extended the (LambdaWorkflowScheduler) class of DEWE v3 that discussed previously. The extension called the (LambdaShardWorkflowScheduler) class where we modified the (setJobAsComplete) method to be called by the (jobCompleted) method. It schedules each predecessor job with its successor jobs that have no other predecessor jobs. Afterwards, Lambda will pull all or some of the jobs with precedence requirements based on its batch size and on their order on a shard. In addition, the remaining jobs will be waiting on the shard for the next Lambda invocation.

Algorithm 1 shows the pseudo-code of the improved algorithm for scheduling a workflow. Here we explain the steps of the improved scheduling algorithm. However, step 1 and step 6 are already in the DEWE v3 algorithm but we will explain them to show the content. Step 2: it reads the XML file of the

---

[5] https://docs.aws.amazon.com/kinesis/latest/APIReference/API_PutRecord.html.

Algorithm 1. The improved scheduling algorithm.

```
1:  procedure SCHEDULING JOBS(T, KS)
2:      Read the workflow definition (dag.xml)
3:      T ← job, KSn ← Kinesis − shard, Ln ← Lambda − function
4:      numJobs ← number − of − batch, maxBatch ← Lambda − batch − number
5:      flag ← max − batch − number, loadBalancing[] ← numberJobs − to − shard
6:      Schedule all jobs that have not predecessor jobs (Ti)
7:      if (Ti has completed processing) then
8:          KSn=select a shard with the minimum number of receiving jobs
9:          numJobs = 0
10:         for each successor job of Ti do
11:             Tj ← successor − job − of − Ti
12:             Remove Ti as a predecessor job from Tj
13:             if (Tj has no other predecessor jobs) then
14:                 schedule Tj to KSn to run on Ln
15:                 numJobs = numJobs + 1
16:                 while (Tj has successor jobs) do
17:                     if (The successor job has only one predecessor job Tj) then
18:                         Remove Tj as a predecessor job from its successor job
19:                         Schedule the successor job of Tj to KSn to run on Ln
20:                         numJobs = numJobs + 1
21:                     end if
22:                     if (numJobs == maxBatch) then
23:                         flag = true
24:                         break
25:                     end if
26:                 end while
27:             end if
28:             if (flag == true) then
29:                 loadBalancing[n] = loadBalancing[n] + numJob
30:                 KSn=select a shard with the minimum number of receiving jobs
31:                 flag = false
32:                 numJobs = 0
33:             end if
34:         end for
35:         loadBalancing[n] = loadBalancing[n] + numJob
36:     end if
37: end procedure
```

workflow definition. Step 3: we denote T, KSn, and Ln for jobs, Kinesis shards, and Lambda functions respectively. Step 4: we symbolize numJob for counting the number of batch jobs that will be sent for each shard in order to be less or equal to the number of a batch size of Lambda (maxBatch). Step 5: we denote flag as a boolean value to alert when the number of jobs that need to send them to shard be equal to the number of a batch size of Lambda. In addition, we symbolize loadBalancing as an array to count the jobs that send to each shard in order to balance the workload across Kinesis shards. Step 6: at the beginning

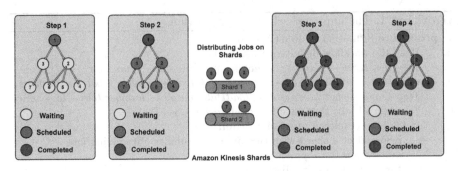

Fig. 2. The scheduling steps of the improved algorithm with a sample workflow example.

of the scheduling, all jobs that have not predecessor jobs will be scheduled across Kinesis shards without their successor jobs such as job 1 in step 1 of Fig. 2 and Fig. 1. In Step 7, if a predecessor job completed the execution, then in step 8: the algorithm will select a shard with the minimum number of receiving jobs among all shards. Step 10: it will traverse all successor jobs of the completed job and in step 12: each successor job will remove the completed job as a predecessor job. Next, in steps 16–21, each predecessor job will be scheduled with its successor jobs that have no other predecessor jobs. For example, job 2 schedules with its successor jobs 4 and 5 on the same Kinesis shard as illustrated in step 2 of Fig. 2. Additionally, job 3 schedules with its successor job 7 on the same Kinesis shard. But job 6 has not been scheduled with its predecessor () because it has two predecessors (jobs 2 and 3). Steps 22–25 are to stop sending jobs to shard due to reaching the maximum number of a batch size of Lambda. Steps 28–31 are to count the jobs that send to each shard. In order to balance the workload across Kinesis shards that is leading to balanced use of all Lambda instances. Moreover, step 30 is to select another Kinesis shard with the minimum number of receiving jobs among all shards to continue scheduling the remaining jobs of the workflow.

Figure 2 shows the steps of the improved scheduling algorithm while Fig. 1 illustrates the steps of the original algorithm. In Step 1, both algorithms have the same assignment to a shard. Step 2 is the difference between Fig. 2 and Fig. 1. In the original algorithm, step 2 as only jobs 2 and 3 are ready and assigned them to shards. While in the improved algorithm, we schedule all these jobs with their successor jobs (4, 5, and 7) except job 6 that has two predecessor jobs (2 and 3). Jobs will be captured in order based on our previous discussion by the shard and Lambda. Where we can put jobs with precedence constraints in a single shard. Subsequently, Lambda will be immediately getting these jobs in a single batch. When jobs 2 and 3 are completed execution in the original algorithm, they will trigger their successor jobs (4, 5, 6, and 7) in step 3 of Fig. 1. Finally, both algorithms have completed the execution of jobs in step 4.

4 Evaluation

In this section, we have evaluated the improved algorithm by comparing its results with the original algorithm. We tested them with a 0.1° and a 6.0° Montage workflows (an astronomy application). We have selected Montage because the previous studies used Montage as well and it allows easier comparison between with past results. Montage was also used for different benchmarks and performance evaluation in the past [7].

First, we tested the Montage workflow degrees by considering the data dependencies between jobs. We placed the Montage workflows on the S3 storage bucket for reading/writing by Lambda. We run the workflow management system on the virtual machine as a management node, where the VM is t2.micro instance as a free tier with 1 vCPU 2.5 GHz, Intel Xeon Family, and 1 GiB memory. In our experiment both systems were evaluated on the same platform configuration as follows:

1. The Lambda Memory sizes were: 512, 1024, 1536, 2048 and 3008 MB
2. The Lambda execution duration was 900 s.
3. The batch size of the Lambda function was 10.
4. The Kinesis shard number was 2.

Figure 3 shows the makespan of both systems. Our improvements outperform the original DEWE v3 system in most cases in these small scale experiments. While the makespan of the improved system is worse than DEWE v3 for the memory 512 MB. Because testing with smaller Montage workflows does not show significant differences with regards to makespan. Memory size will impacts the makespan of workflow execution: if the user has a large-scale workflow, sending more jobs to Lambda will need a higher memory size. CPU is allocated proportionally based on the memory size where the greater size provides more computing power. Our observations here are in alignment with [13]: the lesser memory the Lambda functions have the lesser computing capabilities they have as well.

4.1 Large-Scale Evaluation

We tested both systems with the 6° Montage workflow with data dependencies on Lambda. In this configuration, Montage is a large-scale, compute- and data-intensive scientific workflow that contains a total of 8,586 tasks, 1,444 input data files, and 22,850 intermediate files, with a total size of 38 GB. It contains short jobs such as mProjectPP, mDiffFit, and mBackground while there are six long jobs: mConcatFit, mBgModel, mAdd, mImgtbl, mShrink, and mJPEG. All the short and long jobs are executed on Lambda except the mAdd jobs which are executed on a single virtual machine. The VM is needed because the size of the input/output files for mAdd exceeds the temporary storage space offered in a single Lambda function invocation. The makespan of the large-scale workflow execution of both systems is shown in Fig. 4. In this experiment, both systems were evaluated on the same platform configuration as follows:

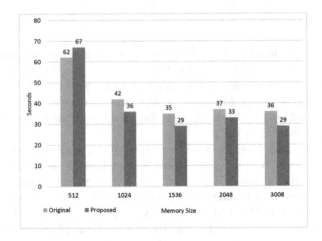

Fig. 3. The execution time of the both systems with a 0.1° Montage workflow with job dependencies running on different Lambda memory sizes.

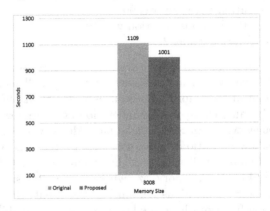

Fig. 4. The execution time of both systems with a 6° Montage workflow with job dependencies running on 3 GB Lambda memory size.

1. The Lambda Memory size was 3008 MB
2. The Lambda execution duration was 900 s.
3. The batch size of the Lambda function was 20.
4. The Kinesis shard number was 30.
5. The virtual machine was t2.xlarge that executed mAdd jobs with its features: 16 GiB of memory and 4 vCPUs.

We used 2 shards for the first experiment because it used a small-scale workflow. While we used 30 shards for the second experiment because it used a large-scale workflow. In addition, we cannot increase the number of shards to indefinitely because some jobs need to execute as single-thread jobs such as mBg-Model and mAdd. Figure 4 shows the reduction in makespan for the 6° Montage workflow. Because scheduling jobs with precedence constraints to be executed in a single function invocation shows the gains. As a result, the improved algorithm can reduce data dependency transfers to speed up the overall makespan of workflow execution as illustrated in Fig. 4.

5 Conclusion

In this paper, we have presented an improvement of the job dispatch algorithm of DEWE v3 to reduce data dependency transfers. DEWE v3 is one of the Workflow Management Systems (WMSs) that provides three different execution modes: traditional cluster, cloud functions, and hybrid mode. Our improved algorithm schedules jobs with precedence constraints to be executed in a single function invocation. Therefore, successor jobs can utilise the output files generated from their predecessor job in the same invocation. This has the potential to reduce the makespan of workflow execution. We have evaluated the improved scheduling algorithm and the original algorithm with small- and large-scale Montage workflows. The experimental results show that the improved algorithm can reduce the overall makespan in contrast to DEWE v3 by about 10%.

In future work, we will extend the improved algorithm to run on heterogeneous memory sizes of cloud functions to reduce the execution time and cost. Moreover, we will extend a Workflow Management System (WMS) tool for the DISSECT-CF [8] simulator in order to be able to simulate the execution of scientific workflows in more reproducible and controlled environments.

Acknowledgements. This work was supported in part by the Hungarian Scientific Research Fund under Grant agreement OTKA FK 131793.

References

1. Abramovici, A., et al.: LIGO: the laser interferometer gravitational-wave observatory. Science **256**(5055), 325–333 (1992)
2. Altintas, I., Berkley, C., Jaeger, E., Jones, M., Ludascher, B., Mock, S.: Kepler: an extensible system for design and execution of scientific workflows. In: Proceedings. 16th International Conference on Scientific and Statistical Database Management, pp. 423–424. IEEE (2004)
3. Deelman, E., et al.: Pegasus: mapping scientific workflows onto the grid. In: Dikaiakos, M.D. (ed.) AxGrids 2004. LNCS, vol. 3165, pp. 11–20. Springer, Heidelberg (2004). https://doi.org/10.1007/978-3-540-28642-4_2
4. Graves, R., et al.: CyberShake: a physics-based seismic hazard model for southern California. Pure Appl. Geophys. **168**(3–4), 367–381 (2011)
5. Jacob, J.C., et al.: Montage: a grid portal and software toolkit for science-grade astronomical image mosaicking. arXiv preprint arXiv:1005.4454 (2010)
6. Jiang, Q., Lee, Y.C., Zomaya, A.Y.: Serverless execution of scientific workflows. In: Maximilien, M., Vallecillo, A., Wang, J., Oriol, M. (eds.) ICSOC 2017. LNCS, vol. 10601, pp. 706–721. Springer, Cham (2017). https://doi.org/10.1007/978-3-319-69035-3_51

7. Juve, G., Deelman, E.: Resource provisioning options for large-scale scientific work-flows. In: 2008 IEEE Fourth International Conference on eScience, pp. 608–613. IEEE (2008)

8. Kecskemeti, G.: DISSECT-CF: a simulator to foster energy-aware scheduling in infrastructure clouds. Simul. Model. Pract. Theory **58**, 188–218 (2015)

9. Kijak, J., Martyna, P., Pawlik, M., Balis, B., Malawski, M.: Challenges for schedul-ing scientific workflows on cloud functions. In: 2018 IEEE 11th International Con-ference on Cloud Computing (CLOUD), pp. 460–467. IEEE (2018)

10. Lee, H., Satyam, K., Fox, G.: Evaluation of production serverless computing envi-ronments. In: 2018 IEEE 11th International Conference on Cloud Computing (CLOUD), pp. 442–450. IEEE (2018)

11. Malawski, M.: Towards serverless execution of scientific workflows-hyperflow case study. In: Works@ Sc, pp. 25–33 (2016)

12. Malawski, M., Gajek, A., Zima, A., Balis, B., Figiela, K.: Serverless execution of scientific workflows: experiments with hyperflow, aws lambda and google cloud functions. Future Gener. Comput. Syst. (2017)

13. Pawlik, M., Figiela, K., Malawski, M.: Performance considerations on execu-tion of large scale workflow applications on cloud functions. arXiv preprint arXiv:1909.03555 (2019)

Resilience - 13th Workshop on Resiliency in High Performance Computing with Clouds, Grids, and Clusters

Workshop on Resiliency in High Performance Computing in Clouds, Grids, and Clusters (Resilience)

Workshop Description

Resilience is a critical challenge as high-performance computing (HPC) systems continue to increase component counts, individual component reliability decreases (such as due to shrinking process technology and near-threshold voltage (NTV) operation), hardware complexity increases (such as due to heterogeneous computing), and software complexity increases (such as due to complex data- and workflows, real-time requirements, and integration of artificial intelligence (AI) technologies with traditional applications).

Correctness and execution efficiency, in spite of faults, errors, and failures, is essential to ensure the success of HPC systems, cluster computing environments, Grid computing infrastructures, and Cloud computing services. The impact of faults, errors, and failures in such HPC systems can range from financial losses due to system downtime (sometimes several tens of thousands of Dollars per lost system-hour), to financial losses due to unnecessary overprovision (acquisition and operating costs of underutilized machines), and financial losses and legal liabilities due to erroneous or delayed output.

The emergence of AI technology opens up new possibilities, but also new problems. Using AI technology for operational intelligence that enables resilience in HPC systems and centers is a complex control problem, while designing resilient AI technology for HPC applications is a difficult algorithmic problem. Resilience for HPC systems encompasses a wide spectrum of fundamental and applied research and development, including theoretical foundations, error/failure and anomaly detection, monitoring and control, end-to-end data integrity, enabling infrastructure, and resilient algorithms.

This workshop brought together experts in the community to further research and development in HPC resilience and to facilitate exchanges across the computational paradigms of extreme-scale HPC, cluster computing, Grid computing, and Cloud computing. The Resilience 2020 workshop program included presentations of 3 high-quality peer-reviewed papers, a keynote by Dr. Petar Radojković of the Barcelona Supercomputing Center, titled *Towards Resilient EU HPC Systems: A Blueprint*, and varying opportunities for discussions among the participants from research, academia, and industry.

Organization

Workshop Chairs

Stephen L. Scott — Tennessee Tech University, USA
Christian Engelmann — Oak Ridge National Laboratory, USA

Workshop Program Chairs

Thomas Naughton — Oak Ridge National Laboratory, USA
Ferrol Aderholdt — Middle Tennessee State University, USA

Workshop Chair Emeritus

Chokchai (Box) Leangsuksun — Louisiana Tech University, USA

Program Committee (PC)

Wesley Bland — Intel Corporation, USA
Hans-Joachim Bungartz — Technical University of Munich, Germany
Marc Casas — Barcelona Supercomputer Center, Spain
Zizhong Chen — University of California, Riverside, USA
Robert Clay — Sandia National Laboratories, USA
Nathan DeBardeleben — Los Alamos National Laboratory, USA
James Elliott — Sandia National Laboratories, USA
Kurt Ferreira — Sandia National Laboratories, USA
Saurabh Hukerikar — NVIDIA, USA
Ignacio Laguna — Lawrence Livermore National Laboratory, USA
Scott Levy — Sandia National Laboratories, USA
Rolf Riesen — Intel Corporation, USA
Yves Robert — ENS Lyon, France
Thomas Ropars — Université Grenoble Alpes, France
Martin Schulz — Lawrence Livermore National Laboratory, USA
Keita Teranishi — Sandia National Laboratories, USA

Predicting Hard Disk Failures in Data Centers Using Temporal Convolutional Neural Networks

Alessio Burrello[1(✉)], Daniele Jahier Pagliari[2], Andrea Bartolini[1],
Luca Benini[1,4], Enrico Macii[3], and Massimo Poncino[2]

[1] Department of Electrical, Electronic and Information Engineering,
University of Bologna, 40136 Bologna, Italy
{alessio.burrello,andrea.bartolini,luca.benini}@unibo.it

[2] Department of Control and Computer Engineering, Politecnico di Torino,
Turin, Italy
danielejahier.pagliari@polito.it

[3] Interuniversity Department of Regional and Urban Studies and Planning,
Politecnico di Torino, Turin, Italy
Massimo.Poncino@polito.it

[4] Department of Information Technology and Electrical Engineering at the ETH
Zurich, 8092 Zurich, Switzerland
lbenini@iis.ee.ethz.ch

Abstract. In modern data centers, storage system failures are major contributors to downtimes and maintenance costs. Predicting these failures by collecting measurements from disks and analyzing them with machine learning techniques can effectively reduce their impact, enabling timely maintenance. While there is a vast literature on this subject, most approaches attempt to predict hard disk failures using either classic machine learning solutions, such as Random Forests (RFs) or deep Recurrent Neural Networks (RNNs). In this work, we address hard disk failure prediction using Temporal Convolutional Networks (TCNs), a novel type of deep neural network for time series analysis. Using a real-world dataset, we show that TCNs outperform both RFs and RNNs. Specifically, we can improve the Fault Detection Rate (FDR) of $\approx 7.5\%$ (FDR = 89.1%) compared to the state-of-the-art, while simultaneously reducing the False Alarm Rate (FAR = 0.052%). Moreover, we explore the network architecture design space showing that TCNs are consistently superior to RNNs for a given model size and complexity and that even relatively small TCNs can reach satisfactory performance. All the codes to reproduce the results presented in this paper are available at https://github.com/ABurrello/tcn-hard-disk-failure-prediction.

Keywords: Predictive maintenance · IoT · Deep learning · Sequence analysis · Temporal Convolutional Networks

© Springer Nature Switzerland AG 2021
B. Balis et al. (Eds.): Euro-Par 2020 Workshops, LNCS 12480, pp. 277–289, 2021.
https://doi.org/10.1007/978-3-030-71593-9_22

1   Introduction

The storage systems of modern data centers can easily include from thousands to millions of hard disk drives. Therefore, despite single hard drives having a very high Mean Time To Failure (MTTF), storage system failures remain one of the main contributors to data center downtimes and maintenance costs [15,17]. One solution to reduce the impact of such failures is to resort to predictive maintenance techniques, where disks operations are continuously monitored. An alarm is raised whenever a drive is predicted to fail shortly, hence allowing timely maintenance actions (replacement of the hard drive, data integrity restoration, etc.) [1–3,14,18,19].

Most hard disk producers adopt Self-Monitoring Analysis and Reporting Technology (SMART) as the tool to enable predictive maintenance [4]. SMART consists of the periodic collection of a set of measurements (SMART *features*) during disk operation, including temperature, seek and read errors, reallocated sectors, etc. These features are then analyzed to determine the likelihood of failure, typically with data-driven approaches based on machine/deep learning models. In particular, most state-of-the-art methods are either based on Random Forests (RFs) or Recurrent Neural Networks (RNNs) [1–3,14,18,19].

Recently, however, many works [5,12] have demonstrated the superiority of Temporal Convolutional Networks (TCNs) for time series analysis. TCNs are particular types of 1-dimensional Convolutional Neural Networks (CNNs), including specific architectural elements (causality and time-dilation) to better adapt to time series. In [5,12], TCNs have been shown to outperform the more expensive and complicated RNNs in many sequence modeling tasks.

In this paper, we assess the effectiveness of TCNs for predicting hard disks failures. To the best of our knowledge, this is the first work to consider Temporal Convolutional Networks for this task. The contribution of this work is three-fold: *i)* we describe a comprehensive analysis of the imbalance management of the failure prediction in hard drives, demonstrating that using a Synthetic Minority Over-sampler improves the performance of up to 43.5% for different classification algorithms. *ii)* We show that the proposed TCN can outperform both RFs and RNNs for failure prediction, mostly thanks to the excellent long-term memory of these networks, which allows them to benefit from a long history of input data. Specifically, with a 90-days input window, we can improve the Fault Detection Rate (FDR) by ≈7.5% compared to state-of-the-art methods, while simultaneously reducing also the False Alarm Rate (FAR) to 0.052%. *iii)* We explore the architectural design space to provide a family of models that offer different trade-offs in terms of processing complexity and memory occupation versus performance. In doing so, we also show that TNCs are consistently superior to RNNs for a given size or complexity. The codes used in all the analysis are public at https://github.com/ABurrello/tcn-hard-disk-failure-prediction.

2   Background and Related Works

2.1   Temporal Convolutional Networks

The main layer type included in TCNs is a particular 1-D Convolution, with two differences compared to standard CNNs:

(1) *Causality*, which implies that each layer output is produced looking only at past samples, i.e. y_{t_N} is obtained from the convolution of x_{t_I} with $t_I \leq t_N$.

(2) *Dilation*, which is the fundamental element behind the success of these nets. Rather than performing convolution on a contiguous time-window of input samples, dilation inserts a fixed step between convolution inputs, thus increasing the receptive field, while keeping the number of parameters low.

Formally, a 1-D causal dilated convolution is computed as:

$$\mathbf{y}_T^m = \text{Dilated-Conv}\left(\mathbf{x}\right) = \sum_{n=0}^{N-1} \sum_{t=0}^{K-1} \mathbf{x}_{T-dt}^n \cdot \mathbf{W}_t^{n,m}$$

where $\mathbf{x}$ is the input feature map and $\mathbf{y}$ the output feature map, T the time index, $\mathbf{W}$ the weights matrix, N the number of input channels, m the output channel, d the dilation parameter, and K the filter size.

2.2   Backblaze Dataset

Our experiments target a real-world hard drive dataset from Backblaze [4], which contains hard drives from many vendors. As [1,18] pointed out, different disk models require dedicated training since they are characterized by different failure modes. Therefore, we focus on one of the most represented models, the Seagate ST300DM001, comprising data between 2014 and 2017, with a high number of failures, i.e. 1009. The dataset is composed of 90 SMART features collected daily, and the date of failure of the drive, if any. It includes a total of 3828 hard drives of the selected model, resulting in more than one million samples. For each of the 1009 failed hard drives, we assigned the failed label to samples in the last week, as suggested in [18]. With this labeling, the algorithm will learn to predict whether *a given hard drive will fail in the upcoming week*.

Table 1 summarises the main characteristics of the dataset, highlighting the strong class imbalance that is intrinsic in the problem (only 0.60% of the samples are labeled as failed).

Table 1. Dataset summary.

Dataset	Backblaze [4]
Model	ST300DM001
# of Hard Disks	3828
# of failed Hard Disks	1009
# of non-failed Hard Disk	2819
Non-failed class samples	1.25M
Failed class samples	7k (0.69%)
# of SMART features (total/after feature sel.)	90/18

2.3   Related Works

Two main formulations of hard disk predictive maintenance have been proposed in the literature, i.e. Failure Prediction (FP) and Remaining Useful Lifetime (RUL) estimation. In FP, predictive maintenance is addressed as a classification problem. The goal is to predict in advance the occurrence of a failure in the monitored drive. RUL estimation, instead, considers the issue as regression and tries to predict the remaining healthy operating life of the target drive [1]. Researchers have been attempting to approach both formulations with different machine learning models. In [3], the authors perform FP with Random Forests (RFs), Support Vector Machines, Gradient Boosted Trees, and Logistic Regression, applied to pre-processed SMART features. They also propose to periodically switch algorithms based on their performance in the previous period. RFs are used for fault prediction also in [18], where the authors focus mostly on using online learning to adapt their model to the variance of SMART features over time. Other works have addressed hard disks predictive maintenance using different flavors of deep Recurrent Neural Networks (RNNs), mostly using the Long-Short Term Memory (LSTM) architecture. RNNs have been used for both failure prediction [19] and RUL estimation [2,14]. The authors of [1] propose to simultaneously perform FP and RUL estimation with a single multi-target LSTM. Interestingly, [2] shows that RFs outperform LSTMs on both continuous and quantized RUL estimation. Moreover, the authors of [14] also experiment with using a standard Convolutional Neural Network (CNN) to estimate the RUL but obtain worse results than those achieved with an LSTM.

3   Methods

In this section, we describe the steps of the pipeline applied to the data to distinguish between failed and healthy hard drives. First, we apply a feature selection stage, followed by the split of train and test data. A re-sampling of the training dataset is then used to manage the strong class imbalance. We conclude with the classification through our proposed Temporal Convolutional Network. Figure 1 depicts the whole flow of our process, described in the next paragraphs, to assess the status of a hard drive from its SMART values.

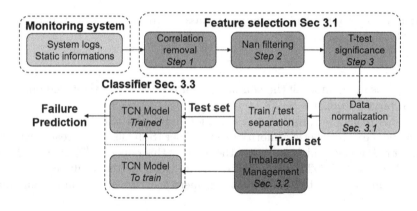

Fig. 1. Pipeline of our method. From raw SMART features to failure prediction.

3.1 Feature Selection

Before classification, we exclude redundant and irrelevant features from the dataset. This step is crucial to reduce the processing time while also increasing the prediction performance. Therefore, we propose a novel three-step feature selection process to reduce from 90 to 18 the features used during classification:

Step 1. Each SMART attribute is characterized by a *raw* and a *normalized* value. The latter is a vendor-specific normalization of the attribute, computed to obtain a similar distribution of features across different hard drive models. However, for a single model, the *raw* and *normalized* values are strongly correlated (Pearson's coefficient $|r| > 0.99$, p-value < 0.001). Therefore, we removed all *normalized* attributes from our analysis, reducing the features from 90 to 45.

Step 2. We removed all the attributes which have more than 60% of NaN in their values, reducing the features from 45 to 25.

Step 3. To verify the effective predictive power of each attribute, we applied a two-coiled t-test with a significant p-value < 0.001. After the test, we selected only attributes that resulted significant for the distinction between failed and non-failed samples, obtaining the final set of 18 features.

Finally, we normalize the 18 features selected using a Min-Max scaler to avoid bias towards features with larger values:

$$x_{norm} = \frac{x - x_{min}}{x_{max} - x_{min}}$$

3.2 Imbalance Management

As anticipated, the failed class is strongly under-represented in our dataset (0.69%). For this reason, the authors of many prior works [2,3,18] propose a random under-sampling of the majority class to reduce the ratio, λ, between the majority and minority class:

$$\lambda = \frac{N_n}{N_f}$$

where N_n is the number of the non-failed samples and N_f of the failed ones. The typical target λ range is $[1, 20]$.

In this paper, we propose to use a more advanced imbalance management technique, i.e. a Synthetic Minority Oversampler (SMOTE). The reader can find details on SMOTE, which are out of the scope of this paper, in [7]. In Sect. 4.2 we show that using SMOTE with a fixed $\lambda = 20$ yields better results compared to those obtained without imbalance management or with random under-sampling.

3.3   TCN Architecture

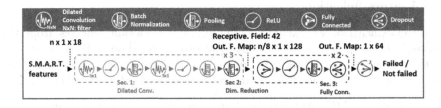

Fig. 2. Topology of the proposed Temporal Convolutional Network.

The TCN architecture used in this work combines dilated 1-D convolutions with max-pooling layers to create a modular structure that progressively reduces the time-length of the input while increasing the number of channels. We designed the network to increase the receptive field through convolutional layers while consuming the time dimension. Note that the architecture is composed of repeated identical *blocks*, as typical in many modern networks, e.g. for computer vision [10,16]. The whole structure is shown in Fig. 2.

The network stacks three convolutional blocks to extract time-relationships between inputs. The three blocks comprise two dilated 1-D convolutions with a 3×1 filter and $d = 2, 2, 4$, respectively, followed by Relu activations and batch normalization. Each block increases the number of channels to 32, 64, and 128, respectively. A final pooling layer halves the time dimension after each block (filter 2×1, stride $= 2$). At the end of the network, three Fully Connected layers with dropout classify the input sequence. A detailed description of the dilated convolutions can be found in [5]. The max-pooling, strided-convolutions, and linear layers are conventional [13].

4   Experimental Results

4.1   Experimental Setup and Metrics

To benchmark our approach, we compared it to the Random Forest of [18] and the LSTM proposed in [1] on the dataset introduced in Sect. 2.2. These two methods are representative of the two most common approaches to hard drives failure prediction in the state-of-the-art. The RF is composed of 30 trees, while the LSTM network has a layer of 384 recurrent neurons followed by two fully connected layers. We refer to [1,18] for further details on the architectures. Note that while the Random Forest receives as an input a single day by construction [18], both the LSTM and the TCN can manage time windows of different lengths. For our experiments, we consider window dimensions between 4 and 90 days.

We use randomly stratified sampling, with 70% of the data used to train all the algorithms and the remaining 30% for testing. On the training dataset, we perform internal validation to search for the best parameters set for the TCN. In detail, we used a batch size of 256 and a learning rate of 0.001, the Adam optimizer, and a decaying factor for the learning rate of 10 every 20 epochs. The maximum number of epochs has been set to 200, using a plateau on the training accuracy of the last 10 epochs as an early stop criterion.

The prediction performance is measured in terms of the following metrics: (1) *Fault Detection Rate* (FDR), i.e. the ratio between the samples predicted as failures and all the real failures, a.k.a. *recall*; (2) *False Alarm Rate* (FAR), i.e. the ratio between the samples wrongly predicted as failures and all the non-failure samples; (3) *Precision*, i.e. the ratio between the correctly predicted failures and all the predicted failures; (4) *F1-score*, i.e. the harmonic mean between precision and recall. All metrics should be maximized except the FAR, which should be minimized. All results are given as mean ± standard deviation, averaging the last 5 models from the training of the networks, or 5 different Random Forests.

4.2   Comparison of the Sampling Techniques

Our first set of experiments targets the different re-sampling methods used for the management of class imbalance. In Fig. 3, we compare three approaches, namely SMOTE, random under-sampling, and "All" (no re-sampling), using both our TCN and the state-of-the-art methods. For the latter, we apply the same pipeline as for our algorithm, replacing only the final classification step. A window of 30 days has been used in these experiments[1]. As the graph of Fig. 3 demonstrates, not applying any re-sampling techniques results in a very poor FDR from 12% to 28%, lower compared to the application of the random under-sampling/SMOTE for all the three classification algorithms. Moreover, although the random under-sampling guarantees a good FDR, it causes the FAR to increase by a factor of 9×/20× compared to the previous case. On the other

---

[1] For this input window size, the TCN achieves a FDR similar to the RF, but the following experiments show that the TCN FDR improves for longer inputs.

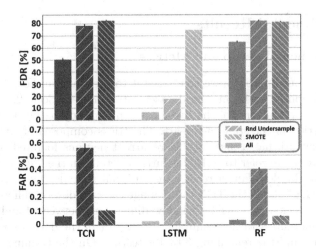

Fig. 3. Effect of different re-sampling methods on the performance of the three classification algorithms.

hand, SMOTE maximizes the FDR for the TCN and the LSTM (for the RF, the FDR is less than 1% lower than with random-undersampling), while achieving a FAR on the TCN and the RF only 1.65×/1.75× higher compared to not applying re-sampling. Overall, the F1-score of the TCN, LSTM, and RF using SMOTE increases of 20.48%, 38.5%, and 9.08% compared to not re-sampling and of 21.38%, 43.5%, and 17.16% compared to the random under-sampling.

Therefore, we use the SMOTE to re-sample our training dataset in all the following experiments.

4.3 Algorithms Comparison

Figure 4 shows the performances of LSTM and TCN with respect to the length of the input data used as input. Note that the RF has been executed on single day input samples as in its original work [18] since it intrinsically doesn't support the analysis of time series. Both the LSTM and our TCN demonstrate better performance by using more days in the input signal. However, for both FDR and FAR, the TCN is capable of taking more advantage from a longer input window. In particular, compared to an input window of size 24, on which the LSTM and the TCN achieve a similar FDR (79.21% vs. 80.23%), the LSTM increases its FDR by less than 2.5% when using a window of 90 days, while the TCN reaches FDR = 89.1%, with an improvement of 8.87% compared to the 24 days case.

Table 2 summarises the comparison of the three methods: the TCN proposed, the LSTM of [1], and the RF presented in [18]. Note that all three algorithms exploit the same steps of pre-processing, differing only in the classification step. When using 90 days of history, the TCN surpasses the competitors by 7.49% (RF) and 7.55% (LSTM) in FDR, achieving slightly lower FAR (0.052 vs. 0.063). We use the F1-score to give an idea of the overall comparison between the

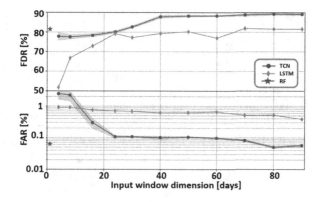

Fig. 4. LSTM and TCN performance for different input window sizes.

Table 2. Performance comparison of the three algorithms.

	RF [18]	TCN – 90 days	LSTM [1] – 90 days
FDR [%]	81,55 ± 0,40	89,10 ± 0,57	81,61 ± 0
FAR [%]	0,063 ± 0,003	0,052 ± 0,004	0,387 ± 0
Precision [%]	89,92 ± 0,47	91,00 ± 0,69	54,8 ± 0
F1-Score [%]	85,52 ± 0,22	90,05 ± 0,13	65,5 ± 0

three methods. Our TCN achieves an average F1-score of 90.05%, compared to the 85.52% obtained by the RF and the 65.5% of the LSTM (the reached performance in our work are almost equal to the ones presented by the authors of the referenced papers). Note that both [1,2] already showed that RF often outperforms LSTM for this kind of task.

These better metrics would directly translate into monetary savings, e.g. for cloud storage providers. Focusing on the FDR, i.e. the number of correctly predicted hard drives failures, we can see that our algorithm mispredicts only 1 failure over 10, compared to the 2 errors over 10 made by the other methods. Considering a realistic cloud storage using a Redundant Array of Independent Disk (RAID) [8] with hot-spare disks, we can link the FDR to a reduction in the number of spare drives with a 1:1 relationship, e.g. 80% FDR allows to reduce the number of the spare disks by 80%. Hence, halving the failure mispredictions implies decreasing by a factor of 2× the extra cost for the redundancy in the data center.

4.4 Model Size Exploration

Finally, inspired by the results in [10], we analyze the impact of the size of the proposed TCN by applying a *width multiplier* and a *depth multiplier* to increase and decrease the number of channels per layer and the number of layers.

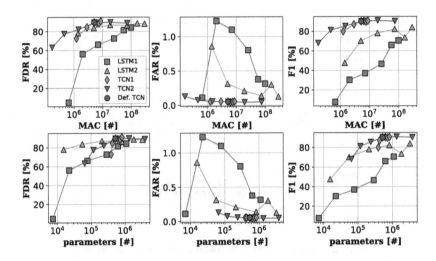

Fig. 5. FDR, FAR and F1 for varying TCN and LSTM model sizes.

Consequently, we increase or reduce both the network size and the number of operations performed for each classification.

Specifically, we regulate the depth of the network considering six models with {1, 2, 3, 4, 5, 6} convolutional blocks respectively (labeled TCN1 in Fig. 5). Convolutional blocks after the third are identical to the first three described in Sect. 3.3 and use 128 channels, $d = 4$, and full padding, but do not include any time dimension reduction. Then, we also multiply the number of channels of each layer by {0.125, 0.25, 0.5, 1, 2, 4}, keeping the default depth of 3, creating six additional models (TCN2 in Fig. 5).

For comparison, we also explore variations of the state-of-the-art RNN architecture using either one or two stacked LSTM layers and {32, 64, 128, 258, 384, 512} hidden layer dimensions. In Fig. 5, we label single-layer models LSTM1 and two-layer models LSTM2. We train all TCNs and LSTMs with identical hyperparameter settings. We do not report any exploration for the Random Forest, since increasing the number of trees does not improve the performance.

Figure 5 shows the FAR, FDR, and F1 score of the twenty-four models considered in this exploration. On the x-axis, the plots report either the number of Multiply-and-Accumulate (MAC) operations or the number of parameters of the corresponding models. The first conclusion that can be drawn from this exploration is that the TCN with channel multiplying factor (CMF) = 1 and three layers (the default structure presented in the paper, shown as a green dot in the figure) is the smallest model that saturates performance, and therefore represents a good trade-off point. Increasing the model size further does not cause a dramatic increase in performance. We obtain the best performance using CMF = 2, reaching an F1 score of 90.9%, only 0.8% better compared to the base architecture. We also note that with progressively bigger architectures, the FAR is almost constant (min 0.44, max 0.55), while we can observe an increase of the

FDR of nearly 30%. Hence, we conclude that small TCNs are sufficient to extract features that distinguish well the *not-failing* category. On the other hand, larger and deeper networks are needed to identify *failing* hard drives correctly, due to the wide range of possible failure modes.

Importantly, for a similar number of MAC operations or parameters, the proposed TCN versions almost always outperform the LSTMs. In particular, the top-right plot of Fig. 5 shows that LSTM architectures are never Pareto optimal in terms of F1-score versus the number of MAC operations. When considering the number of parameters (bottom-right plot), the trend is similar; the only exception is represented by architectures with less than 55k parameters, which, however, reach a F1-score lower than 70%, insufficient for an accurate monitoring system.

5   Conclusions

We have shown that TCNs can outperform state-of-the-art methods for hard disk failure prediction. This improvement is mostly thanks to their excellent long-term memory, which allows them to take advantage of long input time-windows. We have also shown that, for TCNs, applying SMOTE before training helps to improve the FDR while keeping FAR contained. In our future work, we will use TCNs also for RUL estimation, and experiment with unsupervised training to tackle the class imbalance problem. Moreover, this work has shown that small and low-complexity TCNs can still achieve good performance (e.g. the model with CMF=0.25 in Fig. 5 has $32\times/160\times$ fewer parameters/MACs than the biggest TCN, while achieving a decent F1 score of 80.3%, and a FAR <0.1%). This result could allow the execution of TCN-based inference in emerging ultra-low-power MCU architectures, which despite being performance- and memory-limited, offer specific HW and SW features for the execution of tiny ML models [6,9,11]. Our result, combined with these new architectures, could allow the embedding of the TCN in the HDD controller, enabling a scenario in which each hard drive autonomously provides fault prediction alarms to the system. Investigating this scenario will also be part of our future work.

Acknowledgments. This work has been partially supported by the H2020 project IoTwins (g.a. 857191).

References

1. Aggarwal, K., Atan, O., Farahat, A.K., Zhang, C., Ristovski, K., Gupta, C.: Two birds with one network: unifying failure event prediction and time-to-failure modeling. CoRR abs/1812.0 (2018). http://arxiv.org/abs/1812.07142
2. Anantharaman, P., Qiao, M., Jadav, D.: Large scale predictive analytics for hard disk remaining useful life estimation. In: 2018 IEEE International Congress on Big Data (BigData Congress), pp. 251–254 (2018). https://doi.org/10.1109/BigDataCongress.2018.00044

3. Apiletti, D., et al.: iSTEP, an integrated self-tuning engine for predictive maintenance in industry 4.0. In: 2018 IEEE International Conference on Parallel & Distributed Processing with Applications, Ubiquitous Computing & Communications, Big Data & Cloud Computing, Social Computing & Networking, Sustainable Computing & Communications, pp. 924–931 (2018). https://doi.org/10.1109/BDCloud.2018.00136

4. Backblaze: Backblaze dataset (2019). https://www.backblaze.com/b2/hard-drive-test-data.html

5. Bai, S., Kolter, J.Z., Koltun, V.: An empirical evaluation of generic convolutional and recurrent networks for sequence modeling. arXiv preprint arXiv:1803.01271 (2018)

6. Burrello, A., Conti, F., Garofalo, A., Rossi, D., Benini, L.: Work-in-Progress: DORY: lightweight memory hierarchy management for deep NN inference on IoT Endnodes. In: 2019 International Conference on Hardware/Software Codesign and System Synthesis (CODES+ISSS), pp. 1–2 (2019). https://doi.org/10.1145/3349567.3351726

7. Chawla, N.V., Bowyer, K.W., Hall, L.O., Kegelmeyer, W.P.: Smote: synthetic minority over-sampling technique. J. Artif. Intell. Res. **16**, 321–357 (2002)

8. Chen, P.M., Lee, E.K., Gibson, G.A., Katz, R.H., Patterson, D.A.: Raid: high-performance, reliable secondary storage. ACM Comput. Surv. (CSUR) **26**(2), 145–185 (1994)

9. Garofalo, A., Rusci, M., Conti, F., Rossi, D., Benini, L.: PULP-NN: accelerating quantized neural networks on parallel ultra-low-power RISC-V processors. Philos. Trans. Royal Soc. A Math. Phys. Eng. Sci. **378**(2164), 20190155 (2020). https://doi.org/10.1098/rsta.2019.0155

10. Howard, A.G., et al.: MobileNets: efficient convolutional neural networks for mobile vision applications (2017). http://arxiv.org/abs/1704.04861

11. Pagliari, D.J., Poncino, M., Macii, E.: Energy-efficient digital processing via approximate computing. In: Bombieri, N., Poncino, M., Pravadelli, G. (eds.) Smart Systems Integration and Simulation, pp. 55–89. Springer, Cham (2016). https://doi.org/10.1007/978-3-319-27392-1_4

12. Lea, C., Flynn, M.D., Vidal, R., Reiter, A., Hager, G.D.: Temporal convolutional networks for action segmentation and detection. In: 2017 IEEE Conference on Computer Vision and Pattern Recognition (CVPR), pp. 1003–1012 (2016)

13. LeCun, Y., Bottou, L., Bengio, Y., Haffner, P.: Gradient-based learning applied to document recognition. Proc. IEEE **86**(11), 2278–2324 (1998)

14. Lima, F.D.S., Pereira, F.L.F., Leite, L.G.M., Gomes, J.P.P., Machado, J.C.: Remaining useful life estimation of hard disk drives based on deep neural networks. In: 2018 International Joint Conference on Neural Networks (IJCNN), pp. 1–7 (2018). https://doi.org/10.1109/IJCNN.2018.8489120

15. Manousakis, I., Sankar, S., McKnight, G., Nguyen, T.D., Bianchini, R.: Environmental conditions and disk reliability in free-cooled datacenters. In: 14th USENIX Conference on File and Storage Technologies (FAST 16), pp. 53–65 (2016)

16. Sandler, M., Howard, A., Zhu, M., Zhmoginov, A., Chen, L.C.: Mobilenetv 2: inverted residuals and linear bottlenecks. In: The IEEE Conference on Computer Vision and Pattern Recognition (CVPR), June 2018

17. Schroeder, B., Gibson, G.A.: Disk failures in the real world: what does an MTTF of 1,000,000 hours mean to you? In: Proceedings of the 5th USENIX Conference on File and Storage Technologies, p. 1-es. FAST 2007 (2007)

18. Xiao, J., Xiong, Z., Wu, S., Yi, Y., Jin, H., Hu, K.: Disk failure prediction in data centers via online learning. In: Proceedings of the 47th International Conference on Parallel Processing. ICPP 2018 (2018). https://doi.org/10.1145/3225058.3225106

19. Xu, C., Wang, G., Liu, X., Guo, D., Liu, T.: Health status assessment and failure prediction for hard drives with recurrent neural networks. IEEE Trans. Comput. **65**(11), 3502–3508 (2016). https://doi.org/10.1109/TC.2016.2538237

On the Detection of Silent Data Corruptions in HPC Applications Using Redundant Multi-threading

Diego Pérez[1(✉)], Thomas Ropars[2], and Esteban Meneses[1,3]

[1] School of Computing, Costa Rica Institute of Technology, San José, Costa Rica
diperez@estudiantec.cr, emeneses@cenat.ac.cr
[2] Univ. Grenoble Alpes, CNRS, Grenoble INP, Grenoble, France
thomas.ropars@univ-grenoble-alpes.fr
[3] Advanced Computing Laboratory, Costa Rica National High Technology Center,
San José, Costa Rica

Abstract. This paper studies the use of Redundant Multi-Threading (RMT) to detect Silent Data Corruptions in HPC applications. To understand if it can be a viable solution in an HPC context, we study two software optimizations to reduce RMT performance overhead by reducing the amount of data exchanged between the replicated threads. We conduct experiments with representative HPC workloads to measure the performance gains obtained through these optimizations, and the error detection coverage they achieve. In the best case, when running on a processor that features Simultaneous Multi-Threading, our results show that the overhead can be as low as 1.4× without significantly reducing the ability to detect data corruptions.

Keywords: HPC · Silent data corruptions · Redundant multi-threading

1 Introduction

Silent Data Corruptions (SDCs) are alterations of data that go undetected by the hardware. These soft errors are usually attributed to external causes, such as high energy particles that may strike transistors and induce a bit-flip in the memory, the caches or the registers of the processor [12]. Such data corruptions may lead to a crash failure (*e.g.*, a pointer corruption leading to an invalid memory access), or lead to a wrong application output in the worst case.

As supercomputers keep increasing in scale, concerns about SDCs become more serious [1,12,13]. This problem is exacerbated by the current technology trends in processor architectures (*e.g.*, increased number of computing cores or near-threshold voltage) that aim at improving energy efficiency, but also increase the probability of SDCs. Error Correcting Codes (ECC) are usually used to detect and correct soft errors in main memory. However, such solutions

© Springer Nature Switzerland AG 2021
B. Balis et al. (Eds.): Euro-Par 2020 Workshops, LNCS 12480, pp. 290–302, 2021.
https://doi.org/10.1007/978-3-030-71593-9_23

are probably too expensive, both with respect to energy and performance, to be generalized to all caches and processor registers [3].

Several directions are explored to deal with SDCs in supercomputers, each of them having advantages and pitfalls. Some works propose to apply replication at the level of processes [5]. Solutions based on data analysis have also been proposed [2]. In this paper, we study an alternative approach: Redundant Multithreading (RMT). RMT detects SDCs at the level of threads. Hence, it can be cheaper than process replication. However, existing software-based RMT solutions [8,14,16] have major limitations. Either they induce a high performance overhead or they assume very infrequent interactions with other threads or processes, which is typically not a valid assumption with MPI applications.

The main factor that limits the performance of existing RMT solutions is the cost of communicating between threads to compare the output of their execution [8]. In software-based RMT, a *leading* thread has to send the result of each operation it executes to its sibling *trailing* thread that detects soft errors by comparing the values it receives with the result of its own operations. The single-producer/single-consumer (SPSC) queue involved in this communication is central to the performance of RMT.

This paper studies three directions to improve the performance of RMT approaches for HPC. First, it explores the possibility of using Simultaneous Multithreading (SMT) to improve the performance of RMT. The evolution of the hardware (*e.g.*, increased number of cores in processors) makes it difficult for some applications to make good use of all the processors resources [10], thus we think it is worth considering this possibility. Second, we evaluate two solutions to reduce the amount of data that are exchanged between the leading and the trailing RMT threads: i) aggregating multiple produced values together before testing them for SDCs; ii) only testing a subset of the program variables, the ones that are identified as having the potential to corrupt a state outside of the thread context (we call this approach *selective checking*).

We present a detailed evaluation of these optimizations using two representative benchmarks. Our experiments evaluate the performance of the optimizations. Experiments with fault injection are also used to estimate the impact on the coverage offered by RMT. The main conclusion from our experiments is that RMT could be a viable solution for SDC detection at least for some HPC applications. The results obtained with the *selective checking* optimization show that, when taking advantage of SMT hardware threads, the overhead compared to a non-protected execution can be as low as 1.4×, without significantly degrading the error coverage compared to a standard RMT approach.

The paper is organized as follows: Sect. 2 presents the problem of soft-error detection and the related work. Section 3 describes the studied RMT technique and the optimizations. Section 4 presents the evaluation results.

2   Background

2.1   Detecting Soft Errors

This paper considers the case of soft errors due to external causes, such as high energy particles that may invert the state of transistors. These errors are unpredictable by nature. More specifically, we consider soft errors that are not detected by the hardware. Such a soft error might lead to a crash (*e.g.*, a memory reference corruption may generate an invalid memory access), or might go totally undetected: these are silent data corruptions (SDCs). Soft errors can affect different components of a computing node including the main memory, the processor caches, and the processor registers.

Commonly, mechanisms at the hardware level, such as Error Correcting Codes (ECC) and parity bits, are used to protect the main memory and the processor caches [13]. Hence, most often, DRAM and caches are considered safe contrary to the processor registers and the combinational logic [12]. This is the kind of soft errors we are dealing with in this paper.

In today's systems, detecting SDCs has to be done at the software level. In the HPC context, approaches based on process replication have been proposed [5]: each process of the application is replicated and the outputs of sibling processes are compared to detect differences. Such a technique can detect SDCs with high precision, but it is costly as it doubles the amount of resources required to run the application. An alternative is to rely on data analysis to detect unexpected variations in the values of some program variables [2]. Such solutions induce much less overhead than process replication. However, they are only applicable if the data changes in a predictable way, which is not always the case [3].

In this paper, we explore solutions based on thread-level replication to detect SDCs. Such a solution is an alternative to process replication that is expected to be cheaper. Namely, thread-level replication only replicates the computation and not the data. On the other hand, this implies that thread-level replication can only work under the assumption that the memory of the processor is reliable.

Two approaches to thread-level replication exist, ILR (Instruction Level Redundancy) and RMT (Redundant Multi-Threading). ILR duplicates the instructions inside a single thread and compares the results before every write to memory [6]. RMT duplicates each application thread into a *leading* and a *trailing* thread and compares the output to detect SDCs [8,14,16]. Both approaches have advantages and drawbacks. The most appropriate time to run a comparison in ILR is always right after the values have been computed when they are still in the registers of the processor. Since values are produced by two different threads in RMT, comparison checks are more costly. Hence, state-of-the-art ILR techniques are more efficient than best RMT solutions today [6]. However, RMT offers a higher degree of flexibility regarding when to run comparison checks compared to ILR [16], and more opportunities for performance optimizations. Hence, our goal is to explore the potential of RMT approaches in an HPC context.

2.2   Redundant Multi-threading

In RMT approaches, the sibling threads use a Single-Producer-Single-Consumer queue (SPSC) to exchange the values they are generating, to be able to compare them. Hence the performance of RMT depends on the performance of the queue and on how the threads synchronize through this queue.

The synchronization over the queue can be synchronous, asynchronous or *semi-synchronous*. In a synchronous approach, the trailing thread needs to acknowledge the leading thread before any write is made to the memory, which induces a huge performance overhead [16]. On the other hand, in a fully asynchronous approach, performance is promoted over safety [8]. But leaving SDCs undetected for some period of time could result in an uncontrolled propagation of the error to other parts of the application, and lead to an unrecoverable state (for instance, if corrupted data would be saved in a checkpoint).

The *semi-synchronous* approach aims at limiting the synchronization between threads without compromising safety [14]. In this approach, the threads progress most of the time asynchronously and an acknowledgment is sent by the trailing thread to the leading thread only when *volatile* variables, *i.e.*, variables that must never get corrupted, are modified. A volatile variable is a variable that may be modified in ways unknown to the soft-error detection technique or have unknown side effects [16]. HPC applications include many accesses to volatile variables (I/O operations, MPI function calls) which limits the performance improvements that can be gained from the *semi-synchronous* technique.

Another direction to improve RMT performance is to work on the SPSC queue efficiency. Hence, batching has been proposed to improve the performance of SPSC queues [9]. However, fixed-size batching can only be applied with an *asynchronous* technique. Using batches with a *semi-synchronous* communication pattern could lead to a deadlock when the *leading* thread is waiting for an acknowledgment from the *trailing* thread, while the *trailing* thread is waiting for the current batch to be full to start processing data. Hence the most suitable solution for *semi-synchronous* RMT is to use a *dynamic* batching strategy where the leading thread can decide to terminate a batch early if a synchronous communication is required. According to our experiments[1], the queue algorithm proposed by Wang *et al.* [14] is the best queue to implement *semi-synchronous* RMT. Hence, we consider this solution as baseline for our evaluation.

3   Solutions to Improve RMT Performance

To assess the potential of RMT with HPC applications, our study aims at exploring the impact in terms of performance and reliability of different optimizations that could be applied to such a technique. At the hardware level, we consider the impact of Simultaneous Multithreading (SMT). We leverage SMT's ability to run sibling threads on the same physical core. At the software level, we study two optimizations that can be applied to the RMT approach to reduce the stress

---

[1] Results not included in the paper due to the limited space.

on the SPSC queue and, thus, improve performance. In this section, we start by providing details about the *vanilla* RMT algorithm that we use as baseline for our study. Then we present the two optimizations that we propose to evaluate.

3.1 Vanilla Semi-synchronous RMT Algorithm

Our baseline algorithm is designed based on the solution proposed by Wang *et al.* [14]. To obtain efficient communication between sibling threads, they use delayed buffering and lazy synchronization. Delayed buffering means that data are buffered on the producer with the help of a local index and only when K values have been enqueued, the data are made visible to the other thread. Lazy synchronization means that the algorithm avoids checking directly shared variables on each enqueue/dequeue operation, but iterates based on local indexes when possible [14]. Our implementation of this solution, that we call `vanilla-RMT` hereafter, defines the following API that includes 6 methods:

- `Produce()` is called by the leading thread to send a value to the trailing thread. It does not require an explicit acknowledgment. This method is used for *asynchronous* communication.
- `Consume()` is called by the trailing thread to read the next value from the queue and check for a soft error. This method is also used for *asynchronous* communication.
- `Produce_Volatile()` is a blocking method called by the leading thread to enqueue a value and wait for an acknowledgment from the trailing thread before continuing.
- `Consume_Volatile()` is called by the trailing thread to dequeue a value that requires an explicit acknowledgment and sends that acknowledgment.
- `Produce_Drt()` is used to sent data directly from the leading to the trailing thread without any soft-error verification.
- `Consume_Drt()` is used by the trailing thread to receive a value that is not computed locally from the leading thread.

We illustrate the use of this API through the example presented in Fig. 1. Figure 1a shows the original code snippet. The `foo` function computes the sum of the elements of a vector x passed as parameter. The result is stored in the local variable 1. Then a MPI call is made with 1 as input parameter and g as output. Finally, g is returned by the function.

Figure 1b and c illustrates the transformed code that is executed by the leading thread and the trailing thread respectively with RMT. The first thing to mention is that since 1 is an input parameter of a library function call at line 9, it makes it a *volatile* variable. Hence, our RMT approach has to guarantee that this variable is not altered by a SDC before calling the MPI function, and so the leading and the trailing threads respectively have to call `Produce_Volatile()` and `Consume_Volatile()` at line 8. The intermediate values of variable 1 produced at line 5 are also checked for correctness, but since these intermediate values can only alter the local state of the thread, they are checked asynchronously using `Produce()` and `Consume()` calls at line 6.


```
 1  foo(x[]) {
 2    g = 0, l = 0
 3
 4    for (i in 0 : x.lenght) {
 5      l += x[i] * x[i]
 6
 7    }
 8
 9    MPI_Call(l, g)
10
11    return g
12  }
```
(a) Original Code

```
 1  foo_leading(x[]){
 2    g = 0, l = 0
 3
 4    for (i in 0 : x.length) {
 5      l += x[i] * x[i]
 6      Produce(l)
 7    }
 8    Produce_Volatile(l)
 9    MPI_Call(l, g)
10    Produce_Drt(g)
11    return g
12  }
```
(b) Leading thread code

```
 1  foo_trailing(x[]){
 2    g = 0, l = 0
 3
 4    for (i in 0 : x.length) {
 5      l += x[i] * x[i]
 6      Consume(l)
 7    }
 8    Consume_Volatile(l)
 9    //MPI_Call(l, g)
10    g = Consume_Drt()
11    return g
12  }
```
(c) Trailing thread code

Fig. 1. Example of RMT code replication

We should point out that each synchronous exchange (calls to *_Volatile()
functions) makes the leading thread spin-wait for the trailing thread acknowledgment. Since the former might have already enqueued several *non volatile* values, it has to hold until all of them are verified for correctness. Therefore, a *volatile store* implies that the whole execution so far is checked for integrity.

In a RMT approach, instructions and functions calls that correspond to writes to volatile variables should not be replicated [6,8,14,16]. We would not want to print twice a value to the console, or send data twice to a neighbor node. Hence, such calls are only made by the leading thread, as illustrated in line 9 of Fig. 1c. Since the outputs of such calls are required by the trailing thread to continue its execution, these outputs are directly transfered from the leading thread using Produce_Drt() and Consume_Drt() calls, as illustrated in line 10.

3.2 Optimization Techniques for RMT

We present the three techniques studied to improve the performance of RMT.

Leveraging Simultaneous Multi-threading. Most recent processor architectures implement simultaneous multithreading to increase the degree of parallelism in multicore processors. SMT allows having 2 or more threads concurrently executing in the same physical core [11]. It makes a single physical processor appear as (at least) two logical processors. The physical execution resources are shared and the architecture state is duplicated for the logical processors.

The limited scalability of some HPC workloads with SMT threads has been highlighted in several studies [10]. On the other hand, placing a leading thread and its corresponding trailing thread on SMT hardware threads of the same physical core can help to improve the performance of the communication between them, as they will share the same L1 cache. Leveraging SMT for soft-error detection has been proposed in the seminal paper by Reinhardt and Mukherjee [11] but this solution was relying on dedicated hardware. The impact of SMT on RMT has been evaluated in [14] with negative results. As we show in Sect. 4, the conclusions can be different on more recent hardware.

Aggregation of Values. The first software technique we propose to evaluate aims at reducing the contention of the queue between the leading and the trailing thread by aggregating several values together and to compare the aggregated values to detect SDCs. This approach was originally proposed by Mitropoulou *et al.* [8]. Obviously this approach can only be applied to asynchronous communication. We evaluate this idea using the sum (+) operator as aggregation operator. In [8], the authors propose to aggregate 2 values together. We study a generalization of this idea where K values can be aggregated, with K being a power of 2 to be able to compute a modulo very efficiently using bit-wise operations[2].

It should be pointed out that using aggregation could potentially weaken soft-error detection. First, if more than one value is corrupted, there is a small chance that 2 bit-flips or more would compensate each other and go undetected. Second, there is a risk of overflow when computing the aggregated value.

Selective Checking. The second software technique that we evaluate aims at reducing the contention on the queue by limiting the number of values that are checked for correctness. This idea has already been proposed in the context of ILR [7,15]. By definition, writes to *volatile variables* are the points where a thread could make a data corruption visible to the *outside world*. As such, we propose to only check values that are stored in these variables. We refer to this optimization as *selective checking*.

Applying this technique to the example of Fig. 1 would lead to only check the final value of 1 for correctness at line 8. Obviously, with such an approach, there is also a risk of weakening the detection capabilities of the RMT technique. We evaluate this point during our experiments.

4   Evaluation

Our evaluation aims at assessing the efficiency that can be achieved when using an RMT approach to detect SDCs in HPC applications. More specifically, for the three optimizations described in Sect. 3.2, we want to evaluate: i) the performance improvement that can be obtained compared to the vanilla RMT approach presented in Sect. 3.1; ii) the reduction of the capacity of RMT to detect SDCs that they may induce.

4.1   Software Used for Evaluation

RMT Implementation. The implementation of the RMT technique described in Sect. 3.1 has been made in C. The optimizations presented in Sect. 3.2 have been applied to this code base. Special care has been taken to properly align variables and to pad the data structures to avoid any false sharing.

---

[2] The results presented in Sect. 4 are obtained with $K = 16$. Our tests showed that this the value that leads to the best performance for our applications.

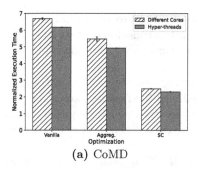
(a) CoMD

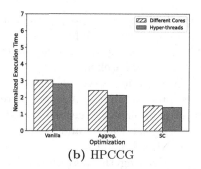
(b) HPCCG

Fig. 2. Performance of RMT with optimizations (`Aggreg`: Performance of RMT with aggregation; `SC`: Performance of RMT with selective checking)

To evaluate the performance of RMT with existing applications, we directly modified the code of the applications to create the leading and trailing threads and to insert API calls when required. Automatically replicating an application for RMT using a compiler approach has already been done in other works [8,14, 16]. Our work focuses on evaluating the efficiency of RMT approaches.

Benchmarks. To run our analysis, we select two applications, HPCCG and CoMD from the Mantevo benchmark suite. HPCCG is representative of finite element methods while CoMD is an implementation of classical molecular dynamics algorithms. We work with the MPI version of these applications.

4.2   Performance Evaluation

The first part of our evaluation focuses on the performance of RMT techniques. We start by presenting the experimental setup used for the evaluation. Then we evaluate the impact of the two software optimizations described in Sect. 3.2. Finally, we evaluate the impact of using SMT threads.

Experimental Setup. All experiments presented below are run on a node equipped with 2 Intel Xeon E5-2630L v4 processors (*Broadwell* architecture) and 128 GB of RAM. Each processor features 10 physical cores with two Hyper-Threads per core. The applications are compiled using the highest level of optimization activated (`-O3`). The presented results are average execution times over 10 runs (with error bars representing the standard deviation).

For the two applications, the problem size considered for the evaluation is the following: a global problem size of $1.28 * 10^8$ for HPCCG and a total number of atoms of $2.4565 * 10^6$ for CoMD.

Performance Impact of the Software Optimizations. Figure 2 presents the performance of the different versions of RMT with the two tested applications. The applications are executed with 20 MPI ranks. This corresponds to running one process per rank in the non-replicated execution and leads to the best performance for these applications with the considered problem sizes[3]. The presented results are normalized execution times with the non-replicated execution as baseline.

We first focus on the results when the leading and the trailing threads of each process are executed on different cores (labeled `Different Cores`). When RMT is applied, we have 40 threads to execute in total[4], which we pin in such a way that the leading and the trailing threads are on a different core but on the same NUMA node.

Comparing the performance of the *vanilla* RMT approach to the performance when optimizations are applied, we observe that the optimizations lead to significant performance improvements. Aggregation leads to 18% and 20% of improvements compared to the default RMT approach with CoMD and HPCCG respectively. The *selective checking* achieves even better performance: 63% for CoMD and 50% for HPCCG.

The obtained performance also show that the *vanilla* RMT approach induces a very high overhead: a 6.7× slowdown for CoMD and a 3× slowdown for HPCCG. We conclude from these results that such an approach is not viable for SDC detection in HPC applications. On the other hand, with *selective checking*, the slowdown reduces to 2.5× for CoMD and to 1.5× for HPCCG. The slowdown could still be too high with CoMD but with HPCCG, the overhead becomes promising and might also even be competitive against ILR techniques [6], where the overall overhead across all applications[5] is 2×. Indeed, in an approach based on full process replication [5], one can expect to achieve a smaller slowdown but at the cost of duplicated the amount of computing resources used to run the application.

Performance Impact of SMT. In Fig. 2, the data labeled `Hyper-threads` correspond to the configuration where the leading and trailing threads of each rank are collocated on the same physical core. The results show that a (limited) performance improvement is always observed. It ranges from 6.2% to 11.6%. Hence, when this approach is combined with *selective checking*, the slowdown reaches 2.3× for CoMD and 1.4× for HPCCG[6].

4.3   Reliability Evaluation

In a second set of experiments, we evaluate the ability of RMT to detect soft errors when the proposed performance optimizations are used. We identify two

---

[3] Trying to take advantage of the SMT threads by running 40 ranks in the non-replicated run does not provide any performance improvement.

[4] We also tested configurations with 10 ranks when RMT was used to have one thread per core. In most cases the performance were equivalent to the results with the default configuration.

[5] Tested applications in [6] are part of different benchmark suites than ours.

[6] These results are not specific to the selected problem size. They remain equivalent for other problem sizes in both applications.

	No RMT	Vanilla	Aggreg.	SC
Benign	29.7	31.2	28.6	31.2
Err. detected	0	63.5	66	48.1
Corrupted	66	0	0	13.6
Crashed	4.3	5.3	5.3	5.2
Timeout	0	0	0.1	1.9

(a) Detection of errors inserted in dot product method (in %)

	No RMT	Vanilla	Aggreg.	SC
Benign	91.5	66.1	61.6	93
Err. detected	0	27.3	31.8	0.5
Corrupted	1.5	0	0	0
Crashed	7	6.6	6.6	6.5
Timeout	0	0	0	0

(b) Detection of errors inserted in HPCCG (in %)

Fig. 3. Performance of RMT with optimizations (**Aggreg**: RMT with aggregation; **SC**: RMT with selective checking)

aspects that can be impacted by changes in the RMT technique with respect to soft errors: i) the capacity of detecting errors might be altered; ii) the probability of experiencing an error might change.

Ability to Detect Soft Errors. To test soft-error detection, we use *FlipIt*, an LLVM-based soft-error injection tool for HPC applications [4]. For these experiments, we consider the HPCCG application.

We configured *FlipIt* to inject a single fault (bit flip) in each execution and we ensure that one fault will be randomly injected in each execution. We allow faults to be injected in arithmetic and control instructions, but not in pointer type instructions because inserting bit flips in these instructions often simply leads to a crash, which is not an interesting case for our evaluation.

In all experiments, HPCCG is run with a single rank, and we deactivate all compiler optimizations to be able to simply relate the executed instructions to the source code described in C. Furthermore, to have a comparable distribution of injected errors in the tests of the RMT techniques and simplify the analysis, we run the tests in the following way: i) We use the same seed for the random number generator that is used to define the sequence of errors that are injected over the different tests for each technique; ii) We configure FlipIt to inject errors only in the application code (and not in the RMT code that can vary in number of instructions depending on the optimization that is used).

In a first step, we focus on the HPCCG routine that computes a dot product between two vectors. This routine is very similar to the one presented in Fig. 1 with local values computed during each iteration of a loop, and the final result of being a volatile variable. Table 3a presents the results of the test. For each configuration, 5000 runs of HPCCG have been executed. We identified 5 possible outcomes for a run: **Benign** (the execution terminated correctly despite the bit flip), **Error detected** (by the RMT technique), **Corrupted** (the application returned a wrong result – a SDC occurred), **Crashed** (for instance due to an illegal memory access), **Timeout** (the execution did not terminate).

Several observations can be made based on the results presented in Fig. 3a. First, it should be noted that HPCCG is rather robust to soft errors injected in that part of the code since about 30% of the executions lead to the correct results in all configurations. On the other hand, 66% of the injected errors lead to an

SDC that corrupted the final result of the application with the non protected version of HPCCG. Our default RMT implementation was able to detect all the SDCs as expected. When applying the optimizations, it is important to notice that the RMT version using aggregation was able to detect all SDCs, while 13% of the executions were corrupted with *selective checking* (SC). This illustrates the trade-off that SC provides: a significant performance improvements at the cost of a reduced error coverage.

Some results presented in Fig. 3a can be a bit surprising at first sight. For instance, there are a bit more executions that terminate correctly with the default RMT approach or when the SC optimization is applied. Also, the version of RMT with aggregation detects more errors than the version without optimizations. We found out that all these *inconsistencies* have the same root cause. They relate to the case where a corruption leads to access an incorrect memory address when loading a value of the vectors used as input of the dot product. Depending on the layout of the data in memory, the incorrect memory address might be not valid (leading to a crash) or might be a valid address which contains a value (which might corrupt the result of the computation or not).

Figure 3b presents the results of the tests when we allow bit flips to be injected in any instruction of the application code. The first thing to observe is that most of the executions of the non-protected version terminate correctly. This implies that HPCCG is in general robust to soft errors. We can also notice that in this case, the SC approach does not experience any corrupted result. The results with the default RMT approach and with the aggregation optimization show that many of the benign errors are detected as soft errors. These are not *false positive* in the sense that real soft errors were detected, but it is still counter-productive since executions that would have otherwise terminated correctly got interrupted. The results obtained with the SC optimization illustrate another advantage of this approach. Since SC only verifies writes done to volatile variables, it almost never detects these benign errors, allowing more often the execution to terminate correctly. We also ran tests where the bit flips are only inserted in the most significant bits. The obtained results are qualitatively equivalent the one of Table 3b with less benign faults being observed.

Probability of Experiencing a Bit-Flip. The results obtained during our evaluation illustrate the trade-offs that are obtained with the different RMT approaches. The SC approach allows reducing the performance compared to the other approaches. On the other hand, it has a negative impact on the ability of RMT to detect SDCs. This is a drawback as it provides a weaker guarantee regarding the validity of the final result of an execution. But it can also be a big advantage as it much less often interrupts an execution because of a detected soft error that would not have corrupted the final result.

To have a full comparison of the RMT approaches, we should also take into account the impact of each approach on the probability to experience a soft error. The duration of the execution and the total number of instructions executed by the applications, are two parameters that can influence this probability. From this point of view, the SC approach is a clear winner. The results presented in Sect. 4.2 show the execution with SC can be up to 63% faster than the default RMT approach. Using the Linux tool *Perf*, we also measured to total number of instructions executed during several runs of HPCCG with the three approaches. We observed that the SC solution reduces the number of instructions to be executed by about 12% compared to the default approach (while the aggregate optimization has not impact on this number). A dedicated analysis would be required to understand the impact of these numbers on the real probability of experiencing soft errors in HPC applications.

5 Conclusion

The paper studies the use of RMT to detect SDCs in HPC applications. To improve the performance of RMT, we evaluate two techniques to reduce the amount of data that need to be exchanged between the replicated threads: aggregation and selective checking. Our evaluation with representative workloads shows that selective checking, which consists in only verifying for correctness the content of variables that can impact the global state of the application, is a promising solution. When running on a multicore processor that features SMT threads, it leads to a performance overhead that can be as low as 1.4× while still ensuring a good error coverage. As future work, we plan to study in details the impact of these optimizations on the probability of experiencing a soft error, to better understand the trade-offs that they offer.

References

1. Bautista-Gomez, L., Zyulkyarov, F., Unsal, O., McIntosh-Smith, S.: Unprotected computing: a large-scale study of DRAM raw error rate on a supercomputer. In: IEEE Supercomputing (2016)
2. Berrocal, E., Bautista-Gomez, L., Di, S., Lan, Z., Cappello, F.: Lightweight silent data corruption detection based on runtime data analysis for HPC applications. In: ACM HPDC (2015)
3. Berrocal, E., Bautista-Gomez, L., Di, S., Lan, Z., Cappello, F.: Toward general software level silent data corruption detection for parallel applications. IEEE TPDS **28**(12), 3642–3655 (2017)
4. Calhoun, J., Olson, L., Snir, M.: FlipIt: an LLVM based fault injector for HPC. In: EuroPar (2014)
5. Fiala, D., Mueller, F., Engelmann, C., Riesen, R., Ferreira, K., Brightwell, R.: Detection and correction of silent data corruption for large-scale high-performance computing. In: IEEE Supercomputing (2012)
6. Kuvaiskii, D., Faqeh, R., Bhatotia, P., Felber, P., Fetzer, C.: HAFT: hardware-assisted fault tolerance. In: ACM Eurosys (2016)
7. Laguna, I., Schulz, M., Richards, D.F., Calhoun, J., Olson, L.: IPAS: intelligent protection against silent output corruption in scientific applications. In: CGO (2016)
8. Mitropoulou, K., Porpodas, V., Jones, T.M.: COMET: communication-optimised multi-threaded error-detection technique. In: ACM CASES (2016)

9. Mitropoulou, K., Porpodas, V., Zhang, X., Jones, T.M.: Lynx: using OS and hardware support for fast fine-grained inter-core communication. In: ACM ICS (2016)
10. Porter, L., et al.: Making the most of SMT in HPC: system-and application-level perspectives. ACM TACO **11**(4) (2015)
11. Reinhardt, S.K., Mukherjee, S.S.: Transient fault detection via simultaneous multithreading. In: IEEE Symposium on Computer Architecture (2000)
12. Snir, M., et al.: Addressing failures in exascale computing. IJHPCA **28**(2), 129–173 (2014)
13. Sridharan, V., et al.: Memory errors in modern systems: the good, the bad, and the ugly. ACM SIGPLAN Notices **50**, 297–310 (2015)
14. Wang, C., Kim, H.S., Wu, Y., Ying, V.: Compiler-managed software-based redundant multi-threading for transient fault detection. In: ACM CGO (2007)
15. Yu, J., Garzaran, M.J., Snir, M.: ESoftCheck: removal of non-vital checks for fault tolerance. In: CGO (2009)
16. Zhang, Y., Lee, J.W., Johnson, N.P., August, D.I.: DAFT: decoupled acyclic fault tolerance. Int. J. Parallel Prog. **40**(1), 118–140 (2012)

A Comparison of Several Fault-Tolerance Methods for the Detection and Correction of Floating-Point Errors in Matrix-Matrix Multiplication

Valentin Le Fèvre[1(✉)], Thomas Herault[2], Julien Langou[3], and Yves Robert[1,2]

[1] Laboratoire LIP, École Normale Supérieure de Lyon, Lyon, France
{valentin.le-fevre,yves.robert}@ens-lyon.fr
[2] University of Tennessee, Knoxville, TN, USA
herault@icl.utk.edu
[3] University of Colorado Denver, Denver, CO, USA
julien.langou@ucdenver.edu

Abstract. This paper compares several fault-tolerance methods for the detection and correction of floating-point errors in matrix-matrix multiplication. These methods include replication, triplication, Algorithm-Based Fault Tolerance (ABFT) and residual checking (RC). Error correction for ABFT can be achieved either by solving a small-size linear system of equations, or by recomputing corrupted coefficients. We show that both approaches can be used for RC. We provide a synthetic presentation of all methods before discussing their pros and cons. We have implemented all these methods with calls to optimized BLAS routines, and we provide performance data for a wide range of failure rates and matrix sizes.

Keywords: Resilience · Matrix-matrix multiplication ·
Algorithm-based fault tolerance (ABFT) · Residual checking (RC) ·
Silent errors

1 Introduction

Reliable computing has become a key challenge when deploying applications on large-scale platforms. These platforms are confronted to many errors striking during execution. These errors are due to the extremely large number of floating-point operations executed by the parallel applications that are deployed on such platforms. Indeed, the probability of facing a corrupted floating-point operation is proportional to the number of such operations that are executed [8]. Even if each processor exhibits a low individual error rate, the probability of several

This work was supported in part by the U.S. National Science Foundation awards 1645514 and 1563744.

© Springer Nature Switzerland AG 2021
B. Balis et al. (Eds.): Euro-Par 2020 Workshops, LNCS 12480, pp. 303–315, 2021.
https://doi.org/10.1007/978-3-030-71593-9_24

errors striking during the execution of the parallel application becomes very high with millions of cores running in parallel for a few days, or even hours.

There are very few ways to ensure that a whole application has executed without error. The only general-purpose method is to replicate the execution and to compare the results of both executions. If they do not coincide, an error has been detected, and the application must be executed a third time. To avoid a-posteriori re-execution, triplication can be enforced, which allows for error correction in addition to error detection, using a simple majority vote. However, triplication is even more costly than replication, which already requires half the resources to execute redundant operations. Fortunately, many scientific applications heavily rely on scientific kernels from numerical linear libraries, and much of their floating-point operations are executed within these kernels. For most linear algebra kernels, application-specific methods have been devised for error detection and correction, with a much lower cost than replication. The most prominent application-specific approaches are Algorithm-Based Fault Tolerance (ABFT) and Residual Checking (RC), which we describe in full details in Sect. 2. Both ABFT and RC are known to enable error detection, but ABFT has received much more attention because it is also deployed for error correction. In theory, ABFT can correct up to k errors with $2k + 1$ checksums [13, 16, 17]. However, the numerical instability of floating-point ABFT currently limits its usage to correct one or two errors within a kernel.

In this paper, we revisit the Residual Checking (RC) approach, and show that it can be an efficient alternative to ABFT for error detection and correction. In particular, we focus on providing a transparent hardened version of some operation: the API, as exposed to the user, does not change, but the result is checked (and corrected if needed) before it is returned to the user. This creates a problem for ABFT, as the efficiency of the technique lies in mixing the user data and the redundant data used for failure detection and correction (see Sect. 2.2). RC can be implemented without modifying the API of the original computation kernel (see Sect. 2.3), which is a key advantage from a software engineering perspective. Another drawback of ABFT compared to RC is the lack of flexibility. By construction, ABFT uses a fixed number of checksums chosen a priori, say $2k + 1$, and will fail if more errors than k errors strike during the kernel. On the contrary, RC adapts the number of verifications on the fly, as a function of the number of errors found.

We adopt a somewhat narrow focus and only deal with protecting matrix-matrix multiplication from floating-point errors. Matrix-matrix multiplication is the archetypal linear kernel and is at the heart of several linear solvers, hence it is one of the most important kernels to study. Assessing the efficiency of residual checking for matrix-matrix multiplication will lay the foundations for the study of a full dense linear algebra library. The major contributions of this paper are the following:

- A synthetic comparison of several fault-tolerance methods for error detection and correction in matrix-matrix multiplication, with novel approaches for RC;

- A publicly-available prototype implementation of all the methods, with calls to optimized BLAS kernels;
- A comparative assessment for a wide range of failure rates and matrix sizes.

2   Methods

2.1   Replication

The first approach to detect computational errors is also the only systemic approach that can apply to any algorithm: it consists in replicating computations, and checking that both executions produce the same result. In the context of mutable data, this also implies to work on a copy of the data to compute, in order to enable the replicated computation [12]. There are multiple ways to implement replication: the computations can be executed sequentially, one after the other, at any level of granularity, or in parallel. Ultimately, the replication process provides two copies of the output of the computation and these copies are compared bit-to-bit, to detect errors.

Any error detected can then be resolved with a voting process: more replicas are computed, and if (at least) two output results converge on a same result, this result is considered valid. The probability that two computation errors produce the same result is considered negligible, since errors are supposed to be independent and identically distributed random variables.

2.2   ABFT

ABFT is an approach introduced in [10], that leverages mathematical properties of the algorithm to introduce redundancy in the data and thus allows to detect, and sometimes locate and correct errors during a computation. Applied to the matrix-matrix multiplication of the $C \leftarrow AB$ as an example, where A is n-by-n and B is n-by-n, the main idea of ABFT is to extend the matrix on which the operation is applied with checksum vectors that are pre-computed before the matrix-matrix multiplication. This gives Aextended as $\begin{pmatrix} A \\ A_c \end{pmatrix}$ with $A_c = v^T A$, Bextended as $\begin{pmatrix} B & B_r \end{pmatrix}$ with $B_r = Bw$ where w and v are checksum generator vectors. Once A and B have been augmented, we perform the matrix multiplication $\begin{pmatrix} C & C^{(r)} \\ C^{(c)} & C^{(\alpha)} \end{pmatrix} \leftarrow \begin{pmatrix} A \\ A^{(c)} \end{pmatrix} \begin{pmatrix} B & B^{(r)} \end{pmatrix}$, and we see that we must have the following relations

$$C^{(r)} = Cw \quad \text{and} \quad C^{(c)} = v^T C \quad \text{and} \quad C^{(\alpha)} = v^T Cw. \tag{1}$$

Therefore, a way to check that the entries of C have been correctly computed is to check that the equalities in Eq. (1) hold. With this scheme, we can, for example, guarantee to detect any single error in C. (In other words, if no more than one entry of C is corrupted, then this scheme will detect the error.) Note that w and v does not have to be vectors, but they can also be block of vectors,

The whole realm of error correction codes (e.g. Reed Solomon error correction code) is now at our doorstep since for each row C_i of C, we have computed C_i and its checksum with respect to w, $C_i w$, and so not only can we detect errors, but we can also locate and recover errors. Using Reed Solomon error correction code, for example, we can detect, locate, and recover k errors with $2k + 1$ checksums (provided that we use an appropriate encoding block of vectors w). However, the Reed Solomon algorithm is notoriously unstable in finite precision arithmetic [6] and does not enable one to recover from many errors or to handle long vectors.

For detection, in practice, one row checksum of the form $C_i w$ is often enough to detect errors in any row of C, C_i. We simply check whether $C_i w = C_i^{(r)}$. This check can fail if the error vector introduced in C is orthogonal to w. However, this is unlikely. Tolerance of the order of machine precision has to be added to the check. Indeed, we only intend to detect errors that are larger than the errors made by the round-off errors of the numerical computation. So we check, for example, that $\|C^{(r)} - Cw\|_2 \leq 10u\|A\|_{\text{fro}}\|B\|_{\text{fro}}\|w\|_{\text{fro}}$, where u is the machine roundoff and the number "10" is taken arbitrarily [9]. A standard way to locate errors is to use *"coordinate checkpointing"*. So if the row checksum $C_i^{(r)}$ is not $C_i w$ and the column checksum $C_j^{(c)}$ is not $v^T C_j$ then we conclude that the entry c_{ij} is false. Once an error is located, we can either recover the c_{ij} through the redundancy introduced by the checksum and therefore solving a system of linear equations with unknown c_{ij}, this leads to the method ABFT-SOLVE, or we can, in the case of matrix-matrix multiplication, simply recompute the entry c_{ij} from the ith row of A and the jth row of B, this leads to the method ABFT-RECOMP.

One advantage of Reed Solomon is that it enables locating and correcting via checksum only on the rows or only the columns, while coordinate checkpointing would need both row and column checksums. For matrix-matrix multiplication, it is convenient to maintain both checksums, while for other linear algebra operations, this is not always natural. Now, how to choose v and w? In the case ABFT-SOLVE, Chen and Dongarra [5,6] showed that taking random matrices enable to recover the solution with high probability during the linear solve to recover the corrupted entries. While less critical, it does seem a good idea to also take random vectors v and w for ABFT-RECOMP.

As for the overhead, we see that to encode and compute with k checksums with $k \ll n$ is $\mathcal{O}(n^3)$ flops, the cost to detect, locate and recover ℓ errors is $\mathcal{O}(n^2 \ell)$ flops. Therefore the cost (in term of flops) of recovery is theoretically negligible compared to the cost of computation.

2.3   Residual Checking (RC)

A closely related method is RC, which exploits the fact that checking the correctness of the result of a computation is usually easier than computing it. In short, still using the $C \leftarrow AB$ matrix-matrix multiplication as an example, to check at low cost whether C is correctly computed, one can compute, on the one hand, Cw and, on the other hand, $A(Bw)$ and check whether these two vectors are similar. And, not surprisingly, the two methods ABFT and RC share similar characteristics: (1) Low cost, (2) if w is in the nullspace of $C - AB$, the error matrix, then we will not detect the errors, however this is unlikely, etc. Hence RC is very similar to ABFT. Historically RC was introduced with "error detection" in mind only. So you would perform the computation, use RC to detect errors, and then redo the computation if any error is detected [14,15]. RC has long be thought to only be able to detect errors, and not able to locate and correct errors. For example, Prata and Silva [14] writes: "*We left out of our comparison one aspect where ABFT would do better than RC, namely fault localization and error recovery, (RC has no such capability).*" Actually, in very much the same way as ABFT, RC is able to detect, locate and correct errors. The two methods (ABFT and RC) are essentially similar and have the same capabilities.

2.4   Differences Between ABFT and RC

There is a fundamental principle difference between RC and ABFT. Given some input, an algorithm computes some output such that a relation is true. For example, given A, (1) LU factorization: compute P, L, and U such that $PA = LU$, (2) QR factorization: compute Q, R such that $A = QR$, (3) SVD decomposition: compute U, Σ, and V^T such that $A = U\Sigma V^T$. RC finds a quick way to check whether this final relation holds. For example, given a vector x, (1) check that $P(Ax) = L(Ux)$, (2) check that $Ax = Q(Rx)$, (3) check that $Ax = U(\Sigma(V^Tx))$. If the relation does not hold, then RC has succeeded in detecting an error. If the relation holds, then RC has succeeded in assessing (with high probability) the correctness of the result.

On the contrary, ABFT starts with checksums on the initial data, and maintains the consistency of the checksums along the algorithm. So the checksums are being modified as the data is being modified so that current data is consistent with current checksum. As a side comment, the difference above explains why that it is easier to derive RC for many more algorithms than for ABFT. (In a few lines, we gave RC for three algorithms, and for ABFT, we barely explained how this concretely worked.) However, in the case of matrix-matrix multiplication and linear algebra in general, once RC and ABFT algorithms are implemented, the differences are not so clear any longer, and we find that the algorithms are often very close. We describe the design space as having three dimensions.

Dimension 1: Appending Checksums or Leaving Checksums Separate. The checksums (for example A_c) can either (case 1ab) be appended to the main matrix (e.g. as extra rows to A) or (case 1rc) left as separate independent blocks of vectors. On the one hand, for RC, the checksums are naturally separate from the matrices. On the other hand, ABFT has been presented with both possibilities. RC is always 1rc. ABFT can be 1ab (e.g., [2,10]) or 1rc (e.g., [18]).

One advantage of leaving the checksums separate from the matrices is to not change the data structures of the original (non fault-tolerant) code. This is much easier to accomplish from a software engineering point of view. One advantage of appending the checksum is to call kernels only once (on the extended data structure). The computation on the checksums is then processed at the same time as the computation on the main matrix. This can be much faster.

Dimension 2: Computing Checksums on Input Data Before Computation or After. If we compute the initial checksums before the matrix-matrix multiplication, we call this 2ab. If we compute the initial checksums after the matrix-matrix multiplication, we call this 2rc. The main distinction between 2ab and 2rc is not really when we compute checksums, but more whether we "can" recompute initial checksums after the main operation. Recomputing the initial checksums after the computation means that we are storing the input data, and we are not overwriting in the initial data with computation. In Numerical Linear Algebra, this is a significant constraints since we often have one operand that is in/out. If we perform 2rc, we must use backup (copy) of all in-out operands.

It seems that, in the literature, ABFT always compute the initial checksums before the computation. One advantage to compute the checksums after is to compute as many initial checksums as needed by the number of errors, which is useful to lower the overhead, and to avoid making any assumption on the maximum number of errors that will be encountered.

Dimension 3: Detect+Recompute or Detect+ Locate+Lazy-Recompute or Detect+Locate+Solve. Case 3rc: detect errors, and recompute the whole computation if some errors are detected 3rc. Case 3lo: detect errors, locate errors and recompute only the corrupted entries (also called *lazy recomputation* in [18].) Case 3ab: detect errors, locate errors and recover the corrupted entries from the redundant information in the checksum, we call this 3ab.

For 3lo and 3ab, in this paper, the localization is done through "coordinate checkpointing". 3lo assumes that entries can be recomputed somewhat easily from only the input data, and maybe some non-corrupted entries. It is not obvious that there are many kernels for which this is possible. Matrix-matrix multiplications is one such kernel. For 3ab, assuming that we can locate the errors, (through coordinate checkpointing, for example,) Chen and Dongarra [5,6] showed that taking random matrices enable to recover the solution with high probability during the linear solve to recover the corrupted entries.

Reed-Solomon encoding enables 3ab with either a row checksum or a column checksum, it does not require both row and column checksum. This is very useful for some operations. (Not matrix-matrix mutiplication though.) However the checksum block of vectors v and w are extremely ill-conditioned and leads to numerically unstable codes. We note that 2ab +3ab is the only way (in this design space) to overwrite in/out operands during the computation and recover from errors. All other methods needs to copy and store in/out operands to extra memory space to be able to recompute from the input in case an error occurs.

Which Dimension Distinguishes ABFT vs RC. Dimension 1: we can distinguish ABFT and RC by defining ABFT as appending checksums to matrices, and RC as having checksum separate from matrices. Dimension 2: we can distinguish ABFT and RC by defining ABFT as computing the initial checksums before computation, and RC as computing the initial checksums after computation. Dimension 3: we can distinguish ABFT and RC by defining RC as detecting and maybe locating errors, and following a detection by recomputation, and defining ABFT as recovering the corrupted entries, after detection and location, from the redundant information contained in the checksum.

3 Related Work

Multitudinous papers have been published on replication, ABFT and RC. A surveys on ABFT is provided in [3]. Due to lack of space, we refer to the extended version [11] for a more comprehensive overview. We have selected below a small set of closely related works, which we classify in Table 1 according to the criteria given in Sect. 2.

Table 1. Taxonomy of related work

Reference	1ab	2ab	3ab	1rc	2rc	3rc	3lo
[10][4]* [2]*	✓	✓	✓				
[14][7]				✓	✓	✓	
[1]				✓	✓	✓	
[18]		✓		✓			✓

*errors are failures and therefore the detection and localization of the error is known

4 Experiments

4.1 Implementations

We implemented variants of all the techniques discussed above. The implementation is in C, relying on the BLAS kernels for all linear algebra operations (namely GEMM and GEMV), and each hardened routine provides the same API as the GEMM routine defined by BLAS, but implements a different error detection and correction strategy. Here is the list of the six routines that we implemented, and that we compare in Sect. 4.3:

- NoFT is a reference point, and is a direct call to the GEMM routine provided by the BLAS library, without any error checking nor correction strategy.
- REPLICATION uses the most simple (and systematic approach): replication, as described in Sect. 2.1: the GEMM operation is computed twice, then resulting elements are compared one by one, and if an error is detected, the entire operation is computed a third time. Elements are then selected by a simple majority vote, and if no majority can be obtained for some element, the operation is applied again, until a pair of matching results can be found.

- ABFT-SOLVE (=1ab +2ab +3ab) is the traditional ABFT method: the input matrices are copied into larger matrices, that are extensions of the inputs with a fixed number of column and row checksums. These checksums are computed from the initial data, and the GEMM operation is applied on the extended matrix. After it completes, we check the checksums to detect errors. If errors are detected, a linear system of equations is solved [2, 4, 13, 16, 17] to compute the corrected values, and the resulting matrix is copied in the output parameter.
- ABFT-RECOMP (=1ab +2ab +3lo) follows the same strategy as ABFT-SOLVE to detect errors, but the matrix is extended with a single column and row as checksums. By crossing the columns in which the row-checksum is incorrect and the rows in which the column-checksum is incorrect, we extract a number of suspected wrong results, and we recompute only these elements from the input data. The result is checked (iterating another step of re-computation if needed), and copied back into the output parameter.
- RC-SOLVE (=1rc +2rc +3ab) uses the RC to compute the checksums (see Sect. 2.3): the GEMM operation is computed, and once it is computed, a single column checksum is generated randomly, and the routine compares how applying the output of GEMM on it differs from applying the two input matrices. If the result differs in any element, there is at least an error on the corresponding row(s). Additional checksums are then generated, until a system of linearly independent equations can be formed. That system is solved to correct the errors.
- RC-RECOMP (=1rc +2rc +3lo) uses the same approach as RC-SOLVE, until the correction phase is reached. When this is the case (there is at least one row with errors), a row-checksum is computed (as the column checksum was), and by crossing the row-checksum errors and the column-checksum errors, we can approximately locate suspected error locations. These elements of the output matrix are recomputed from the initial data to patch the result matrix which is returned by the routine.

4.2 Setup

For introducing errors in the operations, we use a parameter r which is the error rate of one floating-point operation. We compute the probability for an element to be erroneous, knowing it is the result of m operations: $P = 1 - (1 - r)^m$ and we modify each element that has been drawn to be corrupted by multiplying the element by a factor randomly chosen between 0.5 and 1.5, after doing the computation. We first apply this modification on all the elements of the matrix after the GEMM operation, with $m = 2n - 1$, because there are n multiplications and $n - 1$ additions per element when multiplying square matrices of size n. Then, for the recomputed elements of RC-RECOMP and ABFT-RECOMP implementations, we set $m = 2n - 1$ for each element that is recomputed from scratch and we check again the result. For RC-SOLVE and ABFT-SOLVE, $m = c^2$ where c is the number of corrupted columns in the matrix. Finally for REPLICATION, $m = 2n - 1$ for each element of every new matrix computed. In each experiment, the maximum duration of the hardened operation is bounded by 4 iterations of the applied check / correct procedure, and if the matrix is still corrupted at this point, the operation is considered failed. ABFT-SOLVE needs one additional parameter which is the number of checksums to add to the matrix: we set it to $2 \times 2N^3 r$ as $2N^3 r$ is the expected number of failures during the computation and we want a margin to tolerate more errors in bad scenarios. If ABFT-SOLVE cannot solve the system of equations, the operation is considered as failed.

We run the experiments with 16 cores out of a 20-core Intel Xeon CPU E5-2650 v3 at 2.30 GHz, with 64 GB of memory hosted at the University of Tennessee. The code is compiled with GCC 9.2.0, and the BLAS kernels where provided by Intel MKL version 2019.3.199. We evaluate both the sequential and multi-threaded versions of the algorithms. We run 100 iterations of each combination of implementations and parameters (the matrix size N and the error rate r) and we average the execution times of the different parts of the algorithm. *DGEMM* is the time spent doing the main operation (and subsequent DGEMMs for REPLICATION); *Check* is the time spent computing the checksums and finding the location of the errors; *Correct* is the time spent recomputing or solving the systems depending on the chosen implementation. We report the execution times when each of the 100 iterations succeeds; otherwise, we report the number of failed iterations. As a reference, we show the time to execute a GEMM on a $N \times N$ matrix without fault tolerance nor failure injection under the name NoFT. The source code of the implementations used for the experiments is available at https://github.com/vlefevre/abft-rescheck.

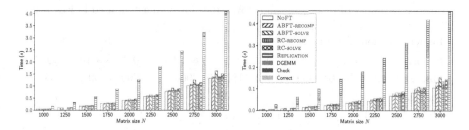

Fig. 1. Sequential (left) and multi-threaded (right) algorithms, error rate of 10^{-9}.

4.3   Results

Figure 1 describes the detailed execution of our 6 implementations for an error rate $r = 10^{-9}$ and a varying matrix size N. The first thing to notice is that replication is always the less efficient technique. Indeed, even without failures, two full DGEMM operations need to be executed to detect failures. Moreover, every time there is at least one error during the computation, we need to compute the resulting matrix a third times to correct it. It is enough to correct in most cases but the cost of a DGEMM operation, especially in sequential, is much bigger than the cost of a detection and the ensuing correction at this error rate.

The overheads of detecting and correcting errors for all methods but REPLI-CATION remain small, even when the matrix size (thus the number of errors) increases: there is only a small proportion of the output matrix that is corrupted, and thus the amount of recomputation or the size of the linear problem to solve to correct are small. Recomputation-based approaches, however, outperform significantly system-solving approaches.

The multi-threaded case shows the same characteristics overall, except the check time of REPLICATION is significantly increased, relative to the duration of the GEMMs. As checking for REPLICATION is a memory-bound problem, when all the cores access the memory simultaneously, the memory bus becomes the bottleneck and limits parallel efficiency. When N increases, both RC-SOLVE and ABFT-SOLVE are likely not to correct everything within 4 re-executions as the correction is done by solving linear systems of size c, the number of corrupted columns, hence with $O(c^3)$ flops. For a given error rate, increasing N will increase both the number of columns and the probability that it is corrupted. Thus the number of operations involved in the solve phase can quickly grow (c^2 compared to $2n - 1$) and require more iterations to finish. ABFT-SOLVE also does not always correct for small error rates or small matrix sizes (see Table 2). As the margin on the number of checksums to add is smaller, it becomes easy to have more errors than what we estimated despite the factor 2 to the expected number of failed operations. This risk is managed by the RC-SOLVE implementation as the checksums are computed after failures hit the initial DGEMM operation, and thus the exact minimal number of checksums is used.

Table 2. Number of failed iterations (over 100) for parameters used in Fig. 1, 2.

Implementation	ABFT-SOLVE							RC-SOLVE	
Error rate r	10^{-10}	10^{-9}				8×10^{-9}	10^{-8}	8×10^{-9}	10^{-8}
Matrix size N	3000	500	750	1000	1250	3000	3000	3000	3000
Sequential	4	2	23	0	7	1	3	11	78
Multi-threaded	3	2	24	4	3	0	4	15	81

Figure 2 shows the same measurements, but with a fixed problem size ($N = 3000$) and a varying error rate. The Solve-based approaches do not produce results at 8×10^{-9} and 10^{-8} error rates in the sequential case, and ABFT-SOLVE only produce an output in a very long time in the multithreaded case with an error rate of 8×10^{-9}. As the number of columns including errors gets closer to N, the size of the system to solve becomes closer to the size of the original matrix. Since errors can also impact these computations, with a higher probability, the solve-based approaches fail, leading to repeated iterations of the correction process. For low error rates, RC-RECOMP and ABFT-RECOMP are the two best performing algorithms and behave very similarly. The main difference between them is that RC-RECOMP is easier (1) to set up since the

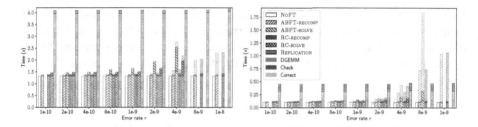

Fig. 2. Sequential (left) and multi-threaded (right) algorithms, matrix size 3000.

check is done after the main computation and does not depend on the algorithm (for detection) and (2) to use as a blackbox for the user with no conversion of data needed. This last point is important as a user-friendly library would take as input $N \times N$ matrices and ABFT needs to add some extra steps to compute a bigger matrix with the checksums in it. The additional memory allocations and copies can quickly increase the execution time and memory footprint, if only a few DGEMM operations are done in a row.

However, as the error rate increases, the recomputation-based approaches start to show slower corrections. This is particularly visible in the multi-threaded case: REPLICATION eventually outperforms RC-RECOMP and ABFT-RECOMP. To explained this: first, REPLICATION's efficiency is independent from the error rate, because errors hit independent elements in the 3 computed matrices; second, as the number of errors in the matrix gets closer to N^2, the recomputation algorithm is less efficient than re-doing a fully optimized GEMM: it implements a parallel loop over the failed elements of sequential dot products. In the multi-threaded case, this is less efficient than recomputing the entire GEMM.

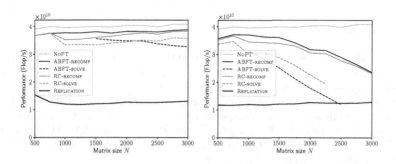

Fig. 3. Performance of the algorithms for $r = 10^{-9}$ (left) and $r = 10^{-8}$ (right).

We sum up these results in Fig. 3. We represent here the performance of the operations, as the ratio between $2N^3$ (the number of floating point operations in a GEMM) and the execution time of the sequential algorithms. It is clearly visible that the error rate has no influence on REPLICATION while ABFT-RECOMP and

RC-RECOMP are the two best performing algorithms and their performance is equivalent. We also see that their performance stays close to that of NoFT as long as both r and N do not become too big. See the extended version [11] for a similar figure where the matrix size is fixed and the error rate is varied.

5 Conclusion

In this paper, we have reviewed and compared ABFT and Residual Checking (RC) for detecting and correcting floating-point errors in matrix multiplication. On the theoretical side, we have detailed both methods, their variants, their common characteristics and their differences. On the practical side, we have implemented two variants for error correction in each method, one based on solving a small linear system, and one based on recomputing only corrupted elements, using coordinate checksumming to locate them. An extensive experimental comparison reveals similar execution times for the core of each method, but ABFT requires to embed the checksum in the user data in order to benefit from the high performance kernel implementation, while RC does not. The flexibility of RC becomes very important when error rates are high, because RC can adapt a posteriori to the number of errors encountered within each particular execution. ABFT requires a fixed number of checksums which will rarely match the exact number of errors striking in a given run. This overhead is acceptable when the number of errors is smaller than expected, but it leads to the failing of the method when the number of errors is higher than this threshold. To summarize, we point out that RC can be extended to correct silent errors in addition to detecting them, in a flexible and adaptive way, and without the burden of the extra memory allocation required by ABFT. Future work will be devoted to extending the approaches to other linear algebra kernels, and to protect from memory corruptions in addition to floating-point errors.

References

1. Argyrides, C., Lisboa, C.A.L., Pradhan, D.K., Carro, L.: A fast error correction technique for matrix multiplication algorithms. In: 15th International On-Line Testing Symposium, pp. 133–137. IEEE (2009)
2. Bosilca, G., Delmas, R., Dongarra, J., Langou, J.: Algorithm-based fault tolerance applied to high performance computing. J. Par. Dist. Comput. **69**, 410–416 (2009)
3. Bouteiller, A., Herault, T., Bosilca, G., Du, P., Dongarra, J.J.: Algorithm-based fault tolerance for dense matrix factorizations, multiple failures and accuracy. ACM Trans. Parallel Comput. 1(2), 1–28 (2015)
4. Chen, Z., Dongarra, J.: Algorithm-based checkpoint-free fault tolerance for parallel matrix multiplications on volatile resources. In: Proceedings IPDPS. IEEE (2006)
5. Chen, Z., Dongarra, J.J.: Condition numbers of gaussian random matrices. SIAM J. Matrix Analysis Appl. **27**(3), 603–620 (2005)
6. Chen, Z., Dongarra, J.: Numerically stable real number codes based on random matrices. In: Sunderam, V.S., van Albada, G.D., Sloot, P.M.A., Dongarra, J.J. (eds.) ICCS 2005. LNCS, vol. 3514, pp. 115–122. Springer, Heidelberg (2005). https://doi.org/10.1007/11428831_15

7. Gunnels, J., Katz, D., Quintana-Ortí, E., Van de Geijn, R.: Fault-tolerant high-performance matrix multiplication: Theory and practice. In: Proceedings of Dependable Systems and Networks (DSN), pp. 47–56 (2001)
8. Herault, T., Robert, Y. (eds.): Fault-Tolerance Techniques for High-Performance Computing. CCN. Springer, Cham (2015). https://doi.org/10.1007/978-3-319-20943-2
9. Higham, N.J., Mary, T.: A new approach to probabilistic rounding error analysis. SIAM J. Sci. Comput. **41**(5), A2815–A2835 (2019)
10. Huang, K., Abraham, J.: Algorithm-based fault tolerance for matrix operations. IEEE Trans. Comput. **33**, 518–528 (1984)
11. Le Fèvre, V., Herault, T., Langou, J., Robert, Y.: A comparison of several fault-tolerance methods for the detection and correction of floating-point errors in matrix-matrix multiplication. Research report RR-9351, INRIA, June 2020
12. Lyons, R.E., Vanderkulk, W.: The use of triple-modular redundancy to improve computer reliability. IBM J. Res. Dev. **6**(2), 200–209 (1962)
13. Plank, J.S.: A tutorial on Reed-Solomon coding for fault-tolerance in RAID-like systems. Softw. Pract. Exp. **27**(9), 995–1012 (1997)
14. Prata, P., Silva, J.G.: Algorithm based fault tolerance versus result-checking for matrix computations. In: 29th International Symposium Fault-Tolerant Computing, pp. 4–11 (1999)
15. Prata, P., Silva, J.G.: Fault-detection by result-checking for the eigenproblem. In: Hlavička, J., Maehle, E., Pataricza, A. (eds.) EDCC 1999. LNCS, vol. 1667, pp. 419–436. Springer, Heidelberg (1999). https://doi.org/10.1007/3-540-48254-7_28
16. Reed, I.S., Solomon, G.: Polynomial codes over certain finite fields. J. Soc. Ind. Appl. Math. **8**(2), 300–304 (1960)
17. Roy-Chowdhury, A., Banerjee, P.: Algorithm-based fault location and recovery for matrix computations on multiprocessor systems. Trans. Comput. **45**(11), 1239–1247 (1996)
18. Smith, T.M., van de Geijn, R.A., Smelyanskiy, M., Quintana-Ortí, E.S.: Towards ABFT for BLIS GEMM. Tech. Rep. 76, FLAME Working Note, June 2015

Complementary Papers

Complementary Papers

The Euro-Par workshops presented in this volume were selected out of submissions made in February. Given the special circumstances as a consequence of the COVID-19 pandemic, the number of submissions was lower than usual, specially for two of the workshops. In fact, the final number of papers accepted by their respective program committees was found to be too low by the Euro-Par workshop organization committee to deserve their organization at the conference. However, even though these two workshops were not formally organized, the papers were also presented for the interest of the audience. We call these papers "complementary papers".

Here is the list of complementary papers:

- "HugeMap: Optimizing Memory-mapped I/O with Huge Pages for Fast Storage". Ioannis Malliotakis, Anastasios Papagiannis, Manolis Marazakis and Angelos Bilas. Presented at the ParaMo workshop.
- "A New Parallel Methodology for the Network Analysis of COVID-19 Data". Giuseppe Agapito, Marianna Milano and Mario Cannataro. Presented at the PDCLifeS workshop.
- "Analysis of Genome Architecture Mapping Data with a Machine Learning and Polymer-Physics-based Tool". Luca Fiorillo, Mattia Conte, Andrea Esposito, Francesco Musella, Francesco Flora, Andrea Maria Chiariello and Simona Bianco. Presented at the PDCLifeS workshop.

We would like to thank the organizers of the workshops which attracted and selected these complementary papers for their work. Their dedication fully contributed to the overall quality of the scientific program of the Euro-Par workshops. We would also like to thank the organizers of the hosting workshop ParaMo, who included one of these complementary papers in their program, providing the authors with the scientific visibility they deserve. Finally, we would like to express our commitment to providing all participants, the authors as well as the attendees, with the best environment for their scientific advances. The committees of these two workshops are detailed below.

Organization

Workshop on Challenges and Opportunities of HPC Storage Systems (CHAOSS)

Organizing Committee

Michael Kuhn — University of Magdeburg, Germany
Kira Duwe — University of Magdeburg, Germany
Margaret Lawson — University of Illinois at Urbana-Champaign, USA
Jay Lofstead — Sandia National Laboratories, USA
Johann Lombardi — Intel Corporation, France

Program Committee

Konstantinos Chasapis — DDN, France
Andreas Dilger — Whamcloud, Canada
Kira Duwe — University of Magdeburg, Germany
Wolfgang Frings — Jülich Supercomputing Centre, Germany
Elsa Gonsiorowski — Lawrence Livermore National Laboratory, USA
Anthony Kougkas — Illinois Institute of Technology, USA
Michael Kuhn — University of Magdeburg, Germany
Margaret Lawson — University of Illinois at Urbana-Champaign, USA
Jay Lofstead — Sandia National Laboratories, USA
Johann Lombardi — Intel Corporation, France
Jakob Lüttgau — German Climate Computing Center, Germany
Anna Queralt — Barcelona Supercomputing Center, Spain
Yue Zhu — Florida State University, USA

Parallel and Distributed Computing for Life Sciences:
Algorithms, Methodologies, and Tools (PDCLifeS)

Organizing Committee

Laura Antonelli	National Research Council of Italy, Italy
Salvatore Cuomo	University of Naples Federico II, Italy

Program Committee

Andrew Adamatzky	University of the West of England, UK
Stefano Berrone	Politecnico di Torino, Italy
Mario Cannataro	Università Magna Graecia, Catanzaro, Italy
Claudia Di Napoli	National Research Council, Italy
Daniela di Serafino	Università della Campania "Luigi Vanvitelli," Italy
Sébastien Limet	Université d'Orléans, France
Lucia Maddalena	National Research Council, Italy
Mario Nicodemi	Università degli Studi di Napoli Federico II, Italy
Domenico Talia	Università della Calabria, Italy
Nicola Tonellotto	University of Pisa, Italy
Carsten Trinitis	Technical University of Munich, Germany
José Carlos Valverde	University of Castilla-La Mancha, Spain
Pierangelo Veltri	Università Magna Graecia, Italy

Analysis of Genome Architecture Mapping Data with a Machine Learning and Polymer-Physics-Based Tool

Luca Fiorillo[iD], Mattia Conte, Andrea Esposito, Francesco Musella, Francesco Flora, Andrea M. Chiariello[(⊠)] [iD], and Simona Bianco[(⊠)] [iD]

Dipartimento di Fisica, Università di Napoli Federico II, and INFN Napoli, Complesso Universitario di Monte Sant'Angelo, 80126 Naples, Italy
{chiariello,simona.bianco}@na.infn.it

Abstract. Understanding the mechanisms driving the folding of chromosomes in nuclei is a major goal of modern Molecular Biology. Recent technological advances in microscopy (FISH, STORM) and sequencing approaches (Hi-C, GAM, SPRITE) enabled to collect quantitative data about chromatin 3D architecture, revealing a non-random and highly specific organization. To transform such tremendous amount of data into valuable insights on genome folding, heavy computational analyses are required. Here, we study the performances of PRISMR, a computational tool based on Machine Learning strategies and Polymer Physics principles, to explore genome 3D structure from Genome Architecture Mapping (GAM) data. Using such data, we show that PRISMR can successfully reconstruct the 3D structure of real genomic regions at various length scales, from mega-base sized loci to whole chromosomes. Importantly, the inferred structures are validated against independent Hi-C data. Finally, we show how PRISMR can be effectively employed to explore differences between experimental methods.

Keyword: Chromatin organization · Machine learning · GAM

1 Introduction

In cell nuclei, chromosomes are organized in a very complex architecture. In recent years, the three-dimensional (3D) structure of chromosomes has been investigated by novel, sophisticated technologies. These include sequencing methods – such as Hi-C [1], Genome Architecture Mapping (GAM) [2], SPRITE [3] - able to detect contacts between pairs of DNA sites genome-wide; microscopy techniques, measuring distances between loci in specific DNA regions [4, 5]. The huge amount of data produced by all these technologies has shown that the 3D organization of chromosome, far from being random, plays a key role for gene activity and transcriptional regulation [6–8]. For instance, it has been shown that chromosomes segregate in specific territories inside nuclei [9] and functional loops occur between promoters and enhancers [10]. Also, interactions are enriched within specific, mega-based sized regions (named topologically associated domains or, shortly, TADs [11, 12]). At larger scales, higher-order spatial patterns like

© Springer Nature Switzerland AG 2021
B. Balis et al. (Eds.): Euro-Par 2020 Workshops, LNCS 12480, pp. 321–332, 2021.
https://doi.org/10.1007/978-3-030-71593-9_25

metaTADs [13] or A/B compartments [1] are found and span tens of mega-bases or entire chromosomes. All these structural features are strongly linked to genome activity [14–16]. However, many aspects of DNA 3D organization remain unclear and the key mechanisms leading to the formation of loops, TADs and so on are currently debated.

To explain the chromosome folding patterns in a coherent framework, Polymer Physics models have been proposed and provided insightful information on chromatin architecture and its folding mechanisms [17, 18]. Furthermore, their combination with the above-mentioned experimental data allowed to increase the accuracy of the description of real genomes. On the other hand, heavy computational efforts are needed to achieve reliable 3D reconstructions [19] and complex computational procedures based, e.g., on Monte Carlo or Molecular Dynamics (MD) simulations, have been developed [20–22].

In the present work, we show how the computational method PRISMR (polymer-based recursive statistical inference method) [21], based on Polymer Physics laws, can be applied on GAM data to infer the 3D structure of chromatin. We summarize the backbone features of the PRISMR algorithm and shortly review its performances when applied on Hi-C data. Since notable computational power is required to the procedure, as massive parallel MD simulations are performed, we describe the usage of High Performance Computing (HPC), involved as in typical other applications [19]. Then, we show how the method can be generally extended to work with different experimental technologies and focus on its application on GAM data [23]. To test the performances of the approach, we show the results from the model of a 6 Mb locus around the *Sox9* gene in mouse embryonic stem cells (mESC, GAM data from [2]). Overall, the 3D structures derived by PRISMR successfully reproduce the input GAM data and match independent Hi-C experimental data [12]. Then, we describe the application of PRISMR on the entire chromosome 7 in mESC [23] and show how the inferred structure can be employed to study the relationship of genomic regions of interest with the surrounding environment. Finally, we briefly discuss how the 3D structures derived *in-silico* by PRISMR can be used to benchmark experimental technologies as GAM and Hi-C, highlighting the potential role that such computational approaches can have in helping the design of experiments. More generally, in this contribution we highlight how the combination of Theoretical Physics, Molecular Biology experimental data and powerful HPC resources allow investigating 3D genome architecture with an increasing level of accuracy [18].

2   The PRISMR Method and Its Extension for GAM Data

2.1   Overview of the PRISMR Method

The PRISMR method is a computational tool designed [21] to derive the 3D structure of a genomic locus starting from experimental data containing its structural features (Fig. 1a). Specifically, PRISMR employs experimental data detecting the pattern of contacts among DNA sites of the considered locus. To deconvolute the architectural information encoded in the data and produce physically meaningful structures, PRISMR is informed with the principles of a Polymer-Physics model of chromatin. Here we use the *Strings&Binders Switch* (SBS) model [24], but any other could be, in principle, employed. The SBS model is based on the biological scenario where diffusive molecules, as transcription factors (TFs), bind to the DNA string and drive its folding. It describes the DNA filament as a self-avoiding walk polymeric chain where diffusive particles called *binders* can attach. Binders can only interact with specific beads of the polymeric chain, known as *binding sites*, and they can attach to more than one binding site simultaneously. In this way, binders allow for the formation of loops between distal polymer sites, driving the spatial conformation of the chain. In general, different types of binding sites can be used with homotypic interaction, i.e. binders can only anchor to the cognate binding sites. The different types of binding sites can be schematically visualized as different colors and all the same colored binding sites along the chain define a *binding domain*. The number of colors of an SBS polymer, the arrangement of binding sites along the chain and the concentration of their respective binders determine the folding properties of the polymer model, that is its possible equilibrium 3D configurations [19, 25, 26]. The equilibrium configurations can be employed as proxy for the real conformations of a genomic locus in nuclei.

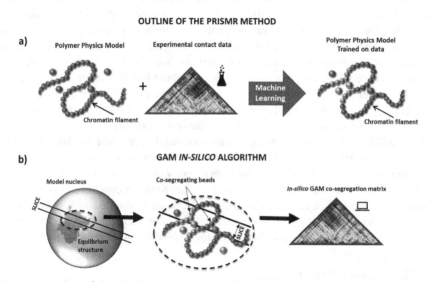

Fig. 1. a) Outline of the PRISMR method [21]. Informed with a Polymer-Physics model of chromatin, PRISMR finds the best polymer to describe a given genomic region. This is done by a Machine Learning approach, i.e. training the polymer model over specific experimental contact data of the region, as Hi-C [1] or GAM [2]. **b)** To use PRISMR on GAM data, an algorithm simulating the GAM experimental method on 3D polymer structures was prepared. Briefly, cell nuclei are modelled as spheres, each one containing a 3D structure. A random plane is generated to simulate a real GAM nuclear profile (NP) for every sphere. Beads inside the simulated NP are counted and hence the segregation frequencies extracted (see text). Finally, the co-segregation frequencies whereby two beads were found in the same simulated NP are arranged in the *in-silico* co-segregation matrix. Adapted from [23].

Given a DNA locus of interest, PRISMR aims to find the best polymer model describing it, that is the best number and arrangements of colors for the SBS polymer chain. The input of PRISMR is the experimental contact data associated to the locus. Typically, they are arranged in a matrix containing the contact frequencies between any pairs of DNA sites. Using a Simulated Annealing Monte-Carlo procedure, PRISMR scans through the huge space of all possible SBS polymer models minimizing a cost function H that measures the difference between the input data and the model contact matrix.

Once the best polymer model is found, its equilibrium 3D structures are obtained by massive parallel Molecular Dynamics (MD) simulations. Typically, the polymer is prepared in a SAW state inside a simulation box and binders are randomly placed in the environment. The simulation is then performed until thermodynamic equilibrium is reached. This is repeated for a large number (hundreds) of independent polymers, so to eventually obtain an ensemble of equilibrium 3D structures. The parameters used (such as the profile of the homotypic bead-binder interaction, the concentration of binders and binding affinity) are described in classical polymer physics studies [27] and are widely used in the field [28, 29].

In order to deal with the large number of particles of an SBS system (typically $10^3 \div 10^4$ for a few mega-base sized locus) and to produce a reliable statistical sampling of the configurations space, High Performance Computing (HPC) resources are needed. To give a sense of the resources involved, a single run with a generic software optimized for parallel computing (as LAMMPS [30]) requires in general a number of processors ranging from 8 to 64, with a time limit of at least 24–48 h, necessary to achieve thermodynamic equilibrium. Additionally, as said, about hundred independent runs are performed to get the final equilibrium ensemble. So, the production of an ensemble of 3D structures through MD simulations is the most computational demanding step and makes the use of HPC one of the key tools for the overall strategy.

The PRISMR procedure has been proven successful in reproducing Hi-C data [26, 31, 32], in predicting the impact of mutations and structural variants [21, 33] and in explaining cell-to-cell structural variability as recently detected in microscopy [34]. We will review in the next sections how PRISMR can work successfully also on GAM data [23]. We recall that other methods have also been developed to reconstruct 3D genome structure, e.g. using polymer models informed with epigenetic data [35, 36] or optimization procedures of restraints given directly by the contact data [37, 38].

2.2 The *in-silico* GAM Algorithm

As explained above, the cost function of PRISMR compares the input experimental contact matrix with the matrix of the polymer model. Thus, it requires an algorithm capable to extract a contact matrix from the 3D structures of a given polymer model and, specifically, the contact matrix must be of the same kind of the input. Hence, for the application on GAM data, an algorithm simulating the generation of a GAM matrix from polymer structures was prepared.

In GAM experiments [2] a random nuclear profile (NP) is cut from each cell of a population. The genomic content of each NP is then sequenced and all the DNA loci are counted. A locus caught in a NP is defined as *segregated*. Hence, the segregation table is extracted, i.e. a table whereby the loci found for each NP are reported. From this, the *co-segregation* frequencies for pairs, triplets etc. of loci in the same NP can be derived. The pairwise co-segregation frequencies are usually arranged in the *co-segregation matrix*. To account for biases as different sequencing mappability, co-segregation matrices can be normalized, e.g. with the *linkage disequilibrium normalization* D' [23]. These matrices can be used as input for PRISMR to find the best polymer structures of a given DNA region.

In order to adapt the PRISMR procedure on GAM data, we realized an *in-silico* version of the GAM pipeline [23]. Precisely, we model cell nuclei as individual spheres containing a polymer 3D structure (Fig. 1b). Then, a plane with random orientation is generated in each sphere and all the beads of the polymer distant from the plane less than a threshold are counted as segregating. This step simulates the NPs extraction and sequencing. Then, the *in-silico* segregation table is generated, the co-segregation frequencies are computed and arranged in a co-segregation *in-silico* matrix, and eventually normalized. The threshold distance from the random plane is set according to the thickness of experimental NPs [2] and the sphere radius is fixed to match typical cell radius estimates taken from mESC cells [2]. In mESC, cell nuclei can be well approximated as spheres, while, for other cell lines, different nuclear geometries can be implemented.

3   The *Sox9* Locus Explored with GAM Data

To test PRISMR on GAM data, we focused on the *Sox9* locus in mESC (data from [2]), i.e. a 6 Mb long region centered around the *Sox9* gene (chr11:109–115 Mb, mm9 genome assembly). Specifically, we applied PRISMR on both the co-segregation and D' normalized GAM data of the *Sox9* locus at 40kb resolution (see Fig. 2a, b, top matrices). The comparison between the PRISMR GAM matrix with the input experimental data is very good in both the co-segregation and D' applications (Fig. 2a, b), as witnessed by the high values of the Pearson (r) and the Stratum Adjusted (scc) [39] correlation coefficients ($r = 0.93$ and $scc = 0.96$ for the co-segregation matrices, while $r = 0.86$ and $scc = 0.97$ for the D' case). These values, together with the visual inspection of the matrices, show that PRISMR results effective on GAM co-segregation as well D' normalized data. To test the robustness of the procedure, we compared the polymer models obtained from the two cases (co-segregation and D'). Importantly, the two best SBS polymers have the same number of colors and appear to have similar arrangements of the binding sites (Fig. 2a, b middle panels). Indeed, we computed the genomic overlap q between the binding domains in the two models, defined as the normalized integral along the locus of the product of the number of their binding sites. We find that the most overlapping domains (equally colored in Fig. 2a,b) have an average overlap $q = 0.70$. As control, we did the same for bootstrapped binding domains, getting $q = 0.47$, which is significantly lower (p-value $= 3e-6$, Mann-Whitney U test). This implies that the PRISMR procedure is robust, as it derives compatible polymer models when fed with raw or normalized GAM data. Also, this indicates that the SBS best polymer can work as a solid model for the 3D structures of a given genomic region.

We then generated a population with up to $5 * 10^2$ equilibrium configurations for the polymer model trained on the co-segregation GAM data, using massive parallel MD simulations. Minute computational details of the simulations can be found in [23]. To test the accuracy of our GAM-derived polymer structures, we computed the contact matrix [26] from them, that is the matrix containing the frequencies whereby pairs of beads are in contact. The contact between two beads is called when their distance is less than a

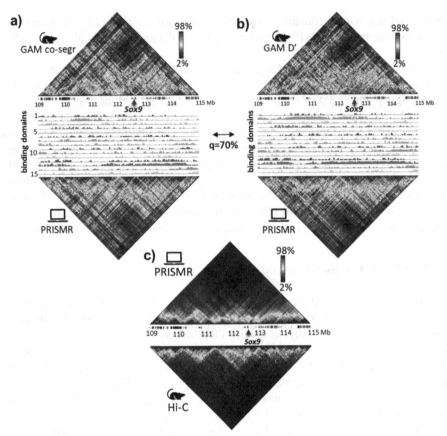

Fig. 2. As first application on GAM data [23], PRISMR was run over the data [2] of the *Sox9* locus (chr11:109–115 Mb) of mESC at 40 kb. **a)** PRISMR is fed with the experimental GAM co-segregation matrix of the locus. In each of these cases, we obtained the best SBS polymer model (Fig. a, b, middle diagrams) and the corresponding *in-silico* GAM matrix (Fig. a, b, bottom matrices). On the top the experimental matrix, on the bottom the PRISMR derived matrix. Color bars indicate the percentiles of the matrices. In the middle, the binding domains found by PRISMR along the best SBS polymer of the locus are shown. The comparison between the two matrices is good ($r = 0.93$ and $scc = 0.96$), as proof of PRISMR effectiveness. **b)** Same as in panel a), but the input experimental matrix is the D' normalized [2] GAM matrix of the *Sox9* locus. Again, the comparison between experiment and model is nice ($r = 0.86$ and $scc = 0.97$). The binding domains found by PRISMR in this case (middle) and those found in the co-segregation case (panel a) have an average overlap $q = 0.70$ (see text). This is significantly higher than a random control case (p-value 3e−6, Mann-Whitney U test), meaning PRISMR inference is very robust to the input data. **c)** To further test the solidity of PRISMR, we considered the 3D structures derived from the co-segregation GAM matrix and extracted an *in-silico* Hi-C matrix from them (top), using an algorithm developed in [26]. We compare this matrix with independent Hi-C data of the same locus [12] (bottom). Strikingly, we get good similarity ($r = 0.90$ and $scc = 0.51$). Adapted from [23].

threshold [26]. Such *in-silico* contact matrix is compared with completely independent Hi-C data [12] for the same *Sox9* genomic locus in mESC, at 40 kb resolution. The comparison reveals good agreement (Fig. 2c), with r = 0.90 and scc = 0.51. This result further supports the robustness of our computational approach when used on GAM data and, importantly, supports the accuracy in the description of the *Sox9* locus from the produced 3D structures.

4   The Chromosome 7 Explored with GAM Data

Here, we show the application of PRISMR trained on GAM data for the entire chromosome 7, in mESC (data from [2]). We used D' GAM data at 250 kb resolution. In line with the previously discussed results, the experimental D' (Fig. 3a, top) and the PRISMR *in-silico* (Fig. 3a, bottom) matrices are similar, with r = 0.67 and scc = 0.96, showing that PRISMR achieves good results even for a system with higher complexity than a locus. As before, from the best SBS polymer (Fig. 3a, middle panel), a population of $5 * 10^2$ equilibrium 3D configurations was derived by use of MD simulations [23]. In Fig. 3b an example of 3D configuration of chromosome 7 is shown, colored according to the color scheme reported in Fig. 3a. From the population of 3D structures, relevant information about specific loci can be extracted, such as the relative location of biologically interesting regions with respect to the architecture of the overall chromosome. In this way, it is possible to reveal systematic tendencies to localize in peripheric or internal positions and, therefore, the possibility to form contacts with other chromosomes. Knowing the preferred contact pattern can be fundamental to understand the impact of mutations occurring on the studied region. We performed this analysis for the mouse orthologue of the human 16p.11.2 locus (chr7: 133.84:134.24 Mb, mm9 genome assembly), which is an interesting region for biomedicine since its mutations (as duplications or deletions) have been associated to the autism disorder [40, 41]. In Fig. 3b the 16p.11.2 locus is marked in red and appears to localize in a peripherical position. To quantitatively understand the preferential localization of the 16p.11.2 locus across all the polymer structures, we computed the distribution of the distance (r) between the locus center of mass and the center of mass of the whole chromosome. Specifically, working with a 250 kb resolution, we took the center of mass of a 2 Mb segment around the 16p.11.2 locus (chr7:133–135 Mb, mm9 genome assembly). Then we normalized dividing by the gyration radius of the chromosome (*location ratio* r/Rg, Fig. 3c). A location ratio larger than 1 indicates a peripheral position, while a value lower than 1 would imply a more internal position inside the chromosome structure. In Fig. 3c we show the distribution of location ratios obtained from the population of structures. We compare against a control case computed for other 300 random loci, all 2Mb sized. The two distributions are not compatible (p-value = 0.01, Mann-Whitney U test), as the histogram of 16p.11.2 is shifted toward higher values. This suggests that the 16p.11.2 tends to be more peripheral than the control. Furthermore, in 10% cases the location ratio of the 16p.11.2 is greater than 1.5, i.e. located in the very periphery of the chromosome. This suggests such locus can give raise to important and functional contacts with other chromosomes nearby. Deeper studies as this, with PRISMR used on increased resolved data, could lead to the rigorous tracking of the contact network for the 16p.11.2. Finally,

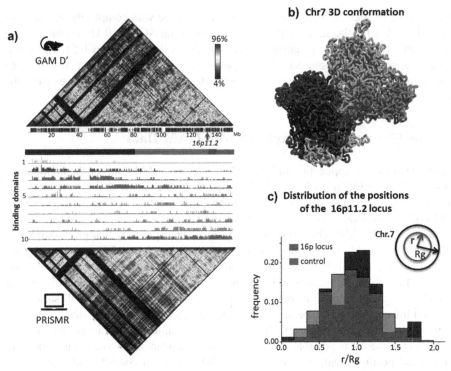

Fig. 3. The PRISMR method was used on the D' normalized GAM data [2] of the chromosome 7 in mESC [23] at 250 kb resolution. **a)** The input experimental matrix of the chromosome is compared against the PRISMR one. Visually and quantitatively they are similar to each other (r = 0.67 and scc = 0.96). In the middle, the binding domains found along the polymer model of the chromosome are reported. **b)** An example of 3D structure inferred by PRISMR is shown. The polymer is colored according to the bar in panel a), under the top matrix. In red, a 2 Mb region (chr7:113–135Mb) containing the mouse orthologue of the human 16p.11.2 locus (chr7:133.85–134.24 Mb). **c)** An example of usage of the PRISMR derived 3D structures. The distribution (blue) of the *location ratio* r/Rg (see text) of the 16p.11.2 mouse orthologue locus across all PRISMR structures is plotted against a control distribution (gray), showing the location ratio for 300 randomly chosen loci of the same size. The distributions are not compatible (p-value = 0.01, Mann-Whitney U test), so that the 16p.11.2 location ratio results shifted toward higher values, indicating more likelihood to be peripheral in the chromosome architecture than the control. This suggests the 16p.11.2 mouse orthologue can establish significant contacts with adjacent chromosomes. Adapted from [23]. (Color figure online)

we note that for both the control case and the specific 16p.11.2 locus, the ratio between standard deviation and the average value is rather high (approximately 36%), hinting that there is a significant structural variability in the conformations. This is in agreement with recent experimental findings highlighting the high degree of structural variability of specific loci among different cells [4, 34, 42].

5 PRISMR-Derived Structures to Compare Different Technologies

In this last section, we compare the results of the PRISMR approach on data from different experimental technologies. To this aim, we consider the ensemble of 3D structures of the *Sox9* locus inferred by PRISMR from GAM data [23] and the ensemble of 3D structures of the same locus derived from Hi-C data in another study [26]. The two *in-silico* populations of structures can be compared rigorously and could be used to understand the differences between the Hi-C and GAM technologies in detecting information about DNA 3D organization [43].

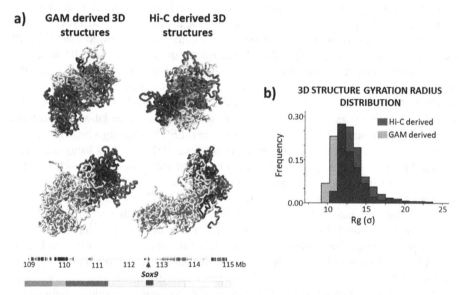

Fig. 4. The structures derived by PRISMR can be interestingly employed to compare experimental technologies, as Hi-C [12] and GAM [2]. **a)** Examples of 3D structures for both the Hi-C and GAM derived cases are shown. Structures are colored according to bar in the bottom, which follows the TADs detected in [12]. These examples of configurations are visually comparable to each other. **b)** The distribution of the gyration radius across the 3D structures is computed. The GAM distribution (red) and the Hi-C distribution (blue) have the same shape, yet the former is shifted to the left, suggesting higher average compaction. Interestingly, such difference could be explored to understand if it reveals differences in how Hi-C and GAM «see» DNA 3D organization [43]. Adapted from [23]. (Color figure online)

For instance, given the 3D structures from Hi-C and GAM, we can compare their geometry by computing the average distance matrix, containing the average Euclidean distances between each possible pair of polymer beads. Comparison between the Hi-C and GAM derived distance matrices reveals good agreement, with r ~ 0.95 and scc ~ 0.60. Conversely, intrinsic differences between the technologies can lower the agreement between the inferred structures at deeper detail than the average distances and could be further explored [43]. In Fig. 4a we show examples of structures taken from the two ensembles and they look, overall, qualitatively similar. The distributions of the gyration radius are quite similar to each other too (Fig. 4b), although GAM structures exhibit slightly lower values.

6 Conclusions

We have shown that PRISMR, a Machine Learning computational method that combines Polymer Physics and data from different experimental methods, can be effectively employed to infer the possible 3D structures of real genomic regions. Among the possible datasets today available, this can be achieved using Genome Architecture Mapping (GAM) data, a recent technique based on sectioning cell nuclear profiles and sequencing their genomic content [2]. We have described the application of PRISMR on GAM data for a 6 Mb locus in mouse embryonic stem cells [2] and showed that PRISMR successfully reproduced the input data. Furthermore, the GAM-derived 3D structures are then used to generate an *in-silico* contact matrix which results compatible with independent Hi-C data [12], supporting the generality and robustness of the computational approach. Next, we showed that the procedure can be extended to study systems with higher complexity as entire chromosomes. So, we generated a population of structures describing chromosome 7 using again GAM data in mESC [2]. Taking advantage of that, we studied the radial position of the mouse orthologue of the 16p.11.2 locus and found a general trend to localize in the peripherical region of the chromosome, with possible implications on its regulation. Finally, we tested the robustness of the 3D reconstruction by comparing the structures inferred from GAM [2] and Hi-C data [12] of the *Sox9* locus and found that both models yield similar results. Differences in the polymer population likely reflect intrinsic differences between the two experimental technologies [43].

The perspective is that sophisticated computational tools combining Machine Learning, Polymer Physics and massively parallel Molecular Dynamics simulations, such as the PRISMR method, will become more and more effective to interpret the constantly increasing amount of data generated by experimental technology, shedding light on the mechanism regulating genome folding.

References

1. Lieberman-Aiden, E., et al.: Comprehensive mapping of long-range interactions reveals folding principles of the human genome. Science **80**(326), 289–293 (2009)
2. Beagrie, R.A., et al.: Complex multi-enhancer contacts captured by genome architecture mapping. Nature **543**, 519–524 (2017)
3. Quinodoz, S.A., et al.: Higher-order inter-chromosomal hubs shape 3D genome organization in the nucleus. Cell **174**, 744-757.e24 (2018)
4. Bintu, B., et al.: Super-resolution chromatin tracing reveals domains and cooperative interactions in single cells. Science **80**(362), eaau1783 (2018)
5. Cardozo Gizzi, A.M., et al.: Microscopy-based chromosome conformation capture enables simultaneous visualization of genome organization and transcription in intact organisms. Mol. Cell. **74**, 212-222.e5 (2019)
6. Misteli, T.: Beyond the sequence: cellular organization of genome function. Cell **128**(4), 787–800 (2007)

7. Bickmore, W.A.: The spatial organization of the human genome. Annu. Rev. Genomics Hum. Genet. **14**, 67–84 (2013)
8. Finn, E.H., Misteli, T.: Molecular basis and biological function of variability in spatial genome organization. Science **365**(6457), eaaw9498 (2019)
9. Cremer, T., Cremer, M.: Chromosome territories (2010)
10. Rao, S.S.P., et al.: A 3D map of the human genome at kilobase resolution reveals principles of chromatin looping. Cell **159**, 1665–1680 (2014)
11. Nora, E.P., et al.: Spatial partitioning of the regulatory landscape of the X-inactivation centre. Nature **485**, 381–385 (2012)
12. Dixon, J.R., et al.: Topological domains in mammalian genomes identified by analysis of chromatin interactions. Nature **485**, 376–380 (2012)
13. Fraser, J., et al.: Hierarchical folding and reorganization of chromosomes are linked to transcriptional changes in cellular differentiation. Mol. Syst. Biol. **11**, 852 (2015)
14. Dekker, J., Misteli, T.: Long-range chromatin interactions. Cold Spring Harb. Perspect. Biol. **7**, a019356 (2015)
15. Dekker, J., Mirny, L.: The 3D genome as moderator of chromosomal communication. Cell **164**, 1110–1121 (2016)
16. Spielmann, M., Lupiáñez, D.G., Mundlos, S.: Structural variation in the 3D genome. Nat. Rev. Genet. **19**, 453–467 (2018)
17. Serra, F., Baù, D., Goodstadt, M., Castillo, D., Filion, G., Marti-Renom, M.A.: Automatic analysis and 3D-modelling of Hi-C data using TADbit reveals structural features of the fly chromatin colors. PLoS Comput. Biol. **13**, e1005665 (2017)
18. Fiorillo, L., et al.: A modern challenge of polymer physics: novel ways to study, interpret, and reconstruct chromatin structure. Wiley Interdiscip. Rev.: Comput. Mol. Sci. **10**(4), e1454 (2019)
19. Conte, M., et al.: Hybrid machine learning and polymer physics approach to investigate chromatin 3D structure. Eur. Conf. Parallel Process. 572–582 (2019, in press)
20. Giorgetti, L., et al.: Predictive polymer modeling reveals coupled fluctuations in chromosome conformation and transcription. Cell **157**, 950–963 (2014)
21. Bianco, S., et al.: Polymer physics predicts the effects of structural variants on chromatin architecture. Nat. Genet. **50**, 662–667 (2018)
22. Sanborn, A.L., et al.: Chromatin extrusion explains key features of loop and domain formation in wild-type and engineered genomes. Proc. Natl. Acad. Sci. U. S. A. **112**, E6456–E6465 (2015)
23. Fiorillo, L., et al.: Inference of chromosome 3D structures from GAM data by a physics computational approach. Methods **S1046–2023**(18), 30485–30487 (2019)
24. Nicodemi, M., Prisco, A.: Thermodynamic pathways to genome spatial organization in the cell nucleus. Biophys. J. **96**, 2168–2177 (2009)
25. Nicodemi, M., Pombo, A.: Models of chromosome structure. Curr. Opin. Cell Biol. **28**, 90–95 (2014)
26. Chiariello, A.M., Annunziatella, C., Bianco, S., Esposito, A., Nicodemi, M.: Polymer physics of chromosome large-scale 3D organisation. Sci. Rep. **6**, 29775 (2016)
27. Kremer, K., Grest, G.S.: Dynamics of entangled linear polymer melts: a molecular-dynamics simulation. J. Chem. Phys. **92**, 5057–5086 (1990)
28. Rosa, A., Becker, N.B., Everaers, R.: Looping probabilities in model interphase chromosomes. Biophys. J. **98**, 2410–2419 (2010)
29. Brackley, C.A., Taylor, S., Papantonis, A., Cook, P.R., Marenduzzo, D.: Nonspecific bridging-induced attraction drives clustering of DNA-binding proteins and genome organization. Proc. Natl. Acad. Sci. U. S. A. **110**, E3605–E3611 (2013)
30. Plimpton, S.: Fast parallel algorithms for short-range molecular dynamics. J. Comput. Phys. **117**, 1–9 (1995)

31. Barbieri, M., et al.: Complexity of chromatin folding is captured by the strings and binders switch model. Proc. Natl. Acad. Sci. U. S. A. **109**, 16173–16178 (2012)

32. Bianco, S., et al.: Modeling single-molecule conformations of the HoxD region in mouse embryonic stem and cortical neuronal cells. Cell Rep. **28**, 1574-1583.e4 (2019)

33. Kragesteen, B.K., et al.: Dynamic 3D chromatin architecture contributes to enhancer specificity and limb morphogenesis. Nat. Genet. **50**, 1463–1473 (2018)

34. Conte, M., Fiorillo, L., Bianco, S., Chiariello, A.M., Esposito, A., Nicodemi, M.: Polymer physics indicates chromatin folding variability across single-cells results from state degeneracy in phase separation. Nat. Commun. **11**, 3289 (2020)

35. Jost, D., Carrivain, P., Cavalli, G., Vaillant, C.: Modeling epigenome folding: formation and dynamics of topologically associated chromatin domains. Nucleic Acids Res. **42**, 9553–9561 (2014)

36. Buckle, A., Brackley, C.A., Boyle, S., Marenduzzo, D., Gilbert, N.: Polymer simulations of heteromorphic chromatin predict the 3D folding of complex genomic loci. Mol. Cell. **72**, 786-797.e11 (2018)

37. Hua, N., Tjong, H., Shin, H., Gong, K., Zhou, X.J., Alber, F.: Producing genome structure populations with the dynamic and automated PGS software. Nat. Protoc. **13**, 915–926 (2018). https://doi.org/10.1038/nprot.2018.008

38. Stefano, M.D., Paulsen, J., Lien, T.G., Hovig, E., Micheletti, C.: Hi-C-constrained physical models of human chromosomes recover functionally-related properties of genome organization. Sci. Rep. **6**, 35985 (2016)

39. Yang, T., et al.: HiCRep: assessing the reproducibility of Hi-C data using a stratum-adjusted correlation coefficient. Genome Res. **27**, 1939–1949 (2017)

40. Stein, J.L.: Copy number variation and brain structure: lessons learned from chromosome 16p11.2. Genome Med. **7**, 13 (2015)

41. Loviglio, M.N., et al.: Chromosomal contacts connect loci associated with autism, BMI and head circumference phenotypes. Mol. Psychiatry. **22**, 836–849 (2017)

42. Nagano, T., et al.: Single-cell Hi-C reveals cell-to-cell variability in chromosome structure. Nature **502**, 59–64 (2013)

43. Fiorillo, L., et al.: Comparison of the Hi-C, GAM and SPRITE methods by use of polymer models of chromatin. bioRxiv. 2020.04.24.059915 (2020).

A New Parallel Methodology for the Network Analysis of COVID-19 Data

Giuseppe Agapito[1,3], Marianna Milano[1,2(✉)], and Mario Cannataro[1,2]

[1] Data Analytics Research Center, Magna Græcia University, 88100 Catanzaro, Italy
{agapito,m.milano,cannataro}@unicz.it
[2] Department of Medical and Surgical Sciences, Magna Græcia University,
88100 Catanzaro, Italy
[3] Department of Legal, Economic and Social Sciences, Magna Græcia University,
88100 Catanzaro, Italy

Abstract. Coronavirus disease (COVID-19) outbreak started at Wuhan, China, and it has rapidly spread across the world. In this article, we present a new methodology for network-based analysis of Italian COVID-19 data. The methodology includes the following steps: (i) a parallel methodology to build similarity matrices that represent similar or dissimilar regions with respect to data; (ii) the mapping of similarity matrices into networks where nodes represent Italian regions, and edges represent similarity relationships; (iii) the discovering communities of regions that show similar behaviour. The methodology is general and can be applied to world-wide data about COVID-19. Experiments was performed on real datasets about Italian regions, and they although the limited size of the Italian COVID-19 dataset, a quite linear speed-up was obtained up to six cores.

Keywords: COVID-19 · Network analysis · Parallel computing

1 Introduction

The global pandemic is caused by a new coronavirus named *Severe Acute Respiratory Syndrome CoronaVirus 2* (SARS-CoV-2) [16], which was first discovered in December 2019 in China [14]. In six months, COVID-19 has spread to more than two hundred countries, infected millions of people and it caused about tens of millions of deaths. COVID-19 has become a global pandemic not only because SARS-COV-2 is new without an effective treatment, but also because it is transmissible from person to person. On March 12, 2020, the World Health Organization (WHO) announces COVID-19 outbreak as a pandemic.

COVID-19 has been recognized in Italy starting from January 31, 2020, [7]. The spread of the disease started from the northern regions of Italy, Lombardy and Veneto on February 21, 2020. From the northern regions of Italy, the disease spread very quickly to the nearest regions and then to the rest ones.

© Springer Nature Switzerland AG 2021
B. Balis et al. (Eds.): Euro-Par 2020 Workshops, LNCS 12480, pp. 333–343, 2021.
https://doi.org/10.1007/978-3-030-71593-9_26

The aim of this study consists of providing a network-based representation of the behaviour of Italian regions with respect to COVID-19 outbreak. To do this, we design an analysis pipeline to model Italian COVID-19 data, daily provided by the Italian Civil Protection, as networks and to perform network-based analysis. We collected data in the period from February 24th to June 7th, 2020. At first, for each type of data, we evaluate the similarity among pair of regions by using a statistical test, i.e. Wilcoxon Sum Rank Test, and according to this, we built similarity matrices (one for each Italian COVID-19 data measure released by Italian Civil Protection). To improve the computation of the similarity matrices, we implemented a parallel methodology. The parallelization of the similarity-matrices calculation is a problem of allocating independent tasks to parallel processors.

In literature, different works recur to network-modelling to analyze COVID-19 data, and most of them recur to network-based representation of data for the application of predictive models. For example, Reich et al. [11] implemented the COVID-19 spread by using SEIRS (Susceptible-Exposed-Infectious-Recovered-Susceptible) agent-based model on a network; Kuzdeuov et al. [6] implemented a network-based stochastic epidemic simulator that models the movement of a disease through the SEIR states of a population; Kumar [5] presents a network-based model for predicting the spread of COVID-19.

To the best of our knowledge, our work is the first study that provides a network-based representation and visualization of COVID-19 data at the regional level and applies network-based analysis to discover communities of regions that show similar behaviour by using a parallel methodology.

The first step of the methodology involves the calculation of the similarity matrix between each pair of regions. This is an easy target for coarse-grained parallelization since all elements of the similarity matrix are independent. We obtain the tasks by considering the input data as a matrix $A_{n \times m}$ with n rows and m columns, from which to extract the squared-blocks SB (i.e., squared sub-matrices between pair of regions) to compute the similarity matrices.

The second step consists in converting the SBs in a network where the nodes represent the Italian regions, and the edges connect statistically similar regions. Finally, we extracted subgroups of regions that form communities based on similarity point of view. The proposed methodology is targeted for multiple CPUs/Cores shared-memory machines.

The main contributions of the paper are: *i)* a parallel preprocessing methodology to improve the multiple pair-wise comparison between Italian regions, *ii)* a network-based representation of COVID-19 diffusion similarity among regions and, *iii)* a graph-based visualization to underline similar diffusion regions, that have a similar diffusion pattern of the disease.

The rest of the paper is organized as follows: Sect. 2 discusses the background on community detection, Sect. 3 presents the implemented pipeline to analyze Italian COVID-19 data, Sect. 4 discusses the results. Finally, Sect. 5 concludes the paper.

2 Background

As a modelling framework, the complex network model has been applied in different fields such as biology, computer science, communication. Once modelled, the network is analysed using some of the many algorithms designed for graph mining. In general, the networks are featured by a heterogeneous structure with specific properties. In particular, the structure presents a heterogeneous distribution of edges that identified the presence of the community. A community presents a group of nodes high densely interconnected respect to the rest of the network [4]. Regardless of the nature of the network, community conveys very important information for the understanding of structural properties. So, community detection in networks is one of the most popular topics in network analysis. In literature, there are many different community detection algorithms.

For example, WalkTrap [10] is a hierarchical clustering algorithm that applies a distance measure based on random walks. Initially, WalkTrap computes the distances between all adjacent nodes in the network. Then, it starts with a node and randomly selects a neighbour of the current node; it merges them in a community, and it updates distances between communities. The idea is that short random walks tend to stay in the same community.

MarkovCluster algorithm [13] works by simulating a stochastic (Markov) flow in a weighted graph, where each node is a data point, while the adjacency matrix stores the edge weights.

Fast Greedy algorithm [2] uses a basic greedy approach [15] starting by single nodes and it joins pairs of ones to form communities.

Louvain [1] includes a community aggregation step to improve communities detection process. The algorithm joins a node with each one of its neighbours community according to the increasing of modularity, otherwise the node stays in its original community.

Spinglass [12] algorithm is based on physical spin glass models. The algorithm aims to find ground state of a spin glass model on the basis that the edges should connect nodes of the same spin state.

3 Parallel Analysis Pipeline

We designed the analysis pipeline with the goal to investigate clusters of Italian Regions with similar behaviour with respect to data provided by the Italian Civil Protection.

The analysis pipeline includes the following steps:

1. Building of similarity matrix. In the first step, the similarity matrix is built. The matrix enters the similarity among pairs of regions respect to an Italian COVID-19 data measure. The similarity is computed by performing the Wilcoxon Sum Rank statical test. Thus, the (h, k) value of the similarity matrix M for data A, e.g., Intensive Care data, is the *p-value* of statistical test obtained by applying the test on the Intensive Care measures of region h with respect to region k. Lower *p-value* implies that regions are dissimilar

with respect to that measure. Otherwise, higher *p-value* implies that regions are similar with respect to that measure. We used the significance threshold of 0.05, thus matrices report only the *p-values* such that: *p-values* >= 0.05, while *p-values* < 0.05 are mapped to zero.

2. Mapping similarity matrices to networks. The second step consists of the building networks starting from the similarity matrices. We map each matrix M(h, k) to a network N, where nodes represent the Italian regions and an edge connects two regions (h, k) if the *p-value* in the similarity matrix is greater than the significance threshold of 0.05. Edges are weighted with the *p-value*.

3. Community detection. The third step consists of the detection of communities on the network by applying an appropriate community detection algorithm. For each network, we extracted subgroups of regions that form a community on the basis of similarity point of view.

Figure 1 shows the main steps of the parallel analysis pipeline.

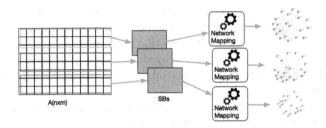

Fig. 1. The main steps of the parallel analysis pipeline.

4   Results

We applied the designed pipeline to analyze the Italian COVID-19 data by considering the period from February 24 to 7 June.

4.1   Input Dataset

The present analysis was carried on the Italian dataset on COVID-19 available at the https://github.com/pcm-dpc/COVID-19 database, provided by the Italian Civil Protection. The dataset consist of the following data collected daily:

- Hospitalised with Symptoms, the numbers of hospitalised patients that present COVID-19 symptoms;
- Intensive Care, the numbers of hospitalised patients in Intensive Care Units;
- Total Hospitalised, the total numbers of hospitalised patients;
- Home Isolation, the numbers of subjects that are infected and in isolation at home;
- Total Currently Positive, the numbers of subjects that are coronavirus positive;

- New Currently Positive, the numbers of subjects that are daily coronavirus positive;
- Discharged/ Healed the numbers of subjects that are healed from the disease;
- Deceased, the numbers of dead patients;
- Total Cases, the numbers of subjects affected by COVID-19;
- Swabs, the numbers of swab test carried on positive subjects and on subjects with suspected positivity.

The data are daily provided for each Italian region.

4.2 Parallel Building of Similarity Matrices

In order to build similarity matrices for Italian COVID-19 data, we performed the Wilcoxon Sum Rank Test. The analysis is performed by using R software [8]. We performed the Wilcoxon test to compute a pair-wise comparison among regions with the goal of evidence statistically similar distributions among them. The pair-wise similarity computation can be executed in parallel since it is an embarrassingly parallelizable task. The problem can be defined as follows: given a matrix $A_{(n \times m)}$ with n rows and m columns, where each elements is denoted as a_{ij} with $1 \leq i \leq n$ and $1 \leq j \leq m$. The matrix A is virtually split in p Square-Blocks SB, where p is the number of available cores, and it is used to balance the workload among the processors/cores available. A SB is built for each couple of regions, and for all the available COVID-19 data (Hospitalised with Symptoms, Intensive Care data, Total Hospitalised, Home Isolation, Total Currently Positive, New Currently Positive, Discharged/Healed, Deceased, Total Cases, Swab). In particular, the main steps necessary to build the similarity matrices are:

1. Partitioning the matrix A in p SquareBlocks SB, to balance the workload among the cores/CPUs available.
2. create independent threads whom is assigned a SB, so that each slave can independently compute its part of the similarity matrix;
3. each computed SB is added to the similarity matrix.

The parallel methodology is currently implemented as a multi-threaded Python application using the *threading* library. The experiments were performed on a workstation equipped with a Pentium i7 2.3 GHz CPU, 16 GB RAM and a 512 GB SSD disk.

The speed-up (S) is defined as the ratio of the time taken using a single processor $(T(1))$ over the time measured using n processors $(T(n))$ (see Eq. 1).

$$S(n) = \frac{T(1)}{T(n)} \tag{1}$$

Figure 2 reports the speed-up obtained by analyzing italian COVID-19 data using 1, 2, 4, and 6 cores, respectively.

Analyzing Fig. 2, it is worth noting that the speed up tends to decrease by increasing the number of computational cores. This is due to the low volume of

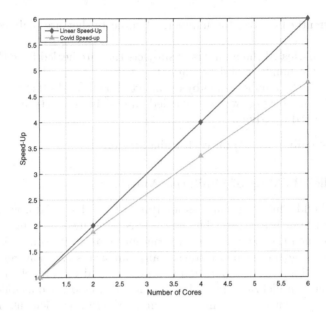

Fig. 2. Figure shows the speedup obtained by the proposed methodology using 1, 2, 4, 6 cores. Blue line represents the linear speed up, whereas the orange line indicates the speed up of the proposed COVID-19 analysis pipeline. (Color figure online)

available COVID-19 data to analyze; in fact, increasing the number of computational cores, the time spent to communicate and synchronize between computational cores, is more expensive than the time necessary to perform computation, leading to low values of speed-up.

4.3 Parallel Mapping Similarity Matrices to Networks

The nodes of the networks are the Italian regions, and the edges link two regions (nodes) with similar trend according to significance level (p-value > 0.05) obtained from Wilcoxon test, otherwise (p-value < 0.05) there is no connection among nodes. The network analysis is performed in parallel by using the igraph library [3]. Results show that according to the type of data, a significant difference exists (p-value less than 0.05) among some regions while for others, it is possible to highlight statistically similar distributions.

4.4 Community Detection

With the goal to identify which regions form a community from the similarity point of view, we applied Walktrap community finding algorithm [10] on the networks, to identify densely connected subgraphs. The extracted communities from Italian COVID-19 networks in the observation period (from February 24th to June 7th, 2020) are reported in Figs. 3, 4, 5, 6, 7, 8, 9, 10, 11 and 12.

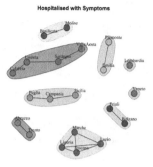

Fig. 3. Communities in Hospitalised with Symptoms Network.

Fig. 4. Communities in Intensive Care Network.

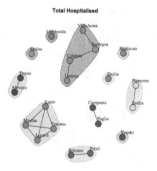

Fig. 5. Communities in Total Hospitalised Network.

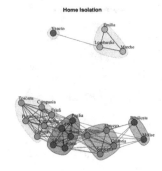

Fig. 6. Communities in Home Isolation Network.

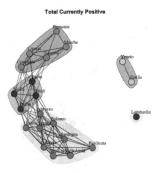

Fig. 7. Communities in Total Currently Positive Network.

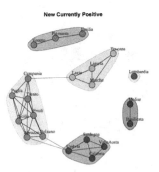

Fig. 8. Communities in New Currently Positive Network.

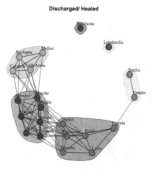

Fig. 9. Communities in Discharged/Healed Network.

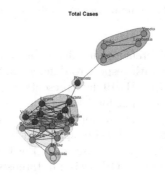

Fig. 10. Communities in Total Cases Network.

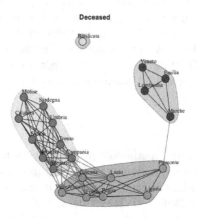

Fig. 11. Communities in Deceased Network.

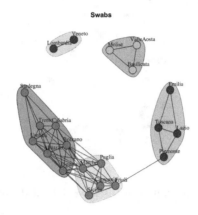

Fig. 12. Communities in Swabs Network.

The results highlight different community structures consisting of groups of regions with similar trends with respect to different data. In fact, each network related to different Italian COVID-19 data presents different detected communities. Furthermore, the regions that form the communities vary according to the diverse data. For example, Lombardia forms a single community in Hospitalised with Symptoms Network (Fig. 3), Total Hospitalised Network (Fig. 5), Total Currently Positive Network (Fig. 7), New Currently Positive Network (Fig. 8), Discharged/Healed Network (Fig. 9). Otherwise, in Intensive Care Network (Fig. 4) and Swabs Network (Fig. 12), Lombardia forms a community together with Veneto. In Home Isolation Network (Fig. 6), a community is composed by Lombardia, Emilia, Marche. In Total Cases Network (Fig. 10) and Deceased Network (Fig. 11), Lombardia forms a community with Lombardia, Emilia, Marche and Veneto. This means that the Italian regions behaved differently with respect to ten different data provided by civil protection. Further analysis about communities in Italian COVID-19 data and their temporal evolution can be found in [9], where a sequential version of this methodology has been used.

5   Conclusion

We proposed a new parallel methodology for network-based representation of COVID-19 similarity among regions and theri graph-based visualization, with the aim to underline similar diffusion regions. We identified similar Italian regions with respect to the available COVID-19 data, and we mapped these ones in different networks. Finally, we performed a network-based analysis to discover communities of regions that show similar behaviour. The experiments performed on real datasets show good speed-up. As future work we plan to implement an R package that incapsulates the presented pipeline.

References

1. Blondel, V.D., Guillaume, J.L., Lambiotte, R., Lefebvre, E.: Fast unfolding of communities in large networks. J. Stat. Mech: Theory Exp. **2008**(10), P10008 (2008)
2. Clauset, A., Newman, M.E., Moore, C.: Finding community structure in very large networks. Phys. Rev. E **70**(6), 066111 (2004)
3. Csardi, G., Nepusz, T., et al.: The igraph software package for complex network research. InterJournal Complex Syst. **1695**(5), 1–9 (2006)
4. Fortunato, S., Hric, D.: Community detection in networks: a user guide. Phys. Rep. **659**, 1–44 (2016)
5. Kumar, A.: Modeling geographical spread of COVID-19 in India using network-based approach. medRxiv (2020). https://doi.org/10.1101/2020.04.23.20076489
6. Kuzdeuov, A., et al.: A network-based stochastic epidemic simulator: controlling COVID-19 with region-specific policies. medRxiv (2020). https://doi.org/10.1101/2020.05.02.20089136
7. Lai, A., Bergna, A., Acciarri, C., Galli, M., Zehender, G.: Early phylogenetic estimate of the effective reproduction number of SARS-CoV-2. J. Med. Virol. (2020). https://doi.org/10.1002/jmv.25723
8. Milano, M.: Computing languages for bioinformatics: R. In: Gribskov, M., Nakai, K., Schonbach, C. (eds.) Encyclopedia of Bioinformatics and Computational Biology, vol. 1, pp. 889–895. Elsevier, Oxford (2019)
9. Milano, M., Cannataro, M.: Statistical and network-based analysis of Italian COVID-19 data: communities detection and temporal evolution. Int. J. Environ. Res. Public Health **17**(12), 4182 (2020)
10. Pons, P., Latapy, M.: Computing communities in large networks using random walks. In: Yolum, I., Güngör, T., Gürgen, F., Özturan, C. (eds.) ISCIS 2005. LNCS, vol. 3733, pp. 284–293. Springer, Heidelberg (2005). https://doi.org/10.1007/11569596_31
11. Reich, O., Shalev, G., Kalvari, T.: Modeling COVID-19 on a network: super-spreaders, testing and containment. medRxiv (2020). https://doi.org/10.1101/2020.04.30.20081828
12. Reichardt, J., Bornholdt, S.: Statistical mechanics of community detection. Phys. Rev. E **74**(1), 016110 (2006)
13. Van Dongen, S.: Graph clustering via a discrete uncoupling process. SIAM J. Matrix Anal. Appl. **30**(1), 121–141 (2008)
14. Wu, Z., McGoogan, J.M.: Characteristics of and important lessons from the coronavirus disease 2019 (COVID-19) outbreak in China: summary of a report of 72 314 cases from the Chinese center for disease control and prevention. JAMA (2020). https://doi.org/10.1001/jama.2020.2648
15. Yang, Z., Algesheimer, R., Tessone, C.J.: A comparative analysis of community detection algorithms on artificial networks. Sci. Rep. **6**, 30750 (2016)
16. Zhu, N., et al.: A novel coronavirus from patients with pneumonia in China, 2019. N. Engl. J. Med. (2020). https://doi.org/10.1056/NEJMoa2001017

HugeMap: Optimizing Memory-Mapped I/O with Huge Pages for Fast Storage

Ioannis Malliotakis[(✉)], Anastasios Papagiannis, Manolis Marazakis, and Angelos Bilas

Institute of Computer Science (ICS), Foundation for Research and Technology – Hellas (FORTH), Heraklion, Greece
{jmal,apapag,maraz,bilas}@ics.forth.gr

Abstract. Memory-mapped I/O (*mmio*) is emerging as a viable alternative for accessing directly-attached fast storage devices compared to explicit I/O with system calls. *Mmio* removes the need for costly lookups in the DRAM I/O cache for cache hits, as they are handled in hardware via the virtual memory mechanism. In this work we present *HugeMap*, a custom *mmio* path in the Linux kernel that uses huge pages for file-backed mappings to accelerate applications with sequential I/O access patterns or large I/O operations. *HugeMap* uses huge pages to reduce CPU processing in the kernel I/O path compared to regular *mmap*. We explore the benefits and trade-offs of huge pages in *HugeMap* using microbenchmarks, IOR, and an in-house persistent key-value store designed for *mmio*. Our experiments show up to 3.7× higher throughput and up to 4.76× lower system time, compared to regular page configurations.

Keywords: Memory-mapped I/O · mmap · Huge pages · Fast storage

1 Introduction

Today, the common approach to access persistent data (e.g., a file or device) is to use read/write system calls. To improve I/O latency and throughput, the Linux kernel uses DRAM caching in the form of a page cache. In addition, applications often employ user-space DRAM caches that allow for custom policies and reduce system call overead, which can further increase performance.

Another approach to access persistent data is to use memory-mapped I/O (*mmio*) i.e., Linux *mmap*. The user can map a file into the process virtual address space. If the requested page is not mapped, a page fault occurs, the kernel allocates a free page, reads the data from the device or file, and updates the page table. The user can access data using regular load/store instructions. Under memory pressure, the kernel evicts I/O pages to reclaim DRAM space.

Also with the Department of Computer Science, University of Crete, Greece.

© Springer Nature Switzerland AG 2021
B. Balis et al. (Eds.): Euro-Par 2020 Workshops, LNCS 12480, pp. 344–355, 2021.
https://doi.org/10.1007/978-3-030-71593-9_27

Mmio provides several benefits compared to explicit I/O, e.g., read/write system calls. With explicit I/O, every I/O operation, including hits, requires an explicit cache lookup which introduces CPU overhead, even if the cache is maintained in user space [6]. On the other hand, *mmio* removes cache lookups for hits. In this case, if a page is cached, a valid translation in the page table exists and the cache lookup is handled in hardware by the Memory Management Unit (MMU). Additionally, *mmio* allows for application-specific optimizations. It can remove the serialization and deserialization in the common path: Applications access data using load/store instructions and this facilitates using the same format for both in-memory and on-device data. Furthermore, it eliminates memory copies between user and kernel space as opposed to system calls. Given these advantages, there are several attempts to use *mmio* in data intensive applications [10].

A disadvantage of *mmio* is that it produces small-sized I/Os to the underlying storage devices. This stems from the fact that the default page size is 4 KB. This significantly reduces I/O performance for sequential accesses. In addition, although this is not a significant issue for random accesses [10], being able to issue large I/Os can still improve performance by reducing overheads in the kernel I/O path. To generate large write I/Os, Linux tries to merge smaller I/Os for consecutive device blocks into larger requests, which incurs CPU overhead. In particular, many HPC applications are designed to issue large I/Os. In these cases, the 4 KB page granularity introduces overhead due to the increased number of page faults.

In this paper, we present *HugeMap*, a custom *mmio* path in the Linux kernel that uses huge pages for file-backed mappings. Our goal is to generate large I/Os where possible and accelerate sequential accesses. Today, *x86_64* processors support both 2 MB and 1 GB huge page sizes. In the rest of this paper we consider only huge pages of size 2 MB, as this page size is enough to achieve peak device throughput. Currently, Linux supports huge pages only for anonymous mappings (i.e., not backed by a file or device), which are mainly used for memory allocation (i.e., malloc) [2]. We extend the *mmio* path with a preallocated buffer of huge pages used only for file-backed mappings, including optimizations for prefetching and fault-around operations. Additionally, we remove merges and complex asynchronous write-backs in the write path. Thus, the CPU processing needed in the common path is reduced, as we show in our evaluation. Our optimizations in the write path also benefit the *msync* system call that synchronizes the memory with the device for file-backed memory mappings. Finally, using huge pages reduces TLB pressure. Huge pages require a single TLB entry for a 2 MB contiguous memory area, whereas the same memory area would require 512 TLB entries of 4 KB small pages. This is an important effect as TLB size does not increase proportionally with DRAM size.

We evaluate *HugeMap* using microbenchmarks, IOR [8], and Kreon [10], an in-house persistent key-value store. Our results show that *HugeMap* achieves up to 54% and 3.7× higher throughput for sequential reads and writes respectively, relative to the corresponding regular page configurations.

2   Background

Linux Huge Pages: The Linux kernel offers two distinct alternatives for huge pages: transparent huge pages (THP) and HugeTLB pages. THP [14] uses sets of 512 sequential, 4 KB pages which are asynchronously and aggressively promoted to a 2 MB huge page by the *khugepaged* kernel daemon. Under conditions of memory pressure, huge pages are demoted back to sets of 512, 4 KB pages and memory compaction is performed. The behaviour of *khugepaged* with respect to page promotion, demotion, and scanning of base page sets, as well as the activation or deactivation of THP are controlled via the sysfs pseudo-filesystem. THP is currently only supported for anonymous mappings and tmpfs/shmem, therefore, we cannot directly use this mechanism over an underlying device/file.

Upon a page fault in the Linux kernel, the function *handle_mm_fault* is central to the fault handling process. In the Linux kernel, a module can register a custom page fault handler for a specific Virtual Memory Area (VMA). This is done through the virtual memory operations struct (*vm_operations_struct*), a member of the *vm_area_struct* (virtual memory area struct). The *vm_operations_struct* contains a function pointer field for handling huge page faults. The Linux kernel calls this handler for huge page faults only in the case where THP is enabled. To bypass these kernel restrictions, THP is activated with the intent of setting the necessary flags for our huge page fault handler to be called; however, huge pages are explicitly allocated by *HugeMap* through the *alloc_pages* function for the DRAM page pool. Therefore, the huge pages allocated by *HugeMap* are not actually handled by *khugepaged*, which only scans sets of 4 KB pages; all huge page operations, such as evictions, swaps, and write-backs are handled by *HugeMap*.

HugeTLB pages [13] are anonymous huge pages residing in kernel space, in a separate pool. These pages must be statically allocated by the user via the HugeTLB pseudo-filesystem (hugetlbfs). A user with the necessary privileges can then mount these pages on a pseudo-filesystem of type *hugetlbfs* with the *mount* command and use them with *mmap*. Due to their static and predefined nature, applications need to be purposely optimized to efficiently use HugeTLB pages. Additionally, as HugeTLB pages only use anonymous mappings and cannot be swapped out under memory pressure, they are not well suited for data intensive applications over fast storage devices.

FastMap: FastMap [11] is an optimized *mmio* path in the Linux kernel that provides a scalable manner to access fast storage devices in multi-core servers. In order to achieve scalable performance, FastMap uses three main optimizations: (1) It maintains clean and dirty pages in separate per-core data-structures, (2) it uses full reverse mappings to keep track of which page tables map a specific page, and (3) it provides a dedicated DRAM cache for increased scalability and to reduce interference with the Linux page cache. FastMap supports only 4 KB pages. *HugeMap* extends FastMap to use 2 MB pages and also provides specific optimizations for huge pages.

3   Design

In this section we outline the design of *HugeMap*, which creates a custom *mmio* path in the Linux kernel from the user down to the device. We implement *HugeMap* as a dynamically loaded kernel module, operating transparently to the user, either directly over the device, or over an underlying filesystem. This is determined at load-time, through the ioctl interface.

HugeMap uses a pre-allocated and configurable in size pool of huge DRAM pages (2 MB). To avoid interfering with the Linux kernel page cache, *HugeMap* maintains a separate memory pool. To provide an efficient page allocation scheme, we use per-core free lists. When the local free list is empty, we steal an empty page from another core. We always return a page to the free-list from which we originally allocated it. Similar to the Linux kernel page cache, we use a radix tree to keep track of pages that are cached by *HugeMap*. This radix tree contains both clean and dirty pages, provides lock-free lookups by using Read Copy Update (RCU), and requires locking for updates.

Furthermore, we keep dirty pages in a separate red-black tree, sorted by page device offset. To separate metadata for dirty pages, we require that a page fault occurs for every write in a read-only page. To achieve this, regardless of the user assigned *mmap* flags, we create read-only mappings in the page table. In the case of a write, an additional page fault occurs that marks the page dirty and inserts it into the red-black tree. In the case where the first access to a page is a write, for optimization purposes we combine these steps and avoid the additional page fault. Keeping the dirty pages sorted in a separate data structure allows us to have efficient *msync* and write-back mechanisms.

When there are no free pages for allocation to serve a page fault, an eviction occurs. In this case we free only clean pages. We have to update the page table, invalidate the associated TLB entries and free the page. It is also necessary to periodically write-back dirty pages to the underlying file/device, so as to have clean pages available to serve page faults. In *HugeMap*, the write-back converts a dirty page to a clean page by writing the page data into the backing device. Furthermore, it has to update the page table to mark the entry as read-only and invalidate the associated TLB entry. A set of threads asynchronously perform these tasks in order to always have clean pages available for eviction. The write-back process is triggered once the amount of dirty pages exceeds 75% of all pages in the page pool. In both eviction and write-back operations the page selection policy is LRU. For this purpose, we keep separate queues for clean and dirty pages. This approach also reduces contention by allowing evictions and write-backs to proceed concurrently.

In the case of sequential accesses, the utilization of huge pages reduces the number of page faults by $2\,MB/4\,KB = 512\times$. Furthermore, it also reduces the complexity of write-back and *msync* operations. In these cases, for 4 KB pages we are forced to perform I/O merging to generate large I/Os from sequentially indexed pages, which is a CPU intensive process. In the case of 2 MB pages there is no need to produce even larger I/Os as (i) it is enough to achieve peak device throughput and (ii) even the Linux kernel does not support issuing larger I/Os for fast storage devices. Huge pages also reduce the overhead of TLB shootdowns. During a TLB shootdown, a core sends a TLB invalidation to all other cores by using inter processor interrupts (IPIs), which cause large overheads and limit scalability [1]. As these invalidations occur in larger granularity, their overhead is less pronounced.

Finally, we provide an efficient *msync* operation. In this case we need to write all dirty pages to the underlying device. With huge pages, this operation always produces 2 MB requests without any merges. Furthermore, we need to move all dirty pages from the dirty queue to the clean queue, update page table entries marking each entry as not writable and dirty, and then invalidate the associated TLB entries. To retrieve all dirty pages, we iterate over the red-black tree. We remove pages from the red-black tree in a batched manner, rather than one at a time, at the end of the *msync* operation.

Huge Page Fault Handling Path: In this section we present the full path of the huge-page fault handling mechanism in *HugeMap*. In the event of a page fault, *HugeMap* first searches the radix tree to check if the requested page already exists in the DRAM cache. If we find the page in the radix tree, then the requested page contains valid data and no I/O is required. Furthermore, it also resides in the appropriate clean or dirty queue. In this scenario, we only update the page table entry with the correct mapping.

If the requested page is not present in the radix tree we try to allocate a free page from the free lists. If we find a free page, we add it to the clean queue, issue an I/O to the underlying device, add the page to the radix tree and finally update the page table, without a TLB invalidation. If we cannot find a free page, we evict a configurable amount of clean pages (we use 16 in our evaluation). Eviction first removes the page from the clean queue, the radix tree, and the page table; then, after a TLB invalidation it inserts the page in the free list.

Write-back threads asynchronously write dirty pages to the backing store, remove pages from the red-black tree, move them from the dirty queue to the clean queue, update the page table and finally, perform TLB invalidations for the associated pages.

Finally, if a write request is issued to a read-only page, the page is already present in the page table as read-only. Thus, the page is moved from the clean to the dirty queue and is inserted to the red-black tree. Last, the associated page table entry is updated and the corresponding mapping is marked as writable, without requiring a TLB invalidation. Figure 1 showcases the algorithm followed by the huge-page fault handler.

Implementation: *HugeMap* is built over *FastMap* [11] and provides a user interface for accessing both block devices and file systems. In both cases we use our custom *mmap* function. All other requests, including read/write calls, are forwarded to the underlying device or file system. Implementation-wise, the utilization of huge pages over devices/files presents a few caveats besides the need to enable THP as explained in Sect. 2. Most notably, one may allocate 2 MB of contiguous memory by calling *alloc_pages* with the proper order argument, however, the kernel still allocates a set of 512, 4 KB pages. To treat these pages

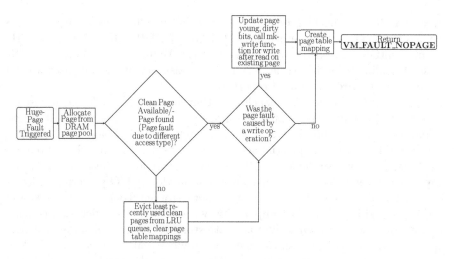

Fig. 1. Huge page fault mechanism

as a single entity (huge page), it is necessary to refer to the page set only through the first page in the 2 MB range. The corresponding *struct page* is treated as a "representative" for the huge page and is used by the various data structures of *HugeMap*, as well as the I/O requests issued to the underlying device. Furthermore, the *__GFP_COMP* flag is used on page allocation to mark the page set as compound [5], similarly to the existing kernel huge page mechanisms.

We also note that *HugeMap* uses the *pgoff* field of the *vm_fault* struct for several purposes. *vm_fault* is the struct used to pass information to a page fault handler regarding a page fault. The *pgoff* field describes the offset of the page fault from the beginning of the device/file, expressed in pages. *HugeMap* insertions and lookups to the page radix tree use it as a key, while the round-robin selection of a per-core clean and dirty page list also relies on it. Additionally, we require the page offset to issue I/O requests to the proper base device sector/file offset. The *pgoff* field is, however, expressed in multiples of 4 KB pages both for regular and huge page faults, meaning that all page faults are 4 KB page aligned. Thus, one must adjust it in order to issue 2 MB aligned I/O requests to the underlying device/file. In our case, this was accomplished by applying a proper bitmask to the *pgoff* field, so that the offset points to the beginning of a 2 MB page set. Presently, our implementation supports defining the page size at compile time via a preprocessor macro. Thus, our module can also work with regular (4 KB) pages as described in Sect. 2. We use this setup for our evaluation.

4   Methodology and Evaluation

Our testbed consists of a dual-socket server that is equipped with two Intel(R) Xeon(R) CPU E5-2630v3 CPUs running at 2.4 GHz, each with 8 physical cores and 16 hyper-threads for a total of 32 hyper-threads. The storage device of the server is a PCIe-attached Intel Optane SSD DC P4800X series with 375 GB capacity. This server is equipped with 256 GB of DDR4 DRAM at 2400 MHz and run CentOS v7.3, with Linux kernel 4.14.72. We disable swapping and CPU frequency scaling to reduce variability in our measurements. In all cases we run the experiments three times and report averages.

First, we use a custom microbenchmark that *mmaps* a block device and issues I/O accesses (*memcpy*) using multiple threads. It supports both sequential and random accesses. As *HugeMap* only supports regular (4 KB) and huge (2 MB) pages, we only evaluate sequential accesses with a single and multiple threads.

Furthermore, we use the Kreon [10] key-value store for our evaluation. Kreon is a persistent key-value store that trades random device I/O patterns for lower CPU consumption. This is possible as modern storage devices (e.g. SSDs and NVMe) provide high I/O throughput even with small I/Os under high concurrency. Kreon relies on *mmap* to interact with storage. It uses a log for allocations, Copy-On-Write (CoW) for persistence and provides scalable insert and lookup operations by using fine-grained locking. The use of the log produces a sequential write access pattern for insert (or update) only workloads; this type of pattern is well-suited to benefit from the use of huge pages.

How does *HugeMap* perform with sequential I/O patterns? Figure 2 shows how *mmap* performs with an increasing number of threads under different configurations. We compare *HugeMap* (both with regular and huge pages) with Linux *mmap*. For Linux we use the *madvise* system call to inform the kernel of the expected I/O pattern. We use both the *MADV_RANDOM* and *MADV_SEQUENTIAL* options. The latter does aggressive read-ahead that can potentially improve sequential performance.

For *HugeMap* with regular pages and Linux with *MADV_RANDOM* we see similar throughput. As we increase the number of threads we observe higher throughput. This happens because of the higher queue depth in the device. Both Linux and *HugeMap* achieve peak throughput with 16 or more threads.

HugeMap with huge pages and Linux with *MADV_SEQUENTIAL*, with 2 or more threads both achieve peak device throughput. With 32 threads, huge pages result in about 12% higher throughput compared to the configurations with regular pages. This shows that high device queue depth is not enough to achieve peak device throughput. Finally, with 1 thread *HugeMap* achieves 54% higher throughput compared to Linux with *MADV_SEQUENTIAL*. Although in Linux the aggressive read-ahead also results in large reads from the device, it requires a page fault per 4 KB, rather than 2 MB in the case of *HugeMap*.

Table 1 shows device performance for all the previously discussed cases, using 32 threads. With huge pages (or aggressive read-ahead) we achieve the peak device throughput of about 2.5 GB/s. Thus, high concurrency to the device is not enough to achieve peak throughput. In all cases we have 100% device utilization. Finally, *HugeMap* for a sequential pattern requires a page fault per 2 MB, instead of 4 KB (i.e., 512× fewer page faults). This results in lower CPU overheads and larger concurrency to the device (i.e., higher queue depth).

With *mmap* a write to a page results in a read-modify-write operation, as the kernel does not know if a page contains useful data. On sequential writes over *HugeMap* using 32 threads, huge pages result in a 3.7× higher throughput compared to regular pages, with the former achieving throughput equal to 1526 MB/s and the latter 412 MB/s.

Specifically, for the write-only microbenchmark (Table 1), due to the read-modify-write operation we observe both reads and writes. *HugeMap* with huge pages always generates 2 MB I/O requests, with minimal CPU processing. Thus, *HugeMap* with huge pages achieves 4.5% and 3.44% higher read and write throughput respectively compared to regular pages. This stems from the fact that with regular pages, all read requests are 4 KB and merging is performed for the write requests. The average request size is 11.38 sectors. In that case the greater number of page faults and the CPU-hungry I/O merging does not allow the microbenchmark to reach 100% device utilization. Finally, *HugeMap* with huge pages provides 74.5× higher I/O queue size.

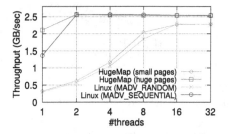

Fig. 2. Throughput scalability for a read-only microbenchmark

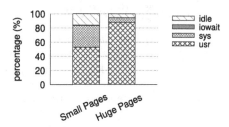

Fig. 3. Execution time breakdown for an insert-only workload with *Kreon*

Table 1. Device performance for a microbenchmarks performing read or write operations with 32 threads. Write operations incur page reads as well.

	Read (MB/s)	Write (MB/s)	avg_rq (sectors)	avg_qz	util (%)
HugeMap *4 KB reads*	2261	–	8	32.2	115
HugeMap *2 MB reads*	2527	–	256	351	100
Linux (MADV_RND) reads	2277	–	8	28.7	114
Linux (MADV_SEQ) reads	2543	–	256	31.2	101
HugeMap *4 KB writes*	273	286	10.4	2.3	32.5
HugeMap *2 MB writes*	1229	985	256	170	100

avg_rq: Average size of requests issued to device
avg_qz: Average queue length of requests issued to device
util: Percentage of CPU time in which I/O requests were issued to device

How does *HugeMap* impact CPU consumption? In this section we examine how much *HugeMap* affects CPU consumption for both read-only and write-only microbenchmarks. Figure 4a shows the execution time breakdown for the

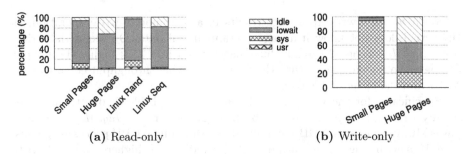

(a) Read-only   (b) Write-only

Fig. 4. Microbenchmark execution time breakdown.

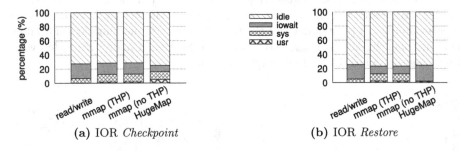

(a) IOR *Checkpoint*   (b) IOR *Restore*

Fig. 5. CPU time breakdown for IOR.

Table 2. Device performance for IOR *Checkpoint* (left) and *Restore* (right).

	xput (MB/s)		avg_rq (sectors)		avg_qz		util (%)	
Read/write	1963	2490	413	257	700	14.5	96	98
mmap (THP)	1940	1743	253	8.9	529	4.1	91	98
mmap (no THP)	1928	1741	257	11.8	479	3.9	90	97
HugeMap	1892	2507	429	257	30	73.2	86	98

read-only microbenchmark. In both *HugeMap* with regular pages and Linux with *MADV_RANDOM* system time is about 10%. In the case of Linux with *MADV_SEQUENTIAL*, system time is 2.3% and in the case of *HugeMap* with huge pages system time is 0.14%. In all cases the majority of execution time is iowait time, which means that the device is the bottleneck. Reducing system time leaves more CPU processing capacity for the user application.

Figure 4b shows that for the write-only microbenchmark the use of huge pages in *HugeMap* reduces the percentage of system time from 94.37% to 20.39%. As we use a microbenchmark in this case the user time in both cases is very low (below 1%). The remainder of system time in the case of huge pages goes to iowait and idle time. This means that an even faster storage device will result in even better performance.

Does *HugeMap* improve checkpoint and restore in HPC? We use the IOR [8] parallel I/O benchmark to evaluate the advantages and drawbacks of *HugeMap* regarding CPU usage and device utilization compared to read/write system calls (without *THP*) and Linux *mmap* (with and without *THP*). We ran experiments on our testbed using an NVMe Optane device. We use two different scenarios in this case. The first scenario is *Checkpoint*, in which 8 processes concurrently write to the NVMe device, for an aggregate write size of 160 GB, or 20 GB per process. This scenario aims to emulate saving the program state in a large scale parallel system. The second scenario is *Restore*, where 8 processes concurrently read the previously written files from the NVMe device, in order to emulate the system restoring itself to a previously saved state. We use 50 GB of main memory in both benchmarks and this includes all page mappings. We report the average over 5 repetitions of each scenario. Before each benchmark the kernel page cache is completely cleared so that no previously cached page is available.

Table 2 showcases these results. The left columns correspond to the *Checkpoint* scenario. In this case we observe that read/write system calls achieve the higher throughput, with Linux *mmap* following closely in performance. *HugeMap* achieves 3.75% lower throughput compared to read/write system calls which is close to the maximum achieved throughput. The columns on the right contain the results for the *Restore* scenario. In this case, we can see that *mmap* achieves 43% lower performance compared to read/write system calls. On the other hand, for *Restore*, *HugeMap* shows the highest performance out of all configurations, with a 44% and 0.6% improvement compared to Linux *mmap* and read/write system calls respectively.

Figure 5a demonstrates the execution time breakdown for the *Checkpoint* scenario. Here we see that *HugeMap* requires slightly greater system time compared to read/write system calls (11% compared to 6%) to achieve almost the same performance, while also enjoying the benefits of *mmio*. Figure 5b shows the CPU breakdown for the *Restore* scenario. In this case, *HugeMap* achieves 9× lower system time compared to read/write system calls and 18.5× compared to *mmap*. Combined with the improvement in throughput, it becomes apparent that *HugeMap* provides the best behaviour for this scenario.

Does *HugeMap* benefit key-value stores? Finally, we use *Kreon* in order to provide a more realistic evaluation under a more complex workload. We use *YCSB* [4] benchmark with an insert-only workload and a dataset of 10M entries (about 10 GBs of keys and values). We provide enough DRAM to ensure that data fits in memory. This experiment examines the impact of 512× fewer page faults on *YCSB* throughput and the balance of system and user CPU time.

Our benchmarks indicate that with huge pages *Kreon* achieves 89.5% higher throughput in terms of ops/s, 1.99 Mops/s compared to 1.05 Mops/s with regular pages. Figure 3 shows that huge pages reduce system time from 30.8% to 6.5%. On the other hand, user time increases from 52.7% to 88%. In both cases iowait percentage is the same and the idle percentage is low compared to user and system pages, we reduce system time and we leave more CPU processing capacity for the user application, i.e. *Kreon* and *YCSB*.

5   Related Work

We briefly review prior work related to huge page management and *mmio* for fast storage devices. Ingens [7] and Hawkeye [9] provide several optimizations for anonymous page mappings in Linux, mainly in the path of promotions and demotions of regular to huge pages and vice-versa. They modify the *THP* mechanism in Linux (Sect. 2) and currently operate only on anonymous mappings. *HugeMap* on the other hand focuses on file/device backed huge page mappings, which are significantly different from anonymous mappings. *DI-MMAP* [15] is a custom *mmio* path in the Linux kernel that tries to optimize it for HPC applications. It uses a dedicated DRAM cache and also provides a FIFO-based eviction policy that is optimized for this type of applications. The authors in [12] optimize the *mmio* path in the Linux kernel. The main improvements are in the case of free page allocation and *Vectored I/O* that optimize write operations, thus showing that fast storage can be used to efficiently extend the available DRAM size. *FastMap* [11] shows that the Linux *mmio* path suffers from scalability limitations with more than 8 threads and provides an evaluation for both storage applications and for extension of DRAM over fast storage devices. In all cases, regular (4 KB) pages are used. *HugeMap* uses *FastMap* and demonstrates the benefits of huge pages in storage applications. The authors in [3] propose the use of read-ahead mechanisms to provide increased throughput for sequential access patterns. We also provide optimizations for sequential access patterns, however, we use huge pages for this purpose. Our approach not only generates larger I/O requests but also reduces the number of page faults and TLB misses.

6   Conclusions

In this paper we present *HugeMap*, a custom memory-mapped I/O path inside the Linux kernel that uses only huge pages for I/O operations. Our approach achieves peak device throughput for sequential I/O patterns. *HugeMap* reduces system time by (1) reducing the number of page faults and TLB invalidations to one per huge page, and (2) reducing the need to perform I/O merging during page write-back. We evaluate *HugeMap* with microbenchmarks, IOR, and the Kreon persistent key-value store. Our results show that *HugeMap* improves I/O throughput by up to up to 3.7× and reduces system time by up to 4.76×. Although we do not explore this further, we believe that *HugeMap* can eventually support a hybrid approach, combining regular and huge pages dynamically.

Acknowledgements. We thankfully acknowledge the support of the European Commission through the H2020 project EVOLVE (GA825061) and the support of the Hellenic General Secretariat for Research and Technology through the MIA-RTDI Research-Create-Innovate project SentiTour (T1EDK-02857). Anastasios Papagiannis is also supported by the Facebook Graduate Fellowship.

References

1. Amit, N.: Optimizing the TLB shootdown algorithm with page access tracking. In: 2017 USENIX Annual Technical Conference (USENIX ATC 2017), Santa Clara, CA. USENIX Association, July 2017
2. Brown, N.: Transparent huge pages in the page cache (2016). https://lwn.net/Articles/686690/
3. Choi, J., Kim, J., Han, H.: Efficient memory mapped file I/O for in-memory file systems. In: 9th USENIX Workshop on Hot Topics in Storage and File Systems (HotStorage 2017), Santa Clara, CA. USENIX Association (2017)
4. Cooper, B.F., Silberstein, A., Tam, E., Ramakrishnan, R., Sears, R.: Benchmarking cloud serving systems with YCSB. In: Proceedings of the 1st ACM Symposium on Cloud Computing. SoCC 2010. Association for Computing Machinery, New York (2010)
5. Corbet, J.: An introduction to compound pages. https://lwn.net/Articles/619514/
6. Harizopoulos, S., Abadi, D.J., Madden, S., Stonebraker, M.: OLTP through the looking glass, and what we found there. In: Proceedings of the 2008 ACM SIGMOD International Conference on Management of Data. SIGMOD 2008, Association for Computing Machinery, New York (2008)
7. Kwon, Y., Yu, H., Peter, S., Rossbach, C.J., Witchel, E.: Coordinated and efficient huge page management with Ingens. In: 12th USENIX Symposium on Operating Systems Design and Implementation (OSDI 2016), Savannah, GA. USENIX Association, November 2016
8. Loewe, W., McLarty, T., Morrone, C.: The IOR Benchmark (2012). https://github.com/hpc/ior
9. Panwar, A., Bansal, S., Gopinath, K.: HawkEye: efficient fine-grained OS support for huge pages. In: Proceedings of the Twenty-Fourth International Conference on Architectural Support for Programming Languages and Operating Systems. ASPLOS 2019. Association for Computing Machinery, New York (2019)
10. Papagiannis, A., Saloustros, G., González-Férez, P., Bilas, A.: An efficient memory-mapped key-value store for flash storage. In: Proceedings of the ACM Symposium on Cloud Computing, SoCC 2018. Association for Computing Machinery, New York (2018)
11. Papagiannis, A., Xanthakis, G., Saloustros, G., Marazakis, M., Bilas, A.: Optimizing memory-mapped I/O for fast storage devices. In: 2020 USENIX Annual Technical Conference (USENIX ATC 20), Boston, MA. USENIX Association (2020)
12. Song, N.Y., Son, Y., Han, H., Yeom, H.Y.: Efficient memory-mapped I/O on fast storage device. ACM Trans. Storage 12(4) 1–27 (2016)
13. The Linux Kernel Documentation: HugeTLB Pages. https://www.kernel.org/doc/html/latest/admin-guide/mm/hugetlbpage.html
14. The Linux Kernel Documentation: Transparent Huge Page Support. https://www.kernel.org/doc/html/latest/admin-guide/mm/transhuge.html
15. Van Essen, B., Hsieh, H., Ames, S., Pearce, R., Gokhale, M.: DI-MMAP-a scalable memory-map runtime for out-of-core data-intensive applications. Cluster Comput. 18(1), 15–28 (2015)

Author Index

Printed in the United States
by Baker & Taylor Publisher Services